The Life of THE ADMIRAL
CHRISTOPHER COLUMBUS

The Life of THE ADMIRAL CHRISTOPHER COLUMBUS BY HIS SON FERDINAND

TRANSLATED, ANNOTATED, AND WITH A NEW INTRODUCTION BY BENJAMIN KEEN

RUTGERS UNIVERSITY PRESS · *New Brunswick, New Jersey*

Library of Congress Cataloging-in-Publication Data

Colón, Fernando, 1488-1539.
The life of the Admiral Christopher Columbus by his son,
Ferdinand. Translated and annotated by Benjamin Keen. New
Brunswick, N. J., Rutgers University Press [1958]

(xxx, 312 p. illus., maps. 25 cm.

Translation of Historie del S. D. Fernando Colombo; nelle quali s'ha par-
ticolare, & vera relatione della vita, & de' fatti dell'Ammiraglio D. Cristoforo
Colombo, suo padre . . .
Bibliographical references included in "Notes" (p. 287-305)
ISBN: 0-8135-0303-5 (cloth) 0-8135-1801-6 (pbk.)

1. Colombo, Cristoforo. 2. Indians of the West Indies. I. Keen, Benjamin,
1913-   ed. and tr.

E111.C737   923.9   58-6288

Library of Congress

Editor's Preface

The biography of Christopher Columbus by his son Ferdinand (Don Fernando Colón) is no ordinary life, and ordinary historical yardsticks do not properly measure its value. Certainly the *Historie* [1] is a work of great authority, written by a son who had at hand all his father's papers and who had personally participated in the events of which it treats. Long ago, Washington Irving called it "the corner-stone of the history of the American continent." Even Henry Vignaud, the severest critic of the materials on which the so-called "Columbus Legend" was based, conceded the *Historie* to be "the most important of our sources of information on the life of the discoverer of America." And the foremost modern American student of Columbus and his voyages, Samuel Eliot Morison, concurs in Vignaud's weighty judgment, dismissing charges of excessive bias against Ferdinand with the common sense observation that his book "needs no more discounting than does any biography of a distinguished father by a devoted son."

Ferdinand's *Historie* is more, however, than a rich and faithful source of information about Columbus, especially about his early years. It is also a moving personal document that vividly re-creates the moral and intellectual atmosphere of Columbus's world and the swirling passions of which he was the center. The intimate, familiar tone of the book, the restrained emotion of a proud and loving son, jealous of his father's honor, that wells up from it, and the autobiographical effect achieved by copious and revealing quotations from Columbus's papers, all enhance its evocative quality. The setting, the figures, and the actions of the drama of discovery emerge from these pages with an enthralling realism and immediacy.

Of special value is the imaginative insight that the book gives into the many-faceted personality and mind of the Discoverer himself. A mass of narrative and descriptive details etches in a convincing literary portrait of the Hero. We receive an impression of the domestic Columbus, "very pleasant to the members of his household, though with a certain gravity"; of a man sensitive to the beauties of nature, tempted by "the little birds and verdure of the fields" to stay in a certain spot forever. We perceive a figure of transition from the dying Middle Ages to the rising world of capitalism and science, blindly credulous and boldly questioning, a medieval mystic incongruously eager for gold and worldly honors. We are told of the superb seaman whom his admiring sailors called "divine"; and between the lines written by Ferdinand's filial piety we discern the weak and fumbling administrator helpless to cope with the violence that the encounter between defenseless Indians and predatory Spaniards unleashed on gold-rich Española.

For the rest, Ferdinand's book has the irresistible virtues of a splendid adventure story. It is in large part a straightforward narrative of action that rises again and again to a stirring climax: the breathless moment of discovery, shipwreck, storm, battle with mutineers or Indians, or a marooning. Often, as in a medieval romance or travel account, the real and the unreal, the probable and the improbable, blend in the most matter-of-fact way. Ferdinand tells casually and unskeptically of griffins, Amazons, and sorcerers. A monstrous fish presages a great storm. A waterspout is dissolved by reading the Gospel according to St. John. This delightful naïveté imparts a true period flavor to the *Historie*.

Ferdinand's style, as well as can be made out from the Italian translation in which it is revealed to us, is simple, unpretentious, tending to an admirable brevity. It is not marred by the long, made-up speeches and other ornate devices affected by Francisco López de Gómara and certain other Spanish chroniclers of Ferdinand's time; nor does it meander and digress interminably like the writing of the garrulous Gonzalo Fernández de Oviedo y Valdés or even that of the great Bartolomé de las Casas. Ferdinand's descriptions of storms, battles, and other crises have a graphic, convincing quality that comes from their very fidelity to the facts, and especially from the mention of many small, sometimes homely, but vividly illuminating details. An occasional anecdote heightens the book's general effect of intimacy and personal involvement, as when Ferdinand recalls how he and his brother Diego, pages to

Queen Isabella, were followed by "shameless wretches" crying, "There go the sons of the Admiral of the Mosquitoes, of him who discovered lands of vanity and illusion, the grave and ruin of Castilian gentlemen."

The facts of Ferdinand's life, a life largely devoted to scholarship and irreproachable by almost every standard, suggest his superb qualifications for his literary task and lend a strong presumption of credibility to his biography.

Ferdinand Columbus was born in August or September of 1488 (most writers prefer the date August 15th) in the Spanish city of Córdoba, where his father was awaiting the report of a committee instructed by the Catholic Sovereigns to study his project of discovery. Ferdinand's mother was a young woman of Córdoba, Beatriz Enríquez de Arana, who became mistress of the thirty-seven-year-old Columbus, a widower and father of a son, Diego. Marriage with a peasant girl was out of the question for the Genoese weaver's son who now dreamed of viceroyships and titles of nobility; and he settled with his conscience by providing for her support and taking her male kin under his wing in the hour of success. Ferdinand, an aristocrat to his fingertips, never mentions his humble mother in his book, though he repeatedly alludes to his father's high-born Portuguese wife.

Ferdinand spent the first years of his life with his mother in Córdoba. Soon after his father's triumphant return from the First Voyage he was appointed a page to Prince Don Juan, heir to the thrones of Castile and Aragón; upon the Prince's early death he entered the service of Queen Isabella. In the Court of the Catholic Sovereigns, patrons of an Italianate Renaissance culture, and perhaps at the feet of one of the Italian humanists and tutors imported by the monarchs, Ferdinand formed the taste for books and scholarship that grew into a ruling passion.

A summons to adventure from his father interrupted the boy's studies. In May, 1502, the thirteen-year-old Ferdinand accompanied Columbus on his Fourth Voyage (May, 1502, to November, 1504). On this voyage, the most difficult and disastrous of all, the lad displayed such staunchness that Columbus praised him highly. "Our Lord gave him such courage," he wrote the King, "that he revived the spirit of the others, and he acted as if he had been a sailor of eighty years, and he consoled me."

Returning to Spain, Ferdinand resumed his studies. He also collaborated with his brother Diego, their uncle Bartholomew, and some other friends in efforts at Court to have the ailing Columbus reinstated in his suspended political rights. In 1509, three years after Columbus's death, Diego was appointed governor of Española and went out accompanied by Ferdinand and Bartholomew. The twenty-one-year-old Ferdinand was charged by the Crown with the erection of churches and monasteries on the island. But Ferdinand preferred to study the wonders and curiosities of the New World at a distance. At the end of a few months he sought and obtained permission from his brother to return to Spain and to his library.

Although Ferdinand never again saw the New World, the Spanish Crown respected and made use of his extensive knowledge of colonial affairs. He was one of the Spanish members of the arbitral commission that met in 1524 to decide the claims of Spain and Portugal to the Moluccas. The next year he presided over a commission of cosmographers and pilots for the correction of marine charts. And in 1526, when Sebastian Cabot set out on an expedition for the Moluccas, Ferdinand assumed his duties of commissioning pilots, examining candidates in his own house.

Ferdinand never married, and no breath of scandal ever touched his serene life. In appearance he resembled his father, being tall and ruddy; in his later years he grew extremely corpulent.

Ferdinand was a wealthy man. In addition to a share of his father's wealth he enjoyed many royal sinecures; his income included the revenue from the labor of four hundred Indian slaves in Española. A major share of this wealth he used for the purchase of books, one of the most important occupations of his life. Every book he bought he carefully numbered, and on the last leaf of each wrote a memorandum of the time and place of its purchase and the sum of money paid for it. This habit of Ferdinand provides us with an itinerary of his book-hunting and other travels, which took him to Italy, the Low Countries, Germany, Switzerland, and England.

In 1526 Ferdinand took possession of a house that he had built in Seville by the river Guadalquivir. In a portion of this building he installed his library, one of the finest private collections in Europe. The historian John Boyd Thacher, himself a noted bibliophile, speaks rapturously of this collection. "Here were gathered no less than 15,370 books and manuscripts, representing the classics, the

Editor's Preface

gems of incunabula, the first fruits of the fecund press, the rarest editions of the poets and of those who had written enduring prose; the sermons and the teachings of the fathers of the Church, the works of the philosophers, the printed fabrics of countless dreams." Ferdinand's house and his library were open to Spanish and foreign scholars; and many regarded him as a colleague and friend. In Brabant he conversed with Erasmus and received a presentation copy of one of his works, proudly recording on the leaf, "Erasmus of Rotterdam gave me this book as a present at Louvain on Sunday, October 7th, in the year 1520: The first two lines of the presentation were written by Erasmus with his own hand."

By the provisions of Ferdinand's will, his library eventually passed into the hands of the cathedral chapter of Seville. In this will Ferdinand set out in meticulous detail a program for the collection's maintenance and increase. It was to be open to all scholars. However, one who wished to consult a book must do so from behind a screen with a hole only large enough for him to introduce his hand in order to turn the pages. Ferdinand justified this restriction by noting that "it is impossible to preserve books though they be chained with a hundred chains." He also devised a plan for indexing and classifying the contents of his library that Thacher calls "worthy of a modern school of the science of bibliography." Ferdinand even dreamed of attaching to his house and library an Imperial College for the study of mathematics and navigation, but death interrupted this plan. He died in his home in Seville on Saturday, July 12, 1539, and was buried in the Cathedral of Seville.

In the hands of the cathedral chapter of Seville, Ferdinand's superb library suffered shameful neglect and losses from vandalism. By the early eighteenth century it seems to have been absolutely abandoned; it is said that children were permitted to play in its galleries and amuse themselves with the miniatures adorning the precious manuscripts. One eyewitness testified that he saw books and manuscripts tossed aside and decaying in the gutters. Today this library, known as the Biblioteca Colombina, contains less than 2,000 of Ferdinand's own books. These, however, include a number of precious works that once belonged to Columbus and bear his marginal annotations. Even in its present diminished state it remains, in Morison's words, "an inspiration for every American scholar; an alembic as it were where a new civilization was distilled from classical scholarship, medieval piety, and modern science."

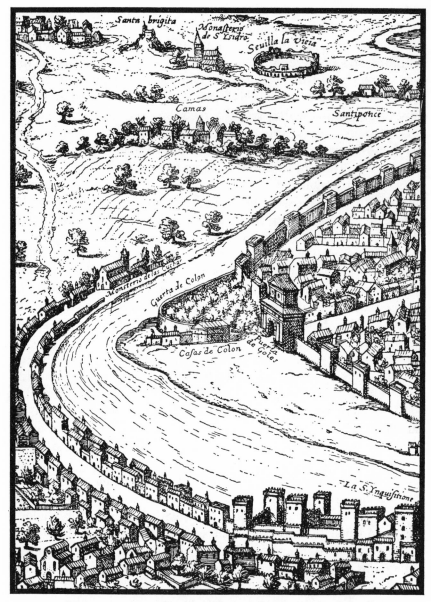

House and Library of Ferdinand Columbus

Editor's Preface

Ferdinand wrote his life of his father during the last years of his life. The tone of the book, frequently polemical and even embittered, reflects the crisis through which the Columbus family was passing at this period. By the capitulations of 1492 and 1493 the Spanish Crown had made sweeping grants of property and political rights in the lands to be discovered, to Columbus and to his descendants. These grants, made with easy generosity to an adventurer whose success was at least problematical, proved inconvenient after Columbus appeared to have made his promises good. The Catholic Sovereigns, who had crushed the power of the lawless barons of Spain, were unwilling to permit the rise of what amounted to a great feudal power in the Indies. The fiasco of Columbus's brief essay at government on Española provided grounds for his removal and replacement by the royal appointee Francisco de Bobadilla. Columbus was never reinstated in his suspended political rights.

His son Diego was appointed governor of Española in 1509, but without the title of viceroy, and two years later the extent of his jurisdiction was specifically limited to Española. Diego and, after his death, his widow Doña María de Toledo fought hard but in vain for the restoration of their hereditary rights. In January, 1536, came the final blow: The Council of the Indies ruled that Columbus's heirs were to renounce, among other rights, the revenues due them and the title of viceroy, in exchange for a perpetual income of 10,000 ducats and the Duchy of Veragua (Panama).[2] Acting on behalf of her infant son Luis, Doña María submitted to the inevitable and accepted the proposed settlement.

Ferdinand was very active in the drawn-out litigation between the Crown and the Columbus family over these matters, acting as legal adviser in turn to Diego and his widow. In connection with these famous *pleitos de Colón* the Crown made every effort to diminish the role of Columbus in the Enterprise of the Indies, attempting to prove by witnesses that Columbus had got the idea of the westward voyage from others and that he had played a minor part in bringing the enterprise to a successful conclusion. For its part, the family summoned witnesses and collected evidence in an attempt to prove the contrary. The Italian scholar Rinaldo Caddeo suggests that Ferdinand first assembled the materials of his *Historie* with these legal needs in mind, and concludes that many of the book's chapters "are an extract, compilation, or copy of the judicial material prepared for this purpose."

If other provocation were needed, the publication of two histories provided sufficient goad for Ferdinand to write his book. In 1535 Oviedo published in Seville the first part of his *Historia general y natural de las Indias*. In this book he advanced the startling view that the Indies had once before belonged to Spain, and that Columbus therefore was not their first discoverer. Two years later appeared the *Castigatissimi annali* of the Genoese Bishop Agostino Giustiniani, with its casual observation that Columbus was of humble birth—a truthful observation but most damaging to the pride of his aristocratic descendants. The importance that Ferdinand attached to these issues is shown by the quite disproportionate space that he devotes initially to answering the two chroniclers and by the fierceness of his polemic.

With all his virtues, public and private, Ferdinand's intellect and heart had limitations that diminish the usefulness of his book. His humanism was of a bookish and pedantic kind, lacking true spirituality and the concern for human well-being that distinguishes the great humanists. Of what might be called "social conscience," as manifested in such generous men among his contemporaries as Sir Thomas More or Bartolomé de las Casas, he was entirely devoid.

Thus the question of Spanish treatment of the Indians, which so deeply touched the heart and conscience of Las Casas, touched Ferdinand not at all. What little he has to say on the subject inclines toward support of the position of Juan Ginés de Sepúlveda, the Spanish jurisconsult who argued that the Indians must be made to serve the Spaniards for their own good as well as that of their masters. Characteristically, Ferdinand ascribes the terrible ravages of disease and famine among the Indians of Española after the coming of the Spaniards to God's avenging hand. Las Casas himself noted that Don Fernando "understood very little about the rights of the Indians and the injustices that his father began against the natives of this island."

As a result, Ferdinand's discussion of Spanish-Indian relations forms one of the weakest portions of his book. The reader of the *Historie* obtains a very inadequate notion of the tragedy that overtook the gentle and virtually defenseless Taino of Española, of whom Columbus wrote: "They are such an affectionate and gen-

Editor's Preface

erous people, and so tractable, that I assure Your Highnesses there are no better people or land in the world. They love their neighbors as themselves, and their speech is the sweetest and gentlest in the world, and they always speak with a smile." For the story of that tragedy, or rather crime, one must go to the thunderous writings of the saintly Las Casas.

We do not know precisely when Ferdinand began or actually completed the writing of his life of his father. There is good reason to believe that he died before he could put the finishing touches to the book. This is suggested not only by certain lacunae in the text that Ferdinand may have deliberately left, with the intention of returning to fill them at a later time, but also by some careless errors of dating and numbering which (if not made by the Italian translator) Ferdinand would certainly have corrected in a final revision.

Why did Ferdinand, a meticulous recorder of his bibliographic treasures and of all his other writings, not list the *Historie* in any of his voluminous catalogues? The Spanish bibliographer Bartolomé José Gallardo (1776-1852), first of all, followed by the famous Americanist Henry Harrisse (1830-1910), seized upon this fact as evidence that the book attributed to Ferdinand had not actually been written by him. But there was ample reason for Ferdinand to keep his authorship and possession of this manuscript a secret. The *Historie* directly challenged positions taken by the Crown in its current litigation with the Columbus family and engaged in severe criticism of Ferdinand the Catholic's treatment of Columbus, criticism that rose in the last pages of the book to an explicit charge of bad faith. There was, of course, an effective censorship of books in Spain at this time. If, as Thacher [3] asserts, the Royal Council forbade Ferdinand to proceed with the writing of an innocuous work on the geography of Spain, how much more it would have frowned on a book of such "dangerous" tendency. Indeed, it is likely that in view of these circumstances Ferdinand himself planned a posthumous publication of his book, and perhaps even selected Italy as the land of its publication.

On the death of Ferdinand in 1539 the manuscript of the *Historie* passed with all the other family papers into the possession of Diego Columbus's widow and eventually into that of her son Don Luis. This playboy grandson of the Discoverer certainly had no

Christopher Columbus's Letter to the Bank of St. George
in Genoa, April 2, 1502

Editor's Preface

interest in books or in the good name of Columbus. But he was chronically hard pressed for money and recognized the commercial value of Ferdinand's manuscript. He found a purchaser in the wealthy and public-spirited Genoese physician Baliano de Fornari.

"We do not know," says Rinaldo Caddeo, "how Don Luis met Fornari, how he consigned the manuscript to him, or what sum was paid for it; but we may assume that the initiative in the affair came from Columbus, that Genoese merchants served as intermediaries, and that Fornari, a generous man much interested in the honor of his house, did not quibble about conditions." In the depth of winter the aged Fornari set out for Venice, the publishing center of Italy, to supervise the translation and publication of the book. The task of rendering the work into Italian was assigned to the professional translator, Alfonso Ulloa, a Spaniard by birth. The book saw the light in 1571. Fornari had projected two other editions, one in Spanish and one in Latin, but on his death these projects were abandoned. And what was worse, the precious Spanish original was lost.

Caddeo offers a harsh judgment on Ulloa's work, charging that he was more of a traitor (*traditore*) than a translator (*traduttore*). In all fairness to Ulloa, it should be said that we have no means of knowing to what extent the errors and anomalies that disfigure the Italian text were caused by the Italian printers, or to what degree they were already present in the Spanish original. It should also be noted that Ferdinand incorporated in his text with little or no change much material from the papers of his father, who frequently wrote in an obscure style.

Although there is no evidence that Ulloa deliberately falsified or altered the meaning of any part of the text, he did allow himself two liberties. In certain places he clarified the meaning of Spanish terms that he wished to keep in the text by adding glosses for the benefit of the Italian reader. It was almost certainly he who marred Ferdinand's impressively simple ending to the book, with its solemn pathos, by the addition of two paragraphs containing some serious factual errors.

I do not propose to survey at length the history of the old and by now very wearisome controversy as to whether Ferdinand actually wrote the biography generally attributed to him. Henry Harrisse, who raised most loudly the cry of "fraud," himself retracted his charge following the first publication in 1875 of the *Historia de las Indias* by Ferdinand's contemporary, Bartolomé de las Casas, who repeatedly cited the lost Spanish original of the *Historie,* made available to him by the Columbus family. The suggestion first advanced by Harrisse, and more recently by the Argentine historian Rómulo D. Carbia, that the book was written by or based on a lost narrative of Hernán Pérez de Oliva, came a cropper when a copy of the missing treatise was found. Leonardo Olschki, who made a critical study of the document, concluded that "the divergency between Ferdinand's *Historie* and Pérez de Oliva's narrative is so deep in every respect and detail that the two works appear irreconcilable at first sight." Carbia's alternative idea that the *Historie* was faked by Las Casas, and the equally humorless suggestion of the distinguished Italian scholar Alberto Magnaghi that it was composed by the worthless Don Luis Columbus, reflect, in the words of Ramón Iglesia, a "total loss of contact with reality." [4]

This is intended to be the first modern and reasonably correct English version of Ferdinand's book. The only other English translation, first prepared for John Churchill, *Voyages* (1732), suffers from many errors and sedulously reproduces the misprints and anomalies of the 1571 Italian edition. In preparing this translation I have had before me the splendid annotated Italian text edited by Rinaldo Caddeo (Milan, 1930, 2 vols.) and the excellent Spanish version of Ramón Iglesia, *Vida del Almirante Don Cristóbal Colón* (México, 1947). My title and some of the paragraphing are lifted directly from Professor Iglesia's edition. Samuel Eliot Morison's superb *Admiral of the Ocean Sea* (Boston, 1942, 2 vols.) was indispensable for the comprehension and rendering of many difficult nautical and astronomical passages.

I have preferred a free to a literal rendering in all cases where strict fidelity to the original would have left a passage unintelligible or obscure in meaning. Where a number or date that is demonstrably false occurs in the Italian text, I have corrected it, with a footnote calling attention to the change. Annotation has been kept to the minimum for the convenience of the nonspecialist reader. Wherever possible, I have given in notes the modern names of places mentioned in the text, or a translation of the names Columbus gave them. Except for Christopher, Bartholomew, Diego, and Ferdinand Columbus, and the Catholic Sovereigns, names of persons have not been Anglicized. Matter interpolated by the translator

Note on the Illustrations and Maps

Ulloa is enclosed in brackets; my own insertions are enclosed in brackets with the initials B.K.

Benjamin Keen

Springfield, Massachusetts
June, 1958

Note on the Illustrations and Maps

The illustrations reproduced in this volume are for the most part of sixteenth-century origin. Some, like the Columbus coat of arms and the sketches of a native house, an Indian canoe, the fruit trees of Española, and the curing of the sick, appeared in the works of Gonzalo Fernández de Oviedo y Valdés or the Italian traveler Girolamo Benzoni, both of whom spent many years in the Spanish colonies. Oviedo, official chronicler of the Indies in the reign of Charles V, published the first part of his *Historia general de las Indias* in Seville in 1535 and, with illustrations, in Salamanca in 1547; Benzoni's *Historia del Mondo Nuovo* was issued in Venice in 1565 and again, with illustrations, in 1572.

The crude woodcuts bearing the inscription "Insula Hyspana"— one supposedly of a landing by Columbus from a forty-oared Mediterranean galley—and the title page cut used to depict the Bahama Islands that Columbus discovered, appeared in the first illustrated Latin edition of Columbus's First Letter concerning America, usually called "Columbus's Letter to Rafael (or Gabriel) Sánchez," treasurer of the Kingdom of Aragón, printed in Basel in 1493. An almost identical letter, addressed to Luis de Santángel and dated a month earlier, was printed in Spanish (unillustrated) in Barcelona in April, 1493. Since the pictures in the Basel edition had all been used before in books printed in Switzerland, they had no connection with the First Voyage. They are of interest, however, as being the first purported pictorial representations of the New World to meet the gaze of European readers.

Note on the Illustrations and Maps

The Jovius portrait is the earliest known engraved likeness of Columbus. Supposedly, it was made from a portrait that the "historian" Paulus Jovius acquired for a gallery of notable people that he started in his villa at Como under the patronage of Pope Leo X. The engraving was included in the second edition of Jovius's *Elogia virorum bellica virtute illustrium* (Basel, 1575).

The Flemish engraver Jean de Bry executed several Columbus scenes for his father Theodore's *Collectiones Peregrinationum in Indiam Orientalem et Indiam Occidentalem* (1590-1634). Some were later used by Antonio de Herrera y Tordesillas, royal historiographer to Philip II, for his *Historia general de los hechos de los Castellanos* (Madrid, 1601-1615). From these two sources we get the scenes of Columbus at Española and Margarita and his parting with the Catholic Sovereigns.

The ships of Columbus's time first appeared in Pedro de Medina's *Arte de navegar*, printed in Valladolid in 1545.

The curious scenes of the "Cannibal Islands" and a Mass on shore are from *Nova typis transacta navigatio novi orbis Indiae occidentalis*, published in 1621. Nothing is known of the author, Franciscus Honorius Philoponus; and it is possible that Casparus Plautius, to whom the book was dedicated, was the real author.

The picture of the house and library of Ferdinand Columbus in Seville is from a sixteenth-century print, probably of Italian origin. It, like several of the foregoing illustrations, was reproduced in Justin Winsor's *Christopher Columbus and How He Received and Imparted the Spirit of Discovery* (Boston: Houghton, Mifflin, 1891); others appeared in the second volume of the collaborative work, *Narrative and Critical History of America*, under the general editorship of Winsor (Boston: Houghton, Mifflin, 1886).

Columbus wrote the Letter to the Directors of the Bank of St. George in Genoa, April 2, 1502, to notify them of his intention to allow a fund to accumulate at the Bank for the purpose of relieving the citizens of Genoa from taxes.

The maps and charts in this volume are largely based on those drawn by Erwin Raisz, copyrighted by Samuel E. Morison, and reproduced in Rear Admiral Morison's *Admiral of the Ocean Sea*, with his permission and that of Little, Brown & Co. Any cartographical errors which may appear in the present maps are not to be imputed to the source maps.

Note to the Second (1992) Edition

I have made only trifling changes in the preface to the first (1959) edition of this book. However, I have taken advantage of this opportunity for revision to correct some errors in my translation of Ferdinand's life of his father that were found by me or by others. I am grateful to Kirkpatrick Sale, *The Conquest of Paradise: Christopher Columbus and the Columbian Legacy* (New York: Alfred A. Knopf, 1990), p. 132n, and to David Henige, *In Search of Columbus: The Sources for the First Voyage* (Tucson: University of Arizona Press, 1991), p. 44n, for noting a few such errors. I have also consulted with profit a new Spanish edition of Ferdinand's book, with a useful introduction and notes by Luis Arranz: Hernando Colón, *Historia del Almirante* (Madrid: Historia 16, 1984).

Benjamin Keen

Santa Fe, New Mexico
December, 1991

Introduction
Christopher Columbus in History: Images of the Man and His Work, 1492–1992

In my preface to Ferdinand Columbus's life of his father I call it a work of great authority. It is in fact a veritable landmark among the flood of writings on Columbus and the Discovery from 1492 to the present. But, given the author's relationship to his subject and the peculiar circumstances in which the book was written—circumstances that I discuss in my preface—it could not be an impartial account of Columbus's life and work. Sometimes it has the defensive tone of a lawyer's brief; sometimes it glosses over or even omits facts that might detract from Columbus's reputation. These qualities make it the primary source of a durable apologetic tradition in the Columbian literature. That tradition is best illustrated by Washington Irving's biography of Columbus (1828), a book whose graceful style and colorful fables helped to create a popular image of Columbus that still defies revisionist efforts to reveal flaws in the character of the Discoverer or to question the unmixed blessings that supposedly resulted from his Discovery.

In fairness to Ferdinand, it must be said that the intense partisanship that pervades his book is not unique; it pervades much if not most of what has been written about Columbus, whatever its viewpoint. I do not refer here to the interminable discussions and polemics about such matters as Columbus's birthplace or nationality, where he made landfall, his navigational skill, or whether he really sought to find the Indies or simply new islands and lands. I have in mind above all the kinds of judgments, for and against, that historians and others make about great historical events and their

Introduction

authors. Like the careers of Napoleon Bonaparte and other movers and shakers of history, Columbus's life and work have from the first been a battleground of opinions. Historians and others have long agreed that the Discovery had prodigious consequences, but disagreed whether they should cause jubilation or regret; whether, weighed in the balance, the Discovery contributed to human welfare or misery. Inevitably, judgments on these matters have also been verdicts regarding the place to be assigned to Columbus in history. Inevitably, too, these diverse judgments have reflected the political, socioeconomic, and ideological backgrounds of the parties to the debate and the prevailing climate of opinion. The importance of the climate of opinion in the formation of such views is suggested by the fact that perhaps the most important work on Columbus and the Discovery published on the eve of the 1992 quincentenary, Kirkpatrick Sale's *The Conquest of Paradise: Christopher Columbus and the Columbus Legacy* (1990), is written from an ecological viewpoint—a viewpoint that could not even have been dreamed of in the times of Ferdinand Columbus or Washington Irving.

Christopher Columbus in the Renaissance

Historians have sometimes complained of the tardy or lethargic response of Renaissance Europe to the discovery of America. Samuel Eliot Morison noted that the great Nuremberg Chronicle, claiming to record all important events since the creation of the world and printed on July 12, 1493, made no reference to the Discovery—but this could reflect the slowness with which news traveled at that time. John H. Elliott speaks of a "blunted impact" that "was in many respects both disappointingly muted and slow in materializing," and suggests that Renaissance Europe "approached the outer world with a combination of prejudice, curiosity, and caution." He cites, as a telling example, the case of the humanist Cochlaeus, who in his introduction to the 1512 edition of Pomponius Mela's *Cosmographia* responded as follows to Amerigo Vespucci's claim that he had discovered a new world that was distinct from and larger than Europe: "Whether this is true or a lie, it has nothing . . . to do with cosmography and the knowledge of History. For the people and places of that continent are unknown and unnamed to us and sailings are only made there with the greatest dangers. Therefore it is of no interest to cosmographers at all."

But this denigration of the Discovery cannot be regarded as a typical reaction of European intellectuals. To be sure, given the initial paucity of information and the uncertainty as to precisely what Columbus had discovered, and the inevitable difficulty of assimilating a mass of new information that so dramatically changed the shape of the world, there was no immediate "intellectual explosion." As early as 1493, however, the Italian humanist at the Spanish Court, Peter Martyr, whose *Decades* (groups of ten letters), published in at least nineteen editions and eight languages between 1504 and 1563, offered Europeans a well-informed running account of the discovery and other events of the New World, wrote: "Raise your spirits. . . . Hear about the new discovery!" Naturally, this note of excitement was sounded earliest and most strongly by Spaniards, who were best informed about the exploits of Columbus and other conquistadors in the New World and appreciated their special importance to Spain. The humanist Juan Luis Vives wrote in 1531: "Truly, the world has been opened to the human race." In his *Historia general y natural de las Indias* (1535) the royal chronicler Gonzálo Fernández de Oviedo y Valdés paid generous tribute to Columbus's achievement: "His is the glory, and only to Columbus, after God, do the past and future Catholic kings of Spain owe praise, as do all the dominions of their Majesties' realm and even foreign kingdoms, because of the great benefit which has redounded to all the world from these Indies, with the countless treasures which have been taken and continue to come from them, and shall be taken as long as men may live." Unstinting in his praise, Oviedo even commended Columbus's harsh colonial rule as necessary to control troublemakers in those distant lands. It remained for Francisco López de Gómara, a chronicler with a gift for lapidary statements, to write in the dedication of his *Historia general de las Indias* (1552) to Charles V: "The greatest event since the creation of the world (excluding the incarnation of Him who created it) is the discovery of the Indies."

To be sure, Spanish praise of Columbus's exploit was sometimes tempered by nationalist resentment of the foreigner Columbus and awareness of the Crown's efforts to curtail the large privileges granted to Columbus in 1492 and 1493 and to diminish his role in the discovery of the Indies. The chronicler Oviedo played into the royal hands by advancing the view that the Indies, then known as the Hesperides, had once before belonged to Spain. Oviedo is also the source

Introduction

of the story of the anonymous pilot who before his death confided to Columbus the secret of the Indies and the way there. Oviedo claimed the story "ran among the common people," but believed it to be false. However, it was picked up and elaborated by Gómara in his own history of the Indies, and was enriched with more undocumented details, half a century later, by Garcilaso de la Vega in his *Royal Commentaries of the Incas.* The myth came to have a life of its own; as late as 1976 a widely respected Spanish scholar, Juan Manzano y Manzano, accepted its truth. In his *Colón y su Secreto* he made it the key to the understanding of Columbus and the genesis of his Enterprise of the Indies.

Praise and blame of Columbus alternate in Fray Bartolomé de las Casas's monumental *Historia de las Indias,* written between 1527 and 1562, but not published until 1875. A friend of the Columbus family, Las Casas had access to many of the Discoverer's papers. The work is in considerable part a biography of Columbus and incorporates the single best source of information on the Discovery, Las Casas's abstract, part summary and part direct quotation, of Columbus's lost *Diario,* the journal of his First Voyage to America. Las Casas also utilized a manuscript copy of Ferdinand's life of his father.

Las Casas passionately admires the Admiral, chosen "among all the sons of Adam" for his providential task of opening "the doors of the Ocean Sea" and making possible the conversion and salvation of the Indians. He sees a divine design in the pattern of Columbus's life before his arrival in Castile, endows him with great virtues, and bitterly criticizes the injustice and ingratitude with which the Spanish monarchs treated him and his family. But when Las Casas turns to discuss Columbus's enslavement of and other cruelties to the Indians his tone changes. The hero Columbus becomes flawed, and Las Casas charges him with "inexcusable ignorance" of the human rights of the Indians. Viewed from this perspective, the sufferings of the Admiral—his imprisonment, the loss of his privileges, and other injustices—are explained by Las Casas as divine punishment for Columbus's offenses against the Indians, a punishment meant to purge him of his sins and save him from eternal damnation. Despite this alternation between praise and blame, Las Casas left no doubt of his overall favorable opinion of the Admiral and his achievement. The 1615 publication of Antonio de Herrera's massive *Historia general de los hechos de los castellanos en las islas y tierra firme del Mar Océano,* whose sources included the manuscript of Las Casas's *His-*

toria, first laid that favorable assessment before Spanish and foreign readers.

News of Columbus's exploits swiftly spread from Spain to Italy, which had close political and cultural links with Spain. In 1516 Agostino Giustiniani published a *Polyglot Psalter* that contained a sketch of Columbus's life, including the casual comment that in his youth he had been an artisan; Giustiniani repeated this comment in his history of Genoa (1537). As noted in my preface, this truthful observation provoked Ferdinand's wrath and provided a goad for writing his own life of his father. Yet Giustiniani was very complimentary to Columbus, calling him "this illustrious man, who if he had lived in the time of the Grecian heroes, without doubt would have been enrolled among the number of the gods," and declaring that "by the marvelous daring of Christopher Columbus of Genoa almost another world has been discovered and added to the company of Christians." Columbus's historic stature was further confirmed by his inclusion in a collection of biographical sketches of famous men, *Elogia virorum illustrium* (1551) by Paolo Giovio, the bishop of Nocera; the work contains the earliest engraved likeness of Columbus. The third volume of the great travel collection *Navigationi et viaggi* (Venice, 1556), compiled by Giovanni Batista Ramusio, Oviedo's friend and business associate, provided a reasonably full account of Columbus's voyages and his troubled rule on Hispaniola, based primarily on Martyr and Oviedo. Finally, in 1565 Girolamo Benzoni published in Venice his famous *Historia del Mondo Nuovo*, the travel account of a Milanese who passed fourteen years in the Indies. Although best known for its moving descriptions of Spanish cruelty to the Indians, the book contains a fairly detailed account of Columbus's life and voyages, based almost entirely on the chronicles of Oviedo and Gómara. However, Benzoni strongly defended the Italian nationality of Columbus against the "inventions" of some Spanish historians who could not abide that "an Italian had conquered such great honor and glory, not only among the Spanish nation but among all the nations of the world." Translated and diffused throughout Europe, especially in the richly illustrated editions published by the de Bry family (described below), Benzoni's book played a major role in the creation of the classic image of a hero who dared greatly, and overcame the opposition of ignorant and bigoted men to achieve his dream, but at last fell victim to his enemies and the ingratitude of princes.

The discovery of a New World inhabited by people described by

Introduction

Columbus, Vespucci, and Peter Martyr as innocent and generous, free from the greed and passions of the Old World, early captured the imagination of French intellectuals. Gilbert Chinard and others have shown that the *Gargantua and Pantagruel* of François Rabelais contains American elements drawn from the letters of Columbus, Peter Martyr, Vespucci, and Jacques Cartier. Rabelais sent Pantagruel sailing westward in order to consult the oracle of the bottle. The priestess of the bottle proclaimed a Utopian message: "Down here, in these circumcentral regions, we place the supreme good not in taking or receiving, but in giving and bestowing." The poet Pierre de Ronsard depicted an Indian Utopia on the shores of Brazil. In his *Discours contre Fortune* (1559), he appealed to the leader of a French colonizing expedition not to carry the evils of European civilization to those blessed shores where men lived free from kings, private property, and lawsuits. As Frenchmen became aware that Columbus and not Vespucci—as a fabricated or doctored letter attributed to Vespucci claimed—had discovered that strange new world, their regard for Columbus grew. The learned royal cosmographer André Thevet, who as late as 1568 gave credence to Vespucci's precedence, made amends by including a sketch of "Christophe Colomb, Genevois," based primarily on Peter Martyr and Benzoni and accompanied by an engraved portrait that he claimed to have acquired in Portugal, in his biographical collection, *Vies des hommes illustres* (1584). Thevet wrote admiringly of the "diligent exploration of that excellent pilot," who after having made vain efforts to secure support for his project in various lands where he acquired the reputation of "a teller of tall tales," "a madman," and "an overheated brain," made good his promise to find "mountains of gold" for the fortunate Spanish rulers who "believed the wise counsel of this Genoese captain." Thevet, it may be noted, also accorded two Indian emperors—Moctezuma and Atahualpa—the honor of inclusion in his work; their biographical sketches were accompanied by engraved portraits, of course done from the artist's imagination. Thevet's biographical encyclopedia, widely read in France and in England, where several editions were published in translation in the seventeenth century, contributed to Columbus's growing public stature.

In Germany, Columbus and his exploits received little attention until the mid-sixteenth century; as late as its 1545 edition, Sebastian Münster's influential *Cosmographia*, the most widely read geographical work of the century, "gave only desultory attention" to the American discoveries. Matters improved in later editions, which included reasonably full accounts of Columbus's first three voyages, based primarily on the reliable Peter Martyr and Spanish chronicles. "All in all," writes Kirkpatrick Sale, "it was what might be called a Germanic treatment, cooler in tone than such Spanish champions as Oviedo and Gómara, but even-handed and as comprehensive as a work based on the tales of others could be expected to be."

The famous Frankfurt publishing house of Jean de Bry and his sons is best known for its contribution to the so-called Black Legend of Spanish cruelty to the Indians through publication of Las Casas's *Brief Account of the Destruction of the Indies* and Benzoni's *Historia del Mondo Nuovo,* illustrated by copperplate engravings whose clarity and beauty of line heightened the horror of the scenes of massacre and outrage that they depicted. However, for his edition of the Latin translation of Benzoni's book, published in three parts between 1594 and 1596, de Bry also prepared a series of plates dealing with Columbus and the Discovery: they included a celebration of Columbus—a triumph with mythological figures—and scenes depicting the famous anecdote of the egg,[1] Columbus's departure on his First Voyage, and his return from the Third Voyage in chains. They are among the earliest and finest pictorial representations of events related to the Discovery and Columbus's life. Thus Benzoni's Italian patriotism and the artistic talent of the de Brys combined to create enduring pictorial and mental images: a heroic Columbus in the moment of his triumph; a brilliant Columbus exposing the incompetence of envious and carping critics; and a tragic Columbus sent home in chains from the new world he had discovered. Moreover, by their silence concerning Columbus's own barbarous mistreatment of the Indians, Benzoni and the de Bry illustrations absolved him from complicity in the crimes charged by the anti-Spanish Black Legend.

In England, which by the last decades of the sixteenth century

[1]The story of the egg tells that Columbus was challenged at a party by a Spaniard who argued that if Columbus had not discovered the Indies it would have been done sooner or later by someone else. Columbus countered by placing an egg on the table and inviting those present to make it stand on its end without the use of any other material. None could, but when Columbus's turn came he crushed one end of the egg, enabling it to stand up. "Wherefore all remained confused, understanding what he meant: that after the deed is done, everybody knows how to do it." The only trouble with this pretty story is that it had been told about other notable figures for at least a century before Benzoni told it.

Introduction

had emerged as the principal threat to Spain's empire in America, promoters of overseas expansion offered Columbus as a model of initiative, daring, and endurance that their own explorers could well emulate. An early promoter of English colonial expansion was Richard Eden, who in 1553 published an English translation of a part of Münster's *Cosmographia*, giving a fairly complete account of Columbus's voyages; two years later he published another collection of translated material dealing with Spanish voyages and conquests, including the first four *Decades* of Peter Martyr. Ignoring Spanish claims of monopoly over America, Eden urged the English to follow Spain's example and explore lands to the north of the regions of Spanish occupation. Following his death, Eden's campaign was taken up by others, most notably by Richard Hakluyt, compiler of a great collection of English travels (1589), who described Columbus as the intrepid pioneer who "stirred up" the Spaniards and "pricked them forward" to their "Western discoveries." The opportunistic nature of the English propaganda in favor of colonization is well illustrated by Hakluyt, who mingled praise for Columbus and Hernán Cortés with denunciations of Spanish cruelty to the Indians. Another compiler of travel accounts, the Anglican clergyman Samuel Purchas, whose monumental collection, *Hakluytus Posthumus, or Purchas His Pilgrimes*, was published in 1625, described Columbus as a man whose patience and endurance had opened up "the Columbian (so fitlier named, than American) World" for Europe. The high standing enjoyed by Columbus in English opinion of the early seventeenth century is suggested by Francis Bacon's proposal in his Utopian novel, *The New Atlantis*, written about 1626, that a statue of Columbus stand in the hall of the "principall inventors" of all time.

In summary, by the middle of the seventeenth century, the familiar heroic figure of Columbus, including most of its mythical elements, had come to dominate writings on the man and his explorations. Renaissance writers had created that image by their emphasis on Columbus's courage and other admirable personal qualities and his alleged mistreatment by the Spanish Crown and by his enemies; by absolving him from complicity in the crimes attributed to Spain by the so-called Black Legend; and above all, perhaps, by their stress on the "mountains of gold" and other opportunities for enrichment or, better said, plunder, that Columbus's discovery came to symbolize for many Europeans. In that connection, Kirkpatrick Sale has noted the sexual symbolism that sometimes tinged English literary references to America. John Donne addressing his mistress:

> Licence my roaving hands, and let them go,
> Before, behind, between, above, below.
> O my America! my new-found-land,
> My kingdome, safeliest when with one man man'd,
> My myne of precious stones, my Emperie,
> How blest am I in this discovering thee!

Similar references appear in various plays of Shakespeare. "The poets," Sale observes, "conveyed the predominant priority: America as the succulent maiden to be seduced, deflowered, and plundered by a virile Europe, which shall bask in her treasures. America, in a phrase, as the land of *exploitation*." That sexual image of America as a maiden to be seduced, it is interesting to note, reappeared as late as 1942 in a major biography of Columbus by the United States historian Samuel Eliot Morison: "Never again may mortal men hope to recapture the amazement, the wonder, the delight of those October days in 1492 when the New World gracefully yielded her virginity to the conquering Castilians."

A few Renaissance writers challenged the conventional heroic image of Columbus: they usually represented the radical wing of Renaissance thought, anti-imperialists and critics of the old European social and political order and the philosophical premises on which that order rested. Such a man was Giordano Bruno, the Italian philosopher who was burned at the stake for heresy in 1600. Bruno used the discovery of America and the Indian to disprove the notion that humans were descended from a common ancestor and cited the intellectual achievements of the Indians to refute charges of their inferiority. He harshly criticized the consequences of the discovery and conquest of America; in his dialogue *La Cena*, he attacked Columbus as one of those "audacious navigators" who in reality only "disturbed the peace of others . . . , increased the vices of nations, spread fresh follies by violence, introduced unheard-of ones where they never existed, taught men a new art and new means of tyranny amongst themselves."

Like Bruno, the French philosopher and essayist Michel de Montaigne used the discovery of America and the Indian to attack the philosophical foundations of Western civilization, to deepen the

Introduction

skeptical crisis of late Renaissance Europe. Although he never mentions Columbus by name, Montaigne severely condemns the European colonial policies and methods that Columbus initiated. In his essay *On Coaches*, the fire of his denunciation recalls the wrathful chapter on "Primitive Accumulation" in Marx's *Capital*:

> Who ever set the utility of commerce and trading at such a price? So many cities razed, so many nations exterminated, so many millions of people put to the sword, and the richest and most beautiful part of the world turned upside down, for the traffic in pearls and pepper! Base and mechanical victories! Never did ambition, never did public enmities, drive men against one another to such horrible hostilities and such miserable calamities.

Columbus in the Age of Reason

In the eighteenth century, many European intellectuals, viewing the Discovery and its consequences with the eyes of Reason, began a reassessment of Columbus's work and its supposed benefits for humankind. Their inquiry into the subject reflected some key elements of the prevailing Enlightenment ideology: anti-colonialism, humanitarianism and reformism, and dislike for the barbaric violence, obscurantism, and fanaticism that they associated with that Age of Darkness, the Middle Ages. For many of these intellectuals Spain in the time of Columbus exemplified that Age of Darkness; they tended to blame the horrors of the Spanish Conquest on Spain's feudal backwardness and intolerant spirit. France, home of the Encyclopedists, was the principal center for dissemination of this negative assessment of the Discovery and its results. Naturally, that assessment found little acceptance in Spain, where writers in this period usually assumed a defensive position, attempting to vindicate Spain's work in America. Typical of this tendency was Juan Nuix's polemical *Reflexiones imparciales sobre la humanidad de los españoles en las Indias* (1782). A more scholarly work that also sought to vindicate Spain's honor was Juan Bautista Muñoz, *Historia del Nuevo Mundo* (1793), heavily based on archival sources.

What is remarkable is that the established image of a heroic and virtuous Columbus suffered little or no damage from the Enlightenment attack on colonialism and the Spanish Conquest. Columbus probably owed this immunity above all to the continuing and growing influence of Ferdinand's *Historie*. The appearance of eight Italian editions in the seventeenth century was followed by the publication of a poor French translation (1681), a more reliable English translation (1732), and the first Spanish translation by A. González Barcia (1749), containing many errors. These translations, used as primary sources by many historians and biographers, diffused ever more widely Ferdinand's hero-worshiping image of his father.

Eighteenth-century French accounts of the discovery of America clearly reflect the influence of Ferdinand's book. Typical of their tone is the *Récherches philosophiques sur la découverte de l'Amérique* (1784) by M. J. Mandrillon, one of a number of entries in a prize contest sponsored in 1782 by the Lyons Academy for the best book on the question: "Was the discovery of America a blessing or a curse to humankind?" Mandrillon not only praised Columbus's merits as a navigator but also depicted him as a humane, compassionate colonizer whose good intentions were thwarted by the Spanish government and other colonists. Had he not met with those obstacles, he could have taught Europe the art of making the peoples of America a "New World of friends." Unhappily, the direction of the enterprise fell into other hands, and its driving force became the Spanish Court's thirst for gold and other riches, a thirst from which Columbus was supposedly free. Spain's rejection of Columbus's mild colonial system was followed by the installation of a "system of barbarism, inhumanity, and greed," resulting in the extermination of the majority of the Indian population and the enslavement of the rest.

Turning to the question of the Discovery's long-range consequences for good and evel, Mandrillon first cited the evils that it had caused in Europe: depopulation, especially of Spain; the introduction of syphilis; and the price inflation resulting from the influx of American gold and silver, especially harmful to wage-earners, whose wages lagged behind prices. Among the benefits, he cited the many new products imported from America; the expansion of commerce; and the advances made in geography, ship construction, navigation, astronomy, and natural science.

Mandrillon concluded: "I dare say that the discovery of America was an evil; the benefits that it has engendered can never compensate for the mass of evils that it has caused." Despite this negative judgment, Mandrillon hailed one long-term consequence of the Discovery, the recently achieved independence of the United States, as a triumph of liberty over tyranny. And he closed with a striking prophecy: "The New World, formerly our slave, largely peopled by our emigrants, will some day come to enslave us. Its industry and

Introduction

power will increase as ours diminishes; the Old World will be subjugated by the New; and that conquering people, having itself suffered the laws of revolution, will in its turn perish, perhaps at the hands of some other people whom it had the misfortune to discover."

The famous Abbé Guillaume Raynal, whose *Histoire philosophique et politique des établissements et du commerce dans les deux Indes* (1770) has been called a *machine de guerre* of the Enlightenment against colonialism, tyranny, superstition, and ignorance, and who had proposed to the Lyons Academy the holding of the prize contest mentioned above, offered his own assessment of the effects of the Discovery in his *Histoire*. Like Mandrillon, he conceded that "this great event" had produced notable advances in science, technology, and knowledge, had made available to Europe some conveniences and luxuries, and that the European colonies have "given splendor, power, and wealth, to the states which have founded them"—but at what a price! The convenience and luxuries were "so cruelly obtained, so unequally distributed, and so obstinately disputed" that it was doubtful whether they justified their cost. The "bold attempts" of Columbus and Vasco da Gama had created "a spirit of fanaticism" for making discoveries in quest of "some continents to invade, some islands to ravage, and some people to spoil, to subdue, and to massacre." The "insatiable thirst for gold" had given rise to "the most infamous and the most atrocious of all traffics, that of slaves," the "most execrable" of crimes against nature. The colonial powers, their resources strained at home and abroad, had "fallen into confusion," and their rivalries led to endless wars that "harassed the globe and stained it with blood." Raynal concluded by asking, if it were possible to do it over again, would we wish to find the way to America and India? Raynal questioned whether "there exists a being infernal enough to answer this question in the affirmative!"

English intellectuals of the time, more conservative than their French colleagues and more interested in the economic side of the question, viewed the results of the Discovery more favorably. In words that seemed to echo Gómara's judgment of more than two centuries earlier, in the *Wealth of Nations* (1776) the economist Adam Smith proclaimed that "the discovery of America and that of the passage to the East Indies by the Cape of Good Hope, are the two greatest and most important events recorded in the history of mankind." In the same book Smith struck a blow at the Noble Savage image of the Indian, sometimes used by French reformers like

Voltaire and Diderot—more or less seriously—to attack the follies and frailties of European civilization. The Indians did not have coined money, carried on all their commerce by barter, and had almost no division of labor. Smith asserted that the Spanish Conquest had led to major advances in American agricultural productivity, thanks to Spain's introduction of cattle, the plow, and other iron tools, with a resulting increase in population. He suggested incorrectly that Mexico and Peru were more populous now than they had been before the Spanish Conquest.

If British scholars in general offered a favorable assessment of the Discovery (although often critical of its Spanish actors and methods) and its consequences, they could do no less for Columbus. Thus, William Robertson's monumental and very popular *History of America* (1777) faithfully followed the line of Ferdinand's *Historie*, unwaveringly taking sides with Columbus and against his enemies in all disputed matters. As concerns Columbus's Indian policy, Robertson wrote that "he adhered scrupulously to the principles of integrity and justice in all his transactions with them, and treated them, on every occasion, not only with humanity but with indulgence." When he deviated from that mild policy—for example, when he imposed the death-dealing gold tribute on the Indians of Hispaniola—Robertson pleads in excuse his need to obtain gold in order to encourage Ferdinand and Isabella to continue supporting his explorations. Robertson concluded his account of Columbus's life with a reverent description of his death: "He died with a composure of mind suitable to the magnanimity which distinguished his character, and with sentiments of piety becoming that supreme respect for religion, which he manifested in every occurrence of his life."

Amid the general chorus of praise for Columbus and his work in eighteenth-century England, at least one dissenting voice was heard. The anti-colonialist Samuel Johnson, who described the dispute between France and England in America as "the quarrel of two robbers over the spoil of a passenger," also wrote: "The Europeans have scarcely visited any coast but to gratify avarice and extend corruption; to arrogate dominion without rights, and practice cruelty without incentive." As for Columbus, he had to travel "from court to court, scorned and repulsed as a wild projector, an idle promiser of kingdoms in the clouds; nor has any part of the world had reason to rejoice that he found at last reception and employment."

Johnson's sour reflections, untypical in England, were unthinkable in England's American colonies, whose rapid material progress

Introduction

and irresistible movement toward independence became "purposefully entwined," in the words of Kirkpatrick Sale, with the image of Columbus. (I speak of the free white population, of course; we have no record of the feelings of the Indians and black slaves on the subject.) As early as 1771, Philip Freneau, the "father of American poetry," offered a tribute to Columbus as his graduation address at Princeton, and in a poem published soon after the battles of Lexington and Bunker Hill (1775) he made the first known use of the name "Columbia" to identify the new nation with the Discoverer. After independence had been won, another poet, Joel Barlow, published (1787) an epic poem, *The Vision of Columbus*. In this poem, Columbus, lying in a Spanish prison, has a prophetic dream in which an angel shows him the future glories of the New World he had discovered, with special attention, of course, to the brilliant progress of the United States. And in 1792, in "A Discourse Intended to Commemorate the Discovery of America by Christopher Columbus," as if rebutting Samuel Johnson, the Reverend Jeremy Belknap, who has been called the "father of American history" for his writings on the explorers, described Columbus as a "genius" who "was not a closet projector, but an enterprising adventurer" whose voyage "opened to the Europeans a new world . . . , gave a new form to their thoughts, to their spirit of enterprise and of commerce . . . enlarged the empire of Spain, and stamped with immortality the name of Christopher Columbus. . . . In the pages of impartial history, he will always be celebrated as a man of genius and science, as a prudent, skillful, intrepid navigator." Citing some of the numerous private and public uses of the name "Columbia" or "Columbian," Kirkpatrick Sale has shown that by the first decades of the nineteenth century Columbia had become "firmly fixed as the allegorical symbol of the United States."

Columbus in the Age of Romance and the Rise of the Scientific School

By the first decades of the nineteenth century, the doubts that skeptics like the Abbé Raynal or Samuel Johnson had raised concerning the merits of Columbus or the benefits of his voyages for humanity had vanished; Columbus and the Discovery had become the objects of a true cult. Europeans and Americans alike now saw the Discovery as the harbinger and first cause of the great economic expansion and the establishment of Western domination over the globe that was under way. Celebrations of the Discovery and Columbus were particularly exuberant in the United States, where a mystic link was seen between them and the spectacular rise of the great Republic of the West.

It was fitting, therefore, that the most popular book ever written about Columbus, the book that incorporated all the legends associated with the man, *The Life and Voyages of Christopher Columbus* (1828), should have been written by an American—Washington Irving. Romanticism was the dominant mode of historical thought and expression in Irving's time; and the same romantic aesthetic criteria that had determined William H. Prescott's choice of the Conquest of Mexico as the subject of his masterpiece (1843), helped Irving decide to write about Columbus and the discovery of America.

Irving had access to a wealth of sources recently brought to light by the Spanish scholar Martín Fernández de Navarrete and published in 1826; they included Las Casas's abstract of Columbus's long-lost journal of the First Voyage, letters between Columbus and the Sovereigns, and the Spanish manuscript of the bizarre *Lettera rarissima* written by Columbus on his Fourth Voyage. With these sources before him Irving could have made a major contribution to the Columbian literature, a truthful work revealing the complex, many-faceted character of Columbus. But he did nothing of the sort. In what Kirkpatrick Sale rightly calls "a glaring abdication of the responsibility of the historian in favor of the license of the novelist," he "created an essentially fictional hero for whose actions it was not necessary to provide documentation; or worse, in favor of the nationalist hoping for popular approval and literary reputation at home." In doing this, Irving was undoubtedly influenced by romantic conventions that required him to assign a suitable grandeur and dignity to his subject; he was also influenced by his political and social conservatism, the conservatism of a gentleman scholar who regarded revolutions, in the words of V. L. Parrington, as "somewhat vulgar affairs." The conventional nature and mediocrity of his thought is well illustrated by his comments on would-be denigrators of Columbus:

There is a certain meddlesome spirit, which, in the garb of learned research, goes prying about the traces of history, casting down its monuments and marring and mutilating its fairest trophies. Care should be taken to vindicate great names from such pernicious erudition. It defeats one of the most salutary purposes of history, that of furnishing examples of what human genius and laudable enterprise may accomplish.

True to his own precept, Irving consistently omits or glosses over the darker sides of Columbus's life, especially his conduct toward the Indians. And, as we have already noted, he readily accepts the most spurious legends about Columbus, including the legend that Columbus's opponents believed the world was flat, the anecdote of the egg, and the story that Isabella offered to pawn her jewels to finance his enterprise. These and other picturesque fables, told in Irving's graceful style, contributed to the book's immense popularity, reflected in the thirty-nine printings and editions published in the United States and Great Britain in the next three decades and the fifty-one editions of translations published in Latin America and Europe in the same period.

Irving's work influenced other biographers who diffused even more widely his romantic vision of Columbus. Most notable among those biographers was the French poet and republican leader Alphonse de Lamartine, whose *Christophe Colomb* (1853), written in elegant prose, faithfully followed the outlines of Irving's story and embroidered his account with all the traditional fables. After Irving's book, Lamartine's life was the most popular nineteenth-century biography of Columbus, published in successive editions in France and in translation in English- and Spanish-speaking countries. Irving and Lamartine were of course not responsible for the romantic excesses committed by imitators or copiers who lacked their talent and sense of proportion, like that Spanish editor who "freely arranged" Lamartine's book (1876) into a fictional biography, dripping with piety and unctuousness. He assigns to Columbus sentiments like the following: "I believe I have a mission to perform, and nothing more. . . . I would feel myself the happiest of men if I had the incomparable satisfaction of knowing that I had succeeded in my enterprise and brought some benefit to the world."

In a more mystic vein, the French writer Antoine Roselly de Lourges insisted in his *Christophe Colomb: Histoire de sa vie at de ses voyages* (1856) and several other works that Columbus had undertaken his voyage in order to convert the heathen and not to gain territory for Spain; accordingly Roselly initiated a movement for Columbus's canonization that won powerful support among Catholic clergy and laypeople in Europe and the United States. But the project encountered serious obstacles; they included the fact that Columbus had fathered an illegitimate son and had engaged in the slave trade, and lack of proof that he had performed an authentic miracle. In the end, the Church tribunal entrusted with such matters voted against Columbus's beatification, the preliminary to sainthood.

After the mid-nineteenth century, positivism and evolutionism gradually replaced romanticism as the ruling ideologies of the Western world, and a more critical, scientific spirit began to appear in writings on Columbus and the Discovery. As a rule, the new approach did not dispute Columbus's greatness or the transcendent significance of his work, but subjected every aspect of his life and his Enterprise of the Indies, and every assertion of the two major sources of information on these subjects, Ferdinand's *Historie* and Las Casas's *Historia de las Indias*, to a searching inquiry. The writings of the great Prussian scholar Alexander von Humboldt, who pioneered in bringing a rigorously scientific, empirical method to the study of ancient America, offer early examples of this same approach toward Columbus and his achievement. For Humboldt one of Columbus's chief glories was the fact that his expedition was prepared in such a way as to leave nothing to chance. "It offers all the characteristics of a scientifically conceived and accomplished plan." Humboldt, stressing Columbus's contributions to scientific knowledge, including the discovery of the variation in terrestrial magnetism, the direction of currents, and the classification of marine plants, left no doubt of his belief in Columbus's greatness: "Columbus served mankind by offering new themes for its reflection; he increased the mass of ideas and, thanks to him, human thought has advanced." Another great Americanist, Henry Vignaud, described Humboldt's *Examen critique de l'histoire de la géographie du Nouveau Continent* (1836–1839) as "the most profound work ever written on the causes of the discovery of America."

As the four-hundredth anniversary of the Discovery approached, there was an outpouring of books, articles, and documents relating to the subject in Europe and America. Las Casas's *Historia de las Indias*, buried in the archives for three hundred years, finally saw the light in 1875. Between 1864 and 1884 the Spanish government published forty-two volumes of documents on the history of colonial Spanish America, especially valuable for the sixteenth century; the

Introduction

collection was enriched by an additional twenty-five volumes between 1885 and 1932. The Italian government commemorated the anniversary by publishing between 1892 and 1896 thirteen volumes of a great *Raccolta di Documenti*; the first three volumes of the set made available Columbus's complete writings in Italian translation, with scholarly commentaries by Cesare de Lollis. In the same period the American bibliophile John Boyd Thatcher published a work in three folio volumes, *Christopher Columbus, His Life, His Works, His Remains* (1903–1904), containing numerous facsimiles and English translations of Columbian documents.

In the same period there also appeared a number of substantial biographies and studies of Columbus. Without questioning the greatness of the man and his work, they approached both with a more critical and realistic posture than Irving's compound of fact and fiction. A Spanish historian of the new realistic school, Cesáreo Fernández Duro, typified this approach when he wrote in his *Colón y la historia póstuma* (1885): "When we censure the tendency . . . to convert heroes into demigods and acknowledge that Columbus, though a great man, was after all a man, subject to human weaknesses and the dominion of passions to which the most famous men have been subject, we do not at all diminish his glory, his prestige, or the opinion that he merits before history." But Spanish historical writing on Columbus and his voyages in this period also had a clear defensive tendency, seeking to vindicate the Spanish Sovereigns and Columbus's Spanish collaborators like Martín Alonso Pinzón against charges that they had mistreated or betrayed the Genoese. A major work of the Spanish realistic school was José María Asensio's richly illustrated biography, *Cristóbal Colón, su vida, sus viajes, sus descubrimientos* (1892).

In Mexico, the statesman and historian Justo Sierra, an exponent of the postivist philosophy of Auguste Comte and Herbert Spencer, reflected the new scientific viewpoint on Columbus in a commemorative address in 1892. Columbus, he observed, was no saint; he was a pirate in his youth, he was greedy and avidly sought authority and honors, he seduced a young woman of Córdoba and abandoned her, and he was cruel to the Indians whom he tried to enslave and sell like merchandise. But Columbus was also "the supreme abbreviator of human evolution," "the genius whose discovery allowed the American tree to shelter in its shade the throne of twentieth-century civilization." Sierra's judgment reflected the positivist view that "history does not absolve or condemn; it investigates, testifies, explains, and that is what makes it a science, that is how it slowly but surely attains the truth."

Traces of the romantic view of Columbus survived longer in Victorian England. The eminent English geographer and historian Clements Markham wrote a short but substantial *Life of Christopher Columbus* (1889), based on the most recent findings. At one point, however, Markham's prudery overcame his critical sense. Against all the evidence to the contrary, he followed Roselly de Lourges in a labored effort to prove that Columbus had married his mistress, Beatriz Enríquez de Arana, Ferdinand's mother. For the rest, Markham's enthusiasm for Columbus and his achievement knew no bounds. Euphoric, like most contemporary intellectuals, at the sight of the West's rapid economic and scientific advance, humankind's growing mastery of nature, and European expansion over the planet, he wrote:

> Looking back at all that has grown out of it in the few centuries that have since elapsed, we now know that the sailing of those three little boats over the bar of Saltes was, since the fall of Rome, the most momentous event in the world's history. . . . Columbus believed that he had discovered a new route to the Indies. He had done infinitely more. He had discovered another continent, and the consequences of his discovery would be vast beyond what it was possible for the greatest genius of the fifteenth century even to conceive.

Two scholars, the French-American Henry Harrisse and the French Americanist Henry Vignaud, produced exhaustive inquiries into various aspects of the Columbian story; their severe questioning of some accepted verities of that story led annoyed critics to dub them writers of the "hypercritical" school. Harrisse is best known for his claim that Ferdinand's life of his father was a fabrication; I noted in my preface that Harrisse himself retracted that charge following the first publication in 1875 of Las Casas's *Historia de las Indias*, which repeatedly cited Ferdinand's book. Vignaud insisted in a series of works that Columbus's great object was not to find a new route to the Indies but to find new lands to the West; his claim found only minority scholarly support but is far from dead today, as shown by Kirkpatrick Sale's recent reopening of the question. Despite some

Introduction

excesses on the part of scholars of the so-called "hypercritical" tendency, they contributed to the advance of Columbian studies by helping to purge the legends that had grown up around Columbus and his voyages. Vignaud called attention to the progress made in the demolition of those legends when he wrote around 1910:

> It has now been shown that the discoverer of America was not of noble origin, that he was not related to the famous Colombos of whom so much was told in the sixteenth century, that none of his relatives was a sailor by profession, that he did not attend any university, that he did not wage a campaign either with the Colombos or for King René or anyone else, and that before his arrival in Portugal in 1476 he was not known to have practiced any other profession than that of weaver.

Despite their critical spirit, most writers of the scientific school had no thought of diminishing the stature of Columbus or detracting from his achievement. On the contrary, in the conclusion to his massive *Nouvelles études critiques* (1911), Vignaud emphasized that his revisionist theory that Columbus believed in the existence of undiscovered lands to the West and had searched for them "obstinately, patiently, intelligently," and that "he discovered America because he had searched for it," enhanced Columbus's greatness and assured him of "the place that belongs to him in the pantheon of great men to whom mankind raises statues."

In the same period, American scholars of the scientific school produced a number of substantial studies; they included Justin Winsor's *Christopher Colombus and How He Received and Imparted the Spirit of Discovery* (1891); John Fiske's *The Discovery of America* (1892); and Filson Young's *Christopher Columbus and the New World of the Discovery* (1906). As a rule, these works accepted the traditional view of Columbus's greatness and the splendor of his Discovery, while rejecting the mythical elements in the Columbus story and admitting that he had made large mistakes and committed cruelties. They usually tempered criticism of his brutal Indian policy, however, by assigning part of the blame to the spirit of the times, to other men, and to the difficult position in which he found himself. But Winsor, the leading Columbian scholar in the United States, provoked remonstrances from his colleagues when, among other critical remarks, he denounced Columbus as a "slave-driver" and "the originator of American slavery." Noting that the great humanitarian Las Casas always spoke of Columbus with admiration and respect, John Fiske asked: "But how could Las Casas ever have respected the feeble, mean-spirited driveller whose portrait Mr. Winsor asks us to accept as the Discoverer of America?" A common defense of Columbus (employed at least since the time of Irving) was the relativist argument that it was unfair to expect him to rise above the accepted practices of his time. "To heap anathemas at this late day upon his head," wrote Charles P. MacKie in *The Last Voyages of the Admiral of the Ocean Sea* (1892), "because, four centuries ago, he did not carry on an anti-slavery crusade as well as one against ignorance and bigotry, seems to be rather hypercritical than just." Winsor had already countered that argument, however, when he observed that "the really great man is superior to his age and anticipates its future"—something that Columbus obviously had not done. A popular biography by John S. C. Abbott, *Christopher Columbus* (1875), sometimes shifted uncomfortably between eulogy and condemnation of its subject. Calling Columbus "one of nature's noblemen," Abbott wrote that "the testimony seems unequivocal that Columbus was, by nature, a kind-hearted man; though, influenced by the darkness of that dark age, he was subsequently guilty of many cruel acts."

But one iconoclastic biographer, Aaron Goodrich, would have nothing to do with such balancing acts. In his *Life of the So-Called Christopher Columbus* (1874), he denounced the Discoverer for his cruelty and other flaws of character. As regards Columbus's Indian policy, "Columbus was inexorable. Gold he must have, if it cost the life of every Indian in the island to procure it." Goodrich even anticipated the skeptical attitude of modern scholars regarding Columbus's claim that the Caribs were cannibals. "Columbus, still bent on the establishment of slavery, sought some excuse, and the most plausible was to represent his victims as monsters, feeding upon human flesh, whom to enslave was to civilize." On the famous oath that Columbus forced his crews to take, to the effect that Cuba was a continent, Goodrich wrote: "He manufactures perjury wholesale, which felony he would perpetuate by the barbarous means of scourging and cutting out the tongues of those who speak the truth. Thus, by a system unknown to Thales and Ptolemy—original if not scientific, did the much-lauded navigator and astronomer, the pious and

Introduction

humane 'admiral,' determine the latitude and longitude of the island of Cuba."

Attacks on Columbus also came from writers who rode one or another historical hobbyhorse. Marie A. Brown, for example, wrote a diatribe, *The Icelandic Discoverers of America, or Honor to Whom Honor Is Due* (1888), in which she denounced Columbus as a usurper, a pirate, a trafficker in human flesh, and the introducer of the sinister Catholic faith.

Such doubts and reservations as Winsor and others may have entertained concerning Columbus's greatness and morality were not permitted to cloud the elaborate official celebration in the United States of the four-hundredth anniversary of the Discovery. Chauncey Depew, president of the New York Central Railroad, echoed Irving when he expressed his strong disapproval of such carping criticism as Winsor had leveled against Columbus: "If there is anything which I detest more than another, it is that spirit of critical historical inquiry which doubts everything; that modern spirit which destroys all the illusions and all the heroes which have been the inspiration of patriotism through all the centuries." The celebrations were capped by the opening of the great Columbian Exposition in Chicago on May 1, 1893. Visitors to the Exposition could admire statues of the Discoverer by Augustus Saint-Gaudens and Frédéric-Auguste Bartholdi and full-size facsimiles of the three ships of the First Voyage on Lake Michigan. "But the real end of the fair," writes Kirkpatrick Sale, "was the presumed end and glory for which Columbus had sailed—that is, those American exhibits devoted . . . to Manufactures and Liberal Arts, Machinery, Agriculture, Transportation, Mines and Mining, Electricity, Horticulture, Forestry, and Fisheries." The official celebrations also served more pragmatic ends; the Spanish embassy in the United States sent its government a translation of a debate in the Senate Foreign Relations Committee in which one speaker observed that the principal objective of the Centenary was the strengthening of the commercial and social ties between the United States and the sister nations of the Americas.

In Spain, as in the United States, there was an outpouring of books, poems, speeches, and festivities to commemorate the fourth centenary of the Discovery. Here, too, in addition to seeking to honor Columbus and arouse patriotic zeal, the commemoration had practical motives; by proclaiming the transcendent significance of the Discovery, Spain's contributions to that event, and the constructive nature of Spain's work in America, the Spanish government, headed by the Conservative prime minister Antonio Canovas del Castillo, hoped to bolster the prestige of a discredited monarchy and strengthen Spain's commercial and political ties with her former colonies, the independent Latin American states. The Spanish commemoration, stresses the Spanish historian Salvador Bernabeu Albert in *1892: El IV Centenario del descubrimiento de América en España* (1987), "must be understood in the context of a broader counteroffensive begun by the Spanish government to counter North American imperialism, very active following the Pan-American Conference [of 1889]."

In Italy, celebrating its recent achievement of national unity (1870), the commemoration had a markedly patriotic character; the Italian government and Church did all in their power to "Italianize" and "dehispanicize" the Columbian enterprise, to claim the Genoese navigator for their own by stressing the obstacles placed in his way by Spaniards and the ingratitude shown to him by the Spanish Crown. Pope Leo XIII contributed to Columbus's pious image by issuing an encyclical (July 16, 1892) proclaiming that Columbus had undertaken his great voyage with the object of preparing and facilitating the way for the diffusion of the Faith, and that all his works conformed to religion and were inspired by piety.

With the encouragement of the Spanish government, official celebrations of the fourth centenary of the Discovery were held in Latin American capitals, and October 12 was proclaimed to be forever "El Día de la Raza" (the Day of the Race), but lingering resentment against Spain's colonial rule, revived by the outbreak of the Cuban struggle for independence, kept the level of popular interest and support low. The most gala commemoration took place in Mexico City; it was attended by the dictator Porfirio Díaz, other public officials, and the diplomatic corps, and was marked by the unveiling of a statue of Columbus and the reading of orations and poems honoring the Hero by Justo Sierra and other luminaries of the Porfirista regime.

Columbus in the Twentieth Century: A Clash of Images

In the last decades of the twentieth century the virtual consensus that had prevailed since about 1800 regarding the heroic stature of Columbus and the value of his achievement broke down. As the

· xliii ·

Introduction

world prepared to mark the fifth centenary of the Discovery in 1992, the dispute as to how it should be commemorated, or whether it should be commemorated at all, reached a peak of intensity. The dramatic change in the climate of opinion since the 1892 celebrations, with their flowery eulogies of Columbus and confident affirmations that his exploit had launched the world on a course of endless progress, reflected the catastrophic experiences of the twentieth century: two world wars, a great depression, the collapse of empires, and the frustration of hopes as the world divided into a handful of dominant "rich" states and a great majority of countries plagued by dependency and desperate poverty, all capped by the growing threat of ecological disaster. Inevitably, these vast transformations provoked ideological changes: some loss of nerve and faith in the future by Western elites; and a rising sense of injustice and resentment among the masses of the so-called Third World and ethnic minorities in the West who suffered the effects of what has been called "internal colonialism." In the Americas, that resentment crystallized into a historical vision of the Discovery as a brutal, genocidal invasion of Indian America, followed by five centuries of systematic colonial and neocolonial enslavement and oppression of its Indian, black, and mixed-blood masses. This influential "Vision of the Vanquished," endorsed by many sympathetic white liberals and radicals, is at the heart of the current dispute. That dispute recalls the controversy two hundred years ago concerning the benefits or evils produced by the Discovery and Raynal's question: If we had to do it over again, would we still want to find the route to America and India?

As might be expected, the traditional image of Columbus and his achievement proved most durable in the United States, in part because of the continuing influence of Irving's biography on the reading public and especially on history textbooks; in part, perhaps, because the United States had withstood more successfully than any other part of the world the great economic and political shocks of the twentieth century and therefore faced the future with greater optimism. The 1942 publication of Samuel Eliot Morison's *Admiral of the Ocean Sea: A Life of Christopher Columbus* was a major event in Columbian studies; it also strengthened the hold of the Irving image of Columbus on the American mind by refining that image, freeing it from its complement of old fables, and basing it on a scholarship that appeared indisputably solid. Morison's account of Columbus's

voyages, in particular, gained in credibility from his efforts to retrace them by following Columbus's routes under sail. Superbly
written, the biography continues to enjoy a justified popularity, but
in recent years some of its assertions and especially its large general-
izations have come under growing criticism. Kirkpatrick Sale, for
example, has called attention to some romantic, fictional touches in
the book and, citing some alleged poor navigational judgments by
Columbus, has even questioned Morison's description of him as a
master mariner. In his *Samuel Eliot Morison's Historical World: In
Quest of a New Parkman* (1991), Gregory M. Pfitzer also notes how
Morison gave his imagination free play in reconstructing Columbus's
movements: "Morison presumes to know where Columbus went,
what he saw, and who saw him, with a confidence that would have
shocked even Irving."

Despite its considerable merits, in its essentials Morison's work
represents an updated version of Irving's romantic interpretation of
Columbus. To be sure, Morison condemns Columbus's Indian policy, speaks of his "monstrous expedient" of sending hundreds of Indians to the slave market of Seville and of his responsibility for the
"ghastly system" of compelling the Indians of Hispaniola to pay tribute in gold. But Morison offers little or no analysis of the driving
forces behind these events or of the dehumanizing ideology with
which Columbus approached the Caribbean Indians. What analysis
Morison provides is superficial, as when he suggests that Columbus
failed as a colonial administrator in part "because his conception of a
colony transcended the desire of his followers to impart, and the
capacity of the natives to receive, the institutions and culture of
Renaissance Europe."

For Morison, in fact, the sufferings of the Indians appear to be the
unfortunate price that must be paid for the "transfer of Christian
civilization across the Ocean Sea" by "the stout-hearted son of Genoa." As late as 1974, in the conclusion to his *European Discovery of
America: The Southern Voyages, 1492–1616*, Morison stressed that
Columbus's main conception was "to carry the Word of God and
knowledge of His Son to the far corners of the globe," and that this
conception had become a fact. "To the people of the New World,
pagans expecting short and brutish lives, devoid of hope for any
future, had come the Christian vision of a merciful God and a glorious Heaven." Today many readers will find those comments anach-
ronistic or even laughable. The respected English scholar David

Introduction

Beers Quinn, in a foreword to the 1983 edition of Morison's *Admiral of the Ocean Sea*, criticized Morison for his scant attention to Columbus's failings, noting that Columbus "cannot be detached from the imperialist exploitation of his discoveries and must be made to take some share of responsibility for the brutal exploitation of the islands and mainlands he found."

Until recently the Irving-Morison interpretation of Columbus and his achievement, representing mainstream public and scholarly opinion in the United States, encountered few challenges. One early dissident from Morison's view of Columbus was the geographer Carl O. Sauer, whose studies in the 1930s anticipated the conclusion of the so-called Berkeley school of historians that American preconquest populations had been much larger than was commonly supposed. In 1966 he published *The Early Spanish Main*, a pioneering study of the geographic environment and economy of the Taino Indians of Hispaniola and the impact of Columbus's policies upon them. He concluded that Taino agriculture was as "productive as in few parts of the world," yielding the "highest returns of food in continuous supply by the simplest methods and modest labor," and that the "Indians lived well and at ease in a generous land which they used competently and without spoiling it." Sauer claimed that Columbus's Indian policy, which he described as "simple, rigid, and unworkable," made impossible demands upon the Indians, leading to the destruction of their economic and social systems and the virtual extinction of the native population. "The government of Columbus," Sauer wrote, "was a continuing series of bad decisions. Always he insisted that he was right and would have succeeded but for his enemies. Experience taught him nothing. The heritage of his mistakes continued long after him."

Throughout most of the twentieth century, few Europeans dissented from the conventional image of Columbus of which Morison's biography offered the prime example. Spanish writers on Columbus and related subjects continued the late nineteenth-century historiographic tradition of realism and scientific rigor, but often combined it with a defensive approach toward Spain's work in America. As concerned Columbus and the Discovery, Spanish scholars tended to stress the sincerity and benignity of the Catholic Sovereigns in their dealings with Columbus and the large services rendered by Spaniards to the success of his enterprise. But some, like Ramón Menéndez Pidal in his *El Padre Las Casas: Su doble personalidad* (1963),

· xlvi ·

contrasted the "avid greed" of Columbus and his slave-trading projects with the supposed humanity of Isabella, who forbade Columbus to enslave her Indian vassals. The best Spanish synthesis remains Antonio Ballesteros y Berreta's massive *Cristóbal Colón y el descubrimiento de América* (1945), especially useful for its exhaustive bibliographies and careful surveys of disputed questions. But Ballesteros never comes to grips with the larger issues of Columbus's life and work, and his final assessment is disappointingly superficial and even banal:

> Columbus was the man of genius whose daring exploit immortalized his name. His life displays outstanding virtues of religiosity and perseverance. Loyal to his monarchs, affectionate with his family, a sincere and constant friend, he was not the saint imagined by Roselly de Lourges. Subject to the weaknesses of human nature, his very defects present him to us as one of the most powerful and interesting individuals in the history of humankind.

In Italy, the principal champion of the traditional interpretation of Columbus and his achievement is Paolo Emilio Taviani, whose *Christopher Columbus: The Grand Design* (1985), reflects a vast scholarship and familiarity with the history of Columbus's and Taviani's native city, Genoa. Taviani subjects to informed and searching inquiry many technical problems and disputed aspects of Columbus's life. But for Taviani, a founder and leader of the conservative Christian Democratic party, such questions as Columbus's treatment of the Indians or the possible negative consequences of the Discovery do not seem to exist. For Taviani, Columbus is simply a "true genius," "one of the giants of human history" who "was ever aware of being an instrument of Divine Providence."

Two twentieth-century biographers, perhaps influenced by Freudian and other contemporary psychoanalytical theories, subjected Columbus to a psychological analysis that sought to reveal and explain the complex, contradictory, troubled personality of the man. In 1929 the German-Jewish novelist Jacob Wasserman published a life, soon translated into English as *Columbus: Don Quixote of the Seas.*[2] The

---

[2] Wasserman, I should note, was not the first to compare Columbus to Cervantes' hero. In a biography containing many fictional touches, *La Véridique aventure de Christophe Colomb* (1927), Marius André commented

Introduction

somber tone of the book probably reflects, in part, the darkening political and social atmosphere of the Weimar Republic in the years just before the Nazi seizure of power. But it also stems from Wasserman's portrayal of Columbus as a disturbed personality who, like Don Quixote, is a trifle mad, his head filled with dreams and illusions. Thus, when Columbus unabashedly writes to the Sovereigns, "I am not the first of my family who has sailed the seas as an Admiral," Wasserman absolves him from the charge of deliberate lying. "Those who do so have little imagination, and a sorry sense of this deep, almost unfathomable nature." For Wasserman, it was precisely Columbus's lack of discrimination, his "flaming hallucinations," his acceptance of the most dubious evidence along with the evidence of sober cartographers like Martin Behaim and Paolo Toscanelli, that accounted for the success of his enterprise. "In that head chaos reigned—a murk and confusion of the mind that no longer recognizes any scale of thoughts and values, and had it not been so, the tremendous deed would never have been accomplished. Knowledge begets cowardice; the will can only drive steadily forward in a half-light."

Reflecting on the Capitulations obtained by Columbus from the Sovereigns, Wasserman writes: "A strange fantastic dream-transaction, without example in history, by which both parties, with the same ceremonial seriousness, drew a bill upon the future without the slightest guarantee that it would ever be met. What a personality must this man have been, and what magnetism he must have had, to make the queen, the king, a clear-headed personage like Santangel, and many others also, feel the spell of the daemonic problems that possessed his soul."

Wasserman unsparingly condemns Columbus's attitude toward the Indians, which he describes as "from the very outset, cowardly, treacherous, and capricious. On the one hand he cannot sufficiently praise their simplicity and honesty, and on the other he racks his brains over the best way to make the most profit out of them, for he

---

on Columbus's claim during his Third Voyage that the Earthly Paradise was in Venezuela and some other curious geographical observations: "The Admiral is in the grip of a total hallucination. He is a Don Quixote driven mad by too much reading of maritime and biblical romances of chivalry. . . . But he is a self-taught Don Quixote, a novice intoxicated with poorly digested knowledge who can only spout the quotations he has collected."

regards them as his own property—primarily as his own, and after that the property of the Spanish Crown." However, Wasserman recognizes that "no Europeans at the end of the fifteenth century would have shown more judgment in dealing with the Indians . . . ; not one would have suspected or sought for the background of human history and culture, the secret of the race, the fear, the awe, the collapse of that ideal world, the subtle change of feeling that produced the delicate, almost impenetrable cunning—using the word in its psychopathic sense—that hid their true nature as though behind a mask."

And Wasserman rightly stresses Columbus's obsession with gold: "He thought and dreamed of nothing but gold. It was his torment, the spur that drove him on, his obsession, and his hope . . . , and that is why he scraped the gold together by any means and everywhere he can, for gold is the only reality that can prevail upon the mind: by means of gold he can make good his claims and prove his statements—it is the very essence of the veiled mystery, the image of his achievement."

Wasserman's book, now little read, had considerable influence, acknowledged or unacknowledged, on later writers about Columbus. The description of Columbus as a Don Quixote and the stress on Columbus's arrogance, mysticism, and obsession with gold, for example, reappear in the work of a Spanish liberal intellectual, Salvador de Madariaga, in *Christopher Columbus* (1939), written in English. Madariaga writes well and brilliantly re-creates the Spanish historical milieu; although he repeats some myths his book is free from Wasserman's more obvious factual errors. But it suffers from a major flaw—Madariaga doggedly adheres to the thesis that Columbus was of Jewish origin and belonged to a secret group of *conversos*, converted Jews. Madariaga employs this notion throughout the book to explain certain actions of Columbus and his supposed traits of fanaticism and avarice. Although the thesis rests on fragile circumstantial evidence, it continues to have its advocates, like Simon Wiesenthal, author of *Sails of Hope* (1973).

Madariaga refines Wasserman's Don Quixote analogy: "Though Colón [Columbus] and Don Quixote go off the deep end as soon as there is a question of Cipango for Colón, and Dulcinea for Don Quixote, they are only mad north-northwest, and for the rest of life they are sensible and even intelligent. . . . Colón may believe in Cipango and Esdras, but he will have nothing to do with D'Ailly's

Introduction

dragons and griffins; Don Quixote believes in giants and enchanters, but stops at the speaking head in Barcelona. And both believe in islands."

For the rest, Madariaga strongly defends the Indian or colonial policies of both Columbus and the Spanish kings. "Are we to condemn [Columbus]," he writes, "for his inability to handle the Indians with the technique of a contemporary anthropologist? He approached his tasks on the whole with honorable intentions and with an amount of freedom from prejudice, of intellectual detachment and of power of observation altogether unusual in his day and possibly also in ours. His limitations were for the most part due to his time and to the novelty and difficulty of his task." Columbus's real problem, Madariaga asserts, was that "*the natives would not work.*" Madariaga's naive references to Columbus's "honorable intentions" and the natives' supposed unwillingness to work reveal his unconscious but unmistakable pro-colonialist bias, his total inability to view the problem from the viewpoint of the Indians and their interests. In the same apologetic vein, Madariaga writes that "this able, well-meaning and straightforward couple [the Spanish Sovereigns] were confronted with all the problems with which colonial life still baffles and tests modern nations. There is ample evidence that . . . Ferdinand and Isabella never put any special stress on the material results of the discovery." To call King Ferdinand, notorious in his own time for his greed and duplicity, "straightforward" and uninterested in the "material results" of the Discovery appears to contradict elementary historical facts.

Two recent studies have deepened our understanding of Columbus's professional and ideological formation. In his *Christophe Colomb* (1981), the historian Jacques Heers describes the Genoese milieu in which Columbus passed his youth, stressing the extent and variety of Genoa's far-flung foreign trade, Genoese advances in ship construction, and the mastery achieved by Genoese sailors in the techniques of long-distance navigation, including the use of winds and currents in sailing. The training Columbus received in this Mediterranean school of navigation undoubtedly helped him to meet the greater challenges of sailing the "Ocean Sea." Columbus emerges from Heers's book as a typical merchant mariner of his time, an adventurer ready to go wherever the opportunity for profit beckoned.

Alain Milhou explores another dimension of Columbus's character, his mysticism and messianism, in his *Colón y su mentalidad*

· 1 ·

mesiánica franciscanista española (1983). These traits grew stronger as Columbus grew older and found their clearest expression in the curious *Libro de las Profecías* (The Book of Prophecies), a collection of passages from the Scriptures and other sources compiled by Columbus on his return from the Third Voyage and designed to prove to the Sovereigns that the time was ripe (Columbus believed that the world would end in 155 years) for a crusade to recover the Holy Land as the prelude to the discovery and conversion of all the heathen nations. Columbus had no doubt about his own providential role in the accomplishment of this sacred mission. "The Lord purposed that there should be something clearly miraculous in this matter of the voyage to the Indies," Columbus wrote in the *Profecías*, "so as to encourage me and others in the . . . Household of God." Milhou rightly observes that Columbus's religiosity, although sincere, did not inspire a "true humility," but rather confirmed his consciousness of being one of the Elect and supported his obsession with power, titles, fame, and wealth.

A more recent work, *The Libro de las Profecías of Christopher Columbus* (1991), a translation of the Book of Prophecies by the late August Kling, with an elaborate commentary by Delno C. West, deepens our understanding of the apocalyptic and messianic side of Columbus's thought and of what West regards as its decisive role in the genesis of the Enterprise of the Indies. West depicts Columbus as "intensely medieval and mystical in his deep spirituality, resolutely tenacious in pursuing his mystical concepts." West is undoubtedly right in this description of Columbus, but does not adequately explore the contradiction between Columbus's mystical side, his "deep spirituality," and his more modern Renaissance side, reflected in his Faustian assertion of self, his striving for worldly wealth and honors, and in his comment: "O, most excellent gold! Who has gold has a treasure with which he gets what he wants, imposes his will on the world, and even helps souls to paradise."

Finally, in recent decades there has appeared a body of revisionist writings that reflects "The Vision of the Vanquished"—the view that the Discovery brought death, misery, and centuries of oppression and enslavement to the native and black masses of the Americas. The new revisionism also reflects the view of those who claim that the main "legacy" of Columbus—the swift spread of capitalism and industrialism over the globe—was accomplished at an excessive social and economic cost, including a problem of environmental degradation that threatens the very existence of human life on the earth.

· li ·

Introduction

As previously noted, these revisionist viewpoints are at the very heart of the current dispute as to how the Discovery should be commemorated or whether it should be commemorated at all.

The new revisionism has a certain affinity with the classic Marxist attitude toward Columbus and the Discovery. Long ago (1867), in a famous passage of his *Capital*, Marx proclaimed that "the discovery of gold and silver in America, the extirpation, enslavement, and entombment in the mines of the aboriginal population, the beginning of the conquest and looting of the East Indies, the turning of Africa into a warren for the commercial hunting of black-skins, signalized the rosy dawn of capitalist production."

Marx's stress on the immense cost of colonialism in human lives and suffering finds an echo in the modern "Vision of the Vanquished." But Marx also assigned a progressive character to the rise of capitalism, and in the *Communist Manifesto* (1848) he and Friedrich Engels celebrated its great productive triumphs:

> The bourgeoisie, during its rule of scarce one hundred years, has created more massive and more colossal productive forces than have all preceding generations together. Subjection of Nature's forces to man, machinery, application of chemistry to industry and agriculture, steam-navigation, railways, electric telegraphs, clearing of whole continents for cultivation, canalisation of rivers, whole populations conjured out of the ground—what earlier century had even a presentiment that such productive forces slumbered in the lap of social labour?

Many writers of the revisionist school, aware of the damage to the earth and society caused by this explosion of productive forces, would disagree with the positive assessment of Marx and Engels.

It is Columbus's image, however, that has perhaps suffered most at the hands of the twentieth-century revisionists. Thus, in his short biography, *Columbus: His Enterprise* (1976), the novelist Hans Koning flatly declared that "the standard Columbus Day image of Columbus is false," branded him as cruel and greedy, and linked him to the process whereby "the West has ravaged the world for five hundred years, under the flag of a master-slave theory which in our finest hour of hypocrisy was called 'the white man's burden.'"

A more subtle and penetrating critique of Columbus appears in *The Conquest of America: The Question of the Other* (1985) by the

French scholar Tzvetan Todorov. Subjecting Columbus's attitude toward the Indians to a careful dissection, Todorov reveals its contradictions. Sometimes Columbus views the Indians as "noble savages"; on occasion, he sees them as "filthy dogs." Todorov explains that both myths rest on a common base: scorn for the Indians and refusal to admit them to be human beings with the same rights as himself. In the last analysis, Columbus regards the Indians not as human beings but as objects. This is well illustrated by a letter he wrote to the Spanish monarchs in September 1498: "We can send from here in the name of the Holy Trinity, all the slaves and brazilwood that can be sold. If my information is correct, one could sell 4,000 slaves that would bring at least twenty millions." Invoking the Holy Trinity, the pious Columbus offers to send the monarchs unlimited quantities of two undifferentiated commodities: slaves and brazilwood!

A major work of the revisionist school is Kirkpatrick Sale's *The Conquest of Paradise: Christopher Columbus and the Columbian Legacy* (1990), repeatedly cited in this essay. The work is based on massive research. Sale, an environmental activist, makes a blistering attack on Columbus and his "legacy," focusing on the process of human and environmental destruction that the Discovery unleashed in the New World, a process that began in Hispaniola (the "Paradise" of the book's title) and gradually spread to other areas. Noting the "darkness" that surrounds Columbus's birthplace and birthdate, Sale depicts Columbus as a lonely, restless person "without a past that he could define, without a home, or roots, or family, without ever a sense, or love, of place. His early years are dark because, in a sense, they are empty." He is a man given to deception or self-deception, self-pity, "fevered mysticism," and sometimes plain looniness. Some of these themes had been sounded by previous biographers, notably Wasserman. But Sale goes further and takes on Admiral Morison and other "salty types" who proclaim that Columbus was a master mariner. In fact, Sale asserts, Columbus "could be a wretched mariner. The four voyages, properly seen, quite apart from bravery and fortitude, are replete with lubberly mistakes, misconceived sailing plans, foolish disregard of elementary maintenance, and stubborn neglect of basic safety."

Conceding the validity of Sale's argument that over large areas of pre-Columbian America (as in the Caribbean) there existed an admirable balance between humans and nature and that the Discovery

· liii ·

Introduction

set in motion a long-range process of human and environmental destruction in the hemisphere; granting, too, that Columbus was cruel and unjust in his dealings with the Indians and had other personal failings, there is a palpable vein of exaggeration running throughout the book. This applies, for example, to the seeming perfection that Sale ascribes to Taino culture, and even more, perhaps, to Sale's closing warning that "there is only one way to live in America, and there can be only one way, and that is as Americans—the original Americans—for that is what the earth of America demands."

We may agree with Sale's argument that the survival of humanity and the earth demands a revival of the communal spirit, the sense of collective good—adapted to twentieth-century conditions—that characterized the lifeways of many ancient American peoples. But one is tempted to ask: The lifeway of which "original Americans" does Sale have in mind? The harmonious lifeway of the Taino, or that of the Aztecs, who combined great cultural achievements with a hateful imperialism based on perpetual war and human sacrifice, or that of the Incas, who combined efficient social engineering with their own brand of exploitive imperialism?

Sale's book was only the most notable example of the rising tide of scholarly and popular criticism of Columbus and his legacy as the quincentennial of his Discovery approached. Protests against a traditional celebration of the Discovery were particularly strong in Latin America. Thus, in September 1991 the prominent Brazilian theologian Leonardo Boff condemned the Discovery and its sequel: "The European Christians invaded the continent. They provoked the greatest genocide in history, reducing the population in a proportion of 25 to 1. They usurped the land, disintegrated the sociopolitical organizations, repressed the native religions, and interrupted the internal logic of development of the native cultures." In place of the traditional celebrations, Boff proposed to celebrate the past and continuing resistance of the Indian and African-American masses to their ages-long exploitation and oppression. Even in Spain, where gala celebrations, including a 500th Year World's Fair in Seville, were planned for 1992, many intellectuals denounced the celebration of what they called a fifteenth- and sixteenth-century genocide.

Popular opposition to the traditional commemoration of the Discovery took various forms. Thus, in July 1990, some 400 Indian people, including a delegation from the United States, met in Quito, Ecuador, to organize public protests against five hundred years of

European "invasion" and "oppression." North American Indian groups, united in a loose confederation, decided to picket all U.S. cities where replicas of Columbus's ships from Spain would dock. And a teachers' organization, Rethinking Schools, published a curriculum guide, *Rethinking Columbus* (1991), containing articles with such titles as "Talking Back to Columbus," "African-Americans: Mourn the Quincentenary," "Let's Leave Columbus Behind," and "Once Upon A Genocide: Christopher Columbus in Children's Literature."

One of the first casualties of this process of "rethinking Columbus" was the use of the word "discovery" to describe his achievement. Awareness of the ethnocentric, Eurocentric connotations of that term has led many scholars and organizations to replace it with the more neutral term "encounter" (*encuentro* in Spanish), first proposed by the Mexican historian Miguel León-Portilla. America, it was argued, was not an empty continent when the Europeans arrived; its true discoverers were the people who had crossed over from Asia by way of the Bering Strait or by sea many thousands of years ago. But the word "encounter," with its suggestion of a peaceful meeting of peoples and cultures, hardly fits the grim reality of the European invasion of Indian America, so I shall continue to use the word "discovery" for lack of a better word.

In the United States, the growing opposition to festivities of the traditional type added to the troubles of the federal commission in charge of the official celebration of Columbus's voyage, already plagued by financial scandal involving the commission's first chair, John Goudie, a real-estate dealer and Republican fund-raiser who subsequently resigned, and by the loss of its main corporate sponsor, Texaco. According to the *Chronicle of Higher Education*, the quincentennial had become so controversial that little or no public funds were available for related research or other programs in 1991. Meanwhile, in many communities opponents of the official celebration were planning to hold "alternative" events.

In a review of Kirkpatrick Sale's *Conquest of Paradise* in the *New York Review of Books* (November 22, 1990), the historian Garry Wills reflected with black humor on the decline of Columbus's reputation as a result of all these developments: "A funny thing happened on the way to the quincentennial observation of America's 'discovery.' Columbus got mugged. This time the Indians were waiting for him. He comes now with an apologetic air—but not, for some, sufficiently apologetic. . . . He comes to be dishonored."

Needless to say, Columbus still had his unreconstructed cham-

· lv ·

Introduction

pions, especially in right-wing circles, who identified unqualified defense of Columbus and his achievement with patriotism. Their attitude was reflected in some actions and policies of the Bush administration. Thus the National Council on the Humanities, headed by Lynne Cheney, wife of the defense secretary, and packed in recent years with diehard conservative Republicans, vetoed a number of commemorative projects proposed to the National Endowment for the Humanities that had been warmly endorsed by peer reviewers. One was a miniseries that presented diverse views of Columbus and his voyage; another miniseries on the same subject, written and narrated by the leftist Mexican novelist Carlos Fuentes, was also turned down, allegedly "at the highest level."

More often than not, however, even those who disagreed with the views of the anti-Columbus, revisionist school offered a defense that was muted or qualified. Thus, asking the question, Was Columbus a great man? John Noble Wilford, in his study *The Mysterious History of Columbus* (1991), replied, "No, if greatness is measured by one's stature among contemporaries," and observed that "the only example Columbus set was one of pettiness, self-aggrandizement, and a lack of magnanimity." But Wilford went on to add: "Yes, if greatness derives from the audacity of his undertaking, its surprising revelation, and the magnitude of its impact on subsequent history." To be sure, Wilford's answer begs the question whether that impact was for good or for ill.

That question cannot be properly answered, I suggest, without noting the very different impact of the Discovery on America and Europe. A balanced assessment must begin by observing that, for the native peoples of America, the Discovery and its sequel of the Conquest were an unmitigated disaster. The combination of new diseases to which the Indians had no acquired immunity, their brutal exploitation, and the resulting social disorganization and loss of will to live led to perhaps the greatest demographic holocaust in recorded history, with an estimated loss of between 90 and 95 percent of the native population between 1492 and 1575. The Discovery and the Conquest also cut short the independent development of Indian societies like the Taino chiefdoms of the Caribbean, notable for their achievements in agriculture; the Chibcha chiefdoms of Colombia, creators of magnificent art; and brilliant civilizations like the Aztec and Inca empires, which, with all their defects, had not exhausted their possibilities for further cultural advance and flowering. The conquistadors, beginning with Columbus, established on the ruins of the Indian societies feudal economic and social structures, admixed with some capitalist elements, that left a legacy of arbitrary rule, corruption, and economic backwardness and dependency to independent Latin America, a legacy that still hampers the area's efforts to modernize and achieve autonomous economic development. One of the most sinister fruits of the Discovery and Conquest was the revival and massive expansion of slavery—which was dying in Europe—as a foundation of American economic life and trade with Europe, with the use first of Indian and later African slaves. Columbus played a major role in the initiation of that process. Columbus also established the first *encomiendas*, a system of forced Indian labor or serfdom that was later transferred to the mainland and had a catastrophic impact on the Indian population. The inhuman conditions in which great numbers of Indian, black, and mixed-blood people live today in the Americas are in large part attributable to the economic and social changes set in motion by the Discovery. For these conditions, Columbus, the first conquistador, bears a considerable share of responsibility.

The impact of the Discovery on Europe and its long-term development was in many respects much more positive. That impact, as noted long ago by Adam Smith and Karl Marx, is clearest in the realm of economics. Historians may debate the influence of American precious metals on Europe's sixteenth-century "price revolution" or the contribution of the slave trade to the "primitive accumulation" of capital in Europe. It is beyond dispute, however, that the combination of these and other events flowing from the discovery of America (like the introduction of the potato, which greatly increased European food production, releasing people from agriculture and making possible a rapid growth of population and urban markets) gave an immense stimulus in Europe's economic modernization and the rise of capitalism, which in turn hastened and facilitated Europe's domination of the globe. The rise of capitalism was accompanied by the enrichment of some elites and the impoverishment or ruin of large numbers of peasants and artisans, and culminated in the Industrial Revolution and its attendant horrors.

The intellectual impact of the Discovery on Europe is more difficult to measure, but it seems indisputable that the expansion of geographic horizons produced by the discovery of America was accompanied by an expansion of intellectual horizons and the rise of new

Introduction

ways of viewing the world that significantly contributed to intellectual progress. One of the first casualties of the great geographic discoveries was the authority of the Ancients and even of the Church Fathers. Thus the Spanish friar Bartolomé de Las Casas (1484–1566), writing on the traditional belief in uninhabitable zones, in one paragraph managed to demolish the authority of Saint Augustine and the Ancients, who, "after all, did not know very much." In the writings of Las Casas and other chroniclers who had actually traveled in America, such phrases as "I can testify from personal experience" or "This I saw with my own eyes" replace the medieval citing of authority as decisive proofs of truthful reporting of the facts.

The discovery of America also produced disputes about the origins and nature of the Indians that led to the founding of the science of anthropology, for the desire to prove the essential humanity and equality of the Indians inspired some sixteenth-century Spanish missionaries like Las Casas to make profound investigations of Indian culture. Reflection on the apparent novelty and strangeness of some Indian ways, and the efforts of pro-Indian friar-anthropologists to understand and explain those ways, also led to the development of a cultural relativism that, like the rejection of authority, represented a sharp break with the past. Thus Michel de Montaigne, who avidly read accounts of Indian customs, observed in his famous essay on the Brazilian Indians, "Of Cannibals": "I think there is nothing barbarous and savage in this nation, from what I have been told, except that each man calls barbarian whatever is not his own practice."

The discovery of America and its people also inspired some Europeans, troubled by the social injustices of Renaissance Europe, to propose radical new schemes of political and economic organization. In 1516, for example, Thomas More published his *Utopia*, portraying a pagan, socialist society whose institutions were governed by reason and justice, so unlike the states of contemporary Europe, which More described as a "conspiracy of the rich against the poor." The principal sources of More's ideas about the evils of private property and the benefits of popular government appear to be the descriptions of Indian customs and beliefs in the writings of Peter Martyr and Vespucci. Examples of the stimulus that the discovery of America gave to European reformist and radical thought could be multiplied.

But if the discovery of America had a beneficial impact on European intellectual life, it also reinforced the negative European attitudes of racism and ethnocentrism. The broad vision of Las Casas, who proclaimed that "all mankind is one," and of Montaigne, who furiously denounced European wars and atrocities against the Indians and proposed "a brotherly fellowship and understanding" as the proper relationship between Europeans and the peoples of the New World, were not typical of contemporary thinking on the subject. Colonial rivals might condemn Spanish behavior toward the Indians, but they usually agreed in regarding native peoples as tainted with vices, and as "poor barbarians." For all these developments, good and bad, Columbus, as the initiator of a great chain of events, bears part of the credit or blame.

In my preface to Ferdinand's life of his father, I call Columbus "a figure of transition from the dying Middle Ages to the rising world of capitalism and science, blindly credulous and boldly questioning, a medieval mystic incongruously eager for gold and worldly honors." To assess the significance of Columbus's achievement properly, it must be understood that he was the instrument of historical forces of which he was unaware, forces of transition from the Middle Ages to that rising world of capitalism, whose success required the conquest of the world and the creation of a world market. That process in turn required an ideological justification, a conviction of the superiority of white European Christians over all other peoples and races. From that to the transformation of the more defenseless or vulnerable of those alien peoples, like the Taino Indians that Columbus met on Hispaniola, into commodities or chattels like brazilwood, was but one step. Columbus's work in the Caribbean represented the first tragic application of that dehumanizing ideology in the New World. If not the father, he is at least one of the fathers of European imperialism, and bears part of the responsibility for the devastating effects of that system of domination.

Some Literary Portraits of Columbus

A survey of Columbus's reputation in history would not be complete without some account of the procession of images of the man and his work that marches through the pages of poems, plays, and novels dealing with the subject. I begin by making two points: the number of such writings is impressively large and their quality, on the whole, very low. A single volume published in 1892 to commemorate the fourth centennial of the Discovery contained six hun-

Introduction

dred poems. In the twentieth century alone, Kirkpatrick Sale counts at least 143 creative works to date, "including 11 book-length poems, 2 short stories, 39 novels, and no fewer than 51 plays and poems, an extraordinary tide to which the United States has contributed well over a third."

The reasons for the mediocrity or worse of the great majority of these creative works are a matter for dispute. One obvious reason is lack of talent on the part of the many poetasters who decided to try their hand at what seemed to be a promising subject. Another is the attitude of uncritical eulogy of Columbus that characterizes the great majority of these writings. Our present knowledge of Columbus's complex, contradictory nature, of the darker side of the man and his work, inevitably gives such pieces a false ring. The Spanish critic Marcelino Menéndez Pelayo, however, argued that it was the very sublimity of the subject matter, and the great amount of information about it, that made for its "intrinsic impossibility" as a theme for poetic or epic writing. Whatever the reasons, the number of poems, plays, and novels about Columbus that have genuine merit is quite small, and I will limit our survey to a few selected pieces.

Lope de Vega's play *El Nuevo Mundo descubierto por Colón* (1614) is not among the best of the great Spanish poet's plays, but aside from the fact that it is the first dramatic work on the Discovery, its treatment of Columbus and his enterprise has some unusual features that give it considerable interest. Lope's primary historical source is Gómara's *Historia de las Indias*; from this source, among other borrowings, he took the story of the dying pilot who confided to Columbus the secret of new lands to the West and the way there. Lope portrays Columbus as a genius impelled by a "secret divinity" to perform his providential mission. But he is aware of the contradictions of the man's character, the mixture of piety and greed, his obsession with gold. Addressing the king, Columbus says:

"Money I must have, for money is all.
Money is the master, the lodestar, the route,
the road, the inspiration, industry and power,
the foundation and the best of friends."

In the course of an interlude featuring a debate among Idolatry, the Devil, and Providence, Lope places in the mouth of the Devil, who wants the Spaniards to leave America to him, a cynical reference to the motives of Columbus and his companions:

"On the pretext of conversion
they come to search for gold and silver. . . ."

Providence does not dispute the Devil's claim:

"Let God judge of men's intentions:
If through this gold He can win the souls you see around you.
Heaven will gain;
it matters not what others gain on earth."

For the rest, Lope's portrayal of the Indians and their reception of the Spaniards after their landing has no relation to reality. The Indians, after recovering from their initial bewilderment, accept the Spaniards as brothers and adore the Cross they have planted on the shore of the island. The Devil admits defeat: "I am vanquished, Thou hast conquered, O Galilean!" And the play closes with a triumphant apotheosis of Columbus in Barcelona, where he is received by the Sovereigns and rewarded with the titles of Duke of Veragua and Admiral of the Ocean Sea and a coat of arms: "Two castles, two lions, for Castile and for Leon."

In *La poesía del Descubrimiento* (1977), José María Gárate Córdoba concedes that only a handful of poems by other Peninsular poets who have written on the Discovery can be called "masterful"; he has special praise for the Catalan poet Jacinto Verdaguer, whose epic poem, *L'Atlantida* (1877), devotes its last two cantos to the Discovery. Written with "the rich sonorities" of the Catalan language, it represents "one of the most valuable Spanish epic poems," according to Gárate. But its treatment of Columbus, mystical and sentimental in the romantic nineteenth-century tradition, lacks veracity; Columbus is portrayed as the "messenger of God" who finds the star of his dreams in the kingdom of Castile; there he secures from Isabella the ships in which he will fly to his promised land, like Moses crossing between the waters of the Red Sea.

A number of Latin American poets have attempted to evoke the greatness of Columbus and his exploit, but few of their productions are memorable. A common theme is praise for Spain's cultural and material gifts to the New World, sometimes contrasted with Indian backwardness; the nineteenth-century Colombian poet José Joaquín Ortiz wrote of "the stupid awe with which the uncultured Indian first saw the haughty war-steed!" The twentieth-century Venezuelan poet Andrés Eloy Blanco depicted America as an Eve awaiting her Spanish Adam:

Introduction

Naked America slept by the sea.
And you took her in your arms and taught her to speak,
and all the excellence of your sacred stock—valor, work, science—
flowered for centuries in the grafted name. . . .

But the greatest Latin American *modernista* poet, the Nicaraguan
Rubén Darío, was sometimes inclined to wish that America had
never been discovered. In his poem to Columbus (1907), he sang:

Unhappy Admiral! Your poor America,
your lovely and hot-blooded Indian maid,
the pearl of your dreams is now hysterical,
her nerves convulsive and forehead pale.

In a biting commentary on the social and political reality of Latin
America four hundred years after Columbus, he wrote:

Christ, gaunt and feeble, walks through the streets,
Barabbas wears epaulets and keeps his slaves,
And the land of the Chibcha, Cuzco and Palenque,
have seen panthers acclaimed and in their glory.

Two authors, the Frenchman Paul Claudel and the Greek Nikos
Kazantzakis (better known as the author of the novel *Zorba the
Greek*), have written plays about Columbus that are notable for their
emotional intensity and originality. A fervent Catholic, a great poet
who combined stylistic innovation with a "spiritual medievalism,"
Claudel published *Le Livre de Christophe Colomb* (The Book of
Christopher Columbus) in 1930; its source was *Le Revelateur du
Globe* (The Revealer of the Globe) by the visionary Catholic writer
Leon Bloy, whose own work was inspired by Roselly de Lourges's
many studies championing the sainthood of Columbus. The play was
staged in Berlin in operatic form by Max Reinhardt, with music by
Darius Milhaud.

A "lyric drama," the play makes large use of such scenic effects as
a flight of doves and the appearance of monstrous Aztec gods, creat-
ing an atmosphere rich in fantasy and symbolism. The play opens in
an inn in Valladolid, where Columbus has come to ask the king for
support for another voyage. "He is old. He is poor. He is sick. He is
about to die." Memories of his life pass through the dying Columbus's mind. He becomes double, a youthful Columbus who reenacts

the scenes of that life and the dying Columbus who passes judgment on himself. A chorus, representing posterity, comments, advises, scolds, and sometimes breaks up, with the chorists moving about and talking in great disorder. From the chorus rises an Accuser who attacks Columbus: "I am talking of you, Christopher, you mountebank, you Bible reader, you confounded ignoramus, slave dealer, liar, rebel, slanderer! Why did you come to make trouble in Spain and to upset all of her worthy traditions? What did Spain care about the other world? Why did you come to take Europe out of her petty routine? Such men as you, if I had my way, should not be imprisoned—they should be shot!" A Defender answers: "All these faults of his, his illusions, suspicions, lies, his jealousy, his egotism, his cruelty, his contempt for things once found and his yearnings for the things yet to be found, all these traits are the faults of a loving heart. Who can rightly judge a loving heart?" And the dispute continues. There is a dialogue between Columbus and the cook who fastened the manacles on him when he was returned to Spain in chains.

On the screen groups of black slaves in chains.
CHRISTOPHER COLUMBUS. Who are those Ethiopians?
COOK. Slaves. Columbus has again brought slavery into the world.
CHRISTOPHER COLUMBUS. Do you mean those Indians I tried to sell as slaves in Seville?
COOK. Hail to the slave driver!
CHRISTOPHER COLUMBUS. I sinned. But I had no gold. I came back goldless from the west. I had to pay with something. Am I not in chains myself?
COOK. You paid with souls.
CHRISTOPHER COLUMBUS. I promised to take darkness out of the world, but never suffering.
COOK. I see men sold as cattle. I see Africa sending to the new world shiploads of human flesh. . . .

The play ends in "the Paradise of the Idea" on a note of high fantasy; Queen Isabella receives from the dying Columbus his last possession, "my mule, my true comrade, who carried me unto the end!" And on that old mule, Isabella, led by Santiago, Spain's patron saint, rides "into the Kingdom which Christopher has made ready

Introduction

for me by unfolding from one shore to a farther shore so splendid a carpet"—a carpet whose name is America.

Nikos Kazantzakis's *Christopher Columbus* (1949) resembles Claudel's play in its qualities of fantasy and symbolism, and in its extensive use of scenographic means to bring visions, portents, and other preternatural events to the stage. Unlike Claudel's play, however, its mood is dark and brooding; a tragic sense of life replaces the religious optimism of Claudel's piece. Kazantzakis freely alters the facts of Columbus's life to suit his poetic ends. His Columbus is a visionary, a Chosen of God who has heard voices calling him Admiral of the Ocean Sea and Viceroy of the Western Indies; he is also a supreme egotist who allows nothing to stand in the way of his grand enterprise.

English-speaking playwrights and poets who have dealt with the themes of Columbus and his Discovery have not produced works (to judge by those which I have been able to examine) that can match the emotional power and originality of Claudel's and Kazantzakis's plays. But the poet Louis MacNeice has a skillfully crafted radio play, *Christopher Columbus* (1944), written to celebrate the 450th anniversary of the Discovery, that he calls "a stylized treatment of a simple heroic theme"; he admits that he has avoided the "temptation to debunk the Columbus legend."

In general, poems about Columbus by modern English-speaking authors, even the most gifted, suffer from the defect to which I alluded above; they tend to idealize him beyond recognition, assigning him a persona that contradicts what is presently known about the man; sometimes they grossly distort the facts of his life.

Alfred Tennyson's "Columbus," written in 1892, is a good example. In an introductory note, Tennyson observed that it was written after "repeated entreaties from certain prominent Americans that he would commemorate the discovery of America," and that it was founded on a passage in Irving's life of Columbus. In the poem an elderly, ailing Columbus, racked with pain, recalls to a visiting nobleman his great services to Spain and bitterly complains of the injustices he has suffered. Inevitably, in view of Tennyson's dependence on Irving, the poem contains a number of legends. Thus Columbus asserts that his opponents at Salamanca believed the world was flat; he also claims that in his old age he had been left "with scarce a coin to buy a meal withal." And he lays the blame for the horrors committed against the "harmless people whom we found in

Hispaniola's island-Paradise" on the "scoundrel scum" for whom he had opened a door to the West, though he concedes that he himself was "not blameless." Despite the musical and stately quality of many of its lines, the poem lacks credibility for the informed modern reader.

An even more unlikely Columbus appears in James Russell Lowell's philosophical poem "Columbus" (1844). Aboard the *Santa Maria*, borne swiftly westward through a "drear waste" of waters, Columbus meditates about the old world he has left behind and the new world that his voyage will bring into being. Lowell, who was troubled by the social injustices that the system of laissez-faire had created and sympathetized with the workers' revolution of 1848 in France, has Columbus say:

> The old world is effete; there man with man
> Jostles, and, in the brawl for means to live,
> Life is trod underfoot. . . .
> Yes, Europe's world
> Reels on to judgment; there the common need,
> Losing God's sacred use, to be a bond
> 'Twixt Me and Thee, sets each one scowlingly
> O'er his own selfish hoard at bay. . . .

Columbus asks how new the new world will be:

> Shall the same tragedy be played anew,
> And the same lurid curtain drop at last
> On one dread desolation . . . ?
> Or shall that commonwealth
> Whose potent unity and concentric force
> Can draw these scattered joints and parts of men
> Into a whole ideal man once more . . .
> Be there built up?

Needless to say, Lowell's effort to transform Columbus into a "transcendental radical" in his own image has no basis in Columbus's own life and beliefs.

In Walt Whitman's moving "Prayer of Columbus" (1876), the Discoverer, "a batter'd, wrecked old man . . . pent by the sea and dark rebellious brows, twelve dreary months"—a reference to his ma-

Introduction

rooning on Jamaica during the Fourth Voyage—also meditates on the future of the new world he has revealed. Like Lowell's Columbus, he hopes that it will be a better, more humane world than old Europe:

> Haply the brutish measureless human undergrowth I know,
> Transplanted there, may rise to stature, knowledge worthy
> [of] Thee,
> Haply the swords I know may there be indeed be turn'd to
> reaping-tools,
> Haply the lifeless cross I know, Europe's dead cross, may bud
> and blossom there.

The poem ends on an optimistic note, natural to "the poet of the democratic ideal":

> As if some miracle, some hand divine unseal'd my eyes,
> Shadowy vast shapes smile through the air and sky,
> And on the distant waves sail countless ships,
> And anthems in new tongues I hear saluting me.

A sampling of the novels dealing more or less directly with Columbus and his voyages indicates that most are adventure stories for whose plots Columbus and his times provide a historical background. One of the better books in this genre is Vicente Blasco Ibañez's, *En busca del Gran Khan* (1929), which reflects careful study of Columbus's life and voyages. C. S. Forester's *To The Indies* (1940) is a deftly written novel whose hero, a Crown attorney, accompanies Columbus on the Third Voyage; Columbus is depicted as a rather pathetic, bumbling, but kindly figure whose powers are failing, and the principal blame for the cruel treatment of the Indians is assigned to his energetic brother Bartholomew, the *Adelantando*. James Street's *The Velvet Doublet* (1953) is a novel of the swashbuckling school; its hero is the sailor Juan Rodrigo Bermejo, who allegedly first sighted land on the First Voyage, was cheated by Columbus of the promised reward, and was so outraged that he converted to the Muslim religion.

In a completely different category is *El arpa y la sombra* (1979), published in English translation as *The Harp and the Shadow* (1990), by the Cuban novelist Alejo Carpentier, a master of the Latin American school of "magical realism." By his own account, Carpentier wrote this book to counter the idealized image of Columbus projected by Catholic writers like Paul Claudel and Leon Bloy. The novel is divided into three principal parts. The first, "The Harp," has as its principal character the Italian nobleman Mastai-Ferrati, the future Pope Pius, who champions the cause of Columbus's beatification in the belief that it would provide an antidote to "the venomous philosophical ideas" of the age. In the second part, "The Hand," Columbus, on his deathbed, awaiting his confessor, recalls and relates the events of his life in a long internal monologue. In the third part, "The Shadow," a Church tribunal hears witnesses for and against Columbus's beatification; the shades of Victor Hugo, Las Casas, and Jules Verne, among others, intervene in this fantastic debate. The tribunal decides against Columbus, and the book ends with a dialogue between him and the shade of another famous Genoese admiral, Andrea Doria.

The Columbus depicted in Carpentier's novel is not an admirable figure. In his monologue he admits to lying about his origins, his education, and his early maritime exploits, and to practicing other deceptions. Carpentier's characterization of Columbus and his motives is based on the most extreme revisionist theses of Vignaud, Madariaga, and others. Thus, his Columbus admits that his true object was not to reach Asia but a rich land to the West of which he had secret knowledge. Carpentier also accepts the thesis of Columbus's Jewish origin. Perhaps the most grotesque feature of the book is its depiction of the relations between Columbus and Queen Isabella. They quarrel, she throws up to Columbus his Jewish origin, but consents to sleep with him. It is difficult to know how much of the novel is satire and irony, and what parts are meant to be taken seriously. In any case, as an antidote to the saintly image of Columbus projected by some of his Catholic biographers it succeeds, perhaps all too well. What is beyond dispute is the power of Carpentier's prose and fantasy, rising to a climax in the last part of the book, with its phantasmagoric account of the last judgment on Columbus.

I must stress that this brief survey of the images of Columbus and his work in historical and other social science writings and in belles-lettres takes account of only a small portion of the vast corpus of published material dealing with the subject, a corpus that recently has been growing by leaps and bounds. Readers who wish to deepen

Introduction

their knowledge of the literature about Columbus are especially advised to consult Foster Prevost, *Columbus: An Annotated Guide to Scholarship on His Life and Writings* (1991) and the copious "Source Notes" in Kirkpatrick Sale's *Conquest of Paradise*, cited above.

The $\mathcal{L}$*ife of* THE ADMIRAL
*C*HRISTOPHER *C*OLUMBUS

The Author's Foreword

I being the son of the Admiral Christopher Columbus, a person worthy of eternal glory for his discovery of the West Indies, it seemed fitting that I, who had sailed with him for some time, and who had written of lesser things, should write the history of his life and marvelous discovery of the New World and the Indies, as his strenuous endless labors and the illness from which he suffered left him no time for the writing of memoirs. I held back from this task, knowing that many others had attempted it; but when I read their books, I found that like most historians they had given too much attention to some matters and not enough to others or passed over in silence precisely what needed to be told in fullest detail. So I decided to assume the burden of this work, thinking it better to suffer criticism of my style and presumption than to leave in oblivion the truth about so illustrious a man. I also console myself with the thought that my book will at least be free from the flaw of most historians, that flaw being the small and doubtful truth of what they write; for I promise to tell the story of the Admiral's life only from his own writings and letters and what I myself observed. And whoever suspects that I have added something of my own invention may be certain that I know such a thing would profit me nothing in the next life and that none but my readers shall reap the fruits of my labor.

Dedication

To the Very Magnificent Signore Baliano de Fornari,[1]
[by] Giuseppe Moleto [2]

The discoverer of a new and useful thing, magnificent lord, has always been much admired by others. The Ancients so esteemed such men that they were not content to render them the praise accorded to mortals, but enrolled them among their gods. Such was the origin of Saturn, Jupiter, Mars, Apollo, Aesculapius, Bacchus, Hercules, Mercury, and Ceres, and, in short, of all the pagan gods of whom the ancient writings are full. In this the Ancients acted reasonably enough, for being without the light of the true faith, they worshiped those from whom they had received some notable benefit; and wise men tell us that we cannot give stronger proof of gratitude toward a benefactor from whom we have received advantages that cannot be repaid in the ordinary way than by honoring him. We honor only what is divine or shows some spark of divinity; and what more convincing sign of divinity can a man give than the discovery of something that is useful to his fellows? Certainly the inventor of a useful thing is much favored of God, the true source of all things good, Who frequently deigns to reveal through a single man what had been hidden for long centuries.

So it was in our time with the New World, which was unknown to all or, if it was ever known, the knowledge was so lost that all that was told of it was regarded as fabulous. Now through the agency of the illustrious Christopher Columbus, a true man of Providence, God has been pleased to disclose it, from which we may conclude that he was much favored of God. More, we may say that in ancient times men not only would have enrolled him among their gods but also would have ranked him at their very head. Certainly our age cannot honor him as his merits deserve, wherefore one who devotes himself to perpetuating his name is worthy of highest praise. That is what your Lordship has done in striving so diligently to give to the world the life of this excellent man, written by the illustrious Don Ferdinand Columbus, second son of the aforesaid Don Christopher and Chief Cosmographer of the invincible Charles V.

Don Ferdinand was no less meritorious than his father, but was much more learned, and left to the Cathedral of Seville, where he had honorable burial, a library that was not only very large but rich, full of rarest works in all the sciences and regarded by all who have seen it as one of the most remarkable things in all Europe. It cannot be doubted that this history is a true one, for it was written by the son, carefully following his father's relations and letters. Nor can it be doubted that it was written by the hand of the aforesaid Don Ferdinand and that your Lordship had the authentic original, for it was given to you as such by your Lordship's close friend, the illustrious Don Luis Columbus. This Don Luis, who today is Admiral of His Catholic Majesty, was nephew of the aforesaid Don Ferdinand and son of the illustrious Don Diego, Don Christopher's first-born son, who inherited the estate and dignity of his father; of the merits of Don Luis one cannot say enough.

Your Lordship, then, being an honorable and generous gentleman, desiring to make immortal the memory of this great man, heedless of your Lordship's seventy years, of the season of the year, and of the length of the journey, came from Genoa to Venice with the aim of publishing the aforesaid book in the Spanish language in which it was written, and in Italian, and even of having it translated into Latin, that the exploits of this eminent man, the true glory of Italy and especially of your Lordship's native city, might be made known. But because of the much time required to do this, and because your many public and private cares obliged you to return to your city, the task was assumed by Signore Giovanni Battista di Marini,[3] a gentleman adorned with most excellent qualities, of great spirit and learning. He being my master and wishing me to aid him in the execution of this project, I agreed thereto, knowing it would please both him and your Lordship. Now, my lord, the book appears under your name, as is fitting, since you labored so zealously that it might be published. Being as it were your Lordship's creation, it is proper that the effect should acknowledge its cause. Receive favorably, then, my lord, this your book, and hold me to be forever your most devoted servant.

Venice
April 25, 1571

Contents

Contents

Contents

Contents

Contents

Contents

Contents

Contents

Chapter 1

Concerning the Birthplace, Family, and Name of the Admiral Christopher Columbus

Two things which are important to know about every famous man are his birthplace and family, because men generally accord more honor to those who were born in great cities and of noble parents. Therefore some wished me to tell how the Admiral came of illustrious stock, although misfortune had reduced his parents to great poverty and need; and how they descended from that Colonus of whom Cornelius Tacitus tells in the twelfth book of his work, saying that he brought King Mithridates a prisoner to Rome, for which exploit the Roman people awarded Colonus the consular dignities, the honor of bearing the standard, and a place among the tribunes. They also wished me to make a great story of those two illustrious Coloni, his relatives, of whom Sabellicus tells that they won a great victory over the Venetians, as will be told in Chapter 5.[1]

But I have spared myself such labor, believing that the Admiral was chosen for his great work by Our Lord, who desired him as His true Apostle to follow the example of others of His elect by publishing His name on distant seas and shores, not in cities and palaces, thereby imitating Our Lord himself, who though his descent was from the blood royal of Jerusalem, yet was content to have his parentage from an obscure source. Similarly, the Admiral, although endowed with all the qualities that his great task required, chose to leave in obscurity all that related to his birthplace and family.

· 3 ·

The Life of the Admiral Christopher Columbus

Therefore some who wish to dim his fame say that he was from Nervi, others from Cugureo, and still others from Bugiasco, all of which are little places near Genoa and situated on the same coast. Others, who would add to his dignity, say that he was from Savona, and still others that he was Genoese.[2] Those who go farthest afield assign him to Piacenza, in which city there are some persons of worth of his family, and tombs with arms and epitaphs bearing the name Colombo; because this was really the name of his ancestors. But he changed the name to make it conform to the language of the country in which he came to reside and raise a new estate, as well as to make it agree with the ancient one and distinguish those who descended from him from all collateral descendants. That is why he called himself Colón.

Reflecting on this, I was moved to believe that just as most of his affairs were directed by a secret Providence, so the variety of his name and surname was not without its mystery. We could cite as examples many names which a hidden cause assigned as symbols of the parts which their bearers were to play. Just so, the Admiral's name foretold the novel and wonderful deed he was to perform. If we consider the common surname of his forebears, we may say that he was truly Columbus or Dove, because he carried the grace of the Holy Ghost to that New World which he discovered, showing those people who knew Him not Who was God's beloved son, as the Holy Ghost did in the figure of a dove when St. John baptized Christ; and because over the waters of the ocean, like the dove of Noah's ark, he bore the olive branch and oil of baptism, to signify that those people who had been shut up in the ark of darkness and confusion were to enjoy peace and union with the Church. So the surname of Colón which he revived was a fitting one, because in Greek it means "member," and by his proper name Christopher, men might know that he was a member of Christ, by Whom he was sent for the salvation of those people. And if we give his name its Latin form, which is Christophorus Colonus, we may say that just as St. Christopher is reported to have gotten that name because he carried Christ over deep waters with great danger to himself, and just as he conveyed over people whom no other could have carried, so the Admiral Christophorus Colonus, asking Christ's aid and protection in that perilous pass, crossed over with his company that the Indian nations might become dwellers in the triumphant Church of Heaven. There is

· 4 ·

reason to believe that many souls that Satan expected to catch be-cause they had not passed through the waters of baptism were by the Admiral made dwellers in the eternal glory of Paradise.

CHAPTER 2

Of the Admiral's Parents and Their Con-dition, and of the False Account That One Giustiniani Gives of His Occupation Before He Acquired the Title of Admiral

Leaving now the etymology or derivation and meaning of the name of the Admiral, and turning to the condition of his parents, I say that they were persons of worth who had been reduced to poverty by the wars and factions of Lombardy. I have not been able to find how or where they lived, although the Admiral him-self says in a letter that he and his ancestors always followed the sea. To inform myself better on this point, in passing through Cugureo I tried to learn what I could from two brothers of the name of Colombo, who were the richest men of that place and were said to be related to the Admiral in some way; but as the younger of the two was more than a hundred years old, I could learn nothing. I do not think that we in whose veins flows his blood should feel less proud on that account, for I think it better that all our glory should come from himself than that we should go about inquiring if his father was a merchant or went hunting with falcons; of such men there are thousands everywhere, and three days after their death the memory of them is lost without a trace among their own townspeople and relations. I believe that such fame and nobility lend less luster than the glory that comes to me from a father whose illustrious deeds had no need of an-cestral riches (which like poverty are the fruit not of virtue but of fortune). Certainly, taking into account his renown and valor, the writers who treat of his occupation should not have described him as one who practiced the mechanical arts.

That, however, some have done, basing themselves on what one Agostino Giustiniani [1] wrote in his chronicle. I shall not attempt to refute this by seeking testimony to the contrary, since in a matter of which living men have no recollection the words of Giustiniani no more constitute proof than it would be proof if I said that I heard the contrary from a thousand persons. Nor shall I try to show it to be false by citing the histories of others who have written about Don Christopher, but rather I shall refute it with the writings and testimony of Giustiniani himself, in whom is verified the proverb that says *mendacem oportet esse memorem*—the liar should have a long memory, else he will contradict what he has said before. That is what Giustiniani did in this case, writing in his edition of the Psalter in four languages, in a gloss on the verse *in omnem terram exivit sonus eorum:*

> This Christopher Columbus, having learned the rudiments of letters as a child, on reaching manhood devoted himself to the art of navigation and went to Lisbon, in Portugal, where he learned geography, which a brother of his who was a map-maker there taught him. As a result of this, of his conversations with men who used to go to the Portuguese fortress of São Jorge da Mina in Africa, and of what he had read in the writings of geographers, he conceived the idea of going to the lands that he later discovered.

These words make it plain that he practiced no manual or mechanical art, since the author writes that he spent his childhood learning letters, his young manhood in navigation, and his later years in discovery. Thus Giustiniani convicts himself of being a false historian and an inconsiderate, prejudiced, and malicious compatriot. Surely, in speaking of a distinguished man and one who so greatly honored the country whose history Giustiniani wrote, even had the Admiral's parents been humble folk, it would have been more honorable for Giustiniani to speak of his family as other writers do, saying *humili loco, seu a parentibus pauperrimis ortus,* [2] rather than use such offensive words as he applied in the said Psalter, falsely calling Columbus an artisan. Even if Giustiniani had not contradicted himself, common sense tells us that a man occupied in some manual art or trade would need to be reared and grow old in it to learn it to perfection, and could not have wandered from youth through so many lands or learned so many languages and sciences as his writings show, especially the four principal sciences that his work required—astronomy, geography, geometry, and navigation.

But it is no wonder that Giustiniani dares lie about a matter of which little is known, since in narrating very simple and familiar things having to do with the Admiral's discovery and navigation he managed to tell more than twelve falsehoods on half a page of his Psalter. In order not to break the thread of my story I shall mention them only briefly, since in the course of this book and with the writings of others I shall prove what he said to be false.

The first lie is that the Admiral went to Lisbon to learn geography from a brother who lived there. The truth is just the opposite; for he had lived before in that city, and taught his brother all he knew.

The second falsehood is that as soon as he came to Castile the Catholic Sovereigns Ferdinand and Isabella accepted his proposals, after all others had rejected them. The truth is that these princes accepted his proposals after seven years.[3]

The third falsehood is that he sailed on his voyage of discovery with two ships, which is not true, since he departed with three caravels.

The fourth falsehood is that the first island he discovered was Española; in reality it was Guanahaní, which the Admiral named San Salvador.

The fifth falsehood is that the aforesaid island of Española was inhabited by cannibals—men who eat human flesh. In reality he found its inhabitants to be the best and most civilized people in those parts.

The sixth falsehood is that he took in battle the first Indian canoe or boat that he found. On the contrary, it will be seen that on that first voyage he warred against no Indians, but kept peace and friendship with them to the day of his departure from Española.

The seventh falsehood is that he returned by way of the Canary Islands, which were not on the return route of those ships.

The eighth falsehood is that from those islands he dispatched a messenger to the most serene Sovereigns aforesaid; the fact is that he did not touch there, as said above, and he himself was his own messenger.

The ninth falsehood is that on his second voyage he sailed with twelve ships, for it is plain there were seventeen.

The tenth lie is that he arrived at Española in twenty days, which is too short a time to come even to the first islands; he actually did not reach Española for two months, arriving much earlier at the others.

The eleventh lie is that he disembarked on Española with two ships, for it is known that he took three ships when he sailed for Cuba from Española.

Giustiniani's twelfth falsehood is that Española is four hours [4] distant from Spain, since the Admiral calculates the distance to be more than five.

To add a thirteenth lie, he says that the western end of Cuba is six hours distant from Española, thus making the distance between Española and Cuba greater than that between Spain and Española.

Considering, then, what little care he took to learn and write the truth about such simple matters, one may judge how well he informed himself about so obscure a point [as Columbus's occupation B. K.] and one concerning which he contradicts himself, as has been shown.

Ending this digression, which I fear has already wearied my readers, I shall only say that because of the many errors and falsehoods contained in the said history and in the Psalter of Giustiniani, the seigniory of Genoa, considering the lying character of his writings, has provided penalties for whoever possesses or reads his history and has ordered that great diligence be shown in searching for copies in all places to which they may have been sent, so that they may be destroyed by public decree.[5]

I return to my principal theme, and conclude by saying that the Admiral was a learned man of great experience and did not waste his time in manual or mechanical labor, which did not comport with the grandeur and immortality of the wonderful deeds he was to perform. And I shall end this chapter with some words taken from his letter to the nurse of the prince Don Juan of Castile, "I am not the first Admiral of my family. Let them call me, then, by what name they will, for after all, David, that wisest of kings, tended sheep and was later made king of Jerusalem, and I am the servant of Him Who raised David to that high estate."[6]

CHAPTER 3

Of the Bodily Disposition of the Admiral
and of the Sciences That He Learned

The Admiral was a well-built man of more than average stature, the face long, the cheeks somewhat high, his body neither fat nor lean. He had an aquiline nose and light-colored eyes; his complexion too was light and tending to bright red. In youth his hair was blonde, but when he reached the age of thirty, it all turned white. In eating and drinking, and in the adornment of his person, he was very moderate and modest. He was affable in conversation with strangers and very pleasant to the members of his household, though with a certain gravity. He was so strict in matters of religion that for fasting and saying prayers he might have been taken for a member of a religious order. He was so great an enemy of swearing and blasphemy that I give my word I never heard him utter any other oath than "by St. Ferdinand!" and when he grew very angry with someone, his rebuke was to say "God take you!" for doing or saying that. If he had to write anything, he always began by writing these words: *IESUS cum MARIA sit nobis in via.* And so fine was his hand that he might have earned his bread by that skill alone.

Leaving his other personal traits and customs for mention at the proper time, let us speak of the sciences to which he most devoted himself. He learned his letters at a tender age and studied enough at the University of Pavia [1] to understand the geographers, of whose teaching he was very fond; for this reason he also gave himself to the study of astronomy and geometry, since these sciences are so closely related that one depends upon the other. And because Ptolemy, in the beginning of his *Geography*, says that one cannot be a good geographer unless one knows how to draw, too, he learned drawing, in order to be able to show the position of countries and form geographic bodies, plane and round.

CHAPTER 4

Of the Activities of the Admiral Before
He Came to Spain

Having gained some knowledge of those sciences, the Admiral began to follow the sea, making several voyages east and west. My knowledge of these voyages and of many other matters touching his early days is imperfect, for he died before I made so bold as to ask him about such things; or, to speak more truly, at the time such ideas were farthest from my boyish mind. But in a letter that he sent in 1501 to the most serene Catholic Sovereigns, to whom he would not have dared write aught but the truth, he wrote the following words:

Very High Kings:
From a very young age I began to follow the sea and have continued to do so to this day. This art of navigation incites those who pursue it to inquire into the secrets of this world. I have passed more than forty years in this business and have traveled to every place where there is navigation up to the present time. I have had dealings and conversation with learned men, priests, and laymen, Latins and Greeks, Jews and Moors, and many others of other sects. I found Our Lord very favorable to this my desire, and to further it He granted me the gift of knowledge. He made me skilled in seamanship, equipped me abundantly with the sciences of astronomy, geometry, and arithmetic, and taught my mind and hand to draw this sphere and upon it the cities, rivers, mountains, islands, and ports, each in its proper place. During this time I have made it my business to read all that has been written on geography, history, philosophy, and other sciences. Thus Our Lord revealed to me that it was feasible to sail from here to the Indies, and placed in me a burning desire to carry out this plan. Filled with this fire, I came to Your Highnesses. All who knew of my enterprise rejected it with laughter and mockery. They would not heed the arguments I set forth or the authorities I cited. Only Your Highnesses had faith and confidence in me.

The Life of the Admiral Christopher Columbus

In another letter which he wrote the Catholic Sovereigns from Española in January, 1495, relating the variations and errors which are commonly found in pilots' sailing directions and charts, he says,

It happened to me that King René[1] (whom God has taken) sent me to Tunis to capture the galleass *Fernandina;* and when I was off the island of San Pietro, near Sardinia, a vessel informed me there were two ships and a carrack with the said galleass, which frightened my people, and they resolved to go no further but to return to Marseilles to pick up another ship and more men. I, seeing that I could do nothing against their wills without some ruse, agreed to their demand, and, changing the point of the compass, made sail at nightfall; and at sunrise the next day we found ourselves off Cape Carthage, while all aboard were certain we were bound for Marseilles.

Likewise, in a memorial or note that he wrote to prove that the five zones are navigable, demonstrating this with the experience of his voyages, he says,

In the month of February, 1477, I sailed one hundred leagues beyond the island of Tile,[2] whose southern part is in latitude 73 degrees N, and not 63 degrees as some affirm; nor does it lie upon the meridian where Ptolemy says the West begins, but much farther west. And to this island, which is as big as England, the English come with their wares, especially from Bristol. When I was there, the sea was not frozen, but the tides were so great that in some places they rose twenty-six fathoms,[3] and fell as much in depth.

The Thule of which Ptolemy speaks does in fact lie where the Admiral says it does; nowadays it is called Frisland. Farther on, seeking to prove that the Equator is habitable, he says, "I visited the fortress of São Jorge da Mina, which belongs to the Portuguese King and lies below the Equator; and I can testify that it is not uninhabitable, as some would have it."

And in the book of his first voyage he says that he "saw some sirens on the coast of Malagueta,[4] but they did not resemble women as much as they are said to do." Elsewhere he says, "Often, in sailing from Lisbon to Guinea, I determined by careful calculation that the degree corresponds to 56⅔ terrestrial miles"; further on he says that on Chios, an island of the Greek Archipelago, he saw mastic

· 11 ·

being drawn from some trees; in another place he writes, "For twenty-three years have I followed the sea without leaving it for any considerable space of time; I have seen all of the East and all of the West" (by which he means that he had sailed northward, that is, to England), "and I have sailed to Guinea, but nowhere have I seen such good harbors as those in the Indies."

Further on he says that he took to the sea at the age of fourteen and followed it ever after. In the book of the second voyage he writes, "It happened to me while in command of two ships that I left one in Pôrto Santo for repairs which took only a day, yet I arrived in Lisbon eight days before that ship because I had a gale from the southwest, while she had only a weak wind from the northeast, which is contrary."

From these examples and citations we may judge how experienced he was in navigation and how many lands and places he had visited before he gave himself up to the enterprise of his discovery.

CHAPTER 5

Of the Admiral's Coming to Spain and of What Happened to Him in Portugal, Which Was the Cause of His Discovery of the Indies

The first cause of the Admiral's coming to Spain and devoting himself to the sea was a renowned man of his name and family, called Colombo,[1] who won great fame on the sea because he warred so fiercely against infidels and the enemies of his country that his name was used to frighten children in their cradles. He must have been a formidable person, indeed, because on one occasion he captured four large Venetian galleys of such great size and armament that they had to be seen to be believed. He was called Colombo the Younger to distinguish him from another Colombo who in his time also won fame on the sea. Marcus Antonius Sabellicus, the Livy of our age, writes in the eighth book of the Tenth Decade of his work that about the time Maximilian, son of the Emperor Frederick III, was elected King of the Romans, Hieronimo Donato was sent as ambassador from Venice to Portugal to thank King João II for having clothed and relieved the people on these great galleys, which were returning from Flanders when they were met and defeated near Lisbon by Colombo the Younger, that famous corsair, who robbed the ships' people and turned them ashore.

The authority of such a serious scholar as Sabellicus reveals the bias of Giustiniani, who made no mention of this affair in his history in order to conceal the fact that the Colombos were not so obscure a family as he would have them to be. And if he kept silent from ignorance, he is still blamable for having omitted from the history of his country a victory so notable that even the enemies of Genoa mention it; for a hostile historian assigns enough importance to this affair to say that on account of it ambassadors were sent to the Portuguese King. This author, Sabellicus, a little later in the same eighth book, though under less obligation than Giustiniani to inform himself about the Admiral's discovery, tells of it without bringing in those twelve lies of Giustiniani's.

I return to my main theme. While the Admiral was sailing in the company of the said Colombo the Younger (which he did for a long time), it was learned that those four great Venetian galleys aforesaid were returning from Flanders. Accordingly Colombo went out to meet those ships and found them between Lisbon and Cape St. Vincent, which is in Portugal. Here they came to blows, fighting with great fury and approaching each other until the ships grappled and the men crossed from boat to boat, killing and wounding each other without mercy, using not only hand arms but also fire pots and other devices. After they had fought from morning to the hour of vespers, with many dead and wounded on both sides, fire spread from the Admiral's ship to a great Venetian galley. As the two ships were grappled tight with hooks and iron chains which sailors use for this purpose, and on both sides there was much confusion and fear of the flames, neither side could check the fire; it spread so swiftly that soon there was no remedy for those aboard save to leap in the water and die in this manner rather than suffer the torture of the fire. But the Admiral, being an excellent swimmer, and seeing land only a little more than two leagues away, seized an oar which fate offered him, and on which he could rest at times; and so it pleased God, who was preserving him for greater things, to give him the strength to reach the shore. However, he was so fatigued by his experience that it took him many days to recover.[2]

Finding himself near Lisbon, and knowing that many of his Genoese countrymen lived in that city, he went there as soon as he could. When they learned who he was, they gave him such a warm welcome that he made his home in that city and married there.

As he behaved very honorably and was a man of handsome presence and one who never turned from the path of honesty, a lady named Dona Felipa Moniz, of noble birth and superior of the Convent of the Saints,[3] where the Admiral used to attend Mass, had such conversation and friendship with him that she became his wife. His father-in-law, Pedro Moniz Perestrello, being dead, they went to live with his widow, who, observing the Admiral's great interest in geography, told him the said Perestrello, her husband, had been a notable seafarer; and she told how he and two other captains had gone with license from the King of Portugal to discover new lands, agreeing to divide all they discovered into three parts and cast lots for the share that should fall to each. Sailing to the southwest, they discovered the islands of Madeira and Pôrto Santo. Since the island of Madeira was the larger of the two, they made two parts of it, the third being the island of Pôrto Santo, which fell to the share of the Admiral's father-in-law, Perestrello, who governed it till his death.

Seeing that her stories of these voyages gave the Admiral much pleasure, she gave him the writings and sea-charts left by her husband. These things excited the Admiral still more; and he informed himself of the other voyages and navigations that the Portuguese were then making to Mina and down the coast of Guinea, and greatly enjoyed speaking with the men who sailed in those regions. To tell the truth, I do not know if it was during this marriage that the Admiral went to Mina or Guinea, but it seems reasonable that he did so. Be that as it may, one thing leading to another and starting a train of thought, the Admiral while in Portugal began to speculate that if the Portuguese could sail so far south, it should be possible to sail as far westward, and that it was logical to expect to find land in that direction.

By His Son Ferdinand

To obtain confirmation on this point, he turned anew to study the writers on geography with whose work he was already familiar, and to consider the astronomical arguments that might support his design; consequently, he noted down any helpful hints that sailors or other persons might drop. He made such good use of all these things that he grew convinced beyond the shadow of a doubt that to the west of the Canary and Cape Verde Islands lay many lands which could be reached and discovered. To show on what weak foundations he raised the vast structure of his project, and in order to satisfy the many persons who wish to know the exact reasons that led him to believe in the existence of these lands and dare launch his enterprise, I shall relate what I have found on this subject in his writings.

CHAPTER 6

Of the Admiral's Principal Reason for Believing That He Could Discover the Indies

Turning to the reasons which persuaded the Admiral to undertake the discovery of the Indies, I say there were three, namely, natural reasons, the authority of writers, and the testimony of sailors. With respect to the first—the natural reasons—he believed that since all the water and land in the world form a sphere, it would be possible to go around it from east to west until men stood feet to feet, one against the other, at opposite ends of the earth. In the second place, he assumed and knew on the authority of approved writers that a large part of this sphere had already been navigated and that there remained to be discovered only the space which extended from the eastern end of India, known to Ptolemy and Marinus,[1] eastward to the Cape Verde and Azore Islands, the westernmost land discovered up to that time. Thirdly, he believed that this space between the eastern end, known to Marinus, and the said Cape Verde Islands could not be more than the third part of the great circle of the sphere, because Marinus had already described in the East fifteen of the twenty-four [astronomical B. K.] hours or parts into which the world is divided; therefore, to reach the Cape Verdes barely required eight more hours, since even Marinus did not begin his description very far to the West.

In the fourth place, he noted that Marinus, having assigned in his *Geography* fifteen hours or parts of the sphere to the East, had not yet come to the end of the eastern lands, which made it reasonable to assume that that end lay much farther beyond; and the farther eastward it extended the closer must it be to the Cape Verdes. Now, if the intervening space were sea, it would be an easy matter to navigate it in a few days; and if it were land, the quicker could it be discovered from the West, because it would be closer to the Cape Verdes. He found support for this reasoning in what Strabo [2] says in Book XV of his *Geography*, that no army ever reached the eastern bounds of India, which Ctesias [3] states to be as large as all the rest of Asia. Onescritus affirms that India is the third part of this sphere, and Nearchus [4] says that to cross India requires four months of travel over flat ground, while Pliny [5] asserts in Chapter 17 of Book VI that it is the third part of the earth. Wherefore the Admiral concluded that India's great size would place it closer to Spain on the West.

The fifth argument, which gave the greatest support to the view that this space was small, was the opinion of Alfragan [6] and his followers, who assign a much smaller size to the earth than all the other writers and geographers, calculating a degree to be only 56⅔ miles; whence the Admiral inferred that since the whole sphere was small, of necessity that space of the third part which Marinus left as unknown had to be small and therefore could be navigated in less time. From this he also inferred that since the eastern end of India was not yet known, that end must be the one which is close to us in the West; therefore any lands that he should discover might be called the Indies.

Here one plainly sees how wrong was a certain Master Rodrigo,[7] formerly Archdeacon of Reina, in Seville, and some others who join him in censuring the Admiral for naming these lands the Indies—which they are not. The Admiral called them the Indies, not because they had been seen or discovered by others, but because they were the eastern part of India beyond the Ganges, to which no geographer had ever set bounds on the east, or made it border on any other country eastward, but only upon the ocean. And because these lands were the unknown eastern part of India and had no name of their own, he named them after the nearest adjoining land, calling them the West Indies. He had the more reason for doing this because he knew all men had heard of the great fame and wealth of India; and by using that name he hoped to arouse the interest of the Catholic Sovereigns (who were doubtful of his enterprise), telling them that he was going to discover the Indies by way of the West. And he desired the support of the rulers of Castile for this plan above that of any other Christian king.

CHAPTER 7

The Second Reason That Encouraged the Admiral to Seek to Discover the Indies

The second reason that inspired the Admiral to launch his enterprise and helped justify his giving the name "Indies" to the lands which he discovered was the authority of many learned men who said that one could sail westward from the western end of Africa and Spain to the eastern end of India, and that no great sea lay between. Aristotle affirms this in the conclusion of the second book of *On the Heavens,* observing that from the Indies to Cádiz is but a few days' sailing; this is confirmed by Averroës in his gloss on this point. Seneca,[1] in the first book of his *Natural Questions,* declaring the wisdom that may be acquired in this life to be as nothing by comparison with what can be gained in the next, says that with a fair wind a ship could sail from the end of Spain to the Indies in a few days. If, as some believe, this Seneca wrote the tragedies attributed to him, we may say that it was apropos of this that he wrote in the chorus of his tragedy *Medea,*

The Life of the Admiral Christopher Columbus

> . . . *venient annis*
> *Secula seris, quibus Oceanus*
> *Vincula rerum laxet, et ingens*
> *Pateat tellus, Tiphysque novos*
> *Detegat orbes, nec sit terris*
> *Ultima Thule.*

This means, "There will come a time in the later years when Ocean shall loosen the bonds by which we have been confined, when an immense land shall be revealed and Tiphys [2] shall disclose new worlds, and Thule will no longer be the most remote of countries." Now it is considered certain that this prophecy was fulfilled in the person of the Admiral.

Strabo, in the first book of his *Geography*, says that the ocean surrounds the whole earth and that it bathes India in the East and Spain and Mauretania in the West. He adds that if it were not for the magnitude of the Atlantic, one could sail from one place to the other along the same parallel; he repeats this statement in the second book. Pliny, in the second book of his *Natural History*, Chapter 3, also says that the ocean surrounds the whole earth and that its length from east to west is that from India to Cádiz. The same author, in Chapter 31 of Book VI, and Solinus,[3] in Chapter 68 of his *Collection of Memorable Things*, say that from the Gorgonas Islands (which are believed to be the Cape Verdes) it is forty days' sailing across the Atlantic to the Hesperides Islands, which the Admiral doubted not were the Indies.

Marco Polo,[4] a Venetian, and John Mandeville [5] tell in their travel accounts that they journeyed far beyond the eastern lands described by Ptolemy and Marinus; they do not speak of the Western Sea, but from their description of the East it could be argued that India neighbors on Africa and Spain. Pierre d'Ailly,[6] in Chapter 8 "Concerning the Size of the Habitable Earth," of his treatise *Concerning the Form of the World*, and Julius Capitolinus,[7] in *Concerning the Habitable Places* and many other treatises, say that India and Spain are near each other in the West. In Chapter 19 of his *Geography* Julius Capitolinus says, "According to the philosophers and to Pliny, the ocean which lies between Spain and Africa, on the west, and India, on the east, is not of very great extent and doubtless could be navigated in a few days with a fair wind. Therefore the beginnings of India in the East cannot be very far from the end of Africa in the West."

The authority of this writer and others like him did more than all else to convince the Admiral that his idea was sound. One Master Paolo,[3] physician to Master Domenico, a Florentine and a contemporary of the Admiral's, also played a large part in encouraging him to undertake his voyage. This Master Paolo was a friend of Fernão Martins, a canon of Lisbon, and they corresponded with each other concerning the voyages being made to Guinea in the time of King Afonso of Portugal and the possibility of similar voyages to the western regions. Their correspondence came to the notice of the Admiral, who was very curious about such matters, and he hastened to write Master Paolo through the agency of Lorenzo Girardi, a Florentine residing in Lisbon, sending him a small sphere on which he showed his design. Master Paolo replied in a letter written in Latin, which translated into the vernacular reads as follows.

CHAPTER 8

The Letters of Paolo, a Physician of Florence, to the Admiral Concerning the Discovery of the Indies

Paolo the physician, to Christopher Columbus, Greetings.[1]

I perceive your noble and grand desire to go to the places where the spices grow; and in reply to your letter I send you a copy of another letter which some time since I sent to a friend of mine, a gentleman of the household of the most serene King of Portugal, before the wars of Castile,[1] in reply to another which by command of His Highness he wrote me on this subject; and I send you another sea-chart like the one I sent him, that your demands may be satisfied. A copy of that letter of mine follows:

The Life of the Admiral Christopher Columbus

Paolo the physician, to Fernão Martins, canon of Lisbon, Greetings.

I was glad to hear of your intimacy and friendship with your most serene and magnificent King. I have often before spoken of a sea route from here to the Indies, where the spices grow, a route shorter than the one which you are pursuing by way of Guinea. You tell me that His Highness desires from me some statement or demonstration that would make it easier to understand and take that route. I could do this by using a sphere shaped like the earth, but I decided that it would be easier and make the point clearer if I showed that route by means of a sea-chart. I therefore send His Majesty a chart drawn by my own hand, upon which is laid out the western coast from Ireland on the north to the end of Guinea, and the islands which lie on that route, in front of which, directly to the west, is shown the beginning of the Indies, with the islands and places at which you are bound to arrive, and how far from the Arctic Pole or the Equator you ought to keep away, and how much space or how many leagues intervene before you reach those places most fertile in all sorts of spices, jewels, and precious stones. And do not marvel at my calling "west" the regions where the spices grow, although they are commonly called "east"; because whoever sails westward will always find those lands in the west, while one who goes overland to the east will always find the same lands in the east.

The straight lines drawn lengthwise on this map show the distance from east to west; the transverse lines indicate distance from north to south. I have also drawn on the map various places in India to which one could go in case of a storm or contrary winds, or some other mishap.

And that you may be as well informed about all those regions as you desire to be, you must know that none but merchants live and trade in all those islands. There is as great a number of ships and mariners with their merchandise here as in all the rest of the world, especially in a very noble port called Zaiton,[2] where every year they load and unload a hundred large ships laden with pepper, besides many other ships loaded with other spices. This country is very populous, with a multitude of provinces and kingdoms and cities without number, under the rule of a prince who is called the Great Khan, which name in our speech signifies King of Kings, who resides most of the time in the province of Cathay. His predecessors greatly desired to have friendship and dealings with the Christians, and about two hundred years ago they sent ambassadors to the Pope, asking for many learned men and teachers to instruct them in our faith; but these ambassadors, encountering obstacles on the way, turned back without reaching Rome. In the time of Pope Eugenius there came to him an ambassador who told of their great feeling of friendship for the Christians, and I had a long talk with him about many things: about the great size of their royal palaces and the marvelous length and breadth of their rivers, and the multitude of cities in their lands, so that on one river alone there are two hundred cities, with marble bridges very long and wide, adorned with many columns. This country is as rich as any that has ever been found; not only could it yield great gain and many costly things, but from it may also be had gold and silver and precious stones and all sorts of spices in great quantity, which at present are not carried to our countries. And it is true that many learned men, philosophers and astronomers, and many other men skilled in all the arts, govern this great province and conduct its wars.

From the city of Lisbon due west there are twenty-six spaces marked on the map, each of which contains two hundred and fifty miles, as far as the very great and noble city of Quinsay.[3] This city is about one hundred miles in circumference, which is equal to thirty-five leagues, and has ten marble bridges. Marvelous things are told about its great buildings, its arts, and its revenues. That city lies in the province of Mangi, near the province of Cathay,[4] in which the king resides the greater part of the time. And from the island of Antillia,[5] which you call the Island of the Seven Cities, to the very noble island of Cipango,[6] there are ten spaces, which make 2,500 miles, that is two hundred and twenty-five leagues. This land is most rich in gold, pearls, and precious stones, and the temples and royal palaces are covered with solid gold. But because the way is not known, all these things are hidden and covered, though one can travel thither with all security.

Many other things could I say, but since I have already

told them to you by word of mouth, and you are a man of good judgment, I know there remains nothing for me to explain. I have tried to satisfy your demands as well as the pressure of time and my work has permitted, and I remain ready to serve His Highness and answer his questions at greater length if he should order me to do so.

Done in the city of Florence, June 25, 1474.

Master Paolo afterwards wrote the Admiral another letter, which read as follows:

Paolo the physician, to Christopher Columbus, Greetings.

I have received your letters together with the things you sent me, and took great pleasure in them. I perceive your grand and noble desire to sail from west to east by the route indicated on the map I sent you, a route which would appear still more plainly upon a sphere. I am much pleased to see that I have been well understood, and that the voyage has become not only possible but certain, fraught with inestimable honor and gain, and most lofty fame among Christians. But you cannot grasp all that it means without actual experience, or without such accurate and copious information as I have had from eminent learned men who have come from those places to the Roman court and from merchants who have traded a long time in those parts and speak with great authority on such matters. When that voyage shall be made, it will be a voyage to powerful kingdoms and noble cities and rich provinces, abounding in all sorts of things that we greatly need, including all manner of spices and jewels in great abundance. It will also be a voyage to kings and princes who are very eager to have friendly dealings and speech with the Christians of our countries, because many of them are Christians; they are also very eager to know and speak with the learned men of our lands concerning religion and all other branches of knowledge, because of the much they have heard of the empires and governments of these parts. For these reasons and many others that might be mentioned, I do not wonder that you, who are of great courage, and the whole Portuguese nation, which has always distinguished itself in all great enterprises, are now inflamed with desire to undertake this voyage.

By His Son Ferdinand

This letter, as was said before, filled the Admiral with even greater zeal for discovery, though its writer was mistaken in his belief that the first lands to which one would come would be Cathay and the empire of the Great Khan, and in the other things that he wrote; for experience has shown that the distance from our Indies to those lands is much greater than the distance from here to our Indies.

CHAPTER 9

The Third Reason and Sign That Gave the Admiral Some Encouragement to Discover the Indies

The Admiral's third and last motive for seeking the Indies was his hope of finding before he arrived there some island or land of great importance whence he might the better pursue his main design. He found support for this hope in the authority of many learned men and philosophers who were certain that the land area of the globe was greater than that of the water. This being so, he argued that between the end of Spain and the known end of India there must be many other islands and lands, as experience has since shown to be true.

He believed this all the more because he was impressed by the many fables and stories which he heard from various persons and sailors who traded to the western islands and seas of the Azores and Madeira. Since these stories served his design, he was careful to file them away in his memory. I shall tell them here in order to satisfy those who take delight in such curiosities.

A pilot of the Portuguese King, Martín Vicente by name, told him that on one occasion, finding himself four hundred and fifty leagues west of Cape St. Vincent, he fished out of the sea a piece of wood ingeniously carved, but not with iron. For this reason and because for many days the winds had blown from the west, he concluded this wood came from some islands to the west.

Pedro Correa, who was married to a sister of the Admiral's wife, told him that on the island of Pôrto Santo he had seen another piece of wood brought by the same wind, carved as well as the aforementioned one, and that canes had also drifted in, so thick that one joint held nine decanters of wine. He said that in conversation with the Portuguese King he had told him the same thing and had shown him the canes. Since such canes do not grow anywhere in our lands, he was sure that the wind had blown them from some neighboring islands or perhaps from India. Ptolemy in the first book of his *Geography*, Chapter 17, writes that such canes are found in the eastern parts of the Indies. Some persons in the Azores also told him that after the wind had blown for a long time from the west, the sea cast on the shores of those islands (especially of Graciosa and Fayal) pine trees that do not grow on those islands or anywhere in that region. On the island of Flores, which is one of the Azores, the sea flung ashore two dead bodies with broad faces and different in appearance from the Christians. Off Cape Verga [1] and elsewhere in that region there once were seen covered boats or canoes which were believed to have been crossing from one island to another when a storm drove them off their course.

In addition to these signs, which seem rather plausible, some claimed to have seen certain islands; among them was one Antônio Leme, a married man of the island of Madeira, who said that once while sailing very far to the west he had seen three islands. The Admiral put no stock in these stories, because from the accounts of these men he knew they had not sailed even one hundred leagues to the west and had taken some reefs for islands. Or these men may have seen some of those floating islands which Pliny also mentions in Chapter 97 of the second book of his *Natural History*, saying that in the northern regions the sea ate away pieces of land on which grow trees with very thick roots, and that these pieces are carried along on the water as if they were rafts or little islands. Seneca, attempting to explain the nature of these islands, says in the third book of his *Natural Questions* that they are composed of stone so spongy and light that the Indian islands formed from it float on the water. Therefore the Admiral supposed that even if Antônio Leme had seen some island, it must have been one of that kind; the islands called St. Brendan,[2] of which so many marvels are told, were probably of the same nature. One finds mention of still others that lie much farther north. In those regions there are other islands that burn perpetually. Juventius Fortunatus [3] tells of two other floating islands supposed to lie to the west and farther south than the Cape Verdes. Cases of this kind may explain why many people on the islands of Ferro, Gomera, and the Azores assured the Admiral that every year they saw some islands to the west, and many persons of worth swore it was so.

The Admiral also tells that in 1484 an inhabitant of the island of Madeira [4] came to Portugal to ask the King for a caravel in order to discover some land which he swore he saw every year and always in the same situation; his story agreed with that of others who claimed to have seen it from an island of the Azores. On the basis of such stories, the charts and maps of ancient days showed certain islands in that region. Aristotle in his book *On Marvelous Things* reports a story that some Carthaginian merchants sailed over the Atlantic to a very fertile island (as I shall presently relate in more detail); this island some Portuguese showed on their charts under the name of Antillia, but in a different situation from Aristotle, though none placed it more than two hundred leagues due west of the Canaries and the Azores. And they hold it for certain that this is the Island of the Seven Cities, settled by the Portuguese at the time the Moors conquered Spain from King Rodrigo, that is, in the year A.D. 714. They say that at that time seven bishops embarked from Spain and came with their ships and people to this island, where each founded a city; and in order that their people might give up all thought of returning to Spain they burned their ships, riggings, and all else needed for navigation. Some Portuguese who speculated about this island conjectured that many of their nation had gone thither but were never able to return.

In particular they say that in the time of the Infante Dom Henrique of Portugal there arrived at this island of Antillia a Portuguese ship, driven there by a storm. After coming ashore, the ship's people were conducted by the inhabitants of the island to their church to see if the visitors were Christians and observed the rites of the Catholic religion. Satisfied that they were Christians, the islanders prayed the ship's people not to leave before the return of their absent lord, whom they would immediately notify of the ship's arrival. They also said that their lord would do great honor to the visitors and give them many presents. But the

Ships of Columbus's Time

ship's master and the sailors feared to be detained, reasoning that because these people did not wish to be known abroad they might burn their ship. So they left for Portugal with their news, expecting to be rewarded by the Infante, who instead rebuked them severely and ordered them to return immediately to the island; but the master took fright and escaped from Portugal with his ship and crew. It is said that while the sailors were in the church on that island the ship's boys gathered sand for the firebox and found that it was one third fine gold.

One Diogo de Teive also went in search of that island. His pilot, Pedro de Velasco by name, a native of Palos de Moguer in Portugal,[5] told the Admiral in Santa María de la Rábida [6] that they had departed from Fayal and sailed more than one hundred and fifty leagues to the southwest. On their return they discovered the island of Flores, to which they were guided by the many birds they saw flying in that direction; as they knew them to be land and not marine birds, they decided they must be flying to some resting place. Then they steered northeast until they reached Cape Clear at the western end of Ireland. Although they encountered very high westerly winds in this region, the sea remained calm. They decided this must be due to the fact that the sea was sheltered by some land on the west; but since it was already August and they feared the onset of winter, they gave up the search for that island. This happened forty years before the discovery of our Indies.

This story was confirmed to the Admiral by a one-eyed sailor in the port of Santa Maria,[7] who told him that on a voyage he had made to Ireland he saw that land, which at the time he supposed to be a part of Tartary; that it turned westward (it must have been what is now called the Land of Cod);[8] and that foul weather prevented them from approaching it. The Admiral says that this account agrees with one given him by Pedro de Velasco, a Galician, who told him in the city of Murcia in Castile that on a voyage to Ireland they sailed so far northwest that they saw land to the west of Ireland; this land, the Admiral thought, was the same that a certain Fernão Dulmo tried to discover. I relate this just as I found it told in my father's writings, that it may be known how from small matters some draw substance for great deeds.[9]

Gonzalo Fernández de Oviedo tells in his history of the Indies that the Admiral had a map on which the Indies were shown by the man who had first discovered them.[10] What actually happened was this:

A Portuguese named Vicente Dias, a citizen of the town of Tavira, going from Guinea to the island of Terceira, having left the island of Madeira on his east, saw or imagined that he saw an island. On arrival at Terceira he told this to a Genoese merchant named Luca di Cazana, a friend of his who was very rich, and urged him to outfit a ship for the conquest of that land. The Genoese agreed and obtained permission from the Portuguese King to do this. Then he wrote his brother Francesco di Cazana, who lived in Seville, praying him to outfit a ship with all speed for the use of that pilot. But his brother jeered at the project, whereupon Luca di Cazana himself outfitted a ship on the island of Terceira. The pilot went three or four times in search of the island, sailing as far as one hundred and twenty to one hundred and thirty leagues from land, but all in vain, for he never found the island. However, neither he nor his comrade abandoned the enterprise until their deaths, because they always hoped to find the island again. The aforesaid Francesco told me he had known two sons of the captain who discovered the island of Terceira, named Miguel and Gaspar Corte-Real, who at various times tried to discover that land; finally, in 1503, they perished in the attempt, one after the other, none knows how or where. Francesco said this affair was known of to many.

Chapter 10

In Which Is Shown the Falsity of the Claim That the Spaniards Once Before Had Possession of the Indies, as Gonzalo de Oviedo Attempts to Prove in His History

If the stories that persons who were almost our contemporaries tell of all these islands and lands are idle fancies and imaginings, what shall we say of the tall tales that Gonzalo Fernández de Oviedo spins in the third chapter of his *Historia natural de las*

Indias? [1] He claims to have proved beyond question that there was an earlier discoverer of the sea route to the Indies and that the Spaniards once before had possession of those lands, citing as proof what Aristotle says of the island of Atlantis, and Sebosus of the Hesperides. His claims are so irrational and baseless in the judgment of certain authors whose works I have carefully examined that I would gladly pass them by in silence to avoid criticizing anyone and boring my readers, were it not that some persons assign great value and importance to these fantasies, to the prejudice of the honor and glory of the Admiral. Moreover, having sought to show accurately the signs and authorities that inspired him to launch his enterprise, I should be remiss in my duty to one to whom I owe so much if I left standing such a great lie. To make plain Oviedo's error, I shall first quote what Aristotle [2] has to say about this in the collection of his propositions made by Fray Teófilo de Ferraris, who in the book *Concerning the Wonders of Nature* has a chapter that contains the following:

It is told that in the Atlantic Ocean, beyond the Columns of Hercules, in ancient times some Carthaginian merchants found an island that had never been inhabited by men, but only by savage beasts. It was thickly wooded, with many navigable rivers, and abounded in all that nature produces, but it was many days' sail from the mainland. On their arrival, finding the island good, with a fertile soil and a temperate climate, these Carthaginian merchants settled there. But the Carthaginian Senate, angered by news of their action, publicly decreed that henceforth none might visit that island; and ordered that those who had first gone there should be put to death, because it was feared that knowledge and possession of that island might be gained by some more powerful empire that would convert it into a threat to the liberties of Carthage.

Having carefully translated this source, I shall explain my reasons for saying that Oviedo's claim that this island was either Española or Cuba is without foundation. In the first place, since Oviedo knew no Latin, he had to use a version that someone else made for him; and that person evidently was not very skilled in translation, since he altered the Latin text at many points. Perhaps these changes led Oviedo astray and made him think the book spoke of some island of the Indies. The Latin text does not say that those mariners sailed through the Strait of Gibraltar, as Oviedo has it. Nor is it stated that the island was large and its trees large, but simply that it was thickly wooded; nor were the rivers said to be marvelous and the island fertile. Nor does it say that it was farther from Africa than from Europe, but only that it was far from the mainland. Nor does it state that towns were founded there, since little of that sort could be done by the merchants who chanced to arrive there. Nor is it written that the island was very famous, but only that the Carthaginian Senate feared its fame might spread to other nations.

As a result of the ignorance of the person who translated that source for him, Oviedo formed a very imperfect conception of the matter. And if he should argue that Aristotle's text differs from the friar's account, which was only a summary of what Aristotle wrote, I would ask Oviedo who made him a judge to distribute kingdoms at his pleasure and to rob of his honor one who had so well earned it. I would also tell him he ought not be content to use a summary in a friar's memorandum book but should go directly to his source in the works of Aristotle. Besides, he was badly informed in this case, for whereas in all his other books Teófilo gives only the substance of what Aristotle said, in this book *Concerning the Wonders of Nature* he states at the outset that he is citing the original text word for word; and it cannot be claimed that there is more or less in Aristotle than what he himself wrote. I may add that Antonio Beccaria of Verona, who translated the book from Greek to Latin, and whose version was used by Teófilo, made more than four changes from the Greek text, as anyone who looks into it can see for himself.

Again, even if Aristotle had written this just as Teófilo renders it, Aristotle cites no authority but uses the word *fertur* ("it is told"), by which he meant that what he wrote about this island was doubtful and had no supporting evidence. He also writes about it as something that happened a long time ago, saying "it is told that in ancient times an island was found." To this one could apply the proverb that long journeys and big lies go together, a proverb all the more applicable to a story containing statements that fly in the face of common sense—like the one in which Oviedo says that the island abounded in everything but had always been uninhabited. A most unlikely statement; for only cultivation makes land productive, and where no men live, nothing useful will grow of itself, and even domesticated plants turn wild and sterile.

Nor is it likely that the Carthaginians would have been displeased because their people had found such an island, nor that they would have slain its discoverers; for if it was as far from Carthage as are the Indies, they had no reason to fear an attack by its inhabitants. But perhaps Oviedo would say not only that the Spaniards once possessed those islands but also that the Carthaginians were prophets whose predictions and fears have been fulfilled in our time through the taking of Tunis or Carthage by the Emperor Charles V with the aid of treasure obtained from the Indies! He would doubtless have written this, too, to ingratiate himself and gain more favors of the kind he gained by writing such fantasies, but it was too late: His book had already been published! Every person of sound judgment will understand how ridiculous it is to say that knowledge of that island was lost because the Carthaginians abandoned it for fear that others would wrest it from them and later use it to attack their city. Surely they had greater reason to fear Sicily and Sardinia, only two days' sail from their city, than Española, a third part of the world away! To the argument that they may have feared that the riches of that land would make their enemies so powerful they might eventually inflict some injury upon them, I reply that they would have had greater hope of being able to repel and defeat the aggressor if they had retained possession of that wealth, while by abandoning the island they would have made of its discovery a gift to others, thus giving rise to the very evil they feared. Surely they would have rather fortified it and protected its approaches, as we know they did in similar cases. Thus, having discovered the islands then called the Casiterides,[3] which we call the Azores, they kept its navigation secret for a long time on account of the tin they obtained from there, as Strabo relates in the conclusion to the third book of his *Geography*.

I therefore conclude that even if Aristotle actually wrote this fable, he may have been referring to the navigation to the Azores; and I believe that Oviedo is led astray by faulty information, by the frailty of old age, or by blind prejudice when he argues that the story refers to the Indies that we possess today and not to the Azores or one of them. And if I am told that this cannot be, because it was not the Carthaginians who held the Azores but the Phoenicians, who traded with Cádiz, I reply that since the Carthaginians came from Phoenicia with Queen Dido they were called Phoenicians at that time, just as today we call Spaniards those Christians who are born and bred in the Indies. And if they come back at me that Aristotle says about this island that it contained many navigable rivers such as are found in Cuba and Española, but not in the Azores, I reply that if we are going to take note of that statement, we must also note that he adds that this island contained many savage animals, which are found neither in Cuba nor Española; and in dealing with a matter of such antiquity Aristotle may well have erred in this particular, as is likely to happen in the telling of such very remote and obscure events.

Now, in point of fact neither Cuba nor Española has navigable rivers such as Aristotle speaks of; true, any ship could enter the larger rivers of those islands, but could not sail up them comfortably. Besides, even if the text were really Aristotle's, the word *navigandum* [navigable] might have been a mistake for *potandum* [drinkable], which fits better in the context, since Aristotle was praising the island for the abundance of its potable water and edible fruits. This could well be said of the Azores, and with greater reason, for neither Cuba nor Española is so situated that the Carthaginians could have been blown there through being near or through mischance.

And if the men who sailed with the Admiral with the single aim of seeking the Indies found the voyage so long that they wanted to turn back, how much longer must it have seemed to men who had no intention of making such a prolonged voyage and would gladly have returned to their homeland whenever the weather permitted? And who ever heard of a storm of such duration and force that it could blow a ship from Cádiz to Española? Nor is it credible that these merchants wanted to remain away from Spain or Carthage any longer than foul weather obliged them to, especially since voyages were not undertaken so lightly or made so easily then as now. That is why in those days very short cruises appeared to be major enterprises, as witness the voyage made by Jason from Greece to Colchis and that of Ulysses in the Mediterranean, both of which took so many years and gained those heroes such renown that the most eminent poets sang their praises—all because of their small experience in navigation. Only in our own time have matters so improved that some have dared to circumnavigate the globe,[4] scorning the proverb that says, "When Cape Nun heaves into sight, turn back me lad, or else—good night!" [5] This Cape Nun is a promontory on the Barbary Coast, not very far from the Canaries.

Besides, it is plainly a mistake to suppose that the island to which the merchants were driven could have been Cuba or Española, because we know for certain that it is almost impossible to approach those islands without first coming to many other islands that surround them on all sides. But if in spite of everything, some should still insist that that land or island was not one of the Azores, as I have suggested, one could top one lie with another by saying that that land was the island mentioned by Seneca in the sixth book of his *Natural Questions,* where he quotes Thucydides as saying that during the Peloponnesian War the whole island of Atlantis, or the greater part of it, was submerged; Plato also tells of this in his *Timaeus.*[6]

Having already spoken too much of this fable, let us go on to another chapter in which Oviedo says that in ancient times the Spaniards had possession of those Indies, basing himself on what Sebosus [7] wrote, that certain islands called the Hesperides were forty days' sail west of the Gorgonas Islands. From this Oviedo concludes that those islands must be the Indies; and being called the Hesperides, they must have received that name from the Hesperus who once ruled over Spain; and consequently that king and the Spaniards must have ruled over those lands. Thus it appears that Oviedo wishes to draw three valid conclusions from a doubtful source, wherein he disagrees with Seneca, who in speaking of these matters in the sixth book of his *Natural Questions* observes that it is risky to make any certain and definite statement on the basis of mere conjecture. Yet that is just what Oviedo did; for Sebosus spoke only of the Hesperides, indicating where they lay, but not stating that they were the Indies or by whom they were named or conquered. As for Oviedo's assertion that Hesperus was a king of Spain, I concede that Sebosus makes that statement; but he says nothing of Hesperus giving his name to Spain or Italy.

Oviedo having noted, like the truthful historian he is, that Sebosus failed him at this point, turned for aid to Hyginus,[8] being careful however not to cite book or chapter, thus "improving" upon his testimony, as the saying goes; for in effect one cannot find a single passage of Hyginus's in which he says anything of the kind. On the contrary, in the single book of his which has been preserved, entitled *Poetic Astronomy,* he not only does not say this, but in three places, speaking of the Hesperides, he observes: "Hercules is depicted as preparing to kill the dragon that guarded the Hesperides"; further on he says that Hercules, having been sent by Eurystheus to seek the golden apples of the Hesperides, went to Prometheus on Mount Caucasus to ask him to show him the way, and this led to the death of the dragon. This story assigns the Hesperides to the East, and Oviedo could just as well say that Hesperus, king of Spain, gave them their name. Farther on, in a chapter on the planets, Hyginus adds that in many stories the planet Venus is called Hesperus because it sets soon after the sun. From all this, we may conclude that if any weight or authority should be assigned to a writer like Hyginus, given to relating the fables of poets, his evidence goes against rather than in favor of Oviedo; and we may assume that those islands were named Hesperides after that star. And just as the Greeks called Italy Hesperia for that reason, as many writers affirm, so Sebosus named those islands the Hesperides, as I believe; and in seeking to establish their location he used the same speculations and reasoning that convinced the Admiral those islands lay in the West.

We may thus conclude not only that Oviedo fakes sources in his writings but also that inadvertently or from a desire to please the person who told him these things (for he certainly did not think them up himself), he inclines to two opposed positions whose contradictory character makes plain how wrong he is. For if, as he claims, the Carthaginians found Cuba or Española inhabited only by animals, how could the Spaniards have possessed it a long time before, and how could their King Hesperus have given it his name? Or could it be that some deluge laid it waste, and afterward a new Noah returned it to the state in which the Admiral discovered it? But I grow weary of this dispute and fear that I have already bored my readers with it, so I will say no more about the matter and continue instead with my history.

CHAPTER 11

How the Admiral Grew Angry with the King of Portugal, to Whom He Had Offered to Discover the Indies

In due time, the Admiral, convinced of the soundness of his plan, proposed to put it into effect and sail over the Western Ocean in search of new lands. But he knew that his enterprise required the cooperation and assistance of some prince; and since he resided in Portugal, he decided to offer it to the king of that country. Although King João [1] listened attentively to the Admiral, he appeared cool toward the project, because the discovery and conquest of the west coast of Africa, called Guinea, had put the prince to great expense and trouble without the least return. At that time the Portuguese had not yet sailed beyond the Cape of Good Hope, which name according to some was given that cape in place of its proper one, Agesingua, because it marked the end of those fine hopes of conquest and discovery; others claim it got that name because it gave promise of the discovery of richer lands and of more prosperous voyages.

Be that as it may, the King was very little inclined to spend more money on discovery; and if he paid some attention to the Admiral, it was because of the strong arguments that the latter advanced. These arguments so impressed the King that the launching of the enterprise waited only upon his acceptance of the conditions laid down by the Admiral. The latter, being a man of noble and lofty ambitions, would not covenant save on such terms as would bring him great honor and advantage, in order that he might leave a title and estate befitting the grandeur of his works and his merits.

So the King, counseled by a Doctor Calzadilla [2] in whom he placed much trust, decided to send a caravel secretly to attempt what the Admiral had offered to do, thinking that if those lands were discovered in this way, he would not have to give the Admiral the great rewards he demanded. With all speed and secrecy, then, the King outfitted a caravel on the pretext of sending provisions and reinforcements to the Cape Verdes, and dispatched it whither the Admiral had proposed to go. But because the people he sent lacked the knowledge, steadfastness, and ability of the Admiral, they wandered about on the sea for many days and returned to the Cape Verdes and thence to Lisbon, making fun of the enterprise and declaring that no land could be found in those waters.[3]

When he learned of this, the Admiral, whose wife had meantime died, formed such a hatred for that city and nation that he resolved to depart for Castile with his little son Diego—who after his father's death succeeded to his estate. But he feared that if the rulers of Castile rejected his enterprise, he would have to propose it to some other prince, which might take a long time; he therefore sent his brother Bartholomew, who lived with him, to England. This Bartholomew knew no Latin, but had much skill and experience in navigation, and made excellent sea-charts, globes, and other instruments of that profession, which his brother the Admiral had taught him. Bartholomew having sailed for England, fate willed that he should fall into the hands of pirates, who despoiled him and all the other people on his ship. For this reason, and also because of the poverty and sickness that he suffered in a foreign land, his mission was for a long time unsuccessful. Eventually, after he had gained some renown through his maps, he obtained interviews with King Henry VII, father of the present King Henry VIII. He presented the King with a map of the world on which were written some verses which I found among my uncle's papers, and which I put down here more for their interest than for their elegance.

> Terrarum quicumque cupis feliciter oras
> Noscere, cuncta decens docte pictura docebit,
> Quam Strabo affirmat, Ptolemaeus, Plinius, atque
> Isidorus: non una tamen sententia quisque.
> Pingitur hic etiam nuper sulcata carinis
> Hispanis zona illa, prius incognita genti,
> Torrida, quae tandem nunc est notissima multis.

And below is written:

> Pro auctore, sive pictore:
> Janua, cui patria est, nomen cui Bartholomaeus
> Columbus de Terra Rubra, opus edidit istud Londonijs
> anno Domini M.CCCC.LXXXX, atque insuper anno octavo,
> decimaque die cum tertia mensis Februarii.
> Laudes Christo cantentur abunde.[4]

By His Son Ferdinand

And because some will note the phrase *Columbus de Terra Rubra*, I may remark that I have seen some signatures of the Admiral before he rose to that estate, in which he signed himself *Columbus de Terra Rubra.*

After the King of England had seen that map and informed himself of the Admiral's offer, he gladly accepted his proposal and summoned him to his Court. But God had reserved that prize for Castile, for by that time the Admiral had successfully completed his enterprise and returned home again, as shall be told at the proper place.

CHAPTER 12

Of the Admiral's Departure from Portugal, and of His Conversations with the Catholic Sovereigns Ferdinand and Isabella

Turning from Bartholomew Columbus's negotiations in England, I come back to the Admiral, who toward the end of the year 1484 secretly departed from Portugal with his little son Diego, fearing that the King might seek to detain him. In fact, the King, after the failure of the people he had sent with the caravel, wished to negotiate again with the Admiral concerning his project; but since he did not move as swiftly as the Admiral, he lost his opportunity, and the Admiral entered Castile to try his fortune there.

Leaving his son in a monastery in Palos, called La Rábida,[1] he proceeded with all haste to the Court of the Catholic Sovereigns, which was then in Córdoba. As he was a person of amiable character and pleasing conversation, he there gained the friendship of men who became his warmest advocates and who were in the best position to urge his cause upon the Sovereigns. One of them was Luis de Santángel,[2] an Aragonese gentleman who was secretary of the exchequer in the royal household, a very intelligent and influential man. But since the affair had more to do with basic scientific doctrine than with words or favors, their Highnesses referred it to the Prior del Prado, later the Archbishop of Granada,[3] order-

Spain in the Time of Christopher Columbus

Kingdom of Castile and León with its dependencies

Kingdom of Aragón with its dependencies

Kingdom of Navarre

Kingdom of Portugal

Kingdom of Granada

50   0   50   100   150
Miles

ing him to form a council of geographers who should study the proposal in detail and then report to them their opinion.

As there were not so many geographers then as now, the members of this committee were not so well informed as the business required. Nor did the Admiral wish to reveal all the details of his plan, fearing lest it be stolen from him in Castile as it had been in Portugal. For this reason the replies and reports that the geographers gave their Highnesses were as varied as their grasp of the subject and their opinions. Some argued in this way: In all the thousands of years since God created the world, those lands had remained unknown to innumerable learned men and experts in navigation; and it was most unlikely that the Admiral should know more than all other men, past and present. Others, who based themselves on geography, claimed the world was so large that to reach the end of Asia, whither the Admiral wished to sail, would take more than three years. For support they cited Seneca, who in one of his books debates the question, saying that many learned men were in disagreement on the question whether the ocean was infinite and doubted that it could ever be navigated; and even if it could be, they questioned whether habitable lands existed at the other end. To this they added that of this inferior sphere of land and water only a small belt or cap was inhabited, all the rest being sea that could be navigated only near the coasts and shores. And even if learned men admitted that one could reach the end of Asia, they did not say that one could go from the end of Spain to the extreme West. Others argued as some Portuguese had done about the navigation to Guinea, saying that if one were to set out and travel due west, as the Admiral proposed, one would not be able to return to Spain because the world was round. These men were absolutely certain that one who left the hemisphere known to Ptolemy would be going downhill and so could not return; for that would be like sailing a ship to the top of a mountain: a thing that ships could not do even with the aid of the strongest wind.

The Admiral gave suitable replies to all these objections, but the more effective his arguments, the less these men understood on account of their ignorance; for when a man poorly trained in mathematics reaches an advanced age, he is no longer capable of apprehending the truth because of the erroneous notions previously imprinted on his mind. Finally, they all repeated the Spanish saying that is commonly used of any doubtful statement, "St. Augustine doubts . . . ," because in Chapter 9 of Book XXI of *The City of God* the saint denies the existence of the Antipodes and holds it impossible to pass from one hemisphere to the other. They also used against the Admiral the fables that say that of the five zones only three are habitable, and other falsehoods which they took for gospel truth. In the end, then, they condemned the enterprise as vain and impossible and advised the Sovereigns that it did not conform with the dignity of such great princes to support a project resting on such weak foundations.

So, having spent much time and money on this project, their Highnesses replied to the Admiral that they were preoccupied with other wars and conquests, especially the War of Granada, which they were then bringing to conclusion, and so could not give their attention to a new enterprise, but that presently they would have a better opportunity to consider the Admiral's offer. Actually, the Sovereigns did not take seriously the large promises made to them by the Admiral.

CHAPTER 13

How the Admiral, Failing to Reach an Agreement with the Catholic Sovereigns, Decided to Offer His Enterprise to France

Meanwhile the Catholic Sovereigns were traveling from place to place on account of the War of Granada, which greatly delayed their coming to a decision and giving the Admiral their reply. The Admiral went to Seville, and finding their Highnesses still undecided, he resolved to bring his project to the attention of the Duke of Medina Sidonia.[1] After many conferences, despairing of a favorable issue to the affair in Spain, and observing that the execution of his project was being much delayed, he decided to go to the Court of the French King, to whom he had already written about the matter. In case he obtained no hearing in France he intended to set out immediately for England in search of his brother, from whom he had had no word.

Accordingly he went to the monastery of La Rábida to call for his son Diego, intending to send him to Córdoba and himself continue on the way to France. But God, Who would not permit His design to be undone, caused the head of that friary, Fray Juan Pérez, to form such a strong friendship for the Admiral and think so highly of his enterprise that he was much distressed at the Admiral's resolution and the loss that Spain would suffer thereby. Fray Juan Pérez therefore prayed him to abandon that resolution, for he himself would see the Queen in the hope that as he was her confessor, she would credit what he might tell her about the affair. By this time the Admiral had lost all hope and was much vexed by the small vision and poor judgment of the advisers of their Highnesses; but his desire that Spain should have the execution of the project (for he already thought of himself as a Spaniard, having spent much time there in connection with his enterprise and having had children born to him there [2]) made him yield to the friar's wishes and entreaties. That is why he rejected the offers that other princes had made him, as he himself states in a letter that he wrote their Highnesses, as follows:

To serve Your Highnesses I refused to listen to France, England, and Portugal, whose princes have written me letters that were shown your Highnesses by Doctor Villalón.[3]

CHAPTER 14

How the Admiral Returned to the Camp of Santa Fé and Took Leave of the Catholic Sovereigns, Having Failed to Reach an Agreement with Them

The Admiral, then, set out with Fray Juan Pérez from the monastery of La Rábida (which is near Palos) for the camp of Santa Fé, where the Catholic Sovereigns were laying siege to Granada. On arrival there the friar saw the Queen and urged the Admiral's cause so fervently that she agreed to reconsider his project. But the Prior del Prado and his henchmen opposed it as before; moreover, my father demanded the titles and offices of admiral and viceroy and other valuable and important things that she was loath to grant. For even if the scheme were sound, the reward he demanded seemed enormous; and if it proved a failure, it would later seem a piece of folly to have given what he asked. As a result the negotiation went up in smoke.

Let me say here that I greatly admire the wisdom, courage, and foresight of the Admiral, who, though so unlucky in his affairs and so desirous of remaining in that kingdom, and reduced at the time to a state in which he should have been content with anything, yet demanded great titles and rewards as if he foresaw the fortunate outcome of his enterprise. For in the end the Queen had to grant all he asked, namely, that he should be Admiral of the Ocean Sea, with the title, prerogatives, and pre-eminencies enjoyed by the admirals of Castile in their jurisdictions, and that he should be viceroy and governor over all the islands and mainland, with the authority and jurisdiction possessed by the admirals of Castile and León; that he should have absolute power to appoint and remove all the officers of administration and justice in all the said islands at his will and pleasure; that all governmental posts and municipal councilorships should be given to one of a list of three persons nominated by him for each position; and that he should appoint justices to sit in every port of Spain that trafficked and traded with the Indies, these justices to decide all matters relating to trade. In addition to the salaries and custom duties appertaining to the said offices of admiral, viceroy, and governor, he demanded a tenth of all that should be bought, bartered, found, or produced within the limits of his admiralty: Thus, if 1,000 ducats were found on a certain island, 100 would be his. And because his enemies were saying that he risked nothing of his own, being only captain of the fleet for the duration of the voyage, he demanded one eighth of all that he brought home, himself paying an eighth part of the total expense of the expedition.

Since their Highnesses would not grant him these important demands, the Admiral took leave of his friends and set out for Córdoba to prepare his journey to France; for he was resolved not to return to Portugal, although the Portuguese King had written to him, as will presently be told.[1]

CHAPTER 15

How the Catholic Sovereigns Ordered
the Admiral to Return and Granted All
He Asked

On the same day that the Admiral departed from Santa Fé, at the beginning of January, 1492, one of the persons who were distressed by his departure and eager to prevent it, that Luis de Santángel of whom I spoke before, presented himself before the Queen and with words that his keen desire to persuade her suggested, told her he was surprised that her Highness, who had always shown a resolute spirit in matters of great weight and consequence, should lack it now for an enterprise that offered so little risk yet could prove of so great service to God and the exaltation of His Church, not to speak of the very great increase and glory of her realms and kingdoms. The enterprise, moreover, was of such nature that if any other ruler should perform what the Admiral offered to do, it would clearly be a great injury to her estate and a cause of just reproach by her friends and of censure by her enemies. Since the project appeared soundly based and the Admiral was a well-informed and intelligent man who sought to take his reward only from what he found, and was ready not only to venture his person but to contribute a part of the costs, her Highness should not consider the enterprise so impossible as claimed by the experts. As for the foolish argument that it would discredit the Queen to have contributed to the project in case the Admiral did not fulfill his promises, he (Santángel) was rather of the opinion that the Sovereigns would be regarded as generous and high-minded princes for having tried to penetrate the secrets of the universe, as other princes and rulers had been praised for doing. Admitted the outcome was doubtful, a large sum of money would be well spent in resolving those doubts; but the Admiral was asking for only 2,500 escudos to equip the expedition, and she should not let it be said that for fear of losing so small an amount she abandoned that enterprise.

The Catholic Queen, who knew Santángel's zeal in her service, thanked him for his good advice and said that she would be glad to accept the Admiral's offer if the business could be put off until she had had a breathing space after the exertions of the War of Granada,¹ and that she was even ready to pledge her jewels for the cost of the expedition. But Santángel, who was grateful to the Queen for accepting on his advice what she had rejected on the advice of others, said this would not be necessary; he would be happy to render her Highness a trifling service by lending her the money. So, having made her decision, the Queen sent a court bailiff posthaste to order the Admiral to return.

The bailiff found him near the bridge of Pinos, which is two leagues distant from Granada; and although the Admiral complained of the delays and difficulties that had been put in the way of his enterprise, on being informed of the Queen's wishes he returned to Santa Fé. There the Catholic Sovereigns received him warmly and ordered their secretary Juan de Coloma to draw up and issue to the Admiral under their royal hand and seal capitulations containing exactly what he had demanded, without changing or taking anything away.

CHAPTER 16

How the Admiral Outfitted Three Caravels for His Voyage of Discovery

Having received the aforesaid capitulations from the very serene Catholic Sovereigns, the Admiral departed on May 12, 1492, from Granada for Palos, that being the port where he was to outfit his expedition because it was obligated to provide their Highnesses with two caravels for a period of three months; these caravels they ordered turned over to the Admiral. He equipped these two ships and one other with due care and diligence. The flagship, in which he himself sailed, was the *Santa María*. The captain of the *Pinta* was Martín Alonso Pinzón; and the *Niña*, which had lateen sails, was commanded by his brother Vicente Yáñez Pinzón of Palos.¹

By His Son Ferdinand

After he had provided these ships with all that was necessary, on August 3d he set sail for the Canaries, having ninety men aboard the fleet. From that date the Admiral was very careful to keep a

Parting of Columbus with the Catholic Sovereigns

journal of all that happened on the voyage: wind directions and currents, the distance run by each ship, and all that they sighted on the way—birds, fish, and any other signs. He did this on all four of his voyages from Castile to the Indies. I do not propose to record these things in detail, however, for while then it was doubtless very useful and proper to describe the route and its navigation, to make observations of the courses and aspects of the stars, and to show how those regions differed in such respects from our seas and lands, I believe that such prolixity would now bore instead of pleasing my readers. I shall therefore mention only such things as appear to be necessary and proper for my readers to know.

CHAPTER 17

How the Admiral Reached the Canaries
and There Took Aboard All He Needed

The day after the Admiral left Palos for the Canaries, Saturday, August 4th, the rudder of the *Pinta* jumped its gudgeons, forcing the crew to strike sails. The sea was too heavy for help to be given, but the Admiral came up, as is the custom of sea captains, to hearten the crew. He approached the more swiftly because he suspected foul play on the part of the ship's owner,[1] who might have hoped by this mishap to prevent the voyage, as he had tried to do before the departure. Pinzón, a skillful and experienced seaman, managed to fasten the rudder with some ropes so that the ship could proceed on her course, but the Tuesday following, the wind blew so hard that the ropes broke and the fleet had to lay to while repairs were made.

This misfortune of the *Pinta*'s twice losing her rudder at the start of the voyage might have caused a superstitious person to augur Pinzón's future disloyalty to the Admiral; for through his malice the *Pinta* twice separated from the fleet, as will presently be told.

Having repaired the damaged rudder as well as they could, they held on their course and at daybreak of Thursday, August 9th, they came in sight of the Canaries, but owing now to contrary winds, now to calms, neither on that nor on the two succeeding days could they land at the Grand Canary, to which they were very close. Accordingly the Admiral left Pinzón there with instructions to try to secure another ship [in place of the disabled vessel B. K.], while he proceeded with the *Santa María* and the *Niña* to the island of Gomera with the same aim.

Sunday, August 12th, the Admiral reached Gomera and immediately sent a boat ashore, but it returned the next morning with news that no ship could be had on the island. The boat's crew added, however, that the people hourly expected the return of Doña Beatriz de Bobadilla, mistress of the island, who was at the Grand Canary with a 40-ton ship belonging to one Grajeda of Seville that suited their needs. The Admiral therefore decided to wait in that port, calculating that if Pinzón had been unable to repair his ship, a replacement could be obtained in Gomera. But after waiting two days more, without any sign of the ship he was told of, the Admiral took advantage of the departure from Gomera of a brig bound for the Grand Canary to put aboard a man who was to inform Pinzón of the *Santa María's* position and help repair the *Pinta's* rudder; the Admiral wrote Pinzón that the only reason he did not return himself to help him was that the *Santa María* was a poor sailer. As he remained without news for a long time after the brig's departure, on August 23d the Admiral decided to return with his two ships to the Grand Canary, leaving the next day. On his course he overtook the brig, which had not yet reached the Grand Canary because of contrary winds.

He took his man aboard again and passed the night near Tenerife, from whose lofty volcano issued immense flames. Observing the astonishment of his crew, he explained to them the cause of this fire, making his point with the example of Mount Etna in Sicily and many other mountains like it. Passing by Tenerife, on Saturday, August 25th, they arrived at the Grand Canary, where Pinzón, though with great difficulty, had arrived the day before. From him he learned that the previous Monday Doña Beatriz had sailed with the ship that he had been at such pains to get. His people were much annoyed by this, but he took it in good part, observing that God must have so disposed; because if they had found that ship, he might have had difficulty in obtaining it and lost time in transferring their cargo aboard, all of which would have delayed the voyage. So, fearing that he might meet that ship on his course if he returned to Gomera, he decided to repair the damaged caravel as well as he could at the Grand Canary, building a new rudder in place of that which had been lost. He also had the *Niña's* rig changed from lateen to round in order to enable her to follow the other ships more easily and safely.

CHAPTER 18

How the Admiral Sailed from the Grand Canary and Continued His Voyage of Discovery, and What Happened to Him on the Ocean

On the afternoon of Friday, September 1st, the ships having been made ready in all respects, the Admiral hoisted sails and set out from the Grand Canary. Next day they reached Gomera, where they passed four more days in taking on meat, wood, and water. And on the morning of the Thursday following, September 6, 1492, which day may be taken to mark the beginning of the enterprise and the ocean crossing, the Admiral sailed westward from Gomera; but he made little headway on account of feeble and variable winds.

At daybreak on Sunday, he found he was nine leagues west of the island of Ferro. This day they completely lost sight of land, and many sighed and wept for fear they would not see it again for a long time. The Admiral comforted them with great promises of lands and riches. To sustain their hope and dispel their fears of a long voyage he decided to reckon less leagues than they actually made, telling them they had covered only fifteen leagues that day, though they had actually gone eighteen. He did this that they might not think themselves so great a distance from Spain as they really were, but for himself he kept a secret accurate reckoning.

Continuing their voyage, at sundown of Tuesday, September 11th, about one hundred and fifty leagues west of the island of

By His Son Ferdinand

Ferro, the Admiral saw a large fragment of mast that may have belonged to a ship of 120 tons and that seemed to have been in the water for a long time. In this region and farther west the currents set strongly to the northeast. At midnight of September 13th, after the fleet had run another fifty leagues westwards, the needles were found to vary half a point to the northwest, and in the morning a little more than half a point to the northeast. From this the Admiral knew that the needle did not point to the polestar, but to some other fixed and invisible point. No one had ever noticed this variation before, so he had good reason to be surprised at it. Three days later, almost one hundred leagues west of that area, he was even more surprised to find that at midnight the needles varied a whole point to the northwest, while in the morning they again pointed directly to the polestar.

Saturday night, September 15th, as they were almost three hundred leagues west of Ferro, a prodigious flame fell from the sky into the sea, some four or five leagues from the ships, toward the southwest, although the weather was as balmy as in April, with a mild wind blowing from the northeast to the southeast and the currents setting to the northeast. The *Niña's* people told the Admiral that the previous Friday they had seen a *garjao* [1] and another bird called *rabo de junco;* [2] they were much surprised by these birds, the first they had seen on the voyage.

They were even more surprised the next day, Sunday, to see the surface of the water covered with a great mass of yellowish green weed, which seemed to have been torn away from some island or reef. [3] The next day they saw much more of this weed; many therefore affirmed they must certainly be near land, especially since they saw a live crab amid these mats of weed; the weed resembled star grass, save that it had long stalks and shoots, and was loaded with fruit like the mastic tree. They also observed that the sea water was less salty by half than before. That night they were followed by many tunny fish that swam about the ships, coming so near that the *Niña's* people killed one with a harpoon.

About three hundred and seventy leagues from Ferro they saw another *rabo de junco;* this bird is so called because its tail forms a long plume [and in Spanish the word *rabo* means "tail"].

The Tuesday following, September 18th, Martín Alonso Pinzón, who had gone ahead in the *Pinta,* a very fast sailer, lay to for the Admiral to come up and informed him he had seen a great flight

of birds moving westward, a sign that made Pinzón hopeful of finding land that night; and at sundown he thought he actually saw
land some fifteen leagues to the north, covered by darkness and
clouds. All the ship's people wanted the Admiral to search in that
direction, but he would not waste his time upon it, because it was
not the place where his calculations made him expect to find land.
That night, after sailing for eleven days under full sail and running ever before the wind, they took in their topsails because the
wind had freshened.

CHAPTER 19

How All the Ship's People, Being Eager
to Reach Land, Were Very Attentive to
the Things They Saw in the Sea

As this was the first voyage of that kind for all the men in the
fleet, they grew frightened at finding themselves so far from land
without prospect of aid, and did not cease to grumble among themselves. Seeing nothing but water and sky all about, they paid the
closest attention to all they observed, as was natural for men who
had gone a greater distance from land than any had ever done
before. So I shall mention all the things to which they assigned
any importance (but only in telling of the first voyage), though
I will not take note of those minor signs that are commonly and
frequently observed at sea.

On the morning of September 19th a pelican flew over the Admiral's ship, followed by others in the afternoon. This gave him
some hope of soon sighting land, for he reflected that these birds
would not have flown far from land. Accordingly, when it grew
calm, the ship's people sounded with two hundred fathoms of line;
they found no bottom, but noted that now the currents set to the
southwest. Again, on Thursday, the 20th of the month, two hours
before noon, two pelicans flew over the ship and a while later came

another; the sailors also caught a bird like a heron, save that it was black, with a white tuft on its head and feet like a duck's, as is common with water birds. They also caught a little fish and saw much weed of the kind mentioned before. At daybreak three little birds flew singing over the ship; they flew away when the sun came out, but left the comforting thought that unlike the other large water birds, which might have come a great distance, these little birds could not have come from afar. Three hours later they saw another bird that came from the west-northwest, and next day, in the afternoon, they saw another *rabo de junco* and a pelican; they also saw more seaweed than ever before, stretching northward as far as they could see. This also comforted them, since they concluded it must come from some nearby land; but at times it caused them great fright, because in places the weed was so thickly matted that it held back the ships. And since fear conjures up imaginary terrors, they even feared lest the weed grow so thick that there might happen to them what is supposed to have happened to St. Amador in the frozen sea that is said to hold ships fast. That is why they kept as clear as possible of those mats of weed.

The next day they sighted a whale, and the Saturday following, September 22d, some *pardelas*[1] were seen. During those three days the wind blew from the southwest, more westerly at some times than at others; and though this wind was contrary to his design, the Admiral wrote that he found it very helpful. For one of the bogeys his people had been scaring themselves with was the idea that since the wind was always at their backs, they would never have a wind in those waters for returning to Spain. Then, when they got such a wind, they would complain that it was inconstant, and that since there was no heavy sea, that proved it would never blow hard enough to return them the great distance they had come from Spain. To this the Admiral would reply that must be because they were near land, which kept the sea smooth, and he sought to convince them as well as he could. But [in his journal B. K.] he wrote that he stood in need of God's aid, such as Moses had when he was leading the Jews out of Egypt and they dared not lay violent hands upon him on account of the miracles that God wrought by his own means. So, says the Admiral, it happened with him on this voyage. For soon after, on Sunday, September 23d, there arose a wind from the west-northwest, with a rough sea such as the people wanted; also, three hours before noon, a turtledove flew over the ship, and in the afternoon they saw a pelican, a small river bird, some white birds, and some crabs among the weed. Next day they saw another pelican, and many *pardelas* flying out of the west, and some little fish, some of which the sailors caught with harpoons, because they would not bite at hooks.

CHAPTER 20

How the Men Grumbled Because of Their Desire to Return, and How Certain Signs and Tokens of Land Made Them Continue Gladly on Their Course

As these signs proved fruitless, the men grew ever more restless and fearful. They met together in the holds of the ships, saying that the Admiral in his mad fantasy proposed to make himself a lord at the cost of their lives or die in the attempt; that they had already tempted fortune as much as their duty required and had sailed farther from land than any others had done. Why, then, should they work their own ruin by continuing that voyage, since they were already running short of provisions and the ships had so many leaks and faults that even now they were hardly fit to retrace the great distance they had traveled? Certainly (said they), none would blame them for deciding to return but rather would hold them for very brave men for having enlisted on such a voyage and having sailed so far. And since the Admiral was a foreigner without favor at Court and one whose views had been rejected and criticized by many wise and learned men, none would speak in his defense and all would believe what they said, attributing to ignorance and ineptitude whatever he might say to justify himself. Others said they had heard enough gab. If the Admiral would not turn back, they should heave him overboard and report in Spain that he had fallen in accidentally while observing the stars; and none would question their story. That, said they, was the best means of assuring their safe return.

The grumbling, lamenting, and plotting went on day after day; and at last the Admiral himself became aware of their faithlessness and wicked designs against him. Therefore at times he addressed them with fair words; again, very passionately, as if fearless of death, he threatened punishment to any who hindered his voyage. By these different means he managed somewhat to calm their fears and check their machinations. To bolster their hopes he reminded them of the signs and tokens mentioned above, assuring them they would soon sight land. After that they looked most diligently for those signs and thought each hour a year until land was reached.

Finally, at sunset of Tuesday, September 25th, while the Admiral was talking with Pinzón, whose ship had come close alongside, Pinzón suddenly cried out, "Land, land, sir! I claim the reward!" And he pointed to a bulk that clearly resembled an island and lay about twenty-five leagues distant. At this the people felt such joy and relief that they offered thanks to God. The Admiral himself gave some credit to that claim until nightfall, and wishing to please them that they might not oppose continuing the voyage, he gratified their wishes and steered in that direction a good part of the night. But next morning they knew that what they had supposed to be land was nothing more than squall clouds, which often resemble land.

So, to the grief and vexation of most of his people, they again sailed westward, as they had done since leaving Spain, save when the winds were contrary. Ever vigilant for signs, they sighted a pelican and a *rabo de junco* and other birds of that kind. The morning of Thursday, September 27th, they saw another pelican flying west to east; they also saw many fish with gilded backs, and caught one of these fish with a harpoon. A *rabo de junco* flew close by; and they noted that for the last few days the currents had not been as constant and regular as before but changed with the tides; the quantity of seaweed also diminished.

Next day all the ships caught fish with gilded backs, and on Saturday they saw a frigate bird. This is a sea bird, but never does it rest upon the water, for it flies through the air pursuing pelicans until from fright they drop their excrement, which it catches in the air for its food; by such tricky hunting does the frigate bird sustain itself in those seas. It is said to be most commonly found near the Cape Verdes. A little later they saw two more pelicans and many flying fish, which are a span long and have two little wings like a bat; these fish sometimes fly about the height of a lance above the water, rising in the air like a harquebus shot, and occasionally they fall into the ships. After dinner the Admiral's people also saw much weed lying in the north-south direction, something they had often seen before, and three more pelicans and a frigate bird, which followed them.

Sunday morning four *rabos de junco* flew over the ship, and the fact that they came together made the people believe that land must be near, especially since a little while later four more pelicans passed by; they also saw many emperor fish, which resemble the fish called *chopos* in that they have a very hard skin and are not good to eat.

Although very attentive to these signs, the Admiral did not neglect the portents of the heavens or the courses of the stars. He was much surprised to observe that in this region the Guards [1] appeared at night directly to the west, while at daybreak they were directly northeast. From this he concluded that during one night the ships traveled only three lines or nine [astronomical в. к.] hours, and by observation he found this to be true every night. He also noted that in the evening the needles varied a whole point, while at dawn they pointed directly to the polestar. This fact greatly disquieted and confused the pilots, until he told them its cause was the circle described by the polestar about the pole. This explanation partly allayed their fears, for these variations on a voyage into such strange and distant regions made them very apprehensive.

CHAPTER 21

How They Continued to See the Above-mentioned Signs and Tokens and Others That Were Even More Hopeful, Which Gave Them Some Comfort

At sunrise on Monday, October 1st, a pelican flew over the ship, and two hours before noon came two more; the direction of the weed was now east to west. In the morning of that day the pilot of the Admiral's flagship said they were 578 leagues west of Ferro, and the Admiral put the figure at 584; but from his secret reckoning he knew they had traveled 707 leagues, a difference of 129 between his count and the pilot's. The reckonings of the other two ships varied even more widely; in the afternoon of the Wednesday following, the *Niña's* pilot claimed they had sailed 540 leagues, while the *Pinta's* set the figure at 634. Allowing for the distance they had covered the past three days, their reckonings still fell far short of the true and reasonable total, for they had always sailed with a stiff wind at their backs. But the Admiral dissembled this error that his people might not grow even more frightened, finding themselves so far from home.

Next day, October 2d, they saw many fish and caught a small tunny. They also saw a white bird like a sea gull and many *pardelas*. The seaweed was now withered and almost reduced to powder.

Next day, seeing no birds save some *pardelas*, the men feared they unknowingly had passed between some islands; for they thought the great multitude of birds they had seen were birds of passage bound from one island to another. The Admiral's people wished to turn off in one or another direction to look for those lands, but he refused because he feared to lose the fair wind that was carrying him due west along what he believed to be the best and most certain route to the Indies. Besides, he reflected that he would lose respect and credit for his voyage if he beat aimlessly about from place to place looking for lands whose position he had claimed to know most accurately. Because of this refusal, the men were on the point of mutiny, grumbling and plotting against him. But God was pleased to assist him with new signs, for on Thursday, October 4th, they saw a flight of more than forty *pardelas* and two pelicans which came so near the ships that a grummet hit one with a stone. They had previously seen another bird like a *rabo de junco* and one resembling a sea gull, and many flying fish fell into the ships. Next day another *rabo de junco* flew over the ship, and a pelican came from the west; many *pardelas* were seen.

At daybreak of the Sunday following, October 7th, they saw what appeared to be land lying westward; but since it was indistinct, none wished to claim having made the discovery, not for fear of being shamed if proved wrong but for fear of losing the 10,000 maravedís promised by the Catholic Sovereigns to the first person sighting land. In order to prevent men from crying "land, land!" at every moment and causing unjustified feelings of joy, the Admiral had ordered that one who claimed to have seen land and did not make good his claim in the space of three days would lose the reward even if afterwards he should actually see it. Being warned of this, none of the people on the Admiral's ship dared cry out "land, land!" but the *Niña*, which was a better sailer and so ranged ahead, fired a gun and broke out flags as a sign that she had sighted land.

But the farther they sailed the more their spirits fell, until at last that illusion of land faded clean away. God, however, was pleased to offer them some small comfort; for they saw many large flocks of birds, more varied in kind than those they had seen before, and others of small land birds which were flying from the west to the southwest in search of food. Being now a great distance from Spain, and convinced that such small birds would not fly far from land, the Admiral changed course from west to southwest, noting [in his journal B. K.] that he was making a slight deviation from his main course in imitation of the Portuguese, who made most of their discoveries by attending to the flights of birds. He did this especially because the birds they saw were flying in almost the very same direction where he always expected land to be found. He reminded the men that he had often told them they must not expect to strike land until they had sailed seven hundred and fifty leagues west of the Canaries; he had also said that the island of Española, then called Cipango, would be found in that area. He would doubtless have found it, too, had he not accepted the truth of the report that that island extended from north to south, and so did not run far enough south to hit it; as a result, Española and the other Caribbean islands now lay on his left, to the south, whither those birds were flying.

Being, then, so near land, they saw a great abundance and variety of birds. On Monday, October 8th, there came to the ship twelve varicolored birds of the kind that sing in the fields; after flying for a while about the ship they continued on their way. The other ships also sighted many birds flying to the southwest; and that night they saw many large birds and flocks of small birds that came from the north and flew after the rest. They also saw many tunny fish, and in the morning they saw a *garjao,* a pelican, ducks, and little birds that flew in the same direction as the others; they noted that the air was as fresh and fragrant as in April in Seville.

But by this time the men's anxiety and desire to sight land had reached such a pitch that no sign of any kind would satisfy them. And though on Wednesday, October 10th, they saw birds passing overhead both night and day, they did not cease to complain nor the Admiral to reprove them for their small spirit, telling them that for better or worse they must go through with the enterprise of the Indies on which the Catholic Sovereigns had sent them.

CHAPTER 22

How the Admiral Sighted the First Land, This Being an Island in the Archipelago Called the Bahamas

Our Lord, perceiving how difficult was the Admiral's situation because of his many opponents, was pleased on the afternoon of Thursday, October 11th, to give them clear indications that they were near land, which cheered the men greatly. First the flagship's people saw a green branch pass near the ship, and later, a large green fish of the kind that is found near reefs. Then the *Pinta's* people saw a cane and a stick; and they fished up another stick skillfully carved, a small board, and an abundance of weeds of the kind that grow on the shore. The *Niña's* crew saw other signs of the same kind, as well as a thorn branch loaded with red berries that seemed to be freshly cut.

These signs, and his own reasoning, convinced the Admiral that land must be near. That night, therefore, after they had sung the Hail Mary as seamen are accustomed to do at nightfall, he spoke to the men of the favor that Our Lord had shown them by conducting them so safely and prosperously with fair winds and a clear course, and by comforting them with signs that daily grew more abundant. And he prayed them to be very watchful that night, reminding them that in the first article of the instructions issued to each ship at the Canaries he had given orders to do no night-sailing after reaching a point seven hundred leagues from those islands, but that the great desire of all to see land had decided him to sail on that night. They must make amends for this temerity by keeping a sharp lookout, for he was most confident that land was near; and to him who first sighted it he would give a velvet doublet in addition to the annuity for life of 10,000 maravedís that their Highnesses had promised.

That same night, about two hours before midnight, as the Admiral stood on the sterncastle, he saw a light, but he says it was so uncertain a thing that he dared not announce it was land. He called Pedro Gutiérrez, butler to the King, and asked him if he saw that light. He replied that he did, so they called Rodrigo Sánchez of Segovia to have a look, but he was too slow in coming to the place from which the light could be seen. After that they saw it only once or twice. This made them think it might be a light or torch belonging to fishermen or travelers who alternately raised and lowered it, or perhaps were going from house to house; for the light appeared and disappeared so quickly that few believed it to be a sign of land.

Being now very watchful, they held on their course until about two hours after midnight, when the *Pinta*, a speedy sailer that ranged far ahead, fired the signal for land. A sailor named Rodrigo de Triana first sighted it while they were still two leagues away. It was not he who received the grant of 10,000 maravedís from the Catholic Sovereigns, however, but the Admiral, who had first seen the light amid the darkness, signifying the spiritual light with which he was to illuminate those parts.[1]

Land being now very near, all the ship's people impatiently awaited the coming of day, thinking the time endless till they could enjoy what they had so long desired.

CHAPTER 23

How the Admiral Went Ashore and Took Possession of the Land in the Name of the Catholic Sovereigns

At daybreak they saw an island about fifteen leagues in length, very level, full of green trees and abounding in springs, with a large lagoon in the middle, and inhabited by a multitude of people who hastened to the shore, astounded and marveling at the sight of the ships, which they took for animals. These people could hardly wait to see what sort of things the ships were. The Christians were no less eager to know what manner of people they had to do with. Their wishes were soon satisfied, for as soon as they had cast anchor the Admiral went ashore with an armed boat, displaying the royal standard. The captains of the other two ships did the same in their boats with the banner of the expedition, on which was depicted a green cross with an F on one side, and crowns in honor of Ferdinand and Isabella on the other.[1]

After all had rendered thanks to Our Lord, kneeling on the ground and kissing it with tears of joy for His great favor to them, the Admiral arose and gave this island the name San Salvador.[2] Then, in the presence of the many natives assembled there, he took possession of it in the name of the Catholic Sovereigns with appropriate ceremony and words. The Christians forthwith accepted him as admiral and viceroy and swore obedience to him as the representative of their Highnesses, with such show of pleasure and joy as so great a victory deserved; and they begged his pardon for the injuries that through fear and little faith they had done him.

Many Indians [3] assembled to watch this celebration and rejoicing, and the Admiral, perceiving they were a gentle, peaceful, and very simple people, gave them little red caps and glass beads which they hung about their necks, together with other trifles that they cherished as if they were precious stones of great price.

CHAPTER 24

Of the Condition and Customs of Those People, and What the Admiral Saw on That Island

The Admiral having returned to his boats, the Indians followed him thither and even to the ships, some swimming and others paddling in their canoes; they brought parrots, skeins of woven cotton, darts, and other things, which they exchanged for glass beads, hawk's bells,[1] and other trifles. Being a people of primitive simplicity, they all went about as naked as their mothers bore them; and a woman who was there wore no more clothes than the men. They were all young, not above thirty years of age, and of good stature. Their hair was straight, thick, very black, and short —that is, cut above the ears—though some let it grow down to their shoulders and tied it about their heads with a stout cord so that it looked like a woman's tress. They had handsome features, spoiled somewhat by their unpleasantly broad foreheads. They were of middle stature, well formed and sturdy, with olive-colored skins that gave them the appearance of Canary Islanders or sunburned peasants. Some were painted black, others white, and still others red; some painted only the face, others the whole body, and others only the eyes or nose.

By His Son Ferdinand

They had no arms like ours, nor knew thereof; for when the Christians showed them a naked sword, they foolishly grasped it by the blade and cut themselves. Nor have they anything of iron, for their darts are sticks with sharpened points that they harden in the fire, arming the end with a fish's tooth instead of an iron point. Some Indians had scars left by wounds on their bodies; asked by signs what had caused them, they replied, also by signs, that the natives of other islands came on raids to capture them and they had received their wounds in defending themselves. They appeared fluent in speech and intelligent, easily repeating words that they had once heard. The only animals of any kind on the island were parrots, which they brought with the things mentioned above for barter. This traffic continued till nightfall.

Next morning, October 13th, many of these people came to the beach and paddled to the ships in their little boats, called canoes; these are made from the bole of a tree hollowed out like a trough, all in one piece. The larger ones hold forty to forty-five persons; the smaller ones are of all sizes, down to one holding but a single man. The Indians row with paddles like baker's peels or those used in dressing hemp. But their paddles are not attached to the sides of the boat as ours are; they dip them in the water and pull back with a strong stroke. So light and skillfully made are these canoes that if one overturns, the Indian rowers immediately begin to swim and right it and shake the canoe from side to side like a weaver's shuttle until it is more than half empty, bailing out the rest of the water with gourds that they carry for this purpose.

That day they brought the same things to barter as the previous day, giving all they had, in exchange for some trifle. They had no jewels or metal objects except some gold pendants which they wear hanging from a hole made through the nostrils. Asked whence came that gold, they replied by signs, from the south, where lived a king who had many tiles and vessels of gold. They added that to the south and southwest there were many other islands and large countries. Being very eager to obtain our things, and having nothing more to give in exchange, they picked up anything they could lay their hands on as soon as they came aboard, were it only a piece of broken crockery or part of a glazed bowl, then jumped into the sea and swam ashore with it. And if they brought anything, they were willing to give all they had for some trifle or for a piece of broken glass. Some of them gave sixteen skeins of

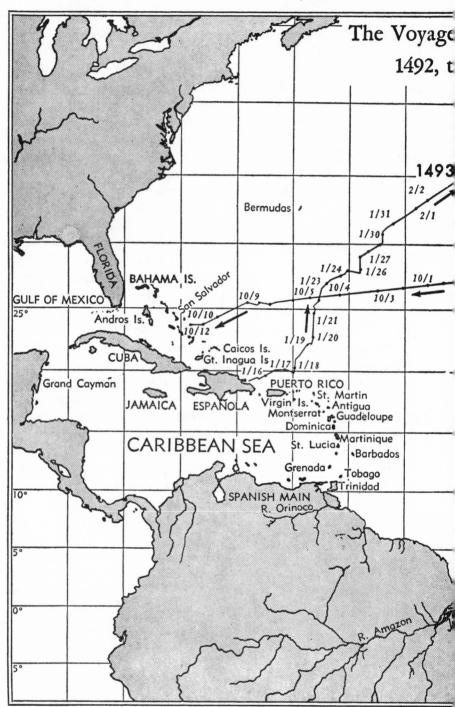

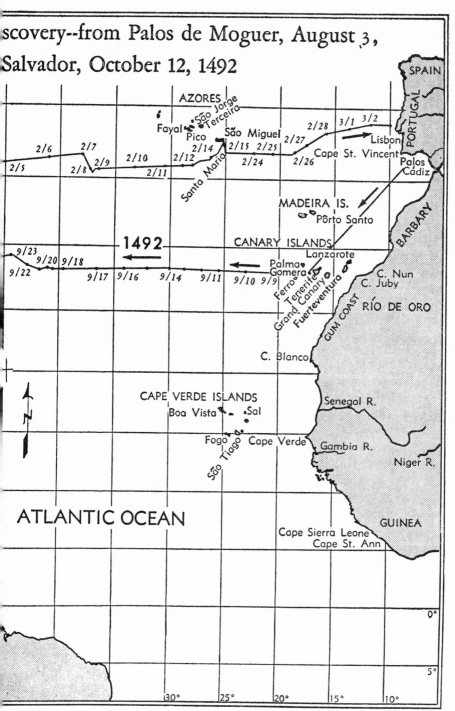

scovery--from Palos de Moguer, August 3,
Salvador, October 12, 1492

AZORES
São Jorge
Terceira
Fayal
Pico
São Miguel
2/28 3/1 3/2
2/14 2/15 2/25 2/27
2/12 2/24 2/26 Lisbon
2/6 2/7 2/10 Cape St. Vincent
2/9 2/11 Santa Maria Palos
2/5 2/8 Cadiz

MADEIRA IS.
Pôrto Santo

1492
CANARY ISLANDS
9/23 Lanzarote
9/20 9/18 Palma
9/22 9/17 9/16 9/14 9/11 9/10 9/9 Gomera
Ferro Tenerife C. Nun
Grand Canary C. Juby
Fuerteventura RÍO DE ORO
GUM COAST

C. Blanco

CAPE VERDE ISLANDS
Boa Vista Sal
Senegal R.

Fogo Cape Verde
São Tiago Gambia R.
Niger R.

ATLANTIC OCEAN GUINEA

Cape Sierra Leone
Cape St. Ann

SPAIN
PORTUGAL
BARBARY

0°
5°
30° 25° 20° 15° 10°

cotton for three Portuguese blancas; [2] these skeins weighed more than twenty-five pounds apiece, and the cotton was very well spun. They passed the day in this traffic, going home in the afternoon.

It may be observed that their liberal terms in this trade did not arise from the great material value they placed upon our things, but from the fact they were ours; for they were convinced our men had come from Heaven, and therefore they wished to have some relic of them.

CHAPTER 25

How the Admiral Left That Island and Went in Search of Others

Next Sunday, October 14th, the Admiral went with his boats along the shore of that island toward the northwest to see what lay on the other side. There he found a large bay or harbor capable of holding all the ships in Christendom. The natives, seeing him go by, ran along the shore crying out, offering him food, and calling others to see the men who had come from Heaven; they prostrated themselves and raised their hands as if giving thanks for the Christians' coming. Many swam or paddled in their canoes to the boats to ask by signs if our men had come from Heaven and to invite them to come ashore to rest. The Admiral gave them all glass beads and pins and took infinite pleasure in the simplicity of these people. At last he came to a peninsula which would have taken three days of hard rowing to round; it was habitable and offered an excellent site for a fort. He saw six Indian huts surrounded by many gardens that were as beautiful as those of Castile in May. But the men were now weary of rowing, and the Admiral could see that this was not the land he sought; nor did it offer such promise of riches as to hold him there any longer. Accordingly, having taken seven Indians to serve him as interpreters, he returned to his ships. From there he sailed toward other islands that could be seen from the peninsula and appeared to be level, green, and thickly inhabited, as was affirmed by the Indians themselves.

One of these islands, which was seven leagues distant, he reached the next day, Monday, October 15th, and named Santa María de la Concepción.[1] The part of the island that faces San Salvador extends five leagues from north to south. But the Admiral sailed down the coast that runs from east to west, and is more than ten leagues long. Casting anchor at the western end of the island, he went ashore to do what he had done on San Salvador. The natives came up quickly to see the Christians and appeared as much surprised as the others.

Finding nothing new on this island, the next day, Tuesday, the Admiral sailed eight leagues westward to a much larger island and anchored on its coast, which extended more than twenty-eight leagues from northwest to southeast; this island too was level and had a fine beach. The Admiral decided to name it Fernandina.[2] Before reaching this island and the island of Concepción they picked up a man in a small canoe who had a piece of the native bread, a gourd filled with water, a lump of earth resembling vermilion, which the natives use to paint their bodies, and some dried leaves which they greatly prize for their fragrance and healthful quality.[3] In a little basket he carried a string of green glass beads and two blancas; from this they concluded that he came from San Salvador and, after stopping at Concepción, was bound for Fernandina to spread the news of the coming of the Christians throughout those islands. As the way was long and he weary, he paddled up to one of the ships and together with his canoe was taken aboard. He had a friendly reception from the Admiral, who sent him ashore as soon as they reached Fernandina in order that he might spread his tidings. The Admiral also gave him some trifles to distribute among the other natives.

This Indian's favorable account of the Christians caused the people of Fernandina to come to the ships in their canoes to barter as the others had done; for these people and all the rest are of the same condition and customs. When the boat was sent ashore for water, the Indians very gladly showed them where to find it and carried the filled casks to the tuns in the boat. They seemed more intelligent and shrewder than the first natives our men had met, driving harder bargains for what they traded. In their huts they had cotton cloths which they used for bed coverings. The women covered their private parts, some with small clouts of woven cotton, others with wrapped skirts of woven cloth.

Among the remarkable things the Christians saw on the island were some trees that bore on a single trunk four or five different kinds of leaves and branches, differing as much as the leaf of the cane from that of the mastic tree; the leaves seemed not to have been grafted but to have grown naturally. They also saw fish of different shapes and fine colors, but found no land animals except lizards and an occasional snake. With a view to learning more about the island, they sailed to the northwest and anchored at the mouth of a beautiful harbor at whose entrance lay a small island, but they could not enter this harbor because it was not deep enough; nor did they try to enter it, because they wanted to stay near a village that was close by. Although this was the largest island they had yet come to, the village consisted of only twelve or fifteen huts shaped like tents and containing no ornament or furniture other than the things the Indians brought to the ships for barter. The beds were nets that had the shape of slings, with the ends attached to two houseposts. They also saw dogs that looked like mastiffs or hunting dogs but could not bark.

CHAPTER 26

How the Admiral Sailed to Other Islands
That Could Be Seen from Where He Was

Finding nothing of importance on Fernandina, on Friday, October 19th, they proceeded to another island, called Saometo, which the Admiral named Isabela.[1] He did this to follow a proper order in the assignment of names. He named the first island, called by the Indians Guanahaní, San Salvador, in honor of God, who had pointed it out to him and saved him from many dangers; the second, Santa María de la Concepción, out of devotion to Our Lady and because she is the principal patroness of Christians; the third, which the Indians called . . . ,[2] Fernandina, in honor of the Catholic King; the fourth, Isabela, in honor of the most serene Queen Isabella; and the island that he next found, Cuba, he named Juana in memory of Prince Juan, heir apparent to the throne of Castile. Thus he aimed to honor both the spiritual and temporal powers.

However, he says that in goodness, extent, and beauty Fernandina far surpassed the other islands. Not only did it abound in springs and beautiful meadows and trees, among which were many aloes,[3] but it had mountains and hills which the others lacked, being very level. Charmed by the beauty of this island, the Admiral decided to take possession of it and went ashore at some meadows as lovely and pleasant as those of Spain in April. They heard the song of nightingales and other small birds, a song so sweet that the Admiral could not tear himself away. These birds flitted among the trees and flew through the air in such swarms that they obscured the sun; most of them were very different from ours, however. That country has many streams and lakes, and near one of these they saw a serpent seven feet long and a foot wide in the middle. Our men pursued the serpent into the lake, which was very shallow, and there they killed it with pikes, though its ferocity and ugliness frightened and surprised them. In due time, however, they came to think it a delicacy, for it is the choicest food the Indians have, and once that horrible skin and scales are removed the flesh is found to be very white, soft, and tasty. The Indians call it iguana.

As it was now late and they wished to learn more about that country, they left the serpent's body there until next day (when they killed another like it), and journeying through that country, they came to a village whose inhabitants fled before them, taking what household goods they could. The Admiral would not permit his men to take anything they had left, that the Indians might not regard the Christians as thieves, and also that the Indians might lose their fear and willingly come to the ships to barter their things as the others had done.

CHAPTER 27

How the Admiral Discovered the Island of Cuba, and What He Found There

Having penetrated the secrets of that island of Isabela and learned the manners and condition of its people, the Admiral would not waste any more time in cruising among those islands, which were very numerous and by the testimony of the Indians resembled each other. He therefore took advantage of a fair wind to sail south toward a very large country called Cuba, that the Indians praised highly; he reached its northern coast on Sunday, October 28th. This island soon proved to be better and richer than the others they had visited, because of the beauty of its hills and mountains, the variety of its trees, its extensive plains, and the great expanse of its coasts and beaches. In order to gain some knowledge of its people, the Admiral anchored in a large river where the trees were very large and tall, with fruit and flowers differing from our own and a multitude of birds. A most delightful place it was, for the grasses were tall and very different from ours; they recognized purslane, wheat, and the like, but the varieties were strange to them. Going up to two huts that they sighted a short distance away, they found that the people had fled for fear, leaving nets and all their other fishing tackle and a dog who could not bark. The Admiral ordered his men not to touch anything, for he was interested only in learning what things the Indians used for their livelihood and service.

Returning to the ships, the Admiral steered northward and came to another large river which he named the Río de Mares.[1] It was superior to the other in that a ship could get up its mouth, and its shores were thickly populated. At sight of the ships the natives fled to the mountains, which were high, round, and covered with trees and pleasant greenery; there the Indians hid all they could take with them. As the timidity of these people kept him from getting information about this island, and he reflected that a landing in force would only frighten them still more, the Admiral decided to send an embassy consisting of two Christians, an Indian he had brought from San Salvador, and a local Indian who had ventured to paddle to the ships in a small canoe.[2] He ordered them to go up country and gain all the information they could, treating the Indians they should meet in a friendly manner. In order not to lose time in their absence, he ordered the ships laid ashore and calked. They discovered that the wood with which they were feeding the fire for this purpose was of the mastic tree, which abounds throughout that country. The leaves and fruit of this tree resemble those of the lentiscus, but it is a much bigger tree than the lentiscus.

CHAPTER 28

How the Two Christians Returned, and the Account They Gave of What They Had Seen

On November 5th, the ships having meantime been repaired and made ready to sail, the two Christians and the Indians returned. They said they had gone twelve leagues into the interior and had reached a village of fifty large wooden huts, thatched with palms, and shaped like tents or pavilions, just as the others had been. There must have been as many as a thousand families in that village, because all the people of the same kindred live in a single house. The principal men of that country came out to meet them and carried them on their shoulders to the village, where they lodged them in the principal house. They seated each in a chair made of one piece and in a strange shape, for it resembled some short-legged animal with a tail as broad as the seat of the chair and lifted up for convenience to lean against; this chair had a head in front with eyes and ears of gold. They call these seats *dujos* or *duchos*. Having seated our men upon them, all the Indians sat down around them and then came up one by one to kiss their hands and feet, believing they came from Heaven. The Indians also gave them some cooked roots that had the flavor of chestnuts.[1] They earnestly prayed the Christians to stay with them or at least to tarry five or six days among them; for the two Indians they had brought as interpreters spoke very well of them. Soon after, many women came in to see them, and the men went out; these women showed the same wonder and reverence, kissing the hands and feet of the Christians as if they were sacred and offering them the presents they had brought.

When it was time for them to return to the ships, many Indians wished to accompany them, but our men would permit only the king, his son, and one servant to go with them. The Admiral received these people very honorably. The Christians related how, both coming and going, they came to many villages where they had the same friendly and hospitable reception; none of these villages contained more than five huts.

On the way they met many people who carried a firebrand to light certain herbs[2] the smoke of which they inhale, and also to make a fire to roast those roots of which they had given the Christians to eat and which are their principal food. The Christians also saw an infinite variety of trees and plants, such as had not been seen on the coast, and a great variety of birds that differed from ours, though there were partridges and nightingales among them. The only four-legged animals they saw were some of those dogs that do not bark.[3] They also saw much land planted to the roots mentioned above, to kidney beans, to some kind of horse beans, and to a grain resembling panic grass that they call maize and is most tasty, boiled, roasted, or ground into flour.

Our people saw a great quantity of cotton made into skeins, and in one house alone they found more than 12,500 pounds of woven cotton. The Indians do not plant it by hand, for it grows wild in the fields, like roses; and the plants open up by themselves when ripe, though not all at the same time. On one plant they saw a tiny bud, another had just opened, and another was fully ripe and ready to fall. The Indians brought a great quantity of this cotton to the ships, giving a basketful for a leather thong. They make no use of it for clothing, but use it rather to make their nets and beds, which they call hammocks, and also to weave the clouts with which their women cover their private parts. Asked if they had any gold, pearls, or spices, they indicated by signs that there was an abundance of all those things to the east in a land called Bohío, which they also called Babeque. We do not yet know for certain to what place they referred.[4]

CHAPTER 29

How the Admiral Left Off Following the Western Coast of Cuba and Turned Eastward Toward Española

Told of this, the Admiral decided to leave the Río de Mares and ordered some of the people of that island made captives; for he intended to take some persons from each island to Spain in order that they might give information about their country. So the Christians seized twelve persons, men, women, and children, who came so peacefully that at sailing time the husband of a woman who had been taken aboard with her two children came up in a canoe and asked by signs to be taken also to Castile that he might not be separated from them. This favor the Admiral willingly granted, and he ordered they should all be well treated.

That day, November 13th, he stood eastward for the island called Babeque or Bohío; but a strong north wind forced him to anchor again on the coast of Cuba among some very high islands near a great harbor which he named Puerto del Príncipe;[1] the islands he named El Mar de Nuestra Señora.[2] These islands were so numerous and close together that less than a quarter-league separated one from another. The channels were so deep and the shores so adorned with trees and greenery that it was most pleasant to sail down them; among the many trees that differed from ours were many mastic and aloe trees,[3] palm trees with smooth green trunks, and a variety of other plants.

These islands were uninhabited, but the Christians found signs of many fires left by fishermen. As we have since learned, bands of Indians come from Cuba in their canoes to these islands and many others that are uninhabited. They feed on fish, birds, crabs, and many other things that they find on them, for the Indians are accustomed to eat such loathsome things as large fat spiders, white worms that breed in rotten wood, and other decayed objects. Frequently, having caught a fish, they eat it almost raw, plucking out the eyes to eat before roasting the rest. They eat many such things that would not only sicken but kill us if we ate them. They hunt and fish according to the season, going first to one island and then to another, like a person who changes his diet when it begins to pall.

On one of the islands of the Mar de Nuestra Señora the Christians killed with their swords an animal like a badger; [4] in the sea they found much mother-of-pearl. Among the fish they caught in their nets was one like a pig, covered with a very hard skin; its only soft spot was the tail.[5] They also noted that in this sea and on its islands the tide rose and fell much more than in the other places where they had been; consequently the tide was the reverse of ours here in Spain, for there, when the moon bore southwest by south, it was low tide.

Chapter 30

How the Admiral Again Sailed Eastward for Española, and How One of His Ships Left Him

Monday, November 19th, the Admiral departed from the Puerto del Príncipe and the Mar de Nuestra Señora in Cuba, steering for the islands of Babeque and Española, but the wind proving contrary, he had to beat about three days between the island of Isabela, which the Indians called Saometo, and Puerto del Príncipe, which lies almost due south about twenty-five leagues from both places. In these waters he found long streamers of weed such as

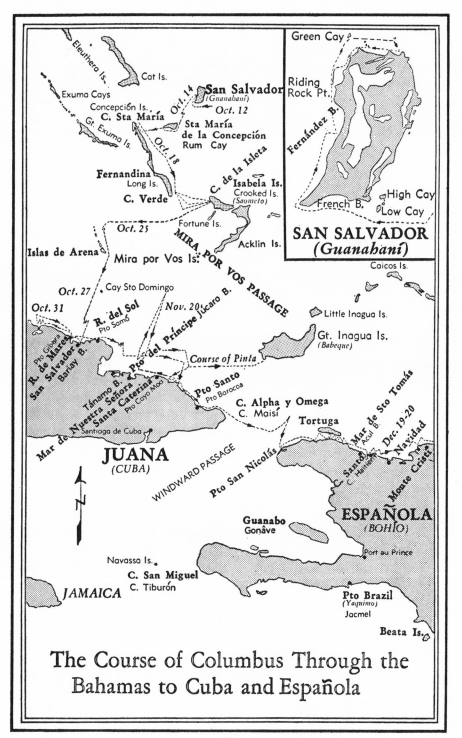

The Course of Columbus Through the Bahamas to Cuba and Española

he had found before in the ocean; he observed that they moved longitudinally with the current and not across it.

Wednesday, November 21st, Martín Alonso Pinzón, having been told by some Indians aboard his ship that there was much gold on the island of Bohío (which was the name they gave to Española), was moved by greed to separate from the Admiral without the excuse of contrary wind or any other cause; for with the wind at his back, he could have followed the Admiral if he chose. Instead, his ship being a smart sailer, he drew farther and farther away, until by nightfall he had completely vanished from sight. The Admiral was thus left with only two ships, and as the wind was unfavorable to go to Española, he returned to Cuba and anchored in a harbor not far from Puerto del Príncipe that he named Santa Caterina,[1] in order to take on wood and water.

In this harbor, by a river where they were getting fresh water, he found some stones with indications of gold. In this region they also found pines so tall they would serve as masts for ships and carracks, or as wood for planking, plentiful enough to make as many ships as desired; evergreen oaks and *madroño* trees and other trees like those of Spain grew there as well. But the Admiral, observing that all the Indians directed him to go to Española, continued on a southeastward course ten or twelve leagues farther down the coast through a region abounding in excellent harbors and numerous large rivers. The Admiral speaks so glowingly of the beauty of this region that I have thought it well to set down his very words concerning the entrance to a river that empties into a harbor that he named Puerto Santo.[2] He writes as follows:

When I went with the boats southward along the mouth of the harbor, I found a river that a galley could easily enter; so hidden was the entrance that it could be seen only from close by. The river's beauty moved me to go upstream, if only a boat's length; I found it had a depth of five to eight fathoms. I proceeded a considerable distance up the river, for I was charmed by the beauty and luxuriant foliage of this river and its pellucid water, through which even the sandy bottom could be seen. I was also taken by the multitude of palm trees of different kinds, the tallest and most beautiful I had yet seen, and by the infinite number of other large and verdant trees. The little birds and the verdure of the fields tempted me to stay there forever. This country, most serene Princes, is of such marvelous beauty that it surpasses all others as the day surpasses the night. That is why I have often said to my men that despite my best efforts to give Your Highnesses a perfect account of it, my tongue could not tell the whole truth nor my pen describe it. Truly, I was so astounded at the sight of so much beauty that I know not how to express myself; for in telling of other regions I wrote all that could be said about their trees and fruits, their plants, harbors, and all their other features; and all affirmed a more beautiful region could not be found. But now I fall silent, only desiring that others may come and show how much better than myself they can describe this most excellent place.

Going on with the boats, the Admiral saw among the trees of this harbor a canoe drawn up on shore under a thatched boathouse; it was made from the bole of a single tree and was as large as a *fusta* [3] with twelve benches. In some huts nearby they found a cake of wax and a man's skull in two baskets hanging from a post. Later they found the same thing in another hut, which made them believe the skull must be that of the ancestor of the family. But they could find no people from whom they could learn anything; for as soon as the Indians saw the Christians, they fled from their homes to the other side of the harbor. Afterwards our men found another canoe, over sixty-three feet long, holding one hundred and fifty persons, and made like the aforementioned one.

CHAPTER 31

How the Admiral Sailed for Española, and What He Saw There

Having sailed one hundred and seven leagues eastward along the coast of Cuba, the Admiral reached its eastern end, which he called Alpha and Omega.[1] Wednesday, December 5th, he departed from there for Española, which lay sixteen leagues to the east; but on account of certain currents that are found there he did not reach it until the next day, when he made a port that he named Puerto San Nicolás because he discovered it on that saint's feast day. This is a very large and good harbor, bordered by many large trees and very deep. However, the land about was rockier [than the land they had seen before B. K.] and the trees smaller, resembling those of Spain; among them were small oaks, myrtles, and *madroños*. Through a plain ran a very peaceful river that emptied into the harbor, which was filled with canoes as large as fifteen-oar *fustas*. As the Admiral could not gain speech with those people, he followed the coast northward till he came to a harbor that he named Puerto de la Concepción,[2] which lies almost due south of a small island that he later named Tortuga and was of the size of the Grand Canary. Perceiving that this island of Bohío was very large, that the land and trees resembled those of Spain, and that the sailors caught in their nets many fish like those of Spain, including soles, skates, salmon, shad, dory, corvinas, sardines, and crabs, he named it Española on Sunday, December 9th.

As all were very curious to learn all they could about this island, three Christians went into the woods while others were fishing on the beach and came on a group of naked Indians, but these fled from them into the thickest part of the forest—something they could easily do, not being hindered by clothing of any kind. The Christians, who needed an interpreter, ran after them and captured a girl wearing only a gold nose plug. They took her to the ships, where the Admiral gave her some trinkets and hawk's bells and sent her ashore unharmed. He ordered three Christians and three Indians brought from other islands to accompany her to her village.

Next day he sent nine armed men ashore. After traveling four leagues they came on a village of more than one thousand huts scattered about in a valley. At sight of the Christians all the inhabitants abandoned their homes and fled into the woods. At this the Indian guide from San Salvador ran after them calling on them to return, saying many good things of the Christians and declaring they came from Heaven; in this way he persuaded the Indians to return, confident and secure. Filled with wonder, they placed their hands on our men's heads as if to honor them, brought them food to eat, and satisfied all their requests. They asked nothing in return, only praying them to stay that night in their village. The Christians did not accept their invitation and returned to the ships with the news that the land was very lovely and abounded in the foods of the Indians, and that the people were lighter-skinned and handsomer than those they had seen on other islands, and friendly and courteous in dealing with them. They also reported that the land of gold was farther east.

Informed of this, the Admiral immediately set sail from that place, though the wind was contrary. Next Sunday, beating about between Española and Tortuga, they met a solitary Indian in a small canoe and marveled that he could keep it afloat in that rough sea. They hoisted him aboard and carried him to Española, sending him ashore with many gifts. He told the other Indians how well he had been treated, and spoke so well of the Christians that soon many of them came to the ship; but they brought nothing of value except some pieces of gold hanging from their ears and noses. Asked whence they got that gold, they told by signs there was much of it farther south.

Next day a large canoe with forty Indians came over from the island of Tortuga to the Admiral's anchorage at a time when the cacique or lord of that harbor of Española was on the beach with his people, trading away a large piece of gold leaf that he had brought. When the cacique's people saw the canoe approaching, they all seated themselves on the ground to show they wished to keep the peace; but most of the Indians in the canoe leaped ashore as if they wanted to fight. The cacique of Española then arose and with threatening words made them turn back; he also splashed water on them and, picking pebbles from the beach, threw them at the canoe.

After those Indians had quietly returned to their canoe, the king took a pebble and placed it in the hand of a servant of the Admiral's that that servant might throw it at the Indians, showing that the Admiral favored the king over them; but as the canoe promptly departed, that servant would not do it. Afterwards, telling of the island to which the Admiral gave the name Tortuga, this cacique declared there was more gold there than in Española. He also said there was more of it on Babeque than anywhere else and that this island was about fourteen days' journey from there.

CHAPTER 32

How the Principal King of That Island Came to the Ships, and of the Great State in Which He Came

Tuesday, December 18th, this cacique, who lived about five leagues from that place, came at the hour of tierce to the village by the sea. Some seamen who were there, sent by the Admiral to see if the Indians were bringing larger samples of gold, went to advise the Admiral of the cacique's coming; they reported he had more than two hundred attendants and was carried in a litter by four men who treated him with great reverence, though he was very young. Having come to the beach, not far from the ships, he rested a while, then came aboard the Admiral's ship with all his people. The Admiral tells of this in his journal:

> Your Highnesses would doubtless think well of the dignity and respect in which they all hold him, though they all go naked. When he came aboard, he found me dining at the table below the sterncastle, and quickly came to seat himself beside me; nor would he let me rise to meet him or get up from the table, but insisted that I should eat. And when he entered below the castle, he signaled with his hand that all his people should remain outside, and they did this with the greatest readiness and respect in the world; and they all seated themselves on the deck, except two men of ripe years whom I took to be his councilors and tutors, who sat at his feet. I thought he might like to eat of our food and ordered that some be brought to him. Of the dishes which were placed before him he took of each only as much as one would take for a taste, and the rest he sent to his people, and they all ate of it; he did the same with the drink, which he only raised to his lips and then gave to the others, all with a wonderful dignity and very few words; and those that he spoke, according to what I could understand, were very weighty and sensible. And those two elders looked at him and spoke for him and with him, with great respect.

After dinner his squire brought a belt like those of Castile in

shape, but of different workmanship, which he gave to me, and
two pieces of worked gold which were very thin, so that I be-

Columbus at Española

lieve they obtain little gold here, though I think they are very
near to where it comes from and that there is much of it. I saw
that a coverlet which I had over my bed pleased him, so I gave
it to him, together with some very good amber beads which I

had about my neck, and some red shoes and a bottle of orange water; with these things he was marvelously content. He and his councilors were much troubled because he understood not me nor I them. Nevertheless, I understood him to say that if I needed anything, the whole island was at my command. I sent for a portfolio of mine, in which I kept as a token a gold excelente [1] on which Your Highnesses are depicted, and I showed it to him and told him again as yesterday that Your Highnesses ruled over the best part of the world and that there were no greater princes; and I showed him the royal banners and the others with the cross. With this he was much impressed and said to his councilors what great lords Your Highnesses must be, since they had sent me such a great distance from Heaven. Many other things were said that I did not understand, except that I clearly perceived he was struck with wonder at everything.

Since it was now late and he wished to go, I sent him ashore in the boat with great honor and caused numerous lombard shots to be fired. On landing, he mounted his litter and departed with more than two hundred men. A son of his was carried on the shoulders of a very important man. He ordered all the Spaniards who were ashore to be supplied with food and shown great courtesy. Afterwards a sailor who met him on the road told me that all the things I had given him were carried in front by a very important man, and that his son did not go with him but followed a little space behind, with as large a retinue as his father. He also said that a brother of the cacique traveled on foot, accompanied by nearly as many men, and was supported under the arms by two principal men. I had given this brother, too, some trifles when he came aboard after his brother.

CHAPTER 33

How the Admiral Lost His Ship on Some Shoals Through the Negligence of His Sailors, and of the Assistance He Received from the King of That Island

I continue with the Admiral's account. He relates that Monday, December 24th, it was very calm, with only light airs that took him from the Mar de Santo Tomás about a league beyond the Punta Santa.[1] At the end of the first watch, about eleven o'clock, he retired to his cabin, for he had gone two days and a night without sleep. Since it was calm, the helmsman turned the tiller over to a grummet, "which," says the Admiral, "I had forbidden throughout the voyage, ordering that wind or no wind, they must never intrust the tiller to boys. But to tell the truth, I felt quite safe from reefs or shoals, for on Sunday, when I sent my boats to the king, they had gone three and a half leagues east of the Punta Santa, and the sailors had surveyed the whole coast and the reefs which extend some three leagues east-southeast from the Punta Santa, and had charted the course we must take, something that had not been done before on the entire voyage."

It pleased Our Lord that at midnight, while I lay in bed, with the ship in a dead calm and the sea as peaceful as the water in a cup, all went to sleep, leaving the tiller in charge of a boy. So it happened that the swells drove the ship very slowly onto one of those reefs, on which the waves broke with such a noise that they could be heard a long league away. Then the boy, feeling the rudder ground and hearing the noise, cried out; hearing him, I immediately arose, for I recognized before anyone else that we had run aground. Very soon the ship's master, whose watch it was, ran up; I told him and the other sailors to take the boat that the ship was towing and cast an anchor astern. He and many others got into the boat, I meanwhile thinking they were going to do what I had told them. But instead they rowed away, fleeing in the boat to the caravel, which was half a league distant. Seeing them flee in the boat, with the water ebbing and the ship in danger, I quickly had the mast cut away to lighten her as much as possible, to see if we could get her off that reef. But the waters ebbing still farther, the ship would not budge, but began to list; her new seams opened up, and she filled up with water. Meanwhile the caravel's boat had come over to help me, and the *Niña's* people, seeing that the men in the boat were escaping to save their own skins, would not let them aboard, and they had to return to the ship.

Seeing no possible way of saving my ship, to save the lives of my crew I left her and went with them to the *Niña*. Since the wind was from the land, and much of the night was already gone, and we knew not our way out of those shoals, I stood by with the caravel until daybreak, when I promptly made for the ship through the reef, having first sent a boat ashore with Diego de Arana of Córdoba, chief constable of the fleet, and Pedro Gutiérrez, butler of Your Highnesses' dais, to let the king know what had happened, informing him that on my way to visit him (as he had invited me to do the previous Saturday) I had lost my ship on a reef a league and a half from his town. Informed of our misfortune, the king shed tears and immediately sent all his people and many large canoes to the ship. So they and we began to unload, and in a short time we had cleared the whole deck, so helpful was the king in this affair. Afterwards, he in person, together with his brothers and relations, kept careful watch both aboard and ashore to see that all was done properly. And from time to time he sent one of his relatives to tell me not to grieve, that he would give me whatever he had. I assure Your Highnesses that nowhere in Castile would better care have been taken of the goods, so that not a shoestring was missing. He caused all our goods to be placed together near the palace, where they remained until the houses that he gave as storehouses had been emptied. He stationed armed men to watch over those goods day and night; and he and all the other natives wept as if our misfortune were their own.

They are such an affectionate and generous people, and so tractable, that I assure Your Highnesses there are no better people or land in all the world. They love their neighbors as themselves, and their speech is the sweetest and gentlest in the world, and they always speak with a smile. They go about naked, men and women, just as their mothers bore them; but believe me,

By His Son Ferdinand

Your Highnesses, they have very good customs, and the king keeps so wonderful a state and displays such dignity that it is a pleasure to watch him. And what excellent memories they have, and how curious they are about everything, asking what such and such a thing is and what is its use.

CHAPTER 34

How the Admiral Decided to Make a Settlement in the Place Where the King Lived, and Named It La Navidad

Monday, December 24th, the principal king of that land returned to the Admiral's caravel and with much show of grief offered to give him liberally of all he had, saying he had already given the Christians three houses in which to store the ship's goods and would have given more were they needed. Meanwhile there came a canoe with Indians from another place, bringing pieces of gold leaf to barter for hawk's bells, which they prized above all else. Sailors also came to report that many Indians from other places were coming to the village with gold objects; these they gave in exchange for lace points and other trifles. They offered to bring more gold if the Christians wanted it. The great cacique, seeing that this pleased the Admiral, told him he would have a great deal of it brought from the Cibao,[1] where most of the gold was found.

Before going ashore he invited the Admiral to dine with him on yams and cassava bread, which is their principal food; and he gave the Admiral some masks with golden eyes and large ears of gold, and other pretty things that they hang about their necks. He complained to the Admiral that the Caribs enslaved his people and carried them away to eat, so he was much comforted when the Admiral showed him our weapons and told him he would use them in his defense. And he was much surprised to see our cannon, which

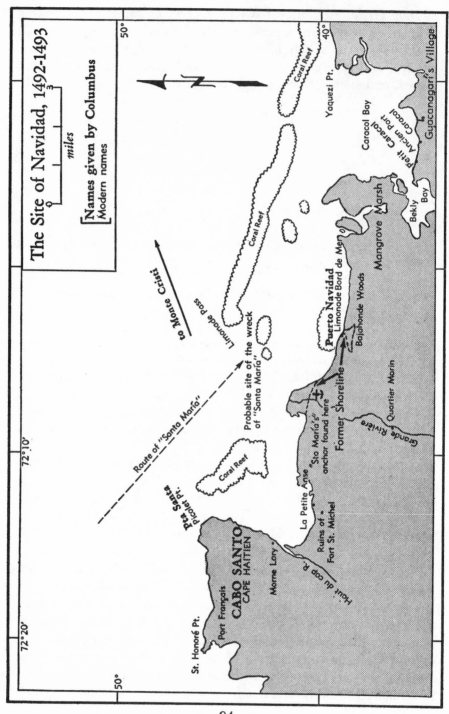

The Site of Navidad, 1492–1493

miles

⌈Names given by Columbus
⌊Modern names

50°

40°

Coral Reef

Yaquezi Pt.

Guacanagarí's Village

Caracol Bay

Petit Caracol
Ancien Port Caracol

Bekly Bay

Mangrove Marsh

to Monte Cristi

Limonade pass

Coral Reef

Puerto Navidad
Limonade Bord de Mer

Bajahonde Woods

Route of "Santa María"

Probable site of the wreck
of "Santa María"

Former Shoreline

Quartier Marin

Grande Rivière

72°10'

Coral Reef

"Sta María's"
anchor found here

La Petite Anse

Pta Santa
Picolet Pt.

CABO SANTO
CAPE HAITIEN

Morne Lory

Ruins of
Fort St. Michel

Haut du cap R.

St. Honoré Pt.

Port Français

72°20'

50°

terrified the Indians so much that they fell down as if dead when they heard the noise.

Having received so many kindnesses and samples of gold from these people, the Admiral quite forgot his grief over the loss of the *Santa María*. He reasoned that God had caused this to pass that he might make a settlement there, so that the Christians he left behind might trade and gain information about that country and its inhabitants by learning their language and trading with that village. Thus, when he returned from Castile with reinforcements, the colonists would be able to guide him in settling and subjugating that land. He inclined toward this decision all the more because many of his men offered to stay behind, declaring they would gladly make their homes in that country. Therefore he resolved to build a fort with the timbers and planking of that ship—of which nothing else remained, all that was useful having been taken out.

Next day, Thursday, December 27th, news came that the caravel *Pinta* was lying in a river at the eastern end of the island. In order to check the truth of this, the cacique Guacanagarí sent a canoe with some Indians and a Christian, but they returned after traveling twenty leagues down the coast without finding any trace of the *Pinta;* therefore no credence was given to an Indian who claimed to have seen it a few days before. The Admiral nevertheless arranged to leave some Christians at that place; for all could see the excellence and wealth of that land. The Indians brought many masks and other objects of gold, telling of many provinces of that island whence came that gold.

When the Admiral was on the point of departure, he spoke to the king about the Caribs, whom those Indians greatly feared. In order that he might be glad to have the Christians for neighbors and also to inspire in the Indians fear of our arms, the Admiral caused a lombard shot to be fired through the hull of the *Santa María;* this gave the cacique a great scare. The Admiral also showed him all our other weapons, explaining the offensive use of some and the defensive use of others; and he told him that as he was leaving those arms for his defense, he need have no fear of the Caribs, for the Christians would kill them all. The Admiral also told him that he was returning to Castile to secure jewels and other gifts for him. The Admiral particularly commended to him Diego de Arana, son of that Rodrigo de Arana mentioned above. To him, to Pedro Gutiérrez, and to Rodrigo de Escobedo, he intrusted the government of the fortress and its garrison of thirty-six men, together with a great store of trading goods and provisions, arms and artillery, the ship's boat, carpenters, calkers, and other men needed for making a settlement, namely, a physician, a tailor, a gunner, and the like.

He then prepared to steer a course directly for Castile without stopping to discover new lands; for he feared that if anything happened to his one remaining ship, the Catholic Sovereigns might never learn of the kingdoms he had gained for them.

CHAPTER 35

How the Admiral Sailed for Castile and Found Pinzón's Caravel

At sunrise on Friday, January 4th, the Admiral left the port that he had named Puerto de la Navidad [1] because it was on Christmas Day that he had landed there, escaping the perils of the sea, and made a beginning of settlement. He shaped a northwest course, with the ship's boat going ahead to get clear of the reefs and shoals that are there. Those reefs and shoals extend from Cabo Santo [2] to the Cabo de la Sierpe, a distance of six leagues, and more than three leagues out to sea. All this coast runs northwest and southeast and is beach and level country for a space of four leagues inland; then begin high mountains and many villages larger than those of other islands.

He then sailed toward a high mountain, which he named Monte Cristi, that lies eighteen leagues east of Cabo Santo. So whoever would go to the town of Navidad, having sighted Monte Cristi (which is round like a tent and resembles a reef), must put out to sea when two leagues distant and sail west till he hits Cabo Santo. Then he will be five leagues from the town of Navidad, and should enter through some channels among the shoals that lie in front. The Admiral thought it well to mention these facts in order to make known the position of the first Christian town founded in the Western World.

After they had sailed with contrary winds farther to the east of Monte Cristi, on Sunday morning, January 6th, a calker sent aloft on the main topsail sighted the *Pinta* running westward before the wind. Coming up to the Admiral, Captain Martín Alonso Pinzón boarded the flagship and began to invent reasons and excuses for having separated from him, saying it had happened unavoidably against his will. The Admiral well knew it was not true, being aware of Pinzón's hostility toward him and the insolence he had displayed at various times on the voyage; but he thought it best to pretend to believe him and dissemble everything lest the whole enterprise come to ruin—and this could have happened very easily, since the majority of the Admiral's crew were Pinzón's townspeople and many were his kinsmen.

Actually Pinzón had separated from the Admiral at the island of Cuba with the intent of going to the island of Babeque because some Indians aboard his caravel told him much gold was to be found there. On arrival there, finding these reports to be untrue, he returned to Española, where other Indians reported the presence of much gold. On this voyage, which had taken him twenty days, he had sailed no more than fifteen leagues west of Navidad as far as a little river that the Admiral had named Río de Gracia. There Martín Alonso tarried sixteen days and found much gold, which he obtained in exchange for objects of trifling worth. Half of this gold he had divided among the crew of his caravel in order to gain their consent to his keeping the rest by virtue of his title of captain. Yet he later sought to convince the Admiral he knew nothing of this gold.

Continuing on his course, the Admiral came to anchor at Monte Cristi. As the wind was contrary for sailing, he went in a boat up a river that lies southwest of the mountain and whose sands abound in gold dust; that is why he named it Río de Oro.[8] This river lies sixteen leagues east of the town of Navidad and is a little smaller than the River Guadalquivir that runs through Córdoba.

Chapter 36

How the First Skirmish Between the Indians and Christians Took Place in Samaná Bay on the Island of Española

Sunday, January 13th, being off Cabo Enamorado [1] in Samaná Bay on the island of Española, the Admiral sent ashore a party which encountered some Indians of ferocious aspect, armed with bows and arrows as if ready for war. Their faces showed anger and surprise, but our men, after striking up a conversation with them, managed to buy two of their bows and some arrows. With great difficulty they prevailed on one to come aboard the caravel to speak with the Admiral. Truly, their speech matched their appearance, which was fiercer than that of any other Indians they had seen. The faces of these Indians were stained with charcoal, for all those people have the custom of painting themselves, some black, some red, and others white; some one way and some another. They wore their hair long and gathered behind the head into nets of parrot's feathers.

One of them, standing before the Admiral as naked as the day his mother bore him, said in a haughty voice that all the people in those parts went about in that manner. The Admiral, thinking he was a Carib,[2] and that the bay separated that people from Española, asked him where the Caribs lived. Pointing with his finger, he indicated that they lived farther to the east, on islands where were found pieces of *guanín* [3] as large as half the caravel's stern. He also related that the island of Matininó [4] was inhabited only by women, with whom the Caribs slept at certain times of the year; if these women bore any sons, they gave them to their fathers to raise. After he had answered all the questions put to him, partly with signs and partly with the help of the Indian interpreters from San Salvador, who knew a little of his speech, the Admiral ordered him fed and given some trifles, such as glass beads and pieces of green and red cloth. Then he sent him ashore to induce the others to bring gold, if they had any.

When the ship's boat landed, the Christians encountered fifty-five Indians among the trees on the beach. These Indians were all naked, wore their hair long as do the women of Castile, and had plumes of parrot's feathers or feathers of other birds tied to the backs of their heads. The Indian who had visited the ship persuaded the others to lay down their bows and arrows and the large cudgels which they use as swords, for they have no iron. The Christians began to buy swords and arrows as the Admiral had instructed them to do, but after the Indians had sold two of their bows they disdainfully refused to sell any more; instead they ran toward the place where they had deposited their weapons, with the design of picking them up and also of getting cords with which to tie our men's hands. But the Christians were prepared for their attack, and though only seven in number, fell upon the Indians with so much spirit that they gave one Indian a slash on the buttocks with a sword and wounded another in the breast with an arrow. Terrified by the valor of our men and the wounds inflicted by our arms, the Indians turned and fled, leaving behind most of their bows and arrows. Many would certainly have been killed had not the pilot of the caravel, who was in charge of the landing party, restrained our men.

The Admiral was not displeased by this incident; for he was convinced these were the Caribs whom the other Indians feared so greatly, or if not Caribs, at least their neighbors. Their appearance, arms, and actions showed them to be a daring and courageous people. The Admiral hoped that when the islanders learned what seven Spaniards had done against fifty-five ferocious Indians, they would feel more respect for the men left behind in the town of Navidad and would not dare annoy them. Later that afternoon the Indians made bonfires on the beach to demonstrate their courage, and a boat was sent to see what they wanted; but nothing our men could do would make the Indians show their faces, so the boat returned.

Their bows are made of yew and are as large as English and French bows; their arrows are stems of cane, very strong and straight, about an arm and a half long. The arrowhead is a small fire-hardened piece of wood about twelve inches long; in this head they insert a fish tooth or bone and coat it with poison. That is why the Admiral named this bay, which the Indians call Samaná, Golfo de las Flechas.[5] Upcountry the Christians saw much fine cotton and chili, which is the Indians' pepper and is very hot; the fruits of this plant are long and partly round. In shallow places there grew much of that weed which our men had seen in long streamers in the ocean; this caused them to surmise that it grew near the shore and when ripe, detached itself and was carried by currents a great distance out to sea.

CHAPTER 37

How the Admiral Departed for Castile and Was Separated from the Pinta by a Great Storm

Wednesday, January 16, 1493, the weather being fair, the Admiral set sail for Castile from the Golfo de las Flechas, now called Samaná Bay. By now both caravels were leaking badly, and it required great toil to keep them afloat. Cape Santelmo,[1] twenty leagues to the northeast, was the last land they saw; here they saw much weed like that they had seen before. After running another twenty leagues they found the sea almost covered with small tunnies; during the next two days, January 19th and 20th, they saw many more; later they saw many marine birds. The weed continued moving with the current, east to west. They had already observed that the currents carry this weed great distances, but not always in the same direction; for sometimes the currents move one way and sometimes another. This they observed every day, until almost half the ocean lay behind them. Proceeding, then, ever with fair winds, they made so much headway that in the opinion of the pilots on February 9th they were south of the Azores. But the Admiral said the Azores were still one hundred and fifty leagues away; and he was right, because they still found much weed, which they had not seen when outward bound until they were two hundred and sixty-three leagues west of Ferro.

As they sailed on, then, with fair weather, the wind began to rise daily, and the sea to run so high that it was all the ships could do to stay alive. The night of Thursday, February 14th, therefore, the ships ran whichever way the wind would take them. As the *Pinta,* commanded by Pinzón, could not take the heavy seas well, she scudded due north before a south wind, while the Admiral kept on a northeast course in order to draw nearer to Spain, which the *Pinta* could not do because of the darkness, although the Admiral made flares all night; thus by daybreak they had lost sight of each other, and each was sure the other had gone down.

In this plight, the Admiral's people gave themselves over to prayers and devotions, making vows and drawing lots to decide who should make a pilgrimage in the name of all to the shrine of Our Lady of Guadalupe.[2] The lot fell upon the Admiral. Then they drew lots for a pilgrimage to Our Lady of Loreto,[3] and it fell upon a sailor of Santa María de Santoña, named Pedro de la Villa. Now they cast lots to select a third pilgrim who should watch all of one night in the church of Santa Clara de Moguer.[4] The lot fell again upon the Admiral. However, the storm grew still more violent, so all the ship's people made a vow to go barefoot and in their shirts to the first shrine of the Virgin they should encounter to say their prayers. Besides these general vows, many persons made their special vows; for the storm now raged with such fury that the Admiral's ship could hardly keep her head for lack of ballast, so much of her provisions having been consumed. To make up for this lack they filled all the empty water casks with sea water, which helped some because it made the ship more stable and thus lessened the danger of capsizing. Of this terrible storm the Admiral wrote as follows:

> I could have endured this storm with less anguish if my life alone had been in danger, not only because I know that I owe my life to the Supreme Creator but also because at other times I have seen death only a hair's breadth away. What caused me infinite grief and anxiety was the thought that after Our Lord had deigned to enlighten me with faith and certainty in this enterprise and had crowned it with victory, in order that my opponents might be abashed and Your Highnesses served by me with honor and increase of your high estate, His Divine Majesty should now seek to hinder this with my death—a fate that I could have borne more easily did it not also threaten the people I had brought with me on the promise of a prosperous outcome. See-

ing themselves so afflicted, these men not only cursed the day they came with me but also lamented that they had let themselves be influenced by my threats and arguments from turning back as they had often resolved to do. Then, my grief was redoubled when I remembered my two sons at school in Córdoba, left friendless in a strange country, before I had done or at least made known to Your Highnesses some service that might dispose you to remember them. And though I comforted myself with the faith that Our Lord would not permit a thing which was so much for the exaltation of His Church, and which I had brought to completion with so much labor and over so much opposition, to be undone and myself destroyed, on the other hand I reflected that He might wish to humiliate me for my demerits, that I might not enjoy so much glory in this world.

Then, with my thoughts in this whirl, I thought upon Your Highnesses, and considered some means whereby, even were I dead and the ship lost, you might get news of the success of my voyage, that the victory I had gained might not be lost. Therefore I wrote on a parchment, as briefly as the state of things required, how I had discovered those lands as I had promised to do; the length of the voyage and the route thither; the goodness of the country and the customs of its inhabitants; and how I had left Your Highnesses' vassals in possession of all I had discovered. This writing, folded and sealed, I addressed to Your Highnesses with a written promise of 1,000 ducats to whoever should deliver it sealed to you; this I did so that if it should fall into the hands of foreigners, they would be restrained by the reward from divulging the information it contained to others. I straightway had a great wooden barrel brought to me, and having wrapped the writing in a waxed cloth and put it in a cake or loaf of wax, I dropped it into the barrel, which I made secure with hoops and cast into the sea; and all thought this was an act of devotion. I still feared the barrel might not reach safety, but as the ships meanwhile were drawing closer to Castile, I placed a similar cask at the head of the stern, so that if the ship sank, it might float on the waves at the mercy of the storm.

Chapter 38

How the Admiral Reached the Azores, and the People of the Island of Santa Maria Seized the Ship's Boat and Its Crew

Running on through this dangerous and terrible storm, at sunrise on Friday, February 15th, one Ruy García, from the port of Santoña, sighted land from the roundtop to the east-northeast. The pilots and the sailors believed it was the Rock of Cintra in Portugal, but the Admiral said it was one of the Azores. Although it was not very distant, the storm prevented them from reaching it that day. Beating about, because the wind blew from the east, they lost sight of that island and caught sight of another about which they ran, struggling with a strong cross wind and foul weather and suffering great privations in their vain efforts to make land. Therefore the Admiral says in his journal:

> In the evening of Saturday, February 16th, I reached one of those islands, but the storm prevented me from learning which one it was. That night I rested a little, for I had not slept since Wednesday; and ever after I was crippled in the legs from always being exposed to cold and water, and from eating little. On Monday morning, after coming to anchor, I learned from the natives that it was Santa Maria, one of the Azores. They all wondered how I had escaped from that very great tempest, which had continued for fifteen days in those parts.

Learning of the Admiral's discovery, these people appeared to rejoice, giving thanks to Our Lord; and three of them came to the ship with refreshments and greetings from the captain of the island,[1] who was away in town. There was nothing in the vicinity of the anchorage but a hermitage which, those people said, was dedicated to the Virgin. Recalling that on Thursday they had taken a vow to march barefoot and in their shirts to the first shrine of the Virgin they should find, the Admiral and all his people decided to fulfill that obligation, especially since the captain and his people had shown such regard and compassion for them, and since the island belonged to a king who was a good friend of the Catholic Sovereigns of Castile. So the Admiral asked those three men to go to town and request the chaplain, who had the keys to the shrine, to come and say a Mass for them. This those men agreed to do, and they entered the ship's boat together with half the crew who would be first to perform their vows; after that portion of the crew had returned aboard the others were to go in their turn.

When the ship's people had landed, barefoot and in their shirts as they had vowed to do, the captain and many of the townsmen, who were waiting in ambush, fell upon them, made them prisoners, and seized their boat, thinking that without it the Admiral could not escape from their hands.

C H A P T E R 39

How the Admiral Rode Out Another Storm and Finally Recovered His Boat and Its Crew

The Admiral now began to think that the men who had gone ashore were much delayed, for they had left at daybreak and it was almost noon; and he began to fear that they had suffered some mishap on land or at sea. Since he could not see the hermitage from where he was anchored, he decided to sail his ship behind a point from which the hermitage could be seen. Drawing nearer, he saw many horsemen who dismounted and entered a boat with the aim of coming out and taking the caravel by armed force. The Admiral ordered his men to arm themselves and be on guard, but not to give the appearance of preparing to resist, in order that the Portuguese might come closer. When they were quite near, the captain stood up and demanded a safe-conduct, which the Admiral granted, thinking to lure him aboard and then hold him as hostage for the return of the boat and men that he had so unjustly seized. But the Portuguese would only come within earshot of the Admiral, who told the captain that he wondered at his unlawful proceeding and asked why the ship's people were not returning in the boat, since they had gone ashore with a safe-conduct in response to offers of help and gifts, and the captain himself had sent messengers to welcome him.

He also asked the captain to consider that his actions not only were unfriendly and contrary to the laws of chivalry but would give serious offense to the King of Portugal, whose subjects received good treatment and every courtesy in the territories of the Catholic Sovereigns, his masters, landing and residing there without any safeguards as safely as if they were in Lisbon. He added that their Highnesses had given him letters of credence to all the princes and lords and nations of the world, which letters he would show him if he came closer. Since those letters obtained respect and good treatment for him and his people in all other parts, they should meet even better reception in Portugal, whose princes were neighbors and kinsmen of the Catholic Sovereigns; the more so as he was their Admiral of the Ocean Sea and viceroy of the Indies that he had lately discovered, in proof of which he was ready to show their letters signed with their royal names and bearing their seals. Then he held up and showed him those letters and told him he might approach without fear, for by reason of the peace and amity between the Catholic Sovereigns and the King of Portugal he had orders to treat with honor and courtesy all the Portuguese ships he should encounter. The Admiral added that even if he persisted in detaining his people, it would not hinder his sailing to Castile, since he had enough men to take the ship to Seville and even to chastise him as his offense merited, should it prove necessary. Besides, his own King might punish him as being responsible for the outbreak of war between him and the Catholic Sovereigns.

The captain and his men replied they knew nothing of the King or Queen of Castile or their letters, nor did they fear them, but would show him what a power was Portugal. This reply made the Admiral wonder if some rupture or discord had arisen between the two countries since his departure, but he answered the captain as tartly as his folly deserved. Finally, as the boat was leaving the captain stood up and told the Admiral to bring the caravel into the harbor, for all that he (the captain) had done was by order of the King, his master. The Admiral asked all his people to bear witness to what the captain said, and called out to the captain and his men, swearing he would not set foot from the caravel until he had depopulated that island and captured two hundred Portuguese to carry home as prisoners. Then he returned to anchor in the harbor where he first lay, because the wind did not permit him to do anything else.

But the next day, the wind rising considerably and the anchorage being poor, he lost his anchors and had no recourse but to make sail for São Miguel. He had resolved that if he could not anchor there because of the terrible storm that continued to rage, he would lie to at sea—a most dangerous thing because of the boisterous sea and because of his crew, of whom there remained only three seamen and some grummets, all the others being landsmen, not counting the Indians who understood nothing of handling sails and riggings. But the Admiral himself supplied the places of the missing men, and so the night passed with great toil and peril till daybreak, when, observing that São Miguel was not in sight and that the weather had improved somewhat, he decided to bear away for Santa Maria to see if he could recover his men, anchors, and boat. He reached the island in the afternoon of Thursday, February 21st.

Soon after his arrival a boat came bearing five seamen and a notary public,[1] who, upon receiving assurance of safety, boarded the caravel; as it was late, they passed the night there. Next day the Portuguese said they came from the captain to learn for certain whence the Admiral came and if he had a commission from the King of Castile. If he would satisfy them on these points, they would treat him with all honor and respect. What caused this change in their bearing was the realization that they could not capture the Admiral or his ship, and that they might be punished for what they had done. The Admiral concealed his resentment and thanked them for their courteous offer, adding that since their request conformed to the customs and usages of the sea he was ready to comply with it. Accordingly, he showed them a general letter of credence from the Catholic Sovereigns, directed to all his subjects and other princes; he also showed the commission and mandate made out to him for that voyage. This satisfied the Portuguese, who went ashore and quickly saw to the return of the boat and the captured sailors. From them the Admiral learned that it was reported on the island that the King of Portugal had notified all his subjects to make the Admiral prisoner by any means they could.

CHAPTER 40

How the Admiral Left the Azores and Was Driven into Lisbon by a Storm

Sunday, February 24th, the Admiral left the island of Santa Maria for Castile in great want of ballast and wood, which bad weather prevented him from taking on, though the wind was fair for his voyage. When they were one hundred leagues from the nearest land, a swallow alighted on the ship; they supposed a storm had driven it out to sea. This was soon confirmed, for next day, February 28th, many other swallows and land birds came to the ship; they also saw a whale.

On March 3d there arose so terrible a tempest that after midnight it split their sails. Finding themselves in such great peril, they made a vow to send a pilgrim, barefoot and in his shirt, to the revered shrine of the Virgin of La Cinta in Huelva. They again cast lots as to who should go, and again the lot fell on the Admiral, as if to show that God found his offerings more acceptable than those of others; many special vows were also made.

So, driving on under bare poles in a terrible sea with high wind and dreadful thunder and lightning, any one of which appeared enough to raise the caravel into the air, they were privileged about midnight by Our Lord to sight land. But this presented no less a danger; and in order to avoid being dashed to pieces or entering some place where they could not save themselves they hoisted a little sail with which they rode out the storm till daybreak, when they saw they were near the Rock of Cintra, within the limits of the kingdom of Portugal.

There the Admiral had to enter, which he did to the great astonishment of the natives and mariners of that country, who came running from all directions to behold the wonder of a ship that had escaped so cruel a storm. For they had received advices of many ships going down in recent days near Flanders and in other parts.

Entering the estuary of Lisbon on Monday, March 4th, he anchored off Restello,[1] and quickly sent a messenger to the Catholic Sovereigns with news of his coming. He also wrote the King of Portugal for permission to anchor off the city, because the place where he lay was unsafe if anyone wished to do him an injury, as some might seek to do on the pretext that the King himself had ordered it in the belief that thereby the victory won by the Crown of Castile might be undone.

C H A P T E R   4 1

How the People of Lisbon Came to Look
upon the Admiral as if He Were a Great
Wonder, and How He Paid a Visit to the
King of Portugal

Tuesday, March 5th, the master of the great ship that the King of Portugal kept in Restello to guard that port[1] came in an armed boat to the Admiral's caravel and requested that he come with him to give an account of himself to the King's ministers, as was the obligation and wont of all the ships that arrived there. The Admiral replied that the admirals of the Kings of Castile, such as himself, were not obliged to obey such a summons, nor might they leave their ships to give such information, on pain of death; and he was determined to do his duty. The master then asked him to send his captain; but the Admiral replied it was all the same thing:

By His Son Ferdinand

He would not even send a grummet; it was useless to ask him to send any member of his crew.

Observing the spirit and good sense of the Admiral's remarks, the master asked him to prove at least that he sailed in the name of the Catholic Sovereigns by showing his credentials. The Admiral found this request reasonable and showed him the letter from the Catholic Sovereigns. This satisfied the master, and he returned to his ship to give an account to his captain, Alvaro Damão, who then came aboard the Admiral's caravel in great state, with many trumpets, fifes, and drums, to congratulate the Admiral and offer his services.

Next day, when the coming of the Admiral of the Indies became known in Lisbon, so many people swarmed aboard to see the Indians and hear the story of the discovery that there was not room for them all; and the surrounding water could not be seen, so full was it of the Portuguese boats and skiffs. Some of the Portuguese praised God for so great a victory; others were angry that the enterprise had slipped through their fingers because of the King's skepticism and indifference. That day, then, passed with much attendance of people.

Next day the King ordered his agents to supply the Admiral with provisions and whatever else he needed for himself and his people, all at the King's expense. He also wrote the Admiral congratulating him on his safe arrival and requesting him to come and visit him, since he was in his kingdom. The Admiral felt some misgiving about this; but in view of the amity between the King and the Catholic Sovereigns and the kindness shown him, and in order to dispel any suspicion that he came from the lands that the Portuguese were conquering, he resolved to go to Valparaíso, where the King was staying, nine leagues from the port of Lisbon; he arrived there Saturday night, March 9th.

By order of the King, all the nobles of his court came out to meet him. And when the Admiral stood in his presence, the King received him with much honor and favor, and bade him be seated and not doff his cap. He heard with a cheerful countenance the details of the Admiral's successful voyage, and offered to do all that might be of service to the Catholic Sovereigns, but he remarked that it seemed to him that by the treaty he had with the Sovereigns the discovered lands belonged to him. The Admiral rejoined that he knew nothing of that treaty but that he had scrupulously observed his orders not to go to the Portuguese possessions of Mina or Guinea. To this the King replied that all was well; he was confident the matter could be amicably and fairly arranged. After they had chatted in this manner for a long time, the King ordered the Prior of Crato, the most important and eminent person there, to provide the Admiral with lodgings and show him every favor and courtesy, which he did.

Having stayed there all Sunday and until after dinner on Monday, the Admiral took leave of the King, who showed him much affection and many courtesies, ordering D. Martin de Noronha to escort him. Many other gentlemen accompanied him to honor him and hear him tell about the great exploits of his voyage.

On the way to Lisbon he passed by a monastery where was staying the Queen of Portugal, who sent word that he must not leave without calling on her. She was much pleased to see him, and showed him such favor and courtesy as might befit a great lord. That night one of the King's gentlemen called on the Admiral to say on the King's behalf that if he wished to go to Castile by land, he would accompany him, obtain lodgings for him on the journey, and provide all he needed as far as the Portuguese border.[2]

CHAPTER 42

How the Admiral Left Lisbon to Go to Castile by Sea

At two in the afternoon on Wednesday, March 13th, the Admiral set sail for Seville; and on Friday, at noon, he put in Saltés and anchored in the harbor of Palos, whence he had departed on August 3d of the preceding year, seven months and eleven days before. All the people received him in procession, giving thanks to Our Lord for this notable gift and victory, which promised so great an increase for the Christian religion and the estate of the Catholic Sovereigns. And all the citizens took pride in the fact that the

By His Son Ferdinand

Admiral had sailed from that place and that the greater and better part of the people who went with him came from there, even though some of them, instigated by Pinzón, had been guilty of disloyalty and disobedience.

It happened that when the Admiral reached Palos, Pinzón had already arrived in Galicia and proposed to go by himself to Barcelona to give an account of the voyage to the Catholic Sovereigns. But they sent him word that he must not come save in the company of the Admiral, with whom he had sailed on that voyage of discovery. This snub caused Pinzón such chagrin and annoyance that he went home to Palos a sick man, and a few days after his arrival died of grief.

Before Pinzón reached Palos, the Admiral had left overland for Seville, intending to go thence to Barcelona, where the Catholic Sovereigns were staying. On the road he was detained some little while by admiring crowds which gathered wherever he passed; for the people came from all the neighboring places to see him and the Indians and the strange things that he brought.

Continuing on his way, he reached Barcelona in mid-April, having previously announced to their Highnesses the prosperous outcome of his voyage. This news caused them great joy and happiness; and they ordered that a solemn reception be held for him, as befitted one who had rendered them so great a service. All the Court and the city came out to meet him; and the Catholic Sovereigns received him in public, seated with all majesty and grandeur on rich thrones under a canopy of cloth of gold. When he came forward to kiss their hands, they rose from their thrones as if he were a great lord, and would not let him kiss their hands but made him sit down beside them. After he had given them a brief account of the voyage and its success they permitted him to retire to his lodgings, to which he went accompanied by the whole Court. So much did their Highnesses favor and honor him that when the King rode about Barcelona the Admiral rode on one side of him and the Infante Fortuna [1] on the other. Never before had anyone been permitted to ride with the King, save his very close kinsman, the Infante.

CHAPTER 43

How It Was Agreed That the Admiral Should Return with a Great Fleet to Settle the Island of Española, and How the Pope Gave His Approval of the Conquest

At Barcelona instructions were carefully drawn up and issued to the Admiral to return to Española to relieve the men who had remained there, to augment the number of settlers, and to complete the conquest of that island, as well as of all others that had been discovered or should be discovered. Soon afterwards, acting on the advice of the Admiral, the Catholic Sovereigns decided to strengthen their title to those lands by securing the Supreme Pontiff's approval and grant of their conquest of the Indies. This donation the ruling Pope, Alexander VI, made on most liberal terms, granting not only all the lands that had already been discovered but all that should be discovered in the future all the way to the East, provided no other Christian prince had actual possession of such land, and forbidding all others to enter within the said limits. The next year the Pontiff confirmed this grant in ample and emphatic terms.

As the Catholic Sovereigns knew that the Admiral had been the prime cause of the favors and grants made to them by the Pope, and that the Admiral's voyage and discovery had given them title and possession of all those lands, they resolved to reward him well for all he had done. Accordingly, on May 28th, in Barcelona, they granted him a new privilege, or rather an explanation and declaration of the first privilege he had received, confirming all they had granted him once before. And in clear and explicit terms they defined the limits and bounds of his admiralship, viceroyalty, and government as extending over all the territory that the Pope had granted them. This privilege and the subsequent declaration were as follows.

Chapter 44

The Privileges Granted by the Catholic Sovereigns to the Admiral[1]

Don Ferdinand and Doña Isabella, by the grace of God King and Queen of Castile, León, Aragón, Sicily, Granada, Toledo, Valencia, Galicia, Majorca, Minorca, Seville, Sardinia, Córdoba, Corsica, Murcia, Jaén, Algarve, Algeciras, Gibraltar, and the Canary Islands; Count and Countess of Barcelona; Lords of Biscay and Molina; Dukes of Athens and Neopatria; Counts of Roussillon and Cerdaña; Marquises of Oristano and Goceano.

Forasmuch as you, Christopher Columbus, are going by our command, with some of our ships and with our subjects, to discover and acquire certain islands and mainland in the Ocean Sea, and it is hoped that by the help of God, some of the said islands and mainland in the said Ocean Sea will be acquired by your pains and industry, therefore it is a just and reasonable thing that since you incur the said danger in our service you should be rewarded for it; And as we desire to honor and favor you on account of what is aforesaid, it is our will and grace that you the said Christopher Columbus, after you have discovered and acquired the said islands and mainland in the said Ocean Sea, or any of the said islands whatsoever, shall be our Admiral of the said islands and mainland which you may thus discover and acquire, and shall be empowered from that time forward to call and entitle yourself Don Christopher Columbus; and that your sons and successors in the said office and charge may likewise entitle and call themselves Don and admiral and viceroy and governor thereof; and that you may have power to use and exercise the said office of admiral, together with the said office of viceroy and governor of the said islands and mainland which you may thus discover and acquire, by yourself or by your lieutenants, and to hear and determine all the suits and causes, civil and criminal, appertaining to the said office of admiral, viceroy, and governor according as you shall find by law, and as the admirals of our kingdom are accustomed to use and exercise it; and that you may have power to punish and chastise delinquents, and exercise the said offices of admiral, viceroy, and governor, you and your said lieutenants, in all that concerns and appertains to the said offices and to each of them; and that you shall have and levy the fees and salaries annexed, belonging and appertaining to the said offices and to each of them, according as our High Admiral in the admiralty of our kingdoms levies and is accustomed to levy them.

And by this our patent, or by the transcript thereof signed by a public scrivener, we command Prince Don Juan, our very dear and well beloved son, and the infantes, dukes, prelates, marquises, counts, masters of orders, priors, commanders, and members of our council, and auditors of our tribunal, alcaldes, and other justices whomsoever of our household, court and chancery, and subcommanders, governors of castles and fortified and unfortified houses, and all councillors and assistants, governors, alcaldes, bailiffs, judges, veinticuatros,[2] jurats, esquires, officers, and liege men of all the cities, towns, and places of our kingdoms and dominions, and of those which you may conquer and acquire, and the captains, masters, mates, officers, mariners, and seamen, our natural subjects who now are or hereafter shall be, and each and any of them, that upon the said islands and mainland in the said ocean being discovered and acquired by you, and the oath or formality requisite in such case having been made and done by you or him who may have your procuration, they shall have and hold you from thenceforth for the whole of your life, and your son and successor after you, and successor after successor for ever and ever, as our Admiral of the said Ocean Sea, and as viceroy and governor of the said islands and mainland, which you the said Don Christopher Columbus may discover and acquire; and they shall treat with you, and with your said lieutenants whom you may place in the said offices of admiral, viceroy, and governor, about everything appertaining thereto, and shall pay and cause to be paid to you the salary, dues, and other things annexed and appertaining to the said offices, and shall observe and cause to be observed toward you all the honors, graces, favors, liberties, pre-eminences, prerogatives, exemptions, immunities, and all other things, and each of them, which in virtue of the said offices of admiral, viceroy, and governor you shall be entitled to have and enjoy, all of which privileges ought to be observed toward you fully and completely, so that nothing may be diminished therefrom; and that neither therein nor in any part thereof shall they place or consent to place hindrance or obstacle against you; for we by this our patent from now henceforth grant to you the said offices of admiral, viceroy, and governor with the right of inheritance for ever and ever, and we give you actual and prospective possession thereof, and of each of them, and power and authority to use and exercise it, and to collect the dues and salaries annexed and appertaining to them and to each of them, according to what is aforesaid.

Concerning all that is aforesaid, if it should be necessary and you should require it of them, we command our chancellor and notaries and the other officers who are at the board of our seals to give, deliver, pass,

By His Son Ferdinand

and seal for you our patent of privilege with the circle of signatures, in the strongest, firmest, and most sufficient manner that you may request and may find needful, and neither one nor the other of you or them shall do contrary thereto in any manner, under penalty of our displeasure and of 10,000 maravedís to our tribunal, upon every one who shall do the contrary. And further we command the man who shall show them this our patent, to cite them to appear before us in our court, wheresoever we may be, within fifteen days from the day of citation, under the said penalty, under which we command every public scrivener who may be summoned for this purpose, to give to the person who shall show it to him a certificate thereof signed with his sign, whereby we may know in what manner our command is executed.

Given in our city of Granada, on the thirtieth day of the month of April, in the year of the nativity of our Lord Jesus Christ one thousand four hundred and ninety-two.

I the King   I the Queen

I, Juan de Coloma, Secretary of the King and of the Queen, our Lords, caused this to be written by their command.

Granted in form, Rodericus, Doctor.

Registered, Sebastián d'Olano. Francisco de Madrid, Chancellor.

And now, since it has pleased our Lord that you should find many of the said islands, and we hope that with His help you will find and discover other islands and mainland in the said Ocean Sea in the said region of the Indies, and you have entreated and prayed us as a favor to confirm to you our said patent, which is above incorporated, and the favor therein contained, in order that you and your sons, descendants, and successors, one after the other, when you shall have ended your days, may be able to hold and may hold the said offices of Admiral, viceroy, and governor of the said Ocean Sea and islands and mainland, which you have thus discovered and found and shall from henceforth discover and find, with all those powers, pre-eminences, and prerogatives which have been and now are enjoyed by our former and present admirals, viceroys, and governors of our said kingdoms of Castile and León, and that you may be paid all the dues and salaries annexed and appertaining to the said offices as used and observed toward the said admirals, viceroys, and governors, or that we should command provision to be made for you in that behalf according to our good pleasure. And we, considering the risk and danger to which you have exposed yourself for our service in going out to search and discover the said islands, and that to which you will now subject yourself in going to seek and discover the other islands and mainland, whereby we have been and hope to be greatly served by you, and in order to confirm a benefit and favor upon you, confirm by these presents to you and to your said sons, descendants, and successors, one after the other, now and for evermore, the said offices of Admiral of the said Ocean Sea, which you have found and discovered, and of viceroy and governor of the said islands and mainland, which you have found and discovered, and of the other islands and mainland which by you or by your industry shall be discovered from this time forth in the said region of the Indies.

And it is our will and pleasure that you, and, after your days are ended, your sons, descendants, and successors, one after the other, shall have and hold the said office of our Admiral of the said Ocean Sea, which is ours, and which commences by a limit or line, which we have caused to be marked, and which passes from the Azores to the Cape Verde islands from north to south, from pole to pole, in such manner that all which is beyond the said line to the westward is ours, and belongs to us; and therefore of all this we make and create you our admiral, and your sons and successors, one after the other, for ever and ever; and likewise we make you, and after your days are ended, your sons, descendants, and successors, one after the other, our viceroy and governor of the said islands and mainland, discovered and to be discovered in the said Ocean Sea in the region of the Indies, as aforesaid; and we give you present and prospective possession of all the said offices of admiral, viceroy, and governor for ever and ever, and power and faculty that you may be able to exercise and may exercise in the said seas the said office of our admiral in all things, and in the form and manner and with the prerogatives, pre-eminences, dues, and salaries, just as our Admirals of the seas of Castile and León exercised and exercise, enjoyed and enjoy it.

And in order that in the country of the said islands and mainland which have been and from henceforth shall be discovered in the said Ocean Sea, in the said region of the Indies, the settlers of the whole of it may be better governed, we give you such power and authority that you may be able as our viceroy and governor, to exercise by yourself and by your lieutenants, alcaldes, bailiffs, and other officials, whom you may thereto appoint, the civil and criminal jurisdiction high and low, /in/ mero / et/ mixto imperio; and that you shall be able to remove or withdraw the said officers and put others in their place, whenever you may choose and may see that it is expedient for our service; and these officers shall be able to hear, dispatch and determine all the suits and causes, civil and criminal, which may arise and be brought forward in the said islands and mainland, and to receive and collect the fees and salaries customary in our kingdoms of Castile and León, annexed and appertaining to the said offices. And you, our said viceroy and governor, shall have power to hear and take cognizance of all the said causes and each of them, whenever you please, by first instance, by way of appeal, or by simple plaint, and to inquire, determine, and dispatch them as our viceroy and governor; and you shall have power to make and shall make, you and your said officers, such inquisitions as of right are incident to the cases, and all other things appertaining to the said offices of viceroy and governor, and which you and your lieutenants and officers whom you may appoint for that purpose shall perceive to be expedient for our service and for the execution of our justice: all which you and they shall have power to do and execute, and to carry into due and effectual execution, just as the said officers would do and would be able to do if they had been appointed by ourselves.

But it is our will and pleasure that the patents and appointments which you may give, be drawn up, expedited, and delivered in our name, saying, Don Ferdinand and Doña Isabella, by the grace of God King and Queen of Castile, León, etc., and be sealed with our seal, which we order to be given to you for the said islands and mainland; and we command all residents, sojourners, and other persons who are or shall be in the said islands and mainland, to obey you as our Admiral of the said Ocean; and they shall all execute your patents and orders, and shall unite with you and with your officers to execute our justice, and shall give and cause to be given to you all the support and help which you may demand and need from them, under the penalties which you shall impose upon them and which we by these presents impose upon them and consider as imposed, and we give you authority to execute them on their persons and property. And likewise it is our will and pleasure that if you should consider it expedient for our service and the execution of our justice that any persons whosoever who are and shall be in the said Indies and mainland should depart from them and should not enter nor be in them, and should come and present themselves before us, you may command it in our name, and make them depart therefrom; and we command such persons by these presents to do so at once and to execute and carry it into effect, without having recourse to or consulting us therein, or expecting to receive any other patent or command from us, notwithstanding any appeal or petition whatsoever which they may make or interpose against such your order. And for all that is aforesaid, and for the other things due and appertaining to the said offices of our admiral, viceroy, and governor, we give you full and complete power, with all its incidents, dependencies, emergencies, annexions, and connections.

Concerning all that is aforesaid, if you shall desire it, we command our chancellor and notaries and the other officials employed at the board of our seals to give and deliver to you and to expedite and seal our patent of privilege with the circle of signatures, as valid, firm and sufficient as you may desire and need, and neither one nor the other of you or them shall act contrary thereto in any manner under penalty of our displeasure and of 10,000 maravedís to our tribunal upon every one who shall do the contrary; and further we command the man who may show you this our patent to cite you to appear before us in our court wheresoever we may be, within fifteen days from the day of citation, under the said penalty, under which we command every public scrivener who may be summoned for this purpose to give thereof to the person who shall exhibit it a certificate signed with his sign, whereby we may know how our command is fulfilled.

Given in the city of Barcelona, on the twenty-eighth day of the month of May in the year of the nativity of our Lord Jesus Christ one thousand four hundred and ninety-three.

I the King   I the Queen

I, Fernán Alvarez of Toledo, secretary of the King and of the Queen, our Lords, caused it to be written by their demand.

Pero Gutiérrez, Chancellor.

Fees of the Seal and Register, nihil.

Granted, Rodericus, Doctor.

Registered, Alonso Pérez.

CHAPTER 45

How the Admiral Departed from Barcelona for Seville, and from Seville for Española

In June, 1493, after he had been supplied with all that he needed to settle those lands, the Admiral sailed from Barcelona for Seville. On arrival there he began diligently to outfit the fleet that the Catholic Sovereigns had ordered him to prepare, and in a short time he had made ready seventeen ships, large and small, well stocked with provisions and carrying all the things and persons needed to settle those lands, including artisans of all kinds, laborers, and peasants to work the land. There came too caballeros, hidalgos, and other men of worth, drawn by the fame of gold and the other wonders of that land. So many offered themselves that it was necessary to restrict the number of those who might go thither, at least until it was known how matters stood in that country and some kind of order had been established there. Even so, the number of people who sailed in the fleet came to fifteen hundred, between gentles and commoners. Some of these people brought horses and beasts of burden and other animals that were very useful in the settlement of Española.

After he had completed all preparations, on Wednesday, September 25, 1493, while my brother and I looked on, the Admiral weighed anchor in the harbor of Cádiz, where the fleet had been assembled, and stood southwest for the Canary Islands, where he intended to take on fresh supplies. They sailed with fair weather, and on September 28th, being one hundred leagues from Spain, many small land birds, turtledoves, and other kinds of small birds came to the Admiral's ship; they appeared to be flying to winter in Africa, and to come from the Azores. Holding on his course, on Wednesday, October 2d, he reached the Grand Canary, where he anchored. At midnight he sailed again for Gomera, which he reached on Saturday, October 5th; there he employed great diligence in taking on all the things that the fleet needed.

CHAPTER 46

How the Admiral, Leaving Gomera, Crossed the Ocean and Discovered the Caribbee Islands

Monday, October 7th, the Admiral set his course for the Indies, having first given to each captain sealed instructions which he must not open unless separated from the fleet by stress of weather. The reason for this secrecy was that in the instructions he showed how to reach the town of Navidad in Española, and he did not want anyone to know that route save in case of great need.

Sailing on with a fair wind, on Thursday, October 24th, having run more than four hundred leagues west of Gomera, he still had not met with the weed that on the first voyage he found after sailing only two hundred and fifty leagues; on that day and the next two days a swallow visited the fleet, to the surprise of all. On Saturday night amid heavy rain and frightful thunder, St. Elmo's fire was seen, with seven lighted candles on top of the mainsail; the sailors call these lights the body of St. Elmo and sing many litanies and say many prayers to the saint, being convinced that storms during which these lights appear hold no danger for anyone. I do not know whether this be true, merely reporting what they say; for according to Pliny, when Roman sailors saw these lights during storms at sea, they said they were Castor and Pollux; Seneca also mentions this at the beginning of the first book of his *Natural Questions*.

I return to my history. On Saturday night, November 2d, the Admiral observed a considerable change in the sky and wind, with dark threatening clouds ahead, which convinced him that land was near. Accordingly he had sails lowered and ordered a careful watch kept—and with good reason, for at daybreak they sighted land to the west. It proved to be a high mountainous island which the Admiral named Dominica because it was discovered on Sunday morning. Soon after, he saw another island to the northeast of Dominica, and then another, and still another farther north.[1] At this all the men gathered aft to sing the Salve and other prayers and hymns devoutly, thanking God for His mercy in letting them reach that land in twenty days' sail from Gomera, a distance which they estimated to be from seven hundred and fifty to eight hundred leagues.

Not finding a suitable anchorage on the east side of this island of Dominica, they sailed over to another island which the Admiral named Maríagalante,[2] after his flagship. There he went ashore and with suitable solemnities renewed the possession that in the name of the Catholic Sovereigns he had taken of all the islands and mainland of the Indies on his first voyage.

CHAPTER 47

How the Admiral Discovered the Island of Guadalupe, and What He Saw There

Monday, November 4th, the Admiral left the island of Maríagalante and sailed northward toward another large island which he named Santa María de Guadalupe, out of devotion and also to comply with the promise he had made to the monks of that house to name some island after their monastery. At a distance of three leagues they saw a very high rock which rose to a peak from which issued a stream or waterfall that appeared to be as thick as a large barrel, and which fell with such a din and force that it could be heard aboard the ships. Some, however, claimed it was a vein of white rock, so white and frothy was the water in its steep fall.

After coming to anchor, the boats went ashore to visit a town that could be seen from the beach; but the people had fled into the hills, and our men found only some children, in whose hands they put hawk's bells in order to reassure the parents when they returned. In the houses they found many geese resembling our own, and many parrots with red, green, blue, and white feathers; these parrots were as large as our roosters. They also saw calabashes and some fruit that looked like green pine cones but were much larger; these were filled with solid pulp, like a melon, but were much sweeter in taste and smell. They grow on plants that resemble lilies or aloe trees and are wild, but it was later learned that the fruit of cultivated plants are better. They also saw other plants and fruits that differed from ours, hammocks of cotton, bows, arrows, and the like; but our men did not take anything in order that the Indians might have more trust in the Christians.

What surprised them most was the discovery of an iron pan,

"The Cannibal Islands"

though I personally believe that some ignorant person found some shiny stone or flint that looked like iron; for up to now no one has found any articles of iron among them, nor did I ever hear the Admiral mention it. And since it was his daily custom to write down all that happened or was told to him, he would certainly have noted down anything that the shore party might have told him of that kind. Even if the pan was of iron, this was no great marvel; for the Indians of that island of Guadalupe being Caribs who went raiding and robbing as far as Española, they may have stolen that pan from the Spaniards or Indians on that island; or they may have taken it from the hull of the ship that the Admiral lost in order to make use of the iron, or from the wreck of some ship carried by winds and currents from Europe to those regions. Be that as it may, the Christians did not take away the pan or anything else that day, and so returned to the ships.

By His Son Ferdinand

Next day, Tuesday, November 5th, the Admiral sent two boats ashore to capture some Indian who could give him an account of that country and inform him how far away was Española, and in what direction. Each of the boats returned with a young Indian. They said they were not natives of that island but of another named Boriquén, now called San Juan,[1] and that the inhabitants of Guadalupe were Caribs, who had captured them and carried them away from their island.

Soon after, when the boats returned ashore to take off some Christians who had remained there, they found with them six women who had fled from the Caribs and who came of their own will aboard the ships. However, the Admiral, not wishing to anger the people of that island, would not let them stay, but gave them some glass beads and hawk's bells and made them go ashore. This he did with a design; for no sooner had they set foot ashore than the Caribs, in full sight of the Christians, took from those women all that the Admiral had given. For this reason, or because of their fear and hatred of the Caribs, when the boats returned for wood and water, these women begged the sailors to take them aboard, indicating by signs that the people of that island ate men and were holding them captives and that they did not wish to stay with them. Moved by their pleas, the sailors again brought them aboard together with two children and a young man who had escaped from the Caribs. For those people felt themselves more secure in the hands of men whom they had never seen before and who differed so greatly from themselves than among those wicked, cruel men who had eaten their children and husbands. It is said the Caribs do not eat or kill women, but keep them as slaves.[2]

One of the women told them that to the south were many islands, some of which were inhabited. This woman and the others called those islands Yaramaqui, Cairoaco, Huino, Buriari, Arubeira, and Sixibey.[3] The mainland, which they said was very large, both they and the people of Española called Zuania. They said that in former times canoes had come from that land to trade, bringing much gold; they said that an island not far from there was two thirds gold. They also said that the king of the land from which they had fled had gone with ten large canoes and three hundred men to raid the neighboring islands and steal their people in order to eat them. From the same women they learned where the island of Española lay. The Admiral had its position charted, but

· 113 ·

for greater security he wished to know what the natives said about it.

He wanted to sail for Española without delay but learned that a captain named Márquez, with eight men, had gone ashore before daybreak and had not returned aboard. A search party was sent ashore; however, the dense forest prevented them from finding any trace of Márquez. Unwilling to leave these men for lost, and equally unwilling to leave a ship to wait for them because she might not find her way to Española, the Admiral decided to stay one more day. As that country is thickly wooded, he ordered the search parties to carry trumpets and harquebuses, that the lost men might be guided by the noise. Having wandered about all day as if they themselves were lost, they returned aboard without having found the missing men or obtained any news of them.

Since it was now Thursday morning and nothing had been heard since Tuesday of those men, who had left without permission, the Admiral decided to continue his voyage or at least to give the appearance of intending to do so, as a warning to others; but at the entreaty of friends and relatives of the missing men he agreed to stay longer. Meantime he had the ships take on wood and water and ordered the men to wash their clothes. He also sent Captain Hojeda [4] ashore with forty men to search for the strays and to learn the secrets of the country. They found maize, aloe, sandalwood, ginger, incense, trees that resembled cinnamon in taste and smell, much cotton, and many falcons, purple herons, crows, pigeons, turtledoves, partridges, geese, and nightingales. They reported that in the space of six leagues they had crossed twenty-six rivers, in many of which the water came to the waist, but I am inclined to believe that owing to the roughness of the country they crossed the same stream many times.

While they were marveling at these things and other groups were going about the island looking for the strays, the latter turned up aboard ship on Friday, November 8th, saying they had lost their way in the dense forest. The Admiral punished them for their rashness, ordering the captain put in chains and placing the others on short rations.

Later he went ashore and entered some houses, where he saw all the things mentioned above, especially much cotton, spun and unspun, looms, and skulls hung from the ceiling, and baskets full

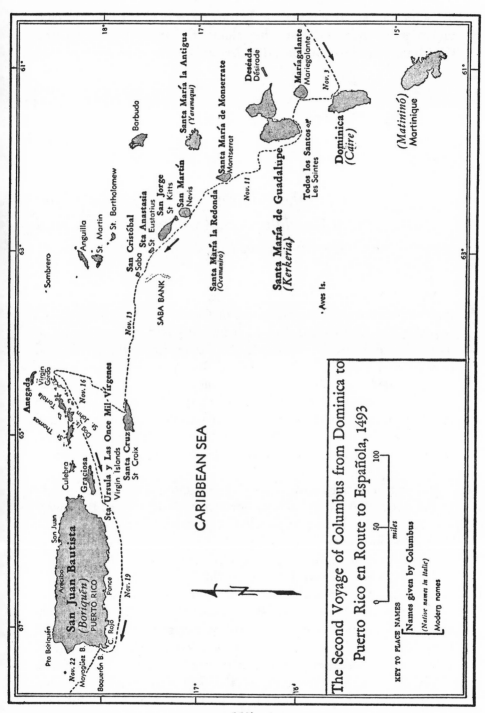

The Second Voyage of Columbus from Dominica to Puerto Rico en Route to Española, 1493

KEY TO PLACE NAMES

Names given by Columbus
(*Native names in italic*)

Modern names

CARIBBEAN SEA

of men's bones. They say these houses were better made and contained more food and the other things the Indians use than the Christians had seen in the other islands on the first voyage.

CHAPTER 48

How the Admiral Sailed from the Island of Guadalupe, and of Some Islands That He Found on the Way

Sunday, November 10th, the Admiral weighed anchor and took the fleet northwest along the coast of Guadalupe for Española. At the island of Monserrate, to which he gave that name because of its height, he learned from the Indians aboard that the Caribs had depopulated that island by eating all its inhabitants. From there he proceeded to Santa María la Redonda, to which he gave that name because it is so round and smooth that it seemed impossible to climb its sides without a ladder; the Indians called this island Ocamaniro. Next he came to Santa María de la Antigua, which the Indians called Yaramaqui; this island has more than eighteen leagues of coast.

Holding on a northwest course, they sighted many other islands to the north that extended in a northwesterly direction; they were all very high and densely wooded. The Admiral anchored at one of these islands and named it San Martín; [1] here they found pieces of coral sticking to the anchor hooks, which made them hopeful of finding other profitable things in this region. Although the Admiral was very eager to learn all he could, he was so anxious to relieve the men he had left on Española that he decided to continue on his course. But on Thursday, November 14th, the wind turned so violent that he had to anchor off an island and send a boat ashore to take some Indian who could tell him where he was. While the boat was returning to the fleet with four women and three children they had seized, they met a canoe with four men and a woman. Seeing that escape was impossible, the Indians picked up their bows and wounded two Christians with arrows shot with such force that one discharged by the woman passed right through a shield; but the boat rammed the canoe with such impetus that it upset and all the Indians were captured as they swam in the sea. One of them continued to shoot arrows while swimming, as if he were ashore. These men had had their virile members cut off, for the Caribs capture them on the other islands and castrate them, as we do to fatten capons, to improve their taste.

After leaving that island the Admiral held on a west-northwest course and found more than fifty islands to the north; the largest he named Santa Ursula and the others Las Once Mil Vírgenes.[2] Next he arrived at an island which he named San Juan Bautista and the Indians called Boriquén. The fleet anchored in a harbor on the west side of the island. There they caught many varieties of fish, such as sea horses, soles, sardines, and shad; they also saw falcons and wild grapevines. On the east side of the island some Christians found well-built Indian houses, placed around a plaza, with a wide road leading to the sea and bordered by towers of cane on both sides; their turrets were roofed with verdure like the garden arbors of Valencia. Near the sea was a high, well-made watch tower that could hold ten or twelve persons.

CHAPTER 49

How the Admiral Arrived at Española and Learned of the Death of the Spaniards

Friday, November 22d, the Admiral reached the northern shore of Española. At Samaná Bay he sent ashore one of the Indians that he had taken to Castile. He was a native of the province of Española who had been converted to our holy faith and had offered to persuade all the Indians to serve the Christians and be at peace with them. The Admiral continued on his course toward the town of Navidad; at Cape Angel some Indians came aboard to trade with the Christians. After they had come to anchor in the harbor of Monte Cristi, a shore party discovered two dead men on the banks of a river. One seemed young; the other, who seemed older, had a rope of esparto grass tied about his neck, his arms extended, and his hands tied to a piece of wood in the form of a cross. The party could not be certain if they were Christians or Indians, but regarded it as an evil omen.

Next day, November 26th, the Admiral again sent men ashore at various places. The Indians came to speak with the Christians in a friendly and fearless manner; touching our men's shirts and doublets, they would say "shirt, doublet," as if to show they knew the names for those things. This allayed the suspicion that the discovery of the dead men had aroused in the Admiral, for he reasoned that the Indians would not be coming aboard so fearlessly if they had harmed the Christians he left there. Next day, past midnight, when they were off the mouth of Navidad harbor, a canoe approached from the shore and the paddlers asked for the Admiral. They were told to come aboard, that he was there; but they would not come until they had seen and recognized him, so the Admiral must come to the ship's side to speak with them. Then two Indians came aboard, each with a mask over his face, and presented those masks to the Admiral in the name of the cacique Guacanagarí, who sent friendly greetings. The Admiral asked about the Christians he had left there and was told that some had died of sickness, some had separated from the rest, and still others had departed for other lands; all had four or five wives apiece. From their words the Admiral gathered that all or most of the Christians must be dead, but since there was nothing he could do for the present, he sent the Indians ashore that night with presents of metal basins and other things for Guacanagarí and his family.

Chapter 50

How the Admiral Found the Town of Navidad Abandoned and Burned, and of His Meeting with King Guacanagarí

Thursday, November 28th, at the hour of vespers, the Admiral moved his fleet in front of the town of Navidad and found it burned to the ground. That day they saw nobody in the vicinity of the town. Next morning the Admiral went ashore and felt much grief at the sight of the ruins of the houses and the fort. Nothing remained of the houses except some smashed chests and such other wreckage as one sees in a land that has been devastated and put to the sack.

As there was no one in the vicinity whom the Admiral could question, he went with some boats up a river that is nearby. He left orders to clean out the well of the fort during his absence; for at the time of his departure for Castile, fearing some untoward event, he had directed all the gold that was found to be thrown into the well. But the well was empty. Going upstream with the boats, the Admiral did not see a single Indian, because all had fled from their huts into the woods. All he found was some clothing that had belonged to the Christians. Returning to Navidad, the Admiral found the bodies of eight Christians; in the fields near the town were three more who were recognized to be Christians by their clothing; these men seemed to have been dead for about a month.

While the Christians were looking around for papers or other traces of the dead men, a brother of the cacique Guacanagarí, accompanied by some other Indians, came to speak to the Admiral. They could say some words in Spanish and knew the names of all the Christians who had been left there. They said that soon after the Admiral's departure those men began to quarrel among themselves, each taking as many women and as much gold as he could. As a result Pedro Gutiérrez and Escobedo slew one Jácome; then, ganging up with nine others, they left with their women for the country of a cacique named Caonabó, who was lord of the mines. Caonabó killed them, and some days later marched with a strong force against Navidad, which was held only by Diego de Arana and ten other men who were willing to remain and guard the fortress, all the others having dispersed to various places on the island. Arriving at the town by night, Caonabó set fire to the houses in which the Christians lived with their women, forcing them to flee in fright to the sea, where eight of them drowned; three others, whom these Indians could not identify, were killed ashore. They also said that Guacanagarí fought against Caonabó in defense of the Christians, but was wounded and had to flee.

This story checked with that told by some Christians whom the Admiral sent ashore to gather information and who visited the principal village. They found Guacanagarí suffering from a wound which he said had kept him from calling on the Admiral and reporting to him what had happened to the Christians. He related that as soon as the Admiral left for Castile they began to quarrel among themselves, each seeking to get gold by barter for himself, and as many women as he could; that they would not be satisfied with what he, Guacanagarí, gave them but instead split up into many gangs, some going in one direction and some in another; and that a band of Biscayans went off to a place where they were all killed. He said they should tell this to the Admiral as the true story of what had happened, and that he should come to visit him, for the cacique was too ill to leave his house.

Next day the Admiral called on the cacique, who appeared very sorrowful and again told his story, relating how he and his men had suffered wounds fighting in defense of the Christians, as was proved by their wounds, which had been made, not by Christian weapons, but by fish-bone spearheads and arrowheads. After they had conversed for a while, the cacique gave the Admiral eight hundred small figured white, green, and red stone beads together with one hundred figured gold beads, a royal gold crown, and three little gourds filled with gold grains that must have weighed 4 gold marks.[1] The Admiral in turn gave him trading truck that may have been worth 4 reales but had for them the value of 1,000.

Although gravely ill, the cacique went with the Admiral to see the fleet and was received with much ceremony. He was much diverted by sight of the horses, of which the Christians had previously given him an account. Because some of the slain Christians had misinformed the cacique concerning our holy faith by telling him that the Christian law was a vain thing, the Admiral undertook to instruct him in it, after which he consented to wear about his neck a silver image of the Virgin, something he had refused to do before.

CHAPTER 51

How the Admiral Left Navidad and Founded a Town That He Named Isabela

Reflecting on the fate of the dead Christians and the misfortunes he had suffered in that country through the loss of his ship at sea and of his garrison and fortress ashore, and observing that a short distance away there were places better suited for settlement, on Saturday, December 7th, the Admiral took the fleet eastward and that afternoon anchored near the islands of Monte Cristi. Next day, passing in front of Monte Cristi, he cruised among the seven low islands there, which have few trees but are not without charm. At that winter season they found flowers and bird's nests, some containing eggs and others fledglings, and all the other things that are proper to the summertime.

From there he proceeded to anchor in front of an Indian village; and having found a plain, with a ravine on one side, that appeared a suitable site for a fortress, he went ashore with all his people, provisions, and equipment. There he founded a town to which he gave the name Isabela, in honor of the Catholic Queen. They believed it to be an excellent site for a town because it had a very large harbor, though open to the northwest, and a lovely river a crossbow shot in width, from which water channels could be led to the town; and beyond the river extended a very charming plain, not far from which, according to the Indians, were the mines of the Cibao. For all these reasons the Admiral (who had already endured great toil on the sea) so drove himself to lay the foundations of that town that not only did he lack time to enter in his journal each day's happenings, as had been his custom, but he even fell ill and was unable to keep a journal at all from December 11, 1493, till March 12, 1494.

In January, after arranging the affairs of the town as well as he could, he sent Alonso de Hojeda with fifteen men in search of the mines of the Cibao. Then, on February 2d, twelve ships of the fleet departed for Castile under the command of Captain Antonio de Torres; he was a brother of Prince Juan's nurse, a man of worth and good judgment, much trusted by the Catholic Sovereigns and by the Admiral. He carried an extensive report of all that had happened, of the character of the country, and of what needed to be done there.

In a few days Hojeda returned and gave an account of his journey. He said that the second day after leaving Isabela they slept in a mountain pass difficult to negotiate, but that afterwards every other league they came to a village whose cacique received them very hospitably. Continuing their journey, they reached the mines of the Cibao on the sixth day after their departure. In Hojeda's presence the Indians took gold out of a brook; they later did the same in many other streams of that province, which Hojeda declared to be very rich in gold. The Admiral, who had by now recovered from his sickness, was overjoyed at this news and decided to go to see for himself the resources of that country and what needed to be done there.

Wednesday, March 12, 1494, the Admiral set out from Isabela to visit the mines of the Cibao; all the able-bodied men who were not required to guard the two ships and three caravels that remained of the fleet rode or marched with him. He had all the munitions and arms on the other vessels taken up and stored in the flagship in order that none might use them to mutiny, as some had attempted to do while he was ill. The cause of this mutiny was that many had embarked on the voyage with the idea that as soon as they landed they could load themselves with gold and return home rich. They did not know that gold may never be had without the sacrifice of time, toil, and privations. As matters did not turn out as they expected, and they were disgruntled at having to work on the construction of the new town, and made ill by the climate and diet of that country, they had conspired to throw off the Admiral's authority, seize the remaining vessels, and return in them to Castile. The instigator and head of the conspiracy was a royal constable, Bernal de Pisa, who had come on the voyage as comptroller for the Catholic Sovereigns. The plot having been discovered, the Admiral, out of respect for his office, did no more than arrest and hold him prisoner aboard the ship, intending to send him to Castile with a formal statement of his crimes; these consisted of mutiny and of having written a paper containing false charges against the Admiral that he tried to hide aboard the ship.

After the Admiral had disposed of all these matters and appointed persons to watch over the government and safety of the town and fleet under his brother, Don Diego Columbus,[1] he set out for the Cibao. He brought implements and all the other things needed to construct a fort that should keep that province at peace and protect Christian gold prospectors from harm by the Indians. In order to show the Indians that they could not do to him what they had done to Arana and his thirty-eight men, and that a large force stood ready to punish them if they molested a single Christian passing through one of their villages, he brought as many men as he could. For greater effect and show, he led his men out of Isabela and other places armed, in military formation, with trumpets sounding and banners displayed.

Having crossed the river that lies a musket shot from Isabela, the Admiral forded a smaller river one league farther on and marched three leagues more to camp that night in a beautiful plain. This plain extends to the foot of a rugged mountain pass, about two crossbow shots high, which he named El Puerto de los Hidalgos [2] in honor of some gentlemen who had gone ahead to supervise the opening up of a road. That was the first road made in the Indies, for the Indian trails are only wide enough to permit one man to walk at a time. Coming out of that pass, they descended to a great plain and next day traveled five leagues, sleeping that night near a large river that they crossed in canoes and rafts. This river, which he named Río de las Cañas,[3] empties into the sea at Monte Cristi.

On the march they passed through many Indian villages of round palm-thatched huts with such small doors that they had to stoop low to enter them. Some Indians that the Admiral had brought from Isabela went into those huts and helped themselves to anything they liked, and the owners gave no sign of displeasure, as if all they had was common property. The natives, thinking we had the same custom, at first went up to the Christians and took anything that caught their fancy, but they were promptly disillusioned. On this journey the Christians passed through mountains covered with pleasant woods where they saw wild grapevines, aloes, wild cinnamon trees, and other trees that had very thick trunks and leaves like those of the apple and yielded a fruit that resembled the fig: It is said that the scammony [4] grows on these trees.

CHAPTER 52

How the Admiral Reached the Province of the Cibao, Where He Found the Gold Mines and Built the Fort of Santo Tomás

Friday, March 14th, the Admiral left the Río de las Cañas and after a march of one and a half leagues reached a larger river which he named Río de Oro [1] because while crossing it they discovered some gold dust. They forded this river with some difficulty and came to a large village. A number of its inhabitants fled to the hills, but most shut themselves up in their homes, barring their huts with crossed bolts of cane. Having no doors of wood or other material, they lock themselves in with these canes; and no native of the country would dare enter a hut that is bolted in this manner. From this village the Admiral proceeded to another beautiful river that he named Río Verde; [2] its banks were covered with shiny round pebbles. There he slept that night.

Next day he continued his journey, passing through some large villages whose inhabitants had barred their huts with bolts of cane as the others had done. The Admiral and his people being weary, they camped that night at the foot of a rugged mountain that he named El Puerto del Cibao. Beyond that mountain, at a distance of eleven leagues from the first mountain they had encountered, begins the province of the Cibao; the country between these two mountains is level, and the way leads ever south. Next day they set out down a difficult trail along which the horses had to be led by the bridle. From this place he sent a mule train to Isabela for bread and wine, for they had begun to run short of provisions

Isabela and the Cibao
The trail followed by the Spaniards····
miles

0 10

Cape Isabela
Isabela
R. de Gracia
Puerto Blanco
Río
Bajabonico
Puerto Plata
C. Angel
Pt. Macoris
Imbert
CORDILLERA
La Cruz de las Guayacanes
Puerto de los Hidalgos
Monte Plata
R. de las Cañas
R. Yaque del Norte
Esperanza
Valverde
Pontón
SETENTRIONAL
VEGA REAL
Loma del Vento
Santiago de los Caballeros
Moca
Amina
R. Jánico
R. Bao
Jánico
Santo Tomás
Concepción de la Vega
CIBAO
CORDILLERA CENTRAL

and the journey was growing long. They suffered all the more from the shortage because they were unaccustomed to the Indian food —unlike the Spaniards who now reside and travel in that region and find the Indian food more digestible and suited to the climate of the country than the food that is brought from Spain, though not so nourishing.

On the return of the men he had sent for provisions, Sunday,

· 125 ·

March 16th, having crossed that mountain, the Admiral entered the province of the Cibao; this is a rough, stony country, full of boulders, with a dense cover of vegetation and drained by many rivers containing gold. The farther they went the rougher the country became, and their way was impeded by high mountains in whose streams they found gold dust. According to the Admiral, heavy rains washed this gold down from the mountain peaks in the form of minute grains. This province is as large as Portugal, and its mines and river sands abound in gold; there are few trees, however, and these grow mostly along the banks of rivers and consist chiefly of pines and palms of different kinds.

Since Hojeda had already journeyed through this country, the Indians knew of the Christians; and wherever the Admiral went, the Indians came out to meet him with gifts of food and gold dust, for they had learned that he came in search of gold. The Admiral had now traveled eighteen leagues from Isabela, and as the country through which he came was very rough, he ordered a fort built in a very attractive and defensible site. This fort he named the Fort of Santo Tomás, and it was to dominate the mining country and serve as a place of refuge in case of need to the Christians who came there.

He left Pedro Margarit, a very worthy man, in command of this fort, with fifty-six men; among them were artisans needed to construct the fort, which was made of earth and wood that it might be able to withstand any number of Indian attackers. After they had broken ground for the foundation and cut through rock to make moats, they were much surprised to find at a depth of two ells below the rock, nests of straw and clay containing, not eggs, but three or four round stones, each the size of a large orange and resembling cannon balls; they seemed to be the work of men. In the river that runs at the foot of the hill on which the fort stands they found stones of different colors, some large and of finest marble, others of pure jasper.

CHAPTER 53

How the Admiral Returned to Isabela and Discovered That the Land Was Very Fertile

After he had provided for the perfect construction of the fort and its defense, on Friday, March 21st, the Admiral returned to Isabela. At the Río Verde he met mules returning with provisions, and since heavy rains had made the river uncrossable, he camped there and sent the provisions on to the fort. While searching for a ford where he could cross that river, and for another ford for the crossing of the Río de Oro, which is larger than the Ebro, he stayed for some days in the Indian villages, eating of their cassava bread and yams, which the Indians willingly exchanged for trifles. Saturday, March 29th, he arrived at Isabela, where the melons were ripe enough to eat, though they had been planted less than two months before; cucumbers had come up in twenty days, and a native wild grapevine had already produced large fine grapes while they were still cultivating it.

Next day, March 30th, a laborer harvested spikes of wheat which had been planted at the end of January; they also picked chickpeas larger than those they had planted. All the seeds they had sown sprouted in three days and were ready to eat by the twenty-fifth day. Fruit stones planted in the ground sprouted in seven days; vine shoots sent out leaves at the end of the same period, and by the twenty-fifth day green grapes were ready to be picked. Sugar canes germinated in seven days. This was due to the temperate climate, very like that of Spain, for it is cool rather than warm; moreover, the waters of that country are very cold, soft, and healthful.

For all these reasons the Admiral was much pleased with the climate and fertility of the country, and with its inhabitants. But the first Tuesday in April a messenger arrived from Santo Tomás, sent by Captain Pedro Margarit with news that the Indians of that province were fleeing and that the cacique Caonabó was preparing to march on the fort and burn it to the ground. The Admiral was not much alarmed by this report, in particular because he relied on the horses; he knew how cowardly were the Indians, and how much they feared to be eaten by the horses, so that they would not even enter the house of a Spaniard who kept a horse. But for a precaution he decided to send Margarit reinforcements and provisions, especially since he intended to go in search of the mainland with the three caravels left to him and wanted to leave the country tranquil and secure. Therefore on Wednesday, April 2d, he sent seventy men with provisions and ammunition to the fort, twenty-five for garrison duty, and the rest to help build a new road, since the first road they had built was very inconvenient for reaching the fords of the rivers.

After these men had departed, and while the caravels were being made ready for the new voyage of discovery, he oversaw work on the town that he had founded, dividing it into streets, with a spacious plaza, and digging a wide channel to the river, for which purpose he had a dam built that should also provide power for a gristmill. This he did because the town lay about a cannon shot from the river, and without that channel the people would have had great difficulty in supplying themselves with water, particularly as most of them were weak and ill with certain diseases caused by the thinness of the air, which did not agree with them. Moreover, all the provisions brought from Castile, except biscuit and wine, were gone, partly because of poor management by the ship captains and partly because food does not keep as well in that country as in Spain. To be sure, they received abundant supplies of food from the Indian villages, but being unaccustomed to this food, they suffered ill effects from it. Therefore the Admiral decided to leave only three hundred men on the island, sending the rest back to Castile. He believed that that number was enough to keep the island and its people peaceful and obedient to the Catholic Sovereigns.

Since the biscuit was almost spent and they had wheat but no flour, he decided to have some gristmills built, but the nearest waterfall that could be used for the purpose was a league and a half away. In this project, as in all others, he had to stand over the workmen and urge them on, because they all shirked work. He also decided to send all the able-bodied men except the artisans and workmen to the Vega Real to pacify that region, make the Indians respect them, and gradually grow accustomed to eating Indian food, for the provisions from Castile were daily in shorter supply. These men were to be commanded by Hojeda until they reached Santo Tomás, where Hojeda should relieve Margarit, who would then take them on a tour of duty about the island. Hojeda, who had worn himself out the previous winter in the discovery of the Cibao (which in the Indian language means "stony"), was to remain as governor of the fort.

Wednesday, April 9th, Hojeda left for Santo Tomás with a force of more than one hundred men; and crossing the Río de Oro, he captured the cacique of that region, together with his brother and nephew, and sent them to the Admiral in chains. He also cut off the ears of one of the cacique's subjects in the square of his village. This he did because some Indians, assigned by that cacique to carry across the river the clothing of certain Spaniards returning from Santo Tomás to Isabela, ran off to their village with that clothing while the Spaniards were in the middle of the stream. Instead of punishing those Indians for their crimes, the cacique had taken the clothes for himself and refused to return them. The cacique who occupied the other bank of the river, trusting in the value of the services he had rendered the Christians, decided to accompany the prisoners to Isabela and intercede for them with the Admiral. The latter received him in a friendly manner but ordered those Indians to be sentenced to death by a public crier, their hands tied behind them. At this the kind cacique shed so many tears that he at last obtained the lives of those men, promising they would never again offend.

After the Admiral had set them all free, a horseman coming from Santo Tomás reported that while passing through the village of the imprisoned cacique he found that the people had captured five Christians bound for Isabela, that he had frightened the Indians with his horse and freed those Christians, putting more than four hundred Indians to flight and wounding two of them in the chase. After he had crossed to the other side he looked back and saw the Indians were preparing to attack those Christians again; at this he turned his horse about and made as if to charge the Indians, so that they fled in panic, believing the horse would fly across the river.

CHAPTER 54

How the Admiral Disposed of the Affairs of the Island and Sailed to Explore the Island of Cuba, Believing It to Be the Mainland

The Admiral having decided to sail in search of the mainland, he appointed a council to govern the island in his absence. Its members were Don Diego Columbus, his brother, with the title of president; Fray Buil[1] and Pedro Fernández Coronel,[2] regents; Alonso Sánchez de Carvajal,[3] councilman of Baeza; and Juan de Luján, a gentleman of Madrid of the household of the Catholic Sovereigns.

In order that the people might not lack flour, he pushed construction of the gristmills, though much hampered by the rains and the flooding of the rivers. The Admiral writes that these rains are the cause of the wetness and consequently of the fertility of that island. So fertile was it that they ate fruit from the trees in No-

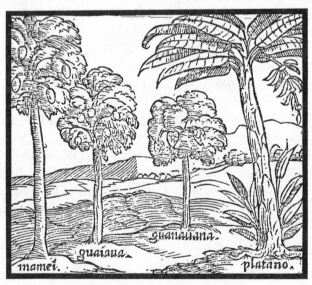

Fruit Trees of Española

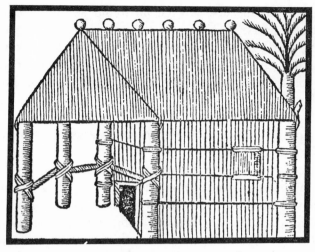

Native House in Española

vember, at which time they flowered again, indicating that they bear fruit twice a year. Plants and seeds continually bear fruit and flower. At all seasons they found in the trees bird's nests containing eggs and young. Moreover, they had daily new confirmation of the wealth of the island; for not a day passed without the return of one of the men the Admiral had dispatched in different directions with news of the discovery of new mines, not to mention the accounts brought by the Indians of the discovery of great quantities of gold in various parts of the island.

But the Admiral was not satisfied with all this and resolved to explore the coast of Cuba, being uncertain whether it was an island or a continent. Thursday, April 24th, after the noon meal, he set sail with three ships, and later that day anchored at Monte Cristi, to the west of Isabela. On Friday he called at Guacanagarí's harbor, hoping to find the cacique there; but at sight of the ships he fled in fear, though his people pretended that he would soon return.[4] Unwilling to stay there without some good cause, the Admiral left this harbor on Saturday, April 26th, and proceeded to the island of Tortuga, which lies six leagues to the west. He lay off it that night with sails set, becalmed in a choppy sea that was thrown back by the current. Next day, with a contrary northwest wind and the current setting from the west, he had to return eastward and anchor off the Río Guadalquivir[5] in Española to await a wind that would enable him to make way against the current, which now as on his first voyage he found setting strongly east-ward in those parts.

Tuesday, April 29th, he reached Puerto San Nicolás with fair weather and thence crossed over to Cuba, beginning to range its southern coast. Having gone one league beyond Cape Fuerte, he put in a large bay with a mouth of great depth and one hundred and fifty feet wide; that is why he named it Puerto Grande.[6] There he anchored and dined on roast fish and hutias,[7] of which the Indians had an abundance. Next day, May 1st, he continued cruising down the coast, encountering commodious harbors, lovely rivers, and very high mountains. From the time they left Tortuga they found the sea covered with the weed they had seen on the way to and from Spain. As they cruised along the shore many islanders paddled to the ships in their canoes; thinking our men had come from Heaven, these Indians brought the Christians cassava bread, water, and fish, asking nothing in exchange. But the Admiral, wishing to send them away happy, ordered them to be paid for everything with glass beads, hawk's bells, and the like.

CHAPTER 55

How the Admiral Discovered the Island of Jamaica

Saturday, May 3d, the Admiral set sail from Cuba for Jamaica to learn if it was true, as they had been told on all the other islands, that Jamaica was very rich in gold. Sunday, the weather being clear and half the voyage behind them, they sighted the island, and anchored off its coast on Monday. The Admiral thought it was the most beautiful island of all that he had seen in the Indies. A multitude of large and small canoes, carrying a great number of natives, came out to the ships. Next day the Admiral cruised down the coast to explore the island's harbors. After he had sent the boats ahead to the mouth of one harbor, there issued from the shore so many armed canoes that the boats had to return to the ships, not so much from fear of the Indians as to avoid hostilities with them. Later, reflecting that an appearance of fear might cause these Indians to grow even more haughty and arrogant, they entered another harbor which the Admiral named El Puerto Bueno.[1] When the Indians again came out, hurling darts at them, the crossbowmen in the boats taught them such a lesson that they had to retreat with the loss of six or seven wounded. The battle ended, a multitude of canoes came peacefully from the neighboring villages to trade their things and provisions for our gewgaws.

In this harbor, which has the form of a horseshoe, they found and repaired a leak in the Admiral's flagship;[2] and on Friday, May 9th, he sailed westward down the coast, keeping close to shore, with the Indians following in their canoes to engage in trade.

But the wind turning foul, the Admiral could not make as much progress as he wished; and finally, on Tuesday, May 13th, he decided to return to Cuba and follow its southern coast until he had sailed some five hundred or six hundred leagues and had made certain whether it was an island or a mainland.

That day, as he was about to sail from Jamaica, a young Indian came aboard saying he wished to go to Castile. Many of his relations and other people followed him in canoes; they begged him to come back but could not turn him from his design. Indeed, in order to escape the tears and lamentations of his sisters he hid where they could not see him. The Admiral marveled at the firm resolution of this Indian and ordered him to be well treated.

CHAPTER 56

How the Admiral Returned from Jamaica to Follow the Coast of Cuba, Believing It to Be the Mainland

Having left Jamaica, on Wednesday, May 14th, the Admiral made the cape that he named Cape Santa Cruz.[1] As he was following the coast there arose a terrible storm of thunder and lightning that, added to the numerous shoals and channels, caused him great danger and toil. He had to guard against two dangers that required contrary measures, the proper precaution against such storms being to strike sail, while to escape running aground he had to carry on; if he had had to face eight or ten leagues more of this, the Admiral's situation would have been intolerable.

But the chief problem was that that whole sea, both to the north and the northeast, was dotted with innumerable small islands. Some were densely wooded, but the majority were sandy and barely visible above the water; they were about a league around, more or less. The nearer they drew to Cuba the higher and lovelier these little islands became. It would have been impossible to name them all; therefore, the Admiral named them collectively El Jardín de la Reina.[2] Next day he sighted still more islands, most of which were larger than those he had seen previously, to the northeast as well as to the northwest and southwest. That day they counted one hundred and sixty islands separated from each other by deep channels through which the ships threaded their way.

On some of those islands they saw many cranes of the size and shape of those of Castile, but bright red.[3] On others they found turtles and many turtle eggs, resembling those of hens but having very hard shells. The turtles lay their eggs in a hole made in the sand, cover them up, and leave them until the heat of the sun has hatched the baby turtles; in time they attain the size of a buckler and sometimes that of a large shield. On those islands, they also saw crows and cranes like those of Spain, cormorants, and a multitude of small birds that sang most sweetly. So fragrant was the air that our men seemed to be amid roses and the most delicate scents in the world. Yet the dangers to navigation were very great here, because there was such a maze of channels that it took a long time to find a way out.

In one of those channels they saw a canoe with Indian fishermen. These men showed no fear but quietly waited until the ship's boat was close, and then made signs not to come nearer until they had done fishing. Their mode of fishing was so strange and novel that our men complied with their wishes. The Indians tied slender cords to the tails of certain fish that we call *revesos*⁴ and that pursue other fish, to which they attach themselves by a rough place on their own bodies that runs from the head to the middle of the back; they stick so fast to any fish they encounter that when the Indian pulls in his cord he draws out both fish together. Our men saw those fishermen pull out a turtle with the pilot fish attached to its neck, that being the place to which the pilot fish fastens itself so that its quarry cannot bite it. I have seen them attach themselves to very large sharks in this manner.

When the Indians were done fishing, having caught two fish and a turtle, they approached very calmly to see what our men wanted. By order of the Christians they accompanied them to the ships, where the Admiral treated them very hospitably; from them he learned that that sea was full of innumerable islands. They offered him all they had, but the Admiral would take only that fish mentioned above, their other possessions being nets, hooks, and calabashes filled with drinking water. He gave them some trifles, and they went away very happy. The Admiral held on his course, though he did not intend to proceed much farther because he was running short of provisions; had he had plenty of food, he would have gone on to return to Spain by way of the East.

By this time the Admiral was quite worn out, both on account of poor diet and because (aside from eight days when he was seriously indisposed) he had not undressed and slept a full night in bed from the time he left Spain till May 19th, the day on which he made this notation in his journal. Great as had been his cares on other voyages, they were redoubled on this one because of the innumerable islands among which they sailed; on the 20th of May alone they sighted seventy-one, not counting the many they sighted at sunset toward the west-southwest. The sight of these islands or shoals all about them was frightening enough, but what was worse was that each afternoon a dense mist rose over them in the eastern sky, with such thunder and lightning that it seemed a deluge was

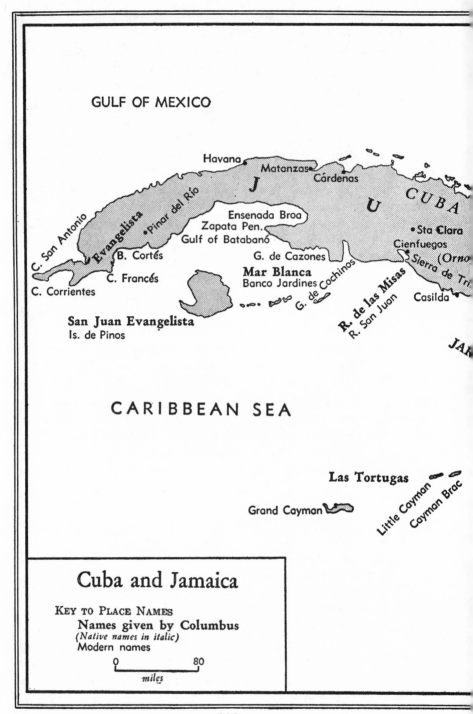

GULF OF MEXICO

CARIBBEAN SEA

Las Tortugas

Grand Cayman

Little Cayman

Cayman Brac

Cuba and Jamaica

KEY TO PLACE NAMES
Names given by Columbus
(Native names in italic)
Modern names

0   80
miles

about to fall; when the moon came out, it all vanished, dissolving part into rain and part into wind. This is such a common phenomenon in those regions that it happened each afternoon on that voyage; and I myself observed it when cruising among those islands in 1503, returning from the discovery of Veragua. The wind which regularly blows at night is from the north because it comes from Cuba; then, at daybreak, it turns easterly and follows the sun till it returns to the west.

CHAPTER 57

How the Admiral Endured Great Hardships and Toil as He Sailed Among Islands Innumerable

Continuing to sail westward among islands innumerable, the Admiral, on Thursday, May 22d, reached an island a little larger than the others and named it Santa Marta. Landing at a village on that island, they found that all the Indians had fled. In the huts they found no food other than fish, which is the whole diet of those Indians; there were many dogs like mastiffs, which also feed on fish. So, without having had speech with anyone or found anything notable, they steered northeasterly among other islands, on which they saw many bright red cranes, parrots, and other varieties of birds, dogs like those mentioned above, and much weed of the kind the Admiral saw in the ocean when he discovered the Indies. This navigation in a maze of shoals and islands caused the Admiral much toil, for he had to steer now west, now north, now south, according to the disposition of the channels. And for all his care in making soundings and keeping lookouts on the roundtop, the ship often scraped bottom, there being innumerable shoals all about.

Navigating in such difficult conditions, he decided to put into

Cuba again to obtain fresh water, of which they were in great need. Because of the dense vegetation on the shore where they touched, they could not see if there was a village, but a sailor who went hunting in the woods with a crossbow encountered thirty Indians who carried their customary arms: darts and the clubs that they use as swords and call macanas. The sailor said that one was dressed in a white tunic that reached to his knees and two others wore tunics that came down to their feet; he said these three were as light-complexioned as our men.[1] He had not spoken with them, however; for taking fright at the sight of all these people, he had called out to his comrades, whereupon the Indians fled and never returned.

Wishing to check the truth of this story, next day the Admiral sent a party ashore, but after proceeding for half a league they were stopped by the dense vegetation and forests; moreover, that whole coast was all marsh and mire for a space of two leagues from the shore to where the hills and mountains began. So they returned with only a report of having seen signs of fishermen on the beach and many cranes like those of Spain but considerably larger.

Continuing ten leagues westward, the fleet sighted huts on the shore; some canoes came out from this village, and the people in them brought fresh water and the things those Indians eat, for all of which they were well paid. The Admiral detained one of them, telling him and the other Indians through an interpreter that he would be released as soon as he had shown him the way and given him other information about that region. The Indian was quite satisfied with this and told the Admiral for a fact that Cuba was an island, that the king or cacique of the western part communicated with his vassals only through signs, by means of which all his orders were swiftly carried out, and that all that coast was very low and fringed by many islands. They found this to be true, for next day, June 11th, seeking to move the ship from one channel to a deeper one, the Admiral had to kedge it with cables over a sandbank less than a fathom deep but two ship lengths in size. Drawing closer to Cuba, they saw turtles two or three ells in size, and so numerous that the sea was covered with them. Then, at daybreak, they saw a flight of cormorants so numerous that they darkened the sun; they came from the sea toward Cuba and soon alighted there. Our men also saw many pigeons and other kinds of birds. Next day so many butterflies flew about the ships that they darkened the air till the afternoon, when a heavy rain squall blew them off.

CHAPTER 58

How the Admiral Returned to Española

Friday, June 13th, observing that the Cuban coast extended far westward, that an infinite number of small islands and shoals made its navigation extremely difficult, and that he was beginning to run short of provisions, the Admiral decided to return to the town of Isabela that he had begun to build on Española. He stopped to take on wood and water at the island of San Juan Evangelista,[1] which is thirty leagues around and seven hundred leagues distant from the island of Dominica.

After he had taken on all he needed, he steered a southerly course, hoping to find deeper water in that direction; and following a channel that he believed to be deepest and most free of obstruction, he found it to be completely surrounded by land on all sides. This greatly frightened his men, who found themselves almost imprisoned, without sufficient provisions or hope of assistance. When the Admiral observed their gloom and anxiety, he shrewdly put on a cheerful countenance, saying he thanked God for forcing him to return by the way he came in, for had they continued sailing in that direction, they might have become hopelessly entangled or lost and without ships or provisions with which to return, whereas now they could easily turn back.[2]

To the general relief and satisfaction, then, he returned to the island of the Evangelista. Wednesday, June 25th, he left that island on a northwest course for some small islands[3] that seemed five leagues distant. Some way beyond, the sea turned green and white, so that it seemed to be one great shoal, though it was two fathoms deep.[4] They sailed over seven leagues of this sea, after which they came to another sea as white as milk; this caused them great surprise, as the water was very dirty. This sea puzzled all who saw it, for it appeared to be all shoal and not deep enough for ships; actually it was about three fathoms deep. After sailing some four leagues over that sea he came to another which was as black as ink and five fathoms deep; over this sea he sailed till he reached Cuba.

Thence he continued eastward with head winds, along channels and sandbanks. On June 30th, while he was entering an account of the voyage in his journal, the ship ran aground with such force that they could not get her off by the stern with the anchors or by any other means; however, with God's aid they managed to pull her off by the prow, though she suffered considerable damage from the shock of the grounding. Having gotten off at last with divine aid, he sailed along as wind and shoals permitted through a sea that was always white and two fathoms deep, neither increasing nor diminishing in depth save when they drew too close to a shoal. Aside from the shoals, every day at sunset he was plagued by rains which issue from the mountains bordering the lagoons that lie next to the sea. He suffered great annoyance from these things until he again approached the island of Cuba from the east, along the route by which they had first come. There, as at his first coming, the air was fragrant with the sweet scent of flowers.

On July 7th the Admiral went ashore to hear Mass. An elderly cacique, the lord of that province, having listened attentively to the Mass, approached the Admiral and communicated to him by signs and as best he could that it was well to thank God, for the souls of the good would go to Heaven, their bodies remaining on earth; but the souls of the wicked would go to Hell. Among other things, he said that he had been on Española and knew the principal Indians of that island. He had also been on Jamaica and had traveled extensively in western Cuba; he said that the cacique of that region dressed like a priest.

CHAPTER 59

Of the Great Hunger and Toil Suffered by the Admiral and His Men, and How He Returned to Jamaica

Leaving that place on Wednesday, July 16th, he sailed on to the accompaniment of terrible rain and wind, and near Cape Cruz off Cuba he was assailed by a thunderburst, so sudden and violent, and with such a downpour of rain, that the deck was placed under water. With the aid of God they were able to strike sails and anchor with the heaviest anchors; but so much water worked down through the floor timbers that the sailors could not get it out with the pumps, especially because they were all very tired and weak from too little food. All they had to eat daily was a pound of rotten biscuits and a pint of wine, and if by great good fortune they caught a fish, they could not keep it from one day to the next because food spoils very quickly in those regions, the climate being warmer than in our country. The shortage of food was felt by all. The Admiral writes in his journal:

I am on the same ration as the others. May it please God that this be for His service and that of Your Highnesses. Were it only for myself, I would no longer bear such pains and dangers, for not a day passes that we do not look death in the face.

With these dangers and afflictions, on July 18th he reached Cape Cruz, where the Indians received him hospitably, bringing much cassava (which is the bread they make by scraping certain roots) and fish and a great quantity of fruit and other food. From this place, being denied a fair wind for Española, on Tuesday, July 22d, he departed for Jamaica and cruised westward down its coast, hugging the land, which was very beautiful and fertile. A league apart he found excellent harbors, and the whole coast was crowded with towns, whose inhabitants followed the ships in their canoes, bringing the Christians food which they liked much better than what they had received on all the other islands. The sky, air, and climate were just the same as in other places; every afternoon there was a rain squall that lasted for about an hour. The Admiral writes that he attributes this to the great forests of that land; he knew from experience that formerly this also occurred in the Canary, Madeira, and Azore Islands, but since the removal of forests that once covered those islands, they do not have so much mist and rain as before.

The Admiral held on his course, always with an adverse wind that forced him to take shelter every afternoon near the land. This was so green and smiling, abounding in food and densely populated, that he thought it unsurpassed by none, especially near a channel that he named the Boca de las Vacas,[1] which contained seven little islands close to land which he said was the highest land he had seen up to that time; he believed that it rose above the zone of the air where storms are born; withal it is all densely populated and very fertile and lovely.

He judged the island must have a circumference of some eight hundred miles, but when he had explored it all, he concluded that it must be only fifty leagues long and twenty wide. Charmed by its beauty, he would have liked to stay longer in order to come to know it better; however, the shortage of provisions and the leaky state of his ships prevented it. Accordingly, whenever a short spell of good weather permitted, he voyaged eastward, and on Tuesday, August 19th, he lost sight of that island and headed directly for Española, naming the eastern point of Jamaica, on the south coast, El Cabo del Farol.[2]

CHAPTER 60

How the Admiral Explored the Southern Shore of the Island of Española Until He Returned Eastward to the Town of Navidad

Wednesday, August 20th, the Admiral sighted the western end of Española, which he named Cape San Miguel; [1] it is thirty miles distant from the eastern end of Jamaica, and sailors nowadays call it Cape Tiburón. While he was off this cape, on Saturday, August 23d, there came out to the ship a cacique who called the Admiral by his name and knew some other Spanish words; this proved to the Admiral that the land was part of Española.

At the end of August he anchored at a small island that he named Alta Vela; and having lost sight of the other two ships, he sent some men ashore to climb to the top of this very high island, from which one could see a great distance in all directions, but they did not sight any sails. As they were leaving that island they killed eight seals which were sleeping in the sand. They also killed many pigeons and other birds, for as that island is uninhabited and the animals are unaccustomed to men, they let themselves be killed with sticks.

The Admiral's people spent the next two days in the same way, waiting for the ships which had been lost since the previous Friday. At last, six days later, they showed up; and all three sailed together for the island of Beata, twelve leagues to the east of Alta Vela. There they sailed by a pleasant plain, about a mile from the sea, and so densely peopled that it seemed to be a continuous settlement, one league long; on this plain was a lake three leagues long from east to west. When the natives learned of the coming of the Christians, they came in their canoes to the caravels to report that some Christians had arrived there from Isabela and that all were in good health. The Admiral was greatly pleased by this news. As he wished to inform the settlers of his safe arrival, he sailed on somewhat farther east and landed nine men who were to cross the island and proceed by way of the forts of Santo Tomás and Magdalena to Isabela. Continuing eastward down the coast, he sent three boats to get water on a beach where a large village could be seen. The Indians, armed with bows and poisoned arrows and carrying cords in their hands, issued from that village making signs that those cords were for tying up the Christians they would capture. But when the boats came ashore, the Indians put aside their arms and offered to bring the Christians bread, water, and all else they had; and, speaking in their native tongue, they asked for the Admiral.

Holding on their course, the ship's people sighted a large fish, big as a whale, with a carapace like a turtle's, a head the size of a barrel protruding from the water, a long tail like that of a tunny fish, and two large wings. From this and from certain other signs the Admiral knew they were in for foul weather and sought a port where they might take refuge. On September 15th by the mercy of God they sighted an island which lies off the eastern end of Española and which the Indians call Adamaney; [2] in the middle of a great storm he anchored behind this island, next to an islet that lies between it and Española. That night he observed an eclipse of the moon and was able to determine a difference in time of about five hours and twenty-three minutes between that place and Cádiz. That, I believe, is the reason the bad weather continued so long. For he had to remain in that port until the twentieth of the month, fearing all the while for the safety of the ships that had not been able to put in; but by the favor of God they were saved. On September 24th, the fleet being reunited, they sailed to the eastern end of Española and from there to an island that lies between Española and San Juan and that the Indians call Amona. [3]

From that point on the Admiral ceased to record in his journal the day's sailing, nor does he tell how he returned to Isabela. He relates only that because of his great exertions, weakness, and scanty diet he fell gravely ill in crossing from Amona to San Juan; he had a high fever and a drowsiness, so that he lost his sight, memory, and all his other senses. [4] Because of his illness, the ship's people decided to abandon the project for exploring the Carib islands and instead make for Isabela, where they arrived five days later, September 29th. There, by God's favor, the Admiral's health was at last restored, though he lay ill for more than five months. This illness was caused by his great exertions on that voyage and the resulting exhaustion, for he sometimes went eight days with less than three hours' sleep. This would seem impossible did he not himself tell it in his writings.

CHAPTER 61

How the Admiral Completed the Conquest of Española, and What He Did to Make It Yield Revenue

On his return to Española from the exploration of Cuba and Jamaica, the Admiral found his brother Bartholomew, who, as told before, had gone to treat with the King of England concerning the discovery of the Indies. On his way back to Castile with an agreement in his possession,[1] he learned in Paris from King Charles of France[2] that his brother the Admiral had already discovered the Indies; the King also presented him with a hundred escudos for his traveling expenses. Bartholomew then made all haste to get to the Admiral in Spain, but when he reached Seville, his brother had already sailed with a fleet of seventeen ships.

Complying with the Admiral's written request, Bartholomew at the opening of the year 1494 conducted Don Diego Columbus, my brother, and myself, to the Court of the Catholic Sovereigns to serve as pages to the most serene Prince Don Juan (whom God keep), by order of the Catholic Queen Isabella, who was then in Valladolid. As soon as we arrived, the Sovereigns summoned Don Bartholomew and sent him to Española with three ships. There he served several years, as appears from a memorandum of his in which he writes the following, "I served as captain from April 14, 1494, until March 12, 1496, when the Admiral sailed for Castile. Then I began to serve as governor and continued in that capacity until August 28, 1498, when the Admiral left on a voyage to discover Paria. At that time I once more began to serve as captain, continuing as such until December 11, 1500, when I returned to Castile."

Returning, then, from Cuba to find his brother on Española, the Admiral named him Adelantado, or governor, of the Indies. Later there was a dispute over this because the Catholic Sovereigns denied they had empowered the Admiral to make such an appointment. To settle their difference they appointed the Admiral's brother to that office again, and thereafter he was called Adelantado of the Indies.

With the aid and advice of his brother the Admiral had some rest and lived very tranquilly, though much troubled both by his illness and because he found that most of the Indians of the country had risen in revolt through the fault of Pedro Margarit, of whom I spoke above. At the time of his departure for Cuba the Admiral had appointed this man captain over three hundred and sixty foot soldiers and fourteen troopers with instructions to patrol the country and reduce it to the service of the Catholic Sovereigns and to compel the Indians to obey the Spaniards—especially in the province of the Cibao, from which the greatest advantage was anticipated. Instead of treating the Admiral with due consideration and respect, Margarit had paid no heed to the Admiral's wishes. Hardly had the Admiral departed when he went off with all his men to the Vega Real, ten leagues from Isabela, with no intention of patrolling or pacifying the island. Instead he proved to be the prime cause of the discords and factions that arose in Isabela, scheming and contriving to have the members of the council established by the Admiral obey his orders, and sending them insolent letters. In the end, seeing he could not achieve his aim of setting himself above all the others, and being unwilling to await the arrival of the Admiral, to whom he would have had to account for his actions in office, he embarked on the first ships that came from Castile, without giving an account of himself or making any disposition of the men left in his charge. As a result each one went where he willed among the Indians, stealing their property and wives and inflicting so many injuries upon them that the Indians resolved to avenge themselves on any that they found alone or in small groups. Thus the cacique of the Magdalena, named Guatiganá, killed ten Christians and secretly ordered fire to be set to a hut in which there were forty sick men. On his return the Admiral severely punished these actions; for though he could not apprehend the cacique, some of his people were seized and sent prisoners to Castile in the fleet of four ships with which Antonio de Torres sailed as commander on February 24, 1495.[3]

He also punished six or seven others who had harmed Christians at various places on the island. Those caciques had already slain many Christians and would have killed many more if the Admiral had not stopped them in time. The Admiral found the island in a pitiful state, with most of the Christians committing innumerable outrages for which they were mortally hated by the Indians, who refused to obey them. The kings and caciques of the island were united in refusing to serve the Christians; and the fact that there were only four principal men among them, whom the other chiefs obeyed, made it easy to obtain the general assent.

These four principal men were Caonabó, Higuanamá, Behechio, and Guarionex. Each had under him seventy or eighty caciques, who rendered no tribute but were obliged to come when summoned to assist them in their wars and in sowing their fields. One of these caciques, Guacanagarí, lord of that part of the island where the town of Navidad had been founded, kept friendship with the Christians; for this reason, as soon as he learned of the Admiral's return, he visited him to let him know that he had no part in the schemes of the other caciques and had given them no aid. As proof of this he recalled the hospitality he had always shown the Christians, of whom no less than a hundred were constantly maintained and supplied by him with all he could provide. For that reason he was hated by the other caciques, especially by Behechio, who had killed one of his wives, and by Caonabó, who had stolen from him another; and that was why he now appealed to the Admiral to restore his wife to him and help him get revenge for his injuries. This the Admiral agreed to do, believing in the good faith of that cacique, for he wept each time he recalled the men who had been killed at Navidad, as if they had been his own sons. Moreover, the Admiral reflected that by taking advantage of the discords among the caciques he might the more easily conquer the island and punish the rebellion of the other Indians and avenge the death of the Christians who had been slain.

On March 24, 1495, therefore, he marched forth from Isabela in warlike array together with his ally and comrade Guacanagarí, who was most eager to rout his enemies. This promised to be a difficult feat, for the rebel caciques had assembled more than one hundred thousand Indians, while the Admiral had only two hundred Christians, twenty horses, and as many hounds. But the Admiral, who understood the Indian character and habits, after a ten days' march from Isabela divided his army into two groups, one under himself and the other under his brother the Adelantado. He intended to attack that scattered horde of Indians from different directions, for he believed that the Indians, frightened by a great din arising simultaneously on various sides, would break and flee in panic; and so it turned out. First the infantry squadrons of the two divisions attacked the Indian host and began to rout them with crossbow and harquebus shots; then the cavalry and hounds fell upon them impetuously to prevent their rallying. As a result those cowardly Indians fled in all directions, hotly pursued by our men, who with God's aid soon gained a complete victory, killing many Indians and capturing others who were also killed. Caonabó, the principal cacique, was taken alive together with his wives and children.[4]

Caonabó afterwards confessed that he had killed twenty of the Spaniards who remained under Arana in Navidad when the Admiral returned to Spain from the discovery of the Indies; and that later, feigning friendship, he had visited Isabela with the true design (which our men suspected) of seeing how he might best attack and destroy it as he had done to the town of Navidad. This the Admiral had already learned from others; and it was to punish Caonabó for this first offense and for his second act of rebellion and assemblage of Indians that he had marched against him. Having made him and one of his brothers prisoners, he sent them to Spain; for he was unwilling to put to death so great a personage without the knowledge of the Catholic Sovereigns; he thought it was enough to have punished many of the guiltiest Indians.

This victory and the imprisonment of those men so improved the position of the Christians that though they numbered only six hundred and thirty, most of them sick, with many children and women among them, the Admiral in the space of a year during which he marched through the country completely pacified the island without having to unsheath his sword again. He reduced the Indians to such obedience and tranquility that they all promised to pay tribute to the Catholic Sovereigns every three months, as follows: In the Cibao, where the gold mines were, every person of fourteen years of age or upward was to pay a large hawk's bell of gold dust; all others were each to pay twenty-five pounds of cotton. Whenever an Indian delivered his tribute, he was to receive a brass or copper token which he must wear about his neck as proof that he had made his payment; any Indian found without such a token was to be punished.

This system would doubtless have produced the desired effects if there had not arisen discords among the Christians, as I shall presently relate. For after the capture of Caonabó the island was so peaceful that a Christian could safely go wherever he pleased, and the Indians themselves offered to carry him pickaback, as they do nowadays at the post stages. The Admiral ascribed this to the favor of God and the good fortune of the Catholic Sovereigns, else it would have been impossible for two hundred poorly armed men, half of them sick, to subdue such a multitude. But the Lord wished to punish the Indians, and so visited them with such shortage of food and such a variety of plagues that he reduced their number by two thirds, that it might be made clear that such wonderful conquests proceeded from His supreme hand and not from our strength or intelligence or the cowardice of the Indians; for even admitting the superiority of our men, it is obvious that the numerical preponderance of the Indians would have nullified this advantage.

CHAPTER 62

Of Some Things That They Saw on the Island of Española, and of the Customs, Ceremonies, and Religion of the Indians[1]

When the Indians had grown more peaceful and lost some of their fear of our men, much was learned about the resources and secrets of that land: that it had mines of copper, sapphires, and amber; brazilwood, ebony, incense, cedars, many fine gums, and different kinds of wild spices that could be brought to perfection by cultivation, such as fine-colored cinnamon (though bitter to the taste), ginger, pepper, and different kinds of mulberry trees for producing silk that bear leaves all year round, and many other useful plants and trees of which nothing is known in our countries.

Our people learned many other things having to do with their customs that seem worthy of being told in this history. Beginning with their religion, I shall cite here the Admiral's own words:

I found neither idolatry nor any other religion among them, but each of their kings (who are many), both on Española and the other islands and the mainland,[2] has a house apart from the town in which there is nothing except some carved wooden images that they called *cemíes;* these houses are used only for the service of the *cemíes,* by means of a certain ceremony and prayer, as is done in our churches. In these houses there is a well-made table, round like a wooden dish, in which is kept a powder that they place on the head of the *cemí* with a certain ceremony; then, through a cane having two branches that they insert in the nose, they sniff up this powder. The words which they spoke none of our men could understand. This powder makes them lose their senses and rave like drunken men. To each statue they assign a name; I believe it must be the name of the father or grandfather or both [of the namer B. K.], for they have more than one, and some more than ten, all in memory of their forebears. I have observed that they praise one statue more highly than another and show more devotion and reverence to some than to others, as we do in processions to the saints in time of need; and the caciques and villages boast of having the best *cemíes.* When they enter the house where they keep their *cemíes,* they keep watch for Christians and will not let them enter. Indeed, if they suspect Christians are coming they take up their *cemíes* and hide them in the woods for fear they will be taken from them; what is even more laughable, they have the custom of stealing each other's *cemíes.*

It once happened that some Christians entered such a house with them, and the *cemí* gave a loud cry and spoke in their language, from which it became clear that the statue was artfully constructed. It was in fact hollow, and to the lower part was attached a blowgun or trumpet which was connected to a dark side of the house, covered by branches and leaves, where was hidden a person who said whatever the cacique wanted him to say (as well as one can speak through a blowgun). The Spaniards suspected the true state of affairs and kicked the *cemí* over, finding what was described above. Seeing that his ruse was discovered, the cacique earnestly pleaded with us to say nothing to his subjects or to any other Indian, because it was by means of that deception that he kept them in obedience to him. We may therefore say that there is a semblance of idolatry among them, at least among those who are not aware of the deception practiced by their caciques, for they believe it is the *cemí* who speaks. In general all the people are deceived. Only the cacique knows of and abets this fraud, by means of which he gets all the tribute he wants from his people.

Likewise, most of the caciques have each three stones, for which they and their people feel great devotion. According to them, one of these stones helps the grains and vegetables grow, the second helps women give birth without pain, and the third secures rain or fair weather when they are in need of either. I sent Your Highnesses three of these stones with Antonio de Torres, and I shall carry three more with me.

When these Indians die, they are buried in various ways. They bury their caciques in this way: They open the cacique up and dry him before a fire that he may keep whole. In the case of others they preserve only the head. Others they bury in a cave and place bread and a calabash full of water above his head. The bodies of others they burn in the house where they have died; when they see them in the last extremity, they strangle them; this they do only to caciques. The bodies of some they throw out of the house, and others they set in a hammock, which is a kind of bed of netting; they place bread and water beside the head, depart, and never come to see him again. Some who are gravely ill they carry to the cacique, who decides whether they should be strangled, and his order is always carried out.

I have taken pains to learn what they believe and know as to where the dead go, especially from Caonabó, who was the principal king of the island of Española; he is a man of mature age, very knowledgeable and sharp-witted. He and others replied that they go to a valley which every principal cacique believes to be in his country; there they find their fathers and forebears; they eat, have wives, and enjoy pleasures and comforts. All this is more fully told in the following account by Fray Ramón,[3] who knew their language and was charged by me to set down all their rites and antiquities. However, it contains so many fictions that the only sure thing to be learned from it is that the Indians have a certain natural reverence for the after-life and believe in the immortality of the soul.

The Relation of Fray Ramón Concerning the Antiquities
of the Indians, Which He, Knowing Their Language,
Carefully Compiled by Order of the Admiral

I, Fray Ramón, a poor anchorite of the Order of St. Jerome, write by order of the illustrious Lord Admiral, viceroy, and governor of the islands and mainland of the Indies what I have been able to learn concerning the beliefs and idolatry of the Indians, and the manner in which they worship their gods. Of these matters I shall give an account in the present treatise.

Each one adores the idols or *cemíes* that he has in his house in some special way and with some special rites. They believe that there is an immortal being in the sky whom none can see and who has a mother but no beginning. They call him Yocahu Vagua Maorocoti, and his mother Atabey, Yermaoguacar, Apito, and Zuimaco, which are five different names.[4] I write only of the Indians of the island of Española, for I know nothing about the other islands and have never seen them. These Indians also know whence they came and where the sun and moon had their beginning, and how the sea was made, and of the place to which the dead go. They believe that the dead people appear on the roads to one who walks alone, but when many go together, the dead do not appear. All this they were taught by their forebears, for they cannot read or count above ten.

I. *Of the place from which the Indians came, and how they came.* In Española there is a province called Caonao, in which is found a mountain called Cauta, having two caves named Cacibajagua and Amayaura. From Cacibajagua came the majority of the people who settled the island. When they lived in that cave, they posted a guard at night, and they intrusted that charge to a man named Macocael; they say that one day the sun carried him off because he was late in coming to the door. Seeing that the sun had carried away this man for neglecting his duties, they closed the door to him, and so he was changed into a stone near that door. They say that others who had gone fishing were caught by the sun and changed into the trees called *jobos* or myrobalans. The reason why Macocael kept guard was to see in what direction he should send or distribute the people; and his lateness was his undoing.

II. *How the women were separated from the men.* It once happened that Guahayona told another man named Yahrubaba to go to pick the herb called *digo* with which they clean their bodies when they bathe. He went out before dawn, and the sun caught him on the road and changed him into a bird which sings in the morning, like the nightingale; it is called Yahubabayael. Guahayona, seeing that the man he had sent to look for *digo* did not return, decided to come out of the cave Cacibajagua.

III. Then Guahayona, angry because the men he had sent to pick *digo* for his bath did not return, decided to go away and said to the women, "Leave your husbands, and we shall go to other lands and take much *digo* with us. Leave your children, for we shall take only the herb with us; later we shall return for the children."

IV. Guahayona left with all the women, and went in search of other lands, and came to Matininó, where he soon left the women and departed for another region called Guanín. The women had left their little children by a brook, and when the latter began to grow hungry, they wept and called on their mothers who had gone away. The fathers could not help their children, and in their hunger the children called out "mama"; they were really asking for the breast. So, weeping and asking for the breast, and saying *too, too* like one who insistently asks for something, they were changed into little animals like frogs, called *tona*, because they had asked for the breast. That is how the men were left without women.

V. *How the women returned to the island of Española, which was formerly called Haiti, that being the name of its inhabitants; and this and the other islands were once called Bohío.* As these Indians have no alphabet or writing, they cannot give a coherent account of these matters, but they have them from their forebears. Therefore their accounts do not agree, not is it possible to write down in an orderly fashion what they say. When Guahayona (he who carried off all the women) went away, he also took with him the wives of his cacique Anacacuya, deceiving these women as he had done the others. There also went a brother-in-law of Guahayona's, named Anacacuya, who entered the sea with him; and when they were in the canoe, Guahayona said to his brother-in-law, "See the beautiful *cobo* in the water." This *cobo* is the periwinkle. When Anacacuya looked into the water, his brother-in-law Guahayona grabbed his feet and threw him in the water; thus Guahayona had all the women to himself and left them on Matininó; it is said that today there are only women on that island. And he departed for another island, called Guanín because of what he took away from there.

VI. *How Guahayona returned to the island of Cauta, whence he had brought the women.* They say that when Guahayona was in the land to which he had gone, he saw that he had left a woman in the sea. He had great pleasure with her, but soon had to look for many bathhouses in which to wash himself because he was full of those sores that we call the French Sickness.[5] She placed him in a *guanara*, which means a place apart; there he was cured of his sores. Afterwards she asked permission to continue on her way, which he granted. This woman was named Guabonito. And Guahayona changed his name, henceforth calling himself Albeborael Guahayona. And Guabonito gave to Albeborael Guahayona many *guanines* and many *cibas* to wear tied on his arms; these *cibas* are stones which much resemble marble and which they wear about their necks and arms; they wear the *guanines* in their ears, which they perforate when they are small; these *guanines* are made of a metal like that of which florins are made. They say that these *guanines* began with Guabonito, Albeborael Guahayona, and the father of Albeborael. Guahayona stayed in that country with his father, named Hivna. His son took from his father the name Híaguaili Guan, which means the son of Hivna; later he called himself Guanín, and is called that today. As the Indians have no alphabet or writing, they do not tell their myths well, nor can I write them down accurately, and I fear that I am telling last things first and the first last; but I put it down just as I had it from the natives of the country.

VII. *How there again were women on the island of Haiti, which is now called Española.* They say that one day the men went to wash themselves; and while they were in the water, it rained hard, and they felt great desire for women; frequently when it rained they sought traces of their wives, but could not find them. However, that day, as they were washing themselves they saw falling from the trees, sliding down the branches, some creatures that were neither men nor women, and had neither male nor female genitals. They tried to catch them, but they slipped away like eels. So by orders of their cacique they summoned two or three men who should see how many of these creatures there were, and who should bring as many men of the kind called *caracaracol*, because they had rough hands, who would be able to catch them and tie them down. They told the cacique there were four of these creatures; so they brought four men who were *caracaracoles*. This *caracaracol* is a sickness like the scab that makes the body very rough. When they had caught them, they considered how they could make women out of them, since they had neither male nor female genitals.

VIII. *How they devised a way of making women of them.* They found a bird now called *inriri*, and in ancient times *inrire cahubabayael*, that is, a woodpecker, which bores holes in trees. Then, seizing those women without male or female genitals, they bound their hands and feet, and tied that bird to the body of each. The bird, thinking they were trees, began his accustomed work, pecking and hollowing out the place where women's genitals are wont to be. The Indians say that is the manner in which they acquired women, as told by their oldest men. As I wrote in haste and had not enough paper, I could not put everything where it belonged, yet I have made no mistake, for they believe everything that is written here. Turning now to what I should have related first, I shall tell their beliefs concerning the origin of the sea.

IX. *How the sea was made.* There was a man called Yaya, whose name they do not know; his son was called Yayael, which means son of Yaya. This Yayael wishing to kill his father, the latter banished him, and he was banished for four months; after that his father killed him and put his bones in a calabash which he hung from the ceiling of his hut, where it hung for some time. One day, wishing to see his son, Yaya said to his wife, "I want to see our son Yayael." She was content and, taking the calabash, turned it over to see the bones of their son. Out of it came many large and small fish. Perceiving that the bones had been changed into fish, they decided to eat them. One day, when Yaya had gone to his maize fields, that were his inheritance, there came four sons of a woman named Itiba Cahubaba, all born at a single birth; for this woman having died in childbirth, they cut her open and took out these four sons. And the first one they took out was *caracaracol*, which means scabby, and his name was . . . ; [6] the others had no name.

X. The four twin sons of Itiba Cahubaba, who died in childbirth, went together to get the calabash in which Yaya kept the bones of his son Yayael who had been changed into a fish; but none of them dared to get it except Deminan Caracaracol, who took it down; and they all had their fill of fish. While they were eating, they heard Yaya coming back from his fields; and in their haste to hang the calabash up again they did not do it right, so that it fell to earth and broke. They say so much water came out of the calabash that it filled the whole earth, and with it came many fish. They say this was how the sea began. After they had left this place they met a man named Conel, who was dumb.

XI. *What happened to the four brothers when they were fleeing from Yaya.* The brothers, coming to the door of Bayamanaco's house, noticed that he had cassava, and said, "Ahiacabo Guarocoel," which means "Let us make the acquaintance of our grandfather." Then Deminan Caracaracol, going ahead of his brothers, entered the house to see if he could find some cassava, which is the bread of that country. Caracaracol, entering the house of Bayamanaco, asked him for some cassava. At this Bayamanaco put his hand to his nose, took out a *guanguayo*, and threw it at Caracaracol's shoulder; this *guanguayo* was full of *cohoba* which he had had made that day and is a powder that they sometimes take as purge and for other purposes which will be told hereafter. They take it by means of a cane half an ell long, putting one end of this cane in the nose and the other in the powder; they snuff this powder into the nose, and it purges them greatly. So he gave them that *guanguayo* instead of bread, and he went away very angry because they had asked him for it. Caracaracol then returned to his brothers and told them what had happened with Bayamanaco, of the blow that he had given him on the shoulder with the *guanguayo*, and that it hurt him sorely. His brothers looked at his shoulder and saw that it was much swollen, and that swelling grew so that he was about to die. They tried to cut it, without success, but taking a stone hatchet, they managed to open it, and out came a live female turtle; so they built a hut and fed the turtle. I could not learn any more about this, and what I have written is of little worth.

They also say that the sun and moon came out of a cave in the country of a cacique named Mautia-Tenuel; this cave is called Iguana, and they feel great reverence for it. It is all painted in their fashion, without any figure, but with many leaves and the like. In this cave there were two stone *cemíes*, about half a man's arm in size, their hands tied; they seemed to be sweating. They held these *cemíes* in much regard; they say that when they needed rain they would visit these *cemíes*, and the rain would immediately come. One of these *cemíes* was called Boinayel, and the other Marohu.

XII. *Their beliefs concerning the wanderings of the dead, of their appearance, and what they do.* They believe the dead go to a place called Coaibai, on one side of an island called Soraya. They say that the first to live there was one Maquetaurie Guayaba, who was lord of Coaibai, home and dwelling place of the dead.

XIII. *Of the forms which they assign to the dead.* They say that during the day the dead live in seclusion, but at night walk about for recreation and eat of fruit called *guayaba*, which has the flavor of [the quince B. K.] [7] and during the day is . . . [8] but at night is changed into fruit; and they have festivities and keep company with the living. The Indians have this method of identifying dead people: They touch the belly of a person with the hand, and if they do not find a navel, they say that person is *operito*, which means dead; for they say that dead persons have no navels. Sometimes one who does not take this precaution and lies with a woman of Coaibai is mocked; for when he holds her in his arms, she suddenly disappears and his arms are empty. They still believe this. When a person is alive, they call his spirit *goeiz;* when he is dead, *opia.* They say that this *goeiz* appears to them often, now in the shape of a man, now of a woman. They say there was a man who wished to fight with a spirit; but when he closed with it, it disappeared, and the man flung his arms about a tree from whose branches he hung. All of them, young and old, believe this; they also believe that the spirits appear to them in the shape of their father, mother, brothers, relatives, or in some other shape. The fruit that they believe the dead eat is the size of a peach. The dead do not appear to them by day, but only by night, and therefore one who walks about at night feels great fear.

XIV. *Whence come these beliefs and why they persist in them.* There are certain men among them, called *bohutís,* who practice great frauds upon the Indians, as shall be explained hereafter, to make them believe that they, the *bohutís,* speak with the dead and that they know all their deeds and secrets, and that when the Indians are ill they cure them. These deceptions I have seen with my own eyes, whereas the other things I told about I heard of only from others, especially from their principal men—because these men believe these fables more firmly than the others. Like the Moors, they have their religion set forth in ancient chants by which they are governed, as the Moors are by their Scripture. When they sing their chants, they play an instrument called *mayohavau* that is made of wood and is hollow, strong, yet very thin, an ell long and half as wide; the part which is played has the shape of a black-smith's tongs, and the other end is like a club, so that it looks like a

Curing the Sick

Indian Canoe

gourd with a long neck; this instrument is so sonorous that it can be heard a league and a half away. To its accompaniment they sing their chants, which they know by heart; and their principal men learn from infancy to play it and sing to it, according to their custom. Now I shall tell many other things concerning the ceremonies and customs of these heathen.

XV. *Of how the* buhuitihus *practice medicine, and what they teach the people, and of the deceptions they practice in their cures.* All the Indians of the island of Española have many different kinds of *cemíes.* In some they keep the bones of their father, mother, relations, and forebears; these *cemíes* are made of stone or wood. They have many of both kinds. There are some that speak, others that cause food plants to grow, others that bring rain, and others that make the winds blow. These simple, ignorant people, who know not our holy faith, believe that these idols or rather demons do all these things. When an Indian falls ill, they bring the *buhuitihu* to him. This doctor must observe a diet just like his patient and must assume the suffering expression of a sick man. He must also purge himself just as the sick man does, by snuffing a powder called *cohoba* up his nose. This produces such intoxication that they do not know what they are doing; and they say many senseless things, declaring that they are speaking with the *cemíes* and that the latter are telling him the cause of the illness.

XVI. *What these* buhuitihus *do.* When a *buhuitihu* goes to call upon a patient, before leaving his hut he takes some soot from a cooking pot, or some charcoal, and blackens his face in order to make the sick man believe whatever he may say about his sickness; then he takes some small bones and a little meat, wraps the whole in something so it will not fall out, and puts it in his mouth. Meanwhile the patient has been purged in the manner described above. Entering the sick man's hut, the doctor sits down, and all fall silent; if there are any children in the hut, they are put out so they will not interfere with the *buhuitihu's* work; only one or two of the principal men remain. Then the *buhuitihu* takes some *güeyo* herb, . . .[9] wide, and another herb, wrapped in an onion leaf four inches long (but the *güeyo* herb is what they all generally use), and taking it between his hands, he mashes it into a pulp; and then he puts it into his mouth at night so as to vomit anything harmful that he may have eaten. Then he begins to sing his chant and, taking up a torch, drinks the juice of that herb. This done, he is quiet for a time; then he rises, goes toward the sick man, who lies alone in the middle of the hut, and walks about him twice or as many times as he thinks proper. Then he stands in front of him and takes him by the legs, feeling of his body from the thighs to the feet, after which he draws his hands away forcefully, as if pulling something out. Then he goes to the door, shuts it, and speaks to it, saying: "Begone to the mountain, or the sea, or where you will"; then, after he has blown like one who blows chaff from his hand, he turns around, joins his hands together as if he were very cold, blows on his hands, and sucks in his breath as if sucking marrow from a bone, then sucks at the sick man's neck, or stomach, or shoulder, or cheeks, or the belly or some other part of the body. Having done this, he begins to cough and make a face as if he had eaten something bitter; then he spits into his hand the stone or bone or piece of meat that he put in his mouth at home or on the road. And if it is a piece of food, he tells the sick man, "You must know that you have eaten something that caused the sickness from which you suffer. See how I have taken it out of your body, where your *cemí* lodged it because you did not pray to him or build him a shrine or give him some land." If it is a stone, he says, "Take good care of it." Sometimes they believe these stones are good and help women in childbirth, and they take good care of them, wrapping them in cotton, placing them in small baskets, and putting food before them; they do the same with the *cemíes* they have in their houses. On a holiday, when they have much food—fish, meat, or bread—they put some of each food in the house of the *cemí*, and next day they carry this food back to their huts after the *cemí* has eaten. But it would truly be a miracle if the *cemí* ate of that or anything else, for the *cemí* is a dead thing of stone or wood.

XVII. *How these physicians are sometimes paid back for their deceptions.* If the sick man should die in spite of having done all these things, and if he has many relations or one who is lord over a village and so can stand up to the *buhuitihu* or doctor (for men of small influence dare not contend with them), then those who wish to do the *buhuitihu* mischief do the following: First, in order to learn if the sick man died through the doctor's fault, or because he did not observe the diet that the doctor prescribed for him, these relations take an herb which is called *güeyo*, whose leaves resemble those of the sweet basil, being thick and long; this herb is also called *zacón*. They squeeze the juice from the leaf, then cut the dead man's nails and the hair above his forehead, pound the nails and hair to a powder between two stones, mix this powder with the juice of the herb, and pour the mixture between the dead man's lips to find out from him if the doctor was the cause of his death and whether he observed his diet. They ask this of him many times, until at last he speaks as distinctly as if he were alive and answers all their questions, saying that the *buhuitihu* did not observe the diet, or was the cause of his death. They say that the doctor asks him if he is alive, and that he can speak very clearly; he replies that he is dead. After they have learned from him what they want to know, they return him to the grave from which they took him. They perform this sorcery in still another way. They take the dead man and make a great fire like that used for making charcoal, and when the wood has turned to live coals, they throw the body into that fierce blaze; then they cover it with earth, as the charcoal-burner does the charcoal, and leave it there as long as they think advisable. Then they ask him the same question as above. The dead man replies that he knows nothing. This they ask of him ten times, and ten times he replies in the same way. Again they ask him if he is dead, but he will speak only those ten times.

XVIII. *How the dead man's relatives avenge themselves when they have had a reply through the sorcery of the potions.* The dead man's relations assemble on a certain day and lie in wait for the said *buhuitihu,* give him such a thrashing that they break his legs, arms, and head, and leave him for dead. At night, they say, there come many different kinds of snakes—white, black, green, and many other colors—that lick the face and whole body of the physician whom the Indians have left for dead. This they do two or three nights in succession; and presently, they say, the bones of his body knit together again and mend. And he rises and walks rather slowly to his home. Those who meet him on the road say, "Were you not dead?" He replies that the *cemíes* came to his aid in the shape of snakes. And the dead man's relations, very angry and desperate because they thought they had avenged the death of their kinsman, again try to lay hands on him; and if they catch him a second time, they pluck out his eyes and smash his testicles, for they say no amount of beating will kill one of these physicians if they do not first tear out his testicles.

How the dead man whom they have burned reveals what they wish to know, and how they take their vengeance. When they uncover the fire, the smoke rises until it is lost from sight, and when it leaves the furnace, it makes a chirping noise. Then it descends and enters the hut of the *buhuitihu* or doctor. If he did not observe the diet, he falls sick that very moment, is covered with sores, and his whole body peels. This they take for a sign that he did not observe his diet, and so they try to kill him in the manner described above. These are the sorceries they perform.

XIX. *How they make and keep their wooden or stone cemíes.* They make the wooden *cemíes* in this fashion. If a man walking along the way sees a tree moving its roots, he stops, filled with fear, and asks who it is. The tree replies, "Summon a *buhuitihu*, and he will tell you who I am." Then that man goes in search of a physician and tells him what he has seen. The sorcerer or warlock immediately runs toward that tree, sits down by it, and prepares a *cohoba* for it, as described in the story of the four brothers. And having made the *cohoba*, he rises, and pronounces all its titles as if it were a great lord, and says to it: "Tell me who you are and what you are doing here, and what you want of me and why you summoned me. Tell me if you want me to cut you down, and if you wish to come with me, and how you want me to carry you; for I shall build a house for you and endow it with land." Then that *cemí* or tree, become an idol or devil, tells him the shape in which it wants to be made. And the sorcerer cuts it down and carves it into the shape that it has ordered, builds a house for it and endows it with land; and many times a year he makes *cohoba* for it.

This *cohoba* is their means of praying to the idol and also of asking it for riches. When they wish to know if they will gain a victory over their enemies, they enter a hut to which only the principal men are admitted. And the lord is the first to make the *cohoba* and plays an instrument; and while he makes the *cohoba* none may speak. After he has finished his prayer he remains for some time with bowed head and arms resting on his knees; then he lifts his head, looks up to the sky, and speaks. All respond to him in a loud voice, and having spoken, they all give thanks; and he relates the vision he had while stupefied with the *cohoba* that he snuffed up his nose and that went to his head. He tells that he has spoken with the *cemí* and that they will gain the victory, or that their enemies will flee, or that there will be many deaths, or wars, or famines, or the like, or whatever comes to his addled head to say. One can imagine the state he is in, for they say the house appears to him to be turned upside-down and the people to be walking with their feet in the air. This *cohoba* they make not only for the *cemíes* of stone and wood but also for the bodies of the dead, as told above.

There are different kinds of stone *cemíes*. Some the doctors extract from bodies of sick people, and it is believed these are the best to induce childbirth in pregnant women. There are other *cemíes* that speak; these have the shape of a large turnip with leaves that trail over the ground and are as long as the leaves of the caper bush; these leaves generally resemble those of the elm, others have three points: The natives believe they help the yucca grow. The root resembles that of the radish, and the leaf generally has six or seven points. I know not with what to compare it, because I have seen no plant like it in Spain or in any other country. The stalk of the yucca is as high as a man.

Now I shall tell of their beliefs concerning their idols and *cemíes,* and how they are greatly deluded by them.

XX. *Concerning the* cemí *Buya y Aiba, which was burned in time of war, and afterwards, being washed with the juice of the yucca, its arms, eyes, and body grew back.* Because the yucca plant was stunted, they washed [this *cemí* B. K.] with water and the aforesaid juice in order to make it large; they say this *cemí* made ill those who had made it because they had not brought it cassava to eat. The name of this *cemí* was Baibrama. And if someone fell ill, they called the *buhuitihu* and asked him the cause of that sickness. The *buhuitihu* replied that Baibrama had caused it because food had not been sent to the caretakers of that *cemí's* house.

XXI. *Concerning the* cemí *of Guamorete.* They say that when they built the house of Guamorete, who was a principal man, they put in it a *cemí,* which he kept on top of his house; the name of this *cemí* was Corocote. Once in time of war the enemies of Guamorete set fire to his house. Then, they say, Corocote got up and walked a crossbow shot from that place, next to the water. They further say that while he lived on the top of that house he would come down at night and lie with the women. After Guamorete died this *cemí* fell into the hands of another cacique, and continued to lie with women. They also say that two crowns grew on his head, and that is why they used to say [of someone B. K.], "since he has two crowns he is certainly the son of Corocote." All this they believed without question. This *cemí* later fell into the hands of another cacique named Guatabanex, and the place where he lived was named Jacagua.

XXII. *Concerning another* cemí *named Opiyelguobirán, who belonged to a principal man named Sababaniobabas, who had many vassals.* They say this *cemí* Opiyelguobirán had four legs, like a dog, and was made of wood, and frequently left his house by night and went into the woods. They would go in search of him, and bring him back to the house tied with cords, but he always returned to the woods. They say that when the Spaniards arrived on the island of Española, this *cemí* fled and went to a lagoon; they followed him there by his tracks, but never saw him again, and know nothing more of him. That is the story they tell, and faithfully do I tell it again.

XXIII. *Concerning another* cemí *named Guabancex.* This *cemí* lived in the land of a principal cacique, named Aumatex. It is a woman, and they say she has two other *cemíes* for companions; one is a herald and the other is the collector and governor of the waters. They say that when Guabancex is angry, she raises the winds and water, throws down houses, and tears up the trees. They say this *cemí* is a woman and is made of stones of that country. Her herald, named Guatauba, carries out her orders by making the other *cemíes* of the province help in raising wind and rain. Her other companion is named Coatrisquié; of him they say that he collects the waters in the valleys between the mountains and then lets them loose to destroy the countryside. The people hold this to be gospel truth.

XXIV. *Their beliefs concerning the* cemí *named Baraguabel.* This *cemí* is an idol who belongs to a principal cacique of the island of Española and goes by various names. He was found in a manner that I shall now relate. They say that one day in the past, before the island was discovered [by the Spaniards B. K.], but they do not know how long ago, some Indians while hunting found an animal which they pursued; it threw itself into a ditch, and when they looked for it, they saw a log that seemed alive. At sight of this the hunter immediately ran to his lord, who was a cacique and the father of Guaraiconel, and told him what he had seen. They went there and found it to be as the hunter had said, so they took that log and built a house for it. They say the *cemí* left that house several times and returned to a place near that place whence they had brought him. The aforesaid lord or his son Guaraiconel sent men to search for the *cemí*, and they found him hiding; they tied him up again and put him in a sack; yet, tied as he was, he got away as before. These ignorant people hold this to be most certain truth.

XXV. *Concerning what is alleged to have been said by two principal caciques of the island of Española, one of them Cacibaquel, father of the aforesaid Guaraiconel, and the other, Guamanacoel.* The great lord who they believe is in heaven (as I wrote at the beginning of this book) ordered Caicihu to fast, which they all generally do, staying in seclusion six or seven days at a time without eating or drinking anything except the juice of the herbs with which they also wash themselves. When the fasting period is finished, they begin to take nourishment. During the time of their fast their bodily and mental weakness causes them to see things that they perhaps wanted to see. They all fast in honor of their *cemíes,* in order to learn from them if they will gain a victory over their enemies, to acquire riches, or to satisfy some other desire. And they say this cacique claimed to have spoken with Yucahu-guamá, who had announced to the cacique that those who succeeded to his power would enjoy it only a short time because there would come to his country a people wearing clothes who would conquer and kill the Indians, and that they would die from hunger. At first they thought he referred to the cannibals; later, reflecting that the cannibals only robbed and then went away, they decided he must have meant some other people. That is why they now believe that the idol prophesied the coming of the Admiral and the people who came with him.

Now I shall tell what I have seen and experienced. When I and other brothers were about to depart for Castile, I, Fray Ramón, a poor anchorite [was ordered B. K.] to remain, and I went to the fortress of La Magdalena, which was built by Don Christopher Columbus, Admiral, viceroy, and governor of the islands and mainland of the Indies, by order of King Ferdinand and Queen Isabella our masters. While I was in that fort, in the company of its captain, Arteaga, God was pleased to enlighten with the light of the Holy Catholic Faith the entire household of the principal chief of the province in which stands the fortress of Magdalena. This province was called Macorix, and its lord is named Guanaoconel, which means "son of Guanaóbocon." In that house were his servants and favorites, who are called *yahu naboriu;* there were sixteen persons in all, all relations of his, including five grown brothers. One of them died, and the other four received the water of holy baptism, and I believe they died martyrs, as is shown by their constancy and the manner of their death. The first to be killed after baptism was an Indian named Guaticavá, who received the baptismal name of Juan. He was the first Christian to suffer a cruel death, and certain am I that he died a martyr's death. I learned from some who were present when he died that he repeatedly said, *Dios naboria daca, Dios naboria daca,* which means, "I am the servant of God." His brother Antonio and another who was with him died in the same manner, uttering the same words. The people of this household always were attentive to my wishes. All those who have survived are still Christians, thanks to the work of the aforesaid Christopher Columbus, viceroy and governor of the Indies; and now, through God's favor, there are many more Christians.

Now I shall tell what happened in the fortress of La Magdalena. While I was there, the Lord Admiral came to relieve Arteaga and some other Christians who were besieged by their enemies, the subjects of a principal cacique named Caonabó. At that time the Lord Admiral told me that the province of Magdalena had a language that was different from any other and was not understood elsewhere on the island, and that I should go to live with another principal cacique named Guarionex, a lord over many vassals, as his language was understood throughout the country. By his order, then, I went to live with Guarionex. However, I said to the governor, Don Christopher Columbus, "Sir, how can your Lordship ask me to stay with Guarionex, when the only language I know is that of Macorix? Let your Lordship permit to come with me one of the Nuhuirey" (these people later became Christians) "who know both languages." He granted my wish, and said I might take along anyone I wished. And God was pleased to give me for companion the best of all the Indians, and the best instructed in the Holy Catholic Faith; afterwards He took him from me: Praised be God who gave him to me and then took him away. Truly I looked upon him as my own good son and brother. He was Guaicavanú, who afterwards became a Christian under the name of Juan.

I, a poor anchorite, shall tell some of the things that befell us there, beginning with how I and Guaicavanú departed for Isabela and there waited for the Lord Admiral until his return from the relief of Magdalena. As soon as he returned, we set out for the place where the Lord Governor had sent us, accompanied by Juan de Ayala, who had command of the fortress of La Concepción that the Governor Christopher Columbus had built half a league from the place where we were going to reside. The Lord Admiral ordered Juan de Ayala to provide us with food from the stores of the fortress. We stayed with the cacique Guarionex almost two years, during which time we instructed him in our holy faith and the customs of the Christians. At first he appeared well disposed toward us, causing us to believe that he would do all we wished and wanted to become a Christian, for he asked us to teach him the Pater Noster, the Ave Maria, the Credo, and all the other prayers and things that are proper for a Christian to know. He learned the Pater Noster, the Ave Maria, and the Credo, as did many other persons of his household; he said his prayers every morning and made the people of his household say them twice a day. But he later grew angry with us and backslid from his good purposes on account of the principal men of that country, who scolded him for obeying the Christian law. They said the Christians were cruel and had taken their lands away by force; therefore they advised him to pay no heed to the Christians; instead they should take counsel together how they might best kill the Christians, since these were insatiable and there was no way of placating them. So he gave up his good ways and we, seeing that he was drawing away from us and abandoning our teachings, decided to go where we might have more success in indoctrinating the Indians in our holy faith. So we left for the country of another principal chief who seemed well disposed toward us and said he wanted to be a Christian. This cacique was named Maviatué.

How we departed for the country of Maviatué, being I, Fray Ramón Pane, a poor anchorite, Fray Juan de Borgoña, of the Order of St. Francis, and Juan Matthew, who was the first to receive baptism on the island of Española. The day after we left the village and dwelling of Guarionex for the land of the cacique Maviatué, the people of Guarionex built a hut next to the chapel, where we had left some images before which the neophytes could kneel and pray and find comfort; these neophytes were the mother, brothers, and relatives of Juan Matthew; afterwards seven others joined them. Eventually all the members of his household became Christians and remained loyal to our holy faith, keeping watch over that chapel and some fields that I had caused to be tilled. On the second day after our departure for Maviatué's village, by orders of Guarionex six men came to the chapel and told the seven neophytes who had it in charge to take the sacred images that I had left in their care and destroy them, because Fray Ramón and his companions had gone away and would not know who had done it. The seven boys who guarded the chapel tried to prevent them from entering; but they forced their way in, took the sacred images, and carried them away.

XXVI. *What happened to the images, and of the miracle that God caused to pass in order to show his power.* After leaving the chapel those men threw the images to the ground, heaped earth on them, and pissed on top, saying, "Now will you yield good and abundant fruit"; they offered this insult because they had buried the images in a tilled field. Seeing this, the lads who watched over the chapel ran to their elders, who were in the fields, and told them that Guarionex's people had desecrated the images and had jeered at them. The Indians immediately left what they were doing and ran crying to tell what had happened to Don Bartholomew Columbus, then governing for his brother the Admiral, who had sailed for Castile. As the viceroy's lieutenant and governor of the islands, he brought those wicked men to trial, and their crime having been established, he caused them to be publicly burned at the stake. However, Guarionex and his people persisted in their evil design of killing all the Christians on the day assigned for them to pay their tribute of gold. The conspiracy being discovered, they were made prisoners on the very day set for their revolt. Yet some persevered in their design, killing four men and Juan Matthew, the chief clerk, and his brother Antonio, who had been baptized.

Then those rebels ran to the place where they had hidden the images and broke them to pieces. Several days later the owner of the field went to dig up some yams (which are roots that look like turnips or radishes), and in the place where the images had been buried two or three yams had grown together in the shape of a cross. This cross was found by the mother of Guarionex—the worst woman I ever knew in those parts. She regarded it as a great miracle, saying to the governor of the fort of Concepción, "God caused this wonder to appear in the place where the images were found, for reasons known only to Himself."

Let me now tell how the first Indians to receive baptism were made Christians, and what is required to make them all Christians. Truly, this island has great need of men who will punish those Indian lords who will not let their people receive instruction in the Holy Catholic Faith; for those people cannot stand up to their lords. I speak with authority, for I have worn myself out in seeking to learn the truth about this matter. But all this is clear from what I have already said: A word to the wise is sufficient. The first Christians on Española, then, were those I have mentioned, namely, Yavauvariú and seventeen persons of his household, all of whom became Christians merely by being taught that there was a God who made all things and created Heaven and earth. There was no need of further discussion or instruction, so well disposed were they to the faith. But with others force and craft are necessary, for we are not all of the same nature. Whereas those I spoke of made a good beginning and a better end, there are others who begin well and afterwards mock what was taught them: Such require the use of force and punishment.

The first Indian to receive baptism on Española was Juan Matthew, baptized on the feast day of St. Matthew the Evangelist in the year 1496, and followed in baptism by all the members of his household. More progress would be made if there were clergy to instruct them in the Holy Catholic Faith, and people to hold them in check. And if I am asked why I think this business so easy, I shall say that I know it by experience, especially in the person of the principal cacique, named Mahuviativiré, who for three years now has continued to be a good Christian, keeping only one wife, although the Indians are accustomed to have two or three wives, and the principal men up to ten, fifteen, and twenty.

This is what I have been able to learn through diligent inquiry of the customs and rites of the Indians of Española, and I seek neither spiritual nor temporal benefit from it. If it redound to the praise and service of Our Lord, may He be pleased to give me strength to persevere; if not, may He deprive me of my understanding.

End of the work
of the poor anchorite Ramón Pane.

CHAPTER 63

How the Admiral Returned to Spain to Give an Account to the Catholic Sovereigns of the State of the Island of Española

Returning to the main theme of my history, I say that the Admiral, having pacified the island and built the little town of Isabela and three forts in that country, decided to return to Spain to report to the Catholic Sovereigns about many things relating to their service. He decided on this especially because many spiteful envious men were giving the Sovereigns false accounts of what was happening in the Indies, to the great prejudice of the Admiral and his brothers. Accordingly, on Thursday, March 10, 1496, he embarked with two hundred and twenty-five Christians and thirty Indians. When it had barely dawned, he hoisted sail and with winds from the east beat up the coast with the *Santa Cruz* and the *Niña*, the same two caravels with which he had explored the island of Cuba. Tuesday, March 22d, he lost sight of the eastern end of Española and sailed directly east as much as the wind permitted. As the winds were easterly, his provisions running low, and his men tired and in bad humor, on April 6th he bore away south for the Caribbees, which he reached three days later, anchoring at Maríagalante on Saturday, April 9th.

Next day he set sail again (although it was not his custom to leave port on Sunday) because the men complained that since they were searching for food, they need not observe the holidays so strictly. So he stood over to Guadalupe, where he anchored and sent some armed boats ashore; but before they reached the beach a multitude of women armed with bows and arrows and with plumes on their heads rushed out of the woods and assumed a menacing attitude. On this account and also because the sea was rather choppy, the men in the boats had two Indians from Española swim ashore to inform the women about the Christians. When told that the Christians only wanted to barter their truck for provisions, the women replied they should go to the northern shore of the island, where their husbands would furnish them with what they needed. Sailing close under the shore, the Admiral's men saw many Indians with bows and arrows who shot at them and uttered great cries, but the arrows fell short. Seeing the armed boats coming ashore, the Indians withdrew to form an ambush; and when our men were about to land, they attacked in order to prevent it. Frightened by the lombard shots fired from the ships, they retreated, leaving their possessions and houses, which the Christians entered, looting and destroying all they found. Being familiar with the Indian method of making bread, they took their cassava dough and made enough bread to satisfy their needs. In the huts they found large parrots, honey, wax, and iron which the Indians used to make little hatchets; and there were looms, like our tapestry looms, on which they weave cloth. The huts were not round in shape, as is customary on the other islands, but square; in one they found a human arm roasting on a spit.

While the bread was being made, the Admiral sent forty men on a reconnaissance of the island to learn something of its nature and resources. Next day they returned with a haul of ten women and three boys, all the others having fled. Among the prisoners was a cacique's wife who almost got the better of a very swift-footed and courageous Canary Islander who had come with the Admiral. She would have escaped from him if, seeing that he was alone, she had not tried to make him prisoner; she grappled with him, threw him to the ground, and would have choked him if the other Christians had not come to his aid.

The women bandage their legs from the calf to the knee with woven cotton to make them look thicker; they call this adornment *coiro* and think it very elegant; they make the bandage so tight that if it is loosened for any reason the leg looks very thin. The

Jamaicans, both men and women, also have this custom and even bandage their arms up to the armpit, so that they look as if they wear armlets such as were once used among us. Their women are excessively stout, so that some of them are an ell and more around; in other respects their bodies are well proportioned. As soon as their sons can stand and walk, bows are placed in their hands so that they may learn to shoot. These Indians wear their hair long, flowing over their shoulders, and go about completely naked. The lady cacique who was made prisoner said the whole island belonged to women, and that the persons who had kept the armed boat from going ashore also were women, with the exception of four men who happened to be there because at a certain period of the year they come to lie with them. This same custom prevailed among the women of another island named Matininó, of whom they told what certain books tell of the Amazons. The Admiral believed it on account of what he had seen of those women and because of the energy and strength they displayed. These women also seemed more intelligent than those of other islands; for the others only measured time by the sun by day and by the moon at night, while these women kept count of time by the other stars, saying: When the Car rises, or such and such a star descends, then is the time to do so and so.

CHAPTER 64

How the Admiral Sailed from the Island of Guadalupe for Castile

After they had made enough bread to last them twenty days, having already an equal amount aboard the ships, the Admiral prepared to continue his voyage to Castile. Observing, however, that that island was as it were the stepping stone and entrance to the others, he decided to gain the friendship of those women by giving them some presents to atone for the injuries that had been done them. He then sent them all ashore except the lady cacique, who agreed to go to Castile with a daughter of hers in the company of some other Indians who had been brought from Española. One of them was that King Caonabó mentioned above, the greatest and most famous Indian of that island, and that because he was not a native of it but of the Caribbees.

Wednesday, April 20th, having taken on water, bread, and wood, the Admiral set sail from the island of Guadalupe. With the wind ahead and much calm, he continued sailing as near the twenty-second degree of latitude as the wind permitted; for at that time men had not learned the trick of running far northward to catch the southwest winds. As they made little way and carried so many people, by May 20th they began to feel great want of provisions, all being reduced to a daily ration of six ounces of bread and a pint and a half of water. Although there were eight or ten pilots aboard the caravels, none of them knew where they were; but the Admiral was very confident that their position was somewhat to the westward of the Azores, stating his reasons in his journal as follows: "This morning the Flemish needles varied a point to the northwest as usual; and the Genoese needles, which generally agree with them, varied slightly to the northwest; later they oscillated between easterly and western variation, which was a sign that our position was somewhat more than one hundred leagues to the west of the Azores; because when we were just at one hundred leagues and there were only a few scattered branches of gulfweed in the sea, the Flemish needles varied to the northwest a point, and the Genoese needles cut the true north-north; and when we shall be farther east-northeast, they will do something else."

This was quickly verified the next Sunday, May 22d, by which indication and the certainty of his dead reckoning he then found that he was one hundred leagues from the Azores; at which he marveled and assigned the cause to the difference of the lodestone with which the needles are magnetized, because up to that meridian they all varied a point to the northwest, and then some held steady, while the others (the Genoese) pointed right to the Star. And the same thing happened the next day, May 24th.

Holding on their course, on Wednesday, June 8th, while all the pilots went about like men who were lost or blind, they came in sight of Odemira, between Lisbon and Cape St. Vincent. The night before, while all the other pilots thought they were several days' sail from land, the Admiral ordered sails taken in for fear of striking land, saying they were near Cape St. Vincent, at which all the pilots laughed, some declaring they were in the Flemish Channel and others that they were near England. Those who were least mistaken said they were off Galicia and therefore should not take in sails, for it was better to die by running on the rocky coast than to perish miserably from hunger at sea. So great was their want of provisions that some, like Caribs, proposed to eat the Indians aboard; others were of the opinion they should save the little food they had by heaving the Indians overboard, and would have done it, too, if the Admiral had not forbidden it, saying that as Christians and human beings, they should not be treated worse than others, for which humanity God rewarded them the next day with the sight of land, as the Admiral had promised.

From that time on the seamen regarded the Admiral as most expert and admirable in matters of navigation.

CHAPTER 65

How the Admiral Came to Court, and of the New Voyage to the Indies That the Catholic Sovereigns Intrusted to Him

On arrival in Castile, the Admiral prepared to set out for the city of Burgos. The Catholic Sovereigns were there to celebrate the marriage of the most serene Prince Don Juan, their son, with the Archduchess Margarita of Austria, the Emperor Maximilian's daughter, who was then brought to the Prince and received with solemn pomp by the majority of the Spanish nobility and the most illustrious concourse of people ever assembled in Spain.[1] But of these matters I shall not speak (though I was present as page to the said Prince), as they are not relevant to my history and the chroniclers of their Highnesses have doubtless done them justice.

· 173 ·

The Life of the Admiral Christopher Columbus

I return to the Admiral's affairs. On arrival at Burgos he was well received by the Catholic Sovereigns, to whom he presented a great quantity of things and specimens that he brought from the Indies, including various birds, animals, trees, and plants, as well as such implements and things as the Indians have for their use and pleasure: many masks and belts with plates of gold set in place of eyes and ears; and gold dust in its natural state, fine or large as beans and chickpeas and some the size of pigeon eggs. Later this was not regarded as remarkable, for they found nuggets weighing more than 30 pounds, but at that time it was held to be a wonderful thing, and to portend what the future might bring, so the Catholic Sovereigns accepted it with rejoicing as a great service.

After he had given the Sovereigns a report about everything that related to the welfare and settlement of the Indies, the Admiral desired to return immediately, fearing that some disaster or misfortune might befall the settlers, especially since he had left them in great want of provisions and other necessities. But insist as he might, since the affairs of that court are usually attended by delay, ten or twelve months passed before he obtained the dispatch of two relief ships under the command of Captain Pedro Fernández Coronel.

Those ships sailed in February, 1497, but the Admiral stayed to attend to the outfitting of the rest of the fleet that he required for his return voyage to the Indies. It was more than a year before he could see the end of this business; during that time he resided at Burgos and Medina del Campo. At Medina del Campo, in 1498,[2] the Catholic Sovereigns granted him many favors and privileges in what related both to the Admiral's affairs and estate and to the better government and administration of the Indies. I shall give account of these things here [3] in order to make clear the good will of the Sovereigns toward him and their desire to reward him for his merits and services. Later, because of the lying reports of spiteful and envious men, they changed their demeanor and permitted injuries and offenses to be done to him, as I shall presently relate.

At Seville, whither the Admiral departed from the Court, the dispatch of the fleet was much delayed through neglect and mismanagement on the part of the royal officials, and especially of Don Juan de Fonseca, Archdean of Seville and later Bishop of Burgos. This gave rise to the mortal hatred that Don Juan ever after bore for the Admiral and his projects, heading the faction that caused him to lose the favor of the Catholic Sovereigns. In order that my brother Diego and I, who had been pages to Prince Don Juan, who had recently died,[4] should not on account of this delay be too long absent from Court, the Admiral on November 2, 1497, sent us from Seville to serve as pages to the most serene Queen Isabella, of glorious memory.

CHAPTER 66

How the Admiral Set Sail from Castile to Discover the Mainland of Paria

Having outfitted his fleet by dint of great toil and diligence, the Admiral on May 30, 1498, set sail from the port of Sanlúcar de Barrameda[1] with six vessels loaded with provisions and other things needed to relieve the settlers on Española. Thursday, June 7th, he arrived at the island of Pôrto Santo, where he heard Mass and stayed long enough to take on water, wood, and other necessities. At nightfall of that day he set sail for the island of Madeira, where he arrived on Sunday, June 10th. The captain of the island received him in the town of Funchal with much kindness and courtesy, and he remained there several days to take on provisions, sailing again on Saturday afternoon.

Tuesday, June 19th, they reached Gomera, where they found a French warship that had captured two Spanish vessels. At the Admiral's approach the Frenchmen slipped cables and made off with their prizes; and the Admiral, thinking they were merchantmen who were fleeing perhaps because they thought our ships were French corsairs, made no effort to pursue. But after they were a considerable way off he learned what had happened and sent three ships after them; and the Frenchmen, taking fright, let one of the captured ships go and fled with the other. But in their fright and haste to escape from port they had not put a sufficient prize crew aboard, so, there being only four Frenchmen and six captive Spaniards aboard that vessel, the latter, seeing that help was on the way, overpowered the French, forced them into the hold, and returned to port under escort of the Admiral's ships. The Admiral ordered the ship returned to its owner and would have punished the Frenchmen if the governor, Alvaro de Lugo, had not intervened on behalf of all the inhabitants of that place, who pleaded with the Admiral to turn the prisoners over to them to be exchanged for six of their people that the Frenchmen had carried away; the Admiral willingly granted their request.

Thursday, June 21st, he set his course for the island of Ferro, and on arrival there he decided to send three of his ships to Española, proceeding with the others to the Cape Verdes, whence he meant to sail in search of the mainland. Accordingly he appointed a captain of each ship in the Española fleet. They were Pedro de Arana,[2] cousin to that Arana who was killed on Española; Alonso Sánchez de Carvajal, councilman of Baeza; and Juan Antonio Colombo, a kinsman of the Admiral.[3] He gave them detailed instructions as to what they must do, ordering that each successively should be captain general of the fleet for a week at a time. Then he departed for the Cape Verdes, and the captains sailed for Española. As the climate of the region through which he sailed was most unhealthy at that season, the Admiral was suddenly seized by grievous pains of gout in the leg, and four days after by a terrible fever, but despite his illness he remained sound of mind and diligently noted the runs made by the ship and the changes in weather, as he had done since the beginning of the third voyage.

Holding on his course, on Wednesday, June 27th, he sighted the island of Sal, one of the Cape Verdes, passed it without calling, and proceeded to another island called Boa Vista—a name that certainly does not correspond to the truth, for it is a miserable and melancholy place. He anchored in a bay on the western shore, nigh to a tiny island and fronting six or seven houses belonging to the island's inhabitants and to the lepers who come there to be cured of their disease. These miserable folk rejoice at sight of a ship as much as and even more than sailors rejoice at sight of land. They hastened to the beach to speak with the sailors sent ashore by the Admiral for water and salt. There is a multitude of goats on this island. Perceiving that the visitors were Castilians, the Portuguese who governed the island for his lord hurried to pay his respects to the Admiral and offered to satisfy all his wants. The Admiral thanked him and ordered that he be shown much courtesy and given refreshments; for as that island is very barren, its inhabitants live very miserably.

Wishing to learn how the lepers cured their disease, the Admiral asked the governor about it and was told the temperate climate of the island was the primary cause of the cure; the second cause was their diet of turtle meat and their smearing of themselves with turtle's blood. By prolonged use of this treatment they are soon cured; but those born with the sickness require a longer treatment.

The reason why there are so many turtles there is that during the months of June, July, and August large numbers of turtles come to the sandy beaches of this island from the coast of Africa; most of these turtles are the size of an ordinary buckler. Each afternoon the turtles come out to sleep and lay their eggs in the sand. At night the Christians go along the beach with lighted torches or lanterns, looking for turtle tracks in the sand. Having found them, they follow them till they come to the turtle; this animal, tired from its long journey, sleeps so soundly that it does not hear the hunter. Then the hunter turns the turtle over on its back and without doing it any other injury goes in search of another, for a turtle cannot, because of its great weight, right itself or move from the place where the hunter has left it. Having caught all they want, they return the next morning to choose those they like best and take them away to eat, letting the smaller ones go.

Such is the wretched mode of life of the lepers, who have no other occupation or food, for the island is very dry and barren, without trees or good water; the water they draw from their wells is very oily and salty. Even the men charged with the defense of that island, being the governor and four others, have nothing more to do than kill goats and salt them for shipment to Portugal. The captain said the goats are so abundant in the mountains that some years they slaughtered a number valued at 3,000 to 4,000 ducats; these goats are all descended from eight goats brought hither by the owner of the island, named Rodrigo Alonso, clerk of the treasury of the King of Portugal. The hunters frequently go four or five months without bread or anything else save goat meat or fish, and that is why they were so grateful for the refreshments that the Admiral had furnished them.

After they had eaten, the governor and his companions, joined by some of the ship's people, went goat-hunting; but to kill as many as were needed for the ship's stores would have taken too long, and the Admiral was in great haste to depart. On Saturday afternoon of the last day in June, therefore, he left for the island of São Tiago, the principal island in the Cape Verde group, which he reached at nightfall the next day, anchoring nigh to a church. He sent a boat ashore to buy some bulls and cows to carry back to Española, but since it was a slow business and he was anxious to go on, he decided not to tarry any longer, especially since he feared his men might fall sick in that unhealthy spot. He writes that from the time of his arrival in those islands he never saw the sky or any star save through a haze so thick and warm that three fourths of the natives of the country were sick, and the rest had a sickly color.

CHAPTER 67

How the Admiral Left the Cape Verdes in Search of the Mainland, and of the Great Heat from Which They Suffered, and of the Clearness with Which He Saw the Pole Star

On Thursday, July 5th, the Admiral left the island of São Tiago, bound for the southwest, intending to sail until he was below the Equator [1] and then sail due west until he struck land or reached a point from which he could sail over to Española. But on account of the very strong north and northwest currents between those islands, he could not make much way. He writes on Saturday, July 7th, that he was in sight of the island of Fogo, which was still one of the Cape Verdes. He says of this island that it is very high toward the south, and from afar resembles a great church with a campanile on its east side in the shape of a very high steep peak, which emits much fire and smoke when the winds blow from the east, as also happens on Tenerife, Mount Vesuvius, and Mount Etna. He held on a southwest course until he found himself five degrees from the Equator, where, after they had sailed continually in the aforementioned haze, the wind fell; this calm lasted eight days, with a heat so excessive that it scorched the ships. None could endure staying below deck, and but for an occasional rain that obscured the sun I believe they would have been burned alive together with their ships. The first day of that calm being clear, the heat was so great that they must have perished if God had not miraculously relieved them with the aforesaid rain and mist. So, having turned somewhat northward and gotten seven degrees above the Equator, he decided not to sail any further south but instead proceed due west, at least until he could see how the weather was shaping up. For on account of the heat he had lost many casks of wine and water, which burst, snapping their hoops, and all their wheat and other provisions were scorched.

He writes that about the middle of July he very carefully took the altitude of the North Star and found a remarkable difference between that parallel and the Azores. In the Azores, when the Guards were at the East Arm, the North Star was lowest, and gradually rose, so that when the Guards were overhead, the North Star was two degrees and a half higher; and being once past that, it began to descend the same five degrees it had ascended. He writes that he had made this observation several times and with favoring weather conditions. But where he now was, in the Torrid Zone, it happened quite otherwise. When the Guards were at the Head position the altitude of the North Star was 6 degrees, and six hours later, when the Guards passed West Arm, the North Star stood 11 degrees above the horizon; and in the morning, when the Guards were below the horizon, the North Star was elevated 16 degrees. So that the difference was ten degrees, and made a circle whose diameter was ten degrees, whereas in the other place it made but five, lowering the position; for there it is lowest at the West Arm, and here when it is at the Head.

He found this very difficult to understand, and after much pondering came to the conclusion that in what relates to the circumference of the star's circle, at the Equator it appears as it is in reality, and the nearer one draws to the Pole the less it seems to be because the heaven is more oblique. As for the northwest variation, I believe the North Star has the same quality of the four quarters as the magnetic needle, which if touched on the east, will point to the east, and similarly to the west, north, or south; that is why the compass-maker covers with a cloth every part of the lodestone except the north part, that is, the part that has the virtue of making the needle point north.

CHAPTER 68

How the Admiral Discovered the Island
of Trinidad and Sighted the Mainland

Tuesday, the last day of July, 1498, having sailed westward so many days, the Admiral concluded the Caribbee Islands must be to the north of him. He therefore decided not to hold on that course any longer but to make for Española, not only because he was in great want of water but also because all his provisions were spoiling. He also feared that in his absence some mutiny or disorder might take place among the people he had left there, as had actually happened. He therefore altered his course from the west and stood north, thinking that on the way he might strike one of the Caribbees, where the sailors could rest and the ships take on wood and water, of which they were very short. One day at noon a sailor from Huelva by the name of Alonso Pérez Nizardo, climbing to the crow's nest, saw land some fifteen leagues to the westward. It had the appearance of three mountains joined at the base; a little later they perceived that this land extended northwestward as far as the eye could reach. So, after all had given many thanks to God and recited the Hail Mary and other devout prayers that sailors are accustomed to say in time of rejoicing as in adversity, the Admiral gave that island the name of Trinidad, both because he had intended to give that name to the first land he should find and because he wished to show his gratitude to God, Who had shown him those three mountains all together.

He then sailed due west toward a cape which lay to the south and cruised along the southern shore of that island till he came to anchor five leagues beyond a point that he called Cabo de la Galera,[1] from a nearby rock that from a distance looked like a galley under sail. As he now had only one cask of water for all his ship's crew, and the other ships were in the same plight, and there was no good watering place there, he continued on Wednesday morning on his course west and anchored at another point that he named Punta de la Playa.[2] The sailors went ashore with much merriment and took water from a pleasant brook; they encountered no people or village in the vicinity, though all along that coast they had seen many huts and villages. They did find signs of fishermen who had fled, leaving their fishing tackle behind; also they found many footprints of animals that seemed to be goats and the skeleton of a hornless animal that they judged to be a macaque or small monkey. They later knew this opinion to be true, from the many animals of that kind they saw in Paria.[3]

That same day (August 1st), sailing southward between Cabo de la Galera and Punta de la Playa, they saw the continent on their left, twenty-five leagues away; but they thought it was another island and the Admiral named it Isla Santa.[4] The coast of Trinidad extends thirty leagues from one point to the other, unbroken by a single harbor its entire length. The whole country was very lovely, with woods reaching down to the water's edge and many villages and huts. They covered this distance in a very short time, because the sea current set so strongly westward that it looked like an impetuous river, both day and night and at all hours, although the tide on this shore rises and falls more than sixty feet; this happens at Sanlúcar de Barrameda, whose waters rise and fall with the tide, yet never cease to flow out to sea.

Chapter 69

How the Admiral Went to the Punta del Arenal, and of a Canoe That Came to Speak to Him

As they had no opportunity to speak with the natives of the country at the Punta de la Playa, and there was no good watering place there, or one in which they could repair their ships or obtain provisions, the Admiral proceeded the next day, August 2d, to another point that seemed to be the western end of that island and named it Punta del Arenal.[1] There he anchored, thinking it offered better protection from the east wind that blew in that region and hindered the boats in coming and going ashore.

As they sailed toward this point a canoe with twenty-five persons began to follow them; a lombard shot away the Indians stopped paddling and called out to them. Our people did not understand a word they said, but the Indians were probably asking what sort of men the Spaniards were and whence they came, as the Indians are accustomed to do. Since words could not persuade the Indians to come nearer, our men tried to coax them by showing brass pots, mirrors, and other things of which Indians are usually very fond. This brought them a little closer, but from time to time they stopped as if in doubt. Then the Admiral tried to lure them by staging a show, with a pipe-and-tabor player mounting the prow, while another sang and played a kettle-drum and some grummets did a dance. At this the Indians assumed a warlike posture, taking up their shields and beginning to shoot arrows at the entertainers, who promptly stopped their performance.[2] Unwilling to let this insolence go unpunished lest they feel contempt for the Christians, the Admiral ordered some crossbowmen to shoot at the Indians, who, finding it difficult to retreat, paddled over to the *Vaqueña* without sign of fear or hesitation. The *Vaqueña's* pilot entered their canoe and gave them some trifles that pleased them greatly; they said that if the Christians came ashore, they would bring them bread from their houses. Then they left for shore, and the ship's people did not detain any for fear of displeasing the Admiral. They said these Indians were of very handsome appearance and had lighter skins than those on the other islands; that they wore their hair long, like women, tied in the back with small strings; and that they covered their private parts with breechclouts.

CHAPTER 70

Of the Danger the Ships Were in While Passing Through the Boca de la Sierpe, and How Paria Was Discovered, Being the First Discovery of the Mainland

As soon as the ships had anchored at Punta del Arenal, the Admiral sent boats ashore for water and to secure an Indian interpreter, but they could do neither, that land being very low and uninhabited. Next day he ordered some wells dug in the sand, but by good fortune they found some already made that contained excellent water; they decided some fishermen must have made them.

Having taken all the water they needed, the Admiral decided to make for another mouth to the northwest that he later named the Boca del Dragón [1] to distinguish it from the one he was in, which he named the Boca de la Sierpe. [2] These mouths are formed by the two western points of Trinidad and two points issuing from the mainland, and they lie almost due north and south of each other. In the middle of the Boca de la Sierpe, where the Admiral was anchored, was a large rock that he named El Gallo. [3] Through this mouth or channel the water ran northward as furiously as if it were the mouth of a vast river, [4] and they named it the Boca de la Sierpe on account of the fright that it gave them.

As they lay securely at anchor there came a wave much greater than usual, running through the mouth northward and making a very great noise. And from the Gulf they now call "of Paria" there issued another wave, racing toward the first, so that they came together like two fighters, with a horrid din, causing the sea to rise up like a mountain or hill the whole length of that channel. This mountainous wave came toward the ships to the great terror of all, who feared to be swamped, but by God's grace it passed below the ships or rather it raised them up and dropped them down again without doing any injury, save that it snapped one ship's cable and swept it from its anchorage, until it hoisted sails and fled from that place. The fury of the wave having soon passed, and seeing how dangerous was that channel, the Admiral set his course through the Boca del Dragón, which lies between the northwest point of Trinidad and the eastern point of Paria. He then sailed westward thinking Paria to be an island and hoping to find an egress northwards toward Española. Though there were many harbors along the coast of Paria, he did not put in any of them, for the whole sea was a harbor, being enclosed by the mainland on all sides.

Chapter 71

How in Paria They Found Gold and Pearls and People of Goodly Condition

August 5th, as he was at anchor and from motives of piety did not wish to set sail that day, which was Sunday, the Admiral sent some boats ashore to a place where they found much fruit of the kind they had seen on the other islands, many trees, and signs of people who had fled for fear of the Christians.[1] Not wishing to tarry there any longer, he proceeded fifteen leagues up the coast. A canoe with three men drew up to the side of the caravel *Correo*, and the pilot, knowing how eager the Admiral was to have speech with those people, pretended he wanted to speak with them, then jumped into the canoe, overturning it. The ship's people picked up those three Indians and their canoe and brought them before the Admiral, who treated them kindly and sent them ashore with many presents. On the shore were many Indians, who, being told by those

· 184 ·

three how well they had been treated, came in their canoes to engage in barter.

They had the same possessions as the other Indians, save that they did not have wooden shields or bucklers; nor did they use the poisonous herb for their arrows, only the Caribs having that practice. For drinking they had a liquor white as milk and another that verged on black and tasted like green wine made of unripe grapes, but our people could not learn from what fruit it was made.[2] They wore well woven cotton cloths in various colors, of the size of handkerchiefs but some larger than others; of our things they prized most articles of brass and especially hawk's bells. They seemed to be of better disposition and more intelligent than the Indians of Española. They cover their private parts with varicolored cloths of the kind mentioned above and wear another cloth about the head. The women cover nothing, not even their genitals; this is also true of the women on the island of Trinidad.

Our men saw nothing here of any value except some small gold mirrors that the Indians wore about their necks; for this reason and because the Admiral lacked the time to investigate the secrets of that country he ordered six Indians taken aboard and continued westward, never suspecting that that land of Paria, which he named Isla de Gracia, was a continent.

Soon afterwards he sighted an island to the south and another of equal size to the west, very mountainous, with sown fields and thickly populated; the Indians here had more gold mirrors about their necks than the others, and many *guanines,* which is a base gold. They said it came from other islands to the west, inhabited by cannibals. The women had on their arms strings of beads interspersed with large and small pearls, some of which the Admiral obtained by barter to send to the Catholic Sovereigns. Asked where they found those things, they indicated by signs that they found them in oyster shells that they gathered to the west and north of the land of Gracia. Therefore the Admiral determined to make a stop there, in order to obtain more certain news of this fortunate discovery. He sent boats ashore, where all the people of that country had gathered. They appeared peaceful and friendly, and begged the Christians to come with them to a nearby house, where they regaled them with food and much of their wine. From this house, which must have been their king's palace, they escorted them to another belonging to a son of his, where they were shown the same

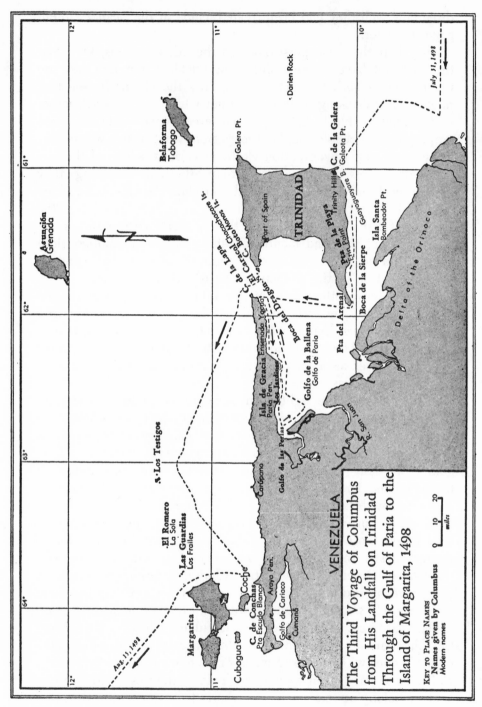

The Third Voyage of Columbus from His Landfall on Trinidad Through the Gulf of Paria to the Island of Margarita, 1498

KEY TO PLACE NAMES
Names given by Columbus
Modern names

courtesy. These Indians were all lighter-skinned than any others they had seen, and acted and looked better, having their hair cut short above the middle of the ear in Castilian fashion. The Spaniards learned from them that that land was named Paria and that they were pleased to be friends with the Christians; thereupon our men took leave of them and returned to the ships.

CHAPTER 72

How the Admiral Sailed Out Through the Boca del Dragón, and of the Danger That He Ran

Holding on his westward course, the Admiral found the depth of the sea ever less, so that having come through four or five fathoms of sea, they found only two and a half at ebb tide, with the tide differing from that at the island of Trinidad. There the water rose three fathoms, and here, forty-five leagues to the westward, it rose only one; there, whether ebb or tide, the current flowed westward, while here at flood it flowed eastward and at ebb to the west; there the water was brackish and here like river water. Observing these differences, and how shallow was the water there, he dared not go on with his ship, which, being almost 100 tons, could not navigate in less than three fathoms. He therefore anchored on that coast, which was very secure because it had a harbor in the form of a horseshoe.

Meanwhile he sent the small caravel *Correo* to survey if there was a passage westward amid those islands. Having gone only a short distance, she returned the next day, August 11th, with a report that at the western end of that sea there was a mouth two leagues wide from south to north, and within, a round bay, with four other smaller bays, one toward each quarter of heaven; from each bay there issued a river whose waters made all that sea so sweet, and farther on the water was much sweeter than where the

Admiral was.[1] From this the Admiral concluded that all that land that he had taken for islands was really but a single continent, especially since in all that sea they had never found more than four or five fathoms of depth, and so much seaweed that they could hardly make their way through it.

Being now very certain he could not get out by sailing westward, that same day he turned eastward with the aim of getting out by the strait that he had seen between the land of Gracia, which the Indians called Paria, and Trinidad. This strait is bounded on the east by the extremity of Trinidad, which the Admiral named Cabo Boto,[2] and on the west by the extremity of the island of Gracia, to which he gave the name Punta de la Lapa; [3] in the middle of this strait are four small islands.

He named it the Boca del Dragón because of the fury with which the fresh water rushes out to sea there, forming three boisterous currents that extend east to west the whole width of the channel. And because the wind failed him as he was sailing through and he ran great danger of being dashed to pieces by the current on some shoal or reef, he had good reason to give it that name. But it pleased Our Lord that what they feared most should prove their salvation, for that same strong current carried them to safety.

Without more delay, on Monday, August 13th, he began to coast westward along the north shore of Paria, intending later to stand over for Española. He gave many thanks to God Who had delivered him from so many trials and dangers, ever pointing out to him new lands filled with peaceable folk and great wealth, and especially that land which he now firmly believed to be a continent because of the great size of the Golfo de las Perlas [4] and of the rivers issuing from it, because all the water in that sea was sweet, because Esdras in Chapter 8 of his fourth book says that of the seven parts of this sphere only one is covered with water, and also because all the Indians in the Cannibal Islands had told them that to the south there lay a very large continent.

CHAPTER 73

How the Admiral Stood Over from the Mainland to Española

Cruising westward along the coast of Paria, the Admiral continually tended offshore to the northwest because the calms and currents set him in that direction, so that on Wednesday, August 15th, he left the cape that he named de Conchas[1] to the south, and Margarita to the west. He gave that island its name, perhaps by divine inspiration, because next to this island lies that of Cubagua, from which an infinite quantity of pearls or margarites has been taken. A similar thing happened on Española, where on his return from Jamaica he named certain mountains Todos de Oro, and in those mountains was later found the greatest quantity of gold dust ever brought from Española to Spain.

I return to the Admiral's voyage. He held on his course by six little islands that he called Las Guardias;[2] three others that lay farther north he named Testigos.[3] They discovered much more land to the west of the coast of Paria, but the Admiral writes that he could not give as full an account of it as he wished because continual watching had made his eyes bloodshot, and therefore he had to write down what he was told by his sailors and pilots. He adds that that same night, Thursday, August 16th, the needles, which until then had not varied to the northwest, suddenly varied more than a point and a half to the northwest, and some more than two points; he could not have been mistaken because he had always kept careful watch. Marveling at this, and regretting that he had not the opportunity to cruise along the coast of the mainland, he held almost due northwest until Monday, August 20th, when he anchored between Beata Island and Española.

From there he sent some Indians with letters to his brother the Adelantado, acquainting him with his safe arrival and the prosperous outcome of his voyage. He was astonished to find himself so far to the west, for he did not think that the deviation produced by the currents could have been so great. Fearing he might run out of provisions, he stood to the eastward for Santo Domingo,

Columbus at the Island of Margarita

putting in this port on August 30th.⁴ The Adelantado had founded
the city on the east bank of the river, where it stands today, naming it in memory of his father, who bore the name Domingo.

CHAPTER 74

Of the Rebellion and Disorders Caused by the Evil Alcalde Mayor, Roldán, That the Admiral Found on His Return to Española

Entering the city of Santo Domingo almost blind from his continual vigils, the Admiral hoped to rest after that difficult voyage
and find his people at peace. But he found all at sixes and sevens,
for all the families of the island were infected with a disorderly
and rebellious spirit. Part of the people he had left were dead, and
of the survivors more than one hundred and sixty were sick with
the French sickness. Many had joined the rebel Roldán. Moreover,
the relief ships he had dispatched from the Canaries had not arrived.

I shall relate the course of events in their order, beginning with
the day on which the Admiral left for Castile. He sailed in March,
1496, thirty months elapsing before the day of his return to Española. At the commencement of this period, anticipating the Admiral's speedy return with relief for themselves, the people remained fairly peaceful. But after the passage of a year, with their
provisions running short and suffering and sickness growing, they
became discontented with their present lot and despaired of the
future. These disaffected persons making their complaints heard,
there arose among them one who sought to stir up the others and
make himself head of a faction. This man was Francisco Roldán,
a native of Torre de Donjimeno, whom the Admiral had appointed
alcalde mayor,¹ by which he obtained so much prestige and au-

thority among both Indians and Christians that he was obeyed as if he were the Admiral himself. For this reason there was not between him and the Adelantado, who was governor, that harmony that the public weal required, as time and events showed. Since the Admiral neither returned nor sent any aid, Roldán began to dream of making himself master of the island, having first killed the Admiral's brothers, the principal obstacles to his scheme; and he only awaited an opportunity to put his plan into effect.

It happened that the Adelantado journeyed to a western province named Xaraguá, about eighty leagues from Isabela, leaving Roldán as his lieutenant but under the authority of Don Diego, the Admiral's younger brother. This gave Roldán such offense that while the Adelantado was away compelling the kings of that province to pay the tribute that the Admiral had imposed on the Indians of the island, Roldán began secretly to form a faction.

But since evil never dares raise its head without some pretext, Roldán seized on the fact that on the beach at Isabela there was a caravel that the Adelantado had had built for sending to Castile if it proved necessary. Although it could not be launched for lack of tackle and other equipment, Roldán claimed this was not so and demanded it be fitted out that some of them might carry to Castile the news of their distress.

On this pretext he demanded the launching of that caravel; and because Don Diego Columbus would not consent, citing the lack of tackle and rigging, Roldán began to conspire ever more brazenly to have it launched in spite of Don Diego. He told his partisans that the Adelantado and Don Diego opposed it only because they wished to remain masters of the island and keep the rest in subjection, fearing lest the Catholic Sovereigns learn of their tyranny. For, said Roldán, they knew how hardly and cruelly the Adelantado treated them, forcing them to work in the fields and build forts; and since they had no hope of the Admiral's return with relief, they would do well to take that caravel and obtain their liberty, disdaining to be ruled by a foreigner for wages that were never paid them, while they could be leading an easy and abundant life. All the wealth of the island should be equally divided among them, and they should be allowed to use the Indians as they pleased, free from interference, whereas now they might not even take for themselves any Indian woman they pleased. The Adelantado not only made them observe the three monastic vows [2] but also imposed fasts and floggings, jailings and chastisements, and that for the most trivial fault. Moreover, he (Roldán) had the wand of justice and royal authority, so that no harm would come to them whatever they might do; they should therefore do as he advised, since they could not go wrong.

With such words, inspired by his hatred for the Adelantado and hope of gain, he attracted so many to his side that one day, the Adelantado having returned from Xaraguá to Isabela, some of them planned to stab him to death, thinking it such easy work that they had ready a rope to hang him up with after he was dead. What wrought them up to do this was the imprisonment of Barahona, a friend of the conspirators. If God had not inspired the Adelantado not to carry out Barahona's death sentence, they doubtless would have killed him then and there.

CHAPTER 75

How Roldán Tried to Seize the Town of
Concepción and Plundered Isabela

Perceiving that his plan to have the Adelantado killed had failed and that his conspiracy was discovered, Roldán determined to seize the town and fortress of Concepción,[1] believing that with that place as his base he could easily subjugate the whole island. It was very convenient for his plan that he was near that town, for in the Adelantado's absence he had been sent by Don Diego with forty men to pacify the Indians of that province, who had risen with the same aim of seizing the fort and killing the Christians. With the pretext of wishing to put an end to this mischief and punish the Indians, Roldán gathered his men on the farm of a cacique named Marque, intending to carry out his plan at the first opportunity. But the commander of the fort, Ballester, who already had some doubts of his loyalty, kept a strong guard and sent word of his danger to the Adelantado. The latter with all speed gathered as many men as he could and hurried to shut himself up in the fort. As his conspiracy was discovered, Roldán went to the fort with a safe-conduct, not so much to discuss a settlement as to see what mischief he could do the Adelantado; and with shameless insolence he demanded that the Adelantado have the caravel launched or let him and his friends do it.

Angered by these words, the Adelantado replied that neither Roldán nor his friends were seamen and so knew nothing of handling a ship; even if they could launch her, they could not sail without rigging and other equipment, the lack of which would expose ship and crew to great danger. The Adelantado spoke as an expert seaman, but they were landlubbers who knew nothing of the business, so the variance of views continued. Having exchanged these and other angry remarks, Roldán marched away in a passion, refusing to resign his office of alcalde mayor or settle their differences as the Adelantado would have him do. He declared he would not do either until the King, whom he represented on the island, had ordered him to do so, for he knew he could expect no justice from the Adelantado, who by one means or another would seek an opportunity to kill him or do him some other injury. Yet (said he) to prove he was a reasonable man he would go to reside where the Adelantado bid him. Told to proceed to the village of the cacique Don Diego Columbus,[2] he refused, saying there were not enough provisions for his men there and so he would seek a more suitable place.

Thereupon he set out for Isabela, and having assembled sixty-five men and found that he could not launch the caravel, he and his henchmen plundered the arsenal and storehouse, taking all the arms, clothing, and food they pleased; nor could Don Diego Columbus, who was there, do aught to stop them. Indeed, his life would have been in danger if he had not taken refuge in the fortress together with some of his servants—though from the testimony that some later gave in this affair it appears that Roldán promised to obey him if he would declare against his brother. This he would not do, and Roldán, unable to do him other injury and fearful of the reinforcements that the Adelantado was sending his brother, marched out of town with all his rebels. As they moved through the countryside they found herds of cattle grazing and killed all the steers they needed for their food and took what beasts of burden they needed for the road. Their goal was the province of Xaraguá, from which the Adelantado had arrived a short time before. They chose to settle in this province because it was the pleasantest and most fertile part of the island, with the most civilized natives and especially the best-looking and best-natured women in the country: This last was their strongest motive for going there.

They did not wish to leave without trying their strength against the Adelantado before he augmented his forces and chastised them as they deserved, so they decided to march on the town of Concepción, take it by surprise, and kill the Adelantado, who was there; they planned to lay siege to the town if their surprise attack failed. But the Adelantado learned of their plan and prepared his defenses, encouraging his men with spirited words and promises of rich rewards and a grant of two slaves apiece. This he did because he knew most of them hankered after the life Roldán offered his followers and were listening to his envoys. It was in fact the hope that all the Adelantado's men would soon come over to his side that encouraged Roldán to begin and persist in his venture. But matters turned out otherwise, for the Adelantado was not only forewarned but was most courageous, had the best men on his side, and had determined to achieve by force of arms what reason and persuasion had failed to gain for him. Gathering his men, then, he marched out of the fort to meet Roldán on the road.

CHAPTER 76

How Roldán Roused the Indians of That Province Against the Adelantado, and How He and His Men Journeyed to Xaraguá

Disappointed in his hope of luring the Adelantado's men to his side, and lacking the courage to meet him in battle, Roldán determined to carry out his first plan of going to Xaraguá. As he marched through the countryside he hurled insults against the Adelantado and spread slanders about him, saying that he (Roldán) had separated from the Adelantado because he was a harsh and vengeful man to Christians and Indians alike, and a very greedy one, as shown by the many obligations and tributes that he imposed on them. It would avail the Indians nothing to pay their tribute regularly, he told them, for the Adelantado would only increase it again, against the wishes of the Catholic Sovereigns, who desired nothing from their subjects but obedience and wished only to maintain them in peace, liberty, and justice. Proclaiming himself their protector and defender, Roldán told the Indians that if they feared to stand up for their rights, he and his men would defend them. Hearing this, the Indians suppressed the tribute that had been levied on them. The result was that the Adelantado could obtain no tribute from the Indians who lived a great distance away, and he feared to collect it from those nearby lest they be provoked to join the rebels.

This policy of forbearance had little effect, for the Adelantado having left Concepción, Guarionex, the chief cacique of that province, undertook with Roldán's aid to lay siege to the town and fortress and kill the Christians who guarded it. To accomplish this he assembled all the caciques subject to him and secretly agreed with them that each should kill the Christians in his province. Because the area cultivated by each Indian is not large enough to support many people, the Christians were obliged to disperse into bands or companies of eight or ten to a district; this gave the Indians hope that by a surprise attack upon the Christians they might succeed in wiping them all out. Their only way of reckoning time or anything else being on their fingers, the Indians agreed to launch the attack on the first day of the next full moon. After Guarionex had instructed the caciques about this, the principal one among them, desiring to gain honor by what he conceived to be an easy feat, and being in any case too poor an astronomer to know for sure the first day of the full moon, attacked the Christians before the appointed day. He was repelled and forced to flee, and when he sought a haven with Guarionex, was instead put to death for prematurely revealing the conspiracy.

This failure caused the rebels great disappointment, for the conspiracy was hatched with their favor and knowledge, and they had awaited its outcome before forming an alliance with Guarionex to destroy the Adelantado. As matters turned out contrary to their hopes, they did not feel secure in the province where they were, and they departed for Xaraguá, still proclaiming themselves protectors of the Indians.

Actually they were naught but plain thieves, having no regard for God or man and seeking only to sate their inordinate appetites, each robbing what he could and their leader Roldán more than all the rest. Thus he urged and ordered the principal men and the caciques to collect all they could from their people, saying he would protect the Indians and the rebels from the tribute demanded by the Adelantado. With this pretext he took an even greater tribute from them, making a single cacique named Manicaotex pay him a calabash filled with gold dust worth 3 marks every three months; and to insure payment he held the cacique's son and nephew hostages, claiming he did this as a mark of friendship. As my readers may wonder why I reduce gold marks to calabash measure, I should explain that I do it to show that in such cases the Indians, having no weights, dealt by the measure.

CHAPTER 77

How Ships Arrived from Castile with Provisions and Relief

The Christians being so divided, and the relief ships from Castile much delayed in coming, neither the Adelantado nor Don Diego could prevent the growth of discontent among their people. Most of them were men of base condition who hankered for the easy life that Roldán promised; and since they feared being left out in the cold, they were reluctant to join in punishing the rebels. So unruly did they become that there was no way of quieting them, and the Adelantado and Don Diego had to bear without recourse the insults of the rebels.

But the Almighty was pleased to assist them, for at this time there arrived those two ships that had been sent out one year after the Admiral's departure from the Indies as a result of his great importunities and pleadings at Court. The Admiral, knowing the situation on Española and the kind of men he had left there and the great dangers that his long absence might occasion, obtained of the Catholic Sovereigns that two of the fleet of eight [1] ships he had been ordered to outfit should go in advance. The arrival of these ships with reinforcements and food, together with the certain knowledge that the Admiral had landed safely in Spain, encouraged the Adelantado's men to serve him more loyally and inspired fear of punishment in Roldán's followers.

As the rebels wished to hear news of Spain and obtain some provisions for their needs, and also to lure some of the new arrivals to their side, they set out for Santo Domingo, where the ships had put in. But the Adelantado was warned of their coming, and being nearer the port, he placed strong guards at certain passes to bar their way while he proceeded to the port to greet the ships and order the affairs of that city. Since he wanted the Admiral to find the island at peace on his return, he again proposed a settlement to Roldán, who was six leagues distant, and sent as emissary the captain of the newly arrived ships, Pedro Fernández Coronel; the Adelantado chose him because he was a man of worth and honor and because as an eyewitness, he could confirm the Admiral's safe arrival in Spain and the friendly reception and the honors he had received from the Catholic Sovereigns. But the rebel leaders feared the impression Coronel might make on their men and would not permit him to address them in public; they came out to meet him with crossbows and arrows ready, and would only allow him to say a few words to persons appointed for that purpose. Consequently he returned without any agreement, and the rebels departed for their quarters in Xaraguá. Some feared lest Roldán and certain other leaders write to friends in the Adelantado's camp to intercede for them with the Admiral on his return, saying that their just complaints were directed only against the Adelantado and not against the Admiral, whose obedient servants they again wished to be.

CHAPTER 78

How the Three Ships Sent by the Admiral from the Canary Islands Arrived at Xaraguá

Having told of those two ships sent by the Admiral from Castile to Española, I shall now tell of the three that separated from him in the Canaries. These ships had fair weather till they reached the Caribbee Islands, which are the first that mariners encounter on the way to the port of Santo Domingo. As the pilots were not as familiar with the navigation of those islands as are the pilots today, they did not steer a proper course to that port, and they were carried by the currents so far westward that they arrived on the coast of Xaraguá, where the rebels were. Learning that these ships were off their course and did not know of the revolt, some of the rebels made their way aboard, pretending to be there by the Adelantado's orders to secure provisions and pacify the country.

But a secret shared by many is no secret, and before long the most alert of the captains, Alonso Sánchez de Carvajal, had learned the truth. He then sought to negotiate a peace with Roldán, hoping to secure his submission to the Adelantado. But the talks and chumming of the rebels with the ship's people caused Carvajal's efforts to fail; for Roldán had received secret assurances from many of the newcomers from Castile that they would join his gang, and with this advantage he was in no mood to make concessions.

Perceiving that the negotiations were dragging on without issue, Carvajal decided with the approval of the other captains to send the laborers they had brought to work for pay in the mines, or at other tasks, overland to Santo Domingo. The winds and currents being very contrary, the ship might be three months at sea without making port; and in that time their people would consume their provisions and might fall sick, losing time that should have been employed in the service for which they came.

This decision made, Juan Antonio Colombo was selected to march overland with the forty laborers; Pedro de Arana should return with the ships; and Carvajal was to remain and try to reach an agreement with the rebels. However, when Juan Antonio got ready to depart the day after landing, those laborers or rather vagabonds deserted to the rebels, leaving their captain with six or seven loyal men.

Seeing this barefaced treason, Captain Colombo fearlessly accosted Roldán and told him that since he claimed to be a loyal servant of the Catholic Sovereigns, he should not allow these men who had come out to colonize and cultivate the land, and who had already received their wages, to idle away their time instead of working at their tasks. He should prove his good faith by dismissing those men; if he allowed them to stay, he would show that he was moved by a rebellious spirit and hatred for the Admiral, and that he wished to obstruct the service of his Sovereigns.

This incident greatly compromised Roldán and his henchmen, but since it served their purposes, and especially since it was easy to plead helplessness in the face of an offense committed by so many, Roldán excused himself from carrying out the captain's request; he said that he could not coerce his people. His monastery, said he, was governed by rules that denied the habit to no man. Juan Antonio decided it was useless and dangerous to insist without hope of success, so he returned to the ships with his few followers. That the same thing might not occur with the remaining men, both captains hastened to depart for Santo Domingo. The weather proved as contrary as they had feared, and they were delayed many days. Their provisions spoiled, and Carvajal's ship suffered great damage on some shoals where he lost his rudder and sprang a leak in the keel, admitting so much water they had great trouble to bring her in.

CHAPTER 79

How the Captains Found the Admiral in
Santo Domingo

On their arrival at Santo Domingo from Xaraguá, the captains found there the Admiral, who had meantime returned from the continent. Although he was fully informed about the rebels, had seen the charges drawn up by the Adelantado against them, and knew they merited severe punishment, he decided to gather new testimony in order to inform the Catholic Sovereigns of what had happened. At the same time he resolved to be as moderate as he could in this affair, that the rebels might more easily be reduced to obedience. Therefore, that none of the people might say he was held there by force, on September 22d [1] he issued a decree promising food and free passage home to all who desired it.

At this time, learning that Roldán and part of his people were bound for Santo Domingo, he ordered Miguel Ballester, alcaide [2] of the fortress of Concepción, to maintain a good watch over that fortress and province. If Roldán came there, he should tell him that the Admiral greatly deplored his sufferings and all that had happened and that he wished to bury the past in oblivion, granting a general pardon to all; Roldán should come to confer with him without fear of reprisal, that they might consider how the interests of the Catholic Sovereigns could best be served; if Roldán felt he needed a safe-conduct, the Admiral would send him one in such form as he desired.

On September 24th [3] Ballester replied that he had certain news that Riquelme had arrived the day before at the village of Bonao, and that Adrián de Mújica and Roldán, the rebel chieftains, were to meet there seven or eight days later, at which time and place he would be able to capture them, as in fact he later did. [4] He added that he had spoken with them according to the Admiral's instructions but found them very stubborn and brazenly defiant. Roldán declared that he had not come to negotiate and did not want or need peace, for he had the Admiral in the hollow of his hand and could help him or destroy him as he pleased. Roldán also declared there could be no talk of pacts or agreements until they had released all the Indians captured in the siege of Concepción, since they had assembled to serve their King, and with the Adelantado's promise of safety. Roldán said other things that showed he wanted no agreement that was not to his very great advantage. Finally, he asked the Admiral to send Carvajal to negotiate with him; Roldán said he would treat only with Carvajal because he was a reasonable and prudent man, as he had shown at the time of the arrival of the three ships at Xaraguá.

This reply caused the Admiral to distrust Carvajal, and with good cause. In the first place, he recalled that before Carvajal's arrival at Xaraguá, where the rebels were, they had often written to friends who were with the Adelantado that they (the rebels) would place themselves in the Admiral's hands as soon as he arrived, and had prayed those friends to intercede for them with him. Second, if they did this on learning of the arrival of the two ships sent to relieve the Adelantado, they had much more reason to seek clemency after learning of the Admiral's arrival—unless the talk they had with Carvajal dissuaded them. Third, had Carvajal desired to do his duty, he could have made Roldán and his principal lieutenants prisoners aboard his caravel, for they were with him two whole days without a safe-conduct. Fourth, since Carvajal knew they were in rebellion, he should not have permitted them to buy fifty-four swords and forty crossbows. Fifth, having received warnings that the men who went ashore with Juan Antonio Colombo intended to desert to the rebels, he should not have let them land; or, learning that they had joined the rebels, he should have made greater efforts to persuade them to return. Sixth, Carvajal went about declaring that he had come to the Indies to stay with the Admiral and see that he did nothing without him, because in Castile it was feared that the Admiral might commit some blunder. Seventh, Carvajal had brought the Admiral a written message from Roldán saying that by Carvajal's advice he had come to Santo Domingo with his people in order to be nearer at hand when the Admiral arrived at Española, that he (Roldán) might treat with him; and now that the Admiral had come it appeared from Roldán's insolent bearing, in such contrast with the tone of his letter, that Carvajal had invited him so that in case the Admiral was delayed or failed to come, Carvajal himself, as the Admiral's associate, and Roldán as alcalde mayor, might rule over the island in defiance of the Adelantado. Eighth, when the other two captains came by sea with the three caravels and Carvajal came overland to Santo Domingo, he was accompanied and guarded by a rebel leader named Gámez, who stayed two days and nights with him aboard his ship and accompanied him to within six leagues of Santo Domingo. Ninth, Carvajal corresponded with the rebels when they went to the Bonao, and sent them gifts and food. Tenth and last, the rebels would treat only with him and unanimously declared that if they had to choose a new leader, they would make him their captain.

The Admiral reflected, on the other hand, that Carvajal was a discreet and prudent man, and an hidalgo as well, that each suspicious circumstance could separately be explained away, and that what he had been told about Carvajal might not be true. And, finally, regarding Carvajal as a person faithful to his trust and one who sincerely wished to quench the flames of discord, the Admiral decided to consult with all his lieutenants about the answer to be given to Roldán. As all were in accord, the Admiral sent Carvajal and the alcaide Ballester to negotiate a pact.

All they could get out of Roldán, however, was that since they had not released the Indians as he demanded, he would not discuss a pact with them. Carvajal made an effective reply, and argued so well that he persuaded Roldán and three or four of his lieutenants to come to confer with the Admiral. This incensed the other rebels, and when Roldán and some others were mounting their horses to depart with Carvajal, these rebels surrounded them and would not allow them to go. They said that if any agreement was to be made, it must be done in writing, that all might know what it contained. Some days later, therefore, on October 15th, Roldán wrote the Admiral a letter approved by all the rebels in which he put all the blame for the revolt on the Adelantado. He wrote that since the Admiral had not sent them a written safe-conduct so that they might come to explain to him all that had happened, they had decided to send him their conditions for peace in writing.

Their demands were immoderate and insolent; but the next day Ballester wrote the Admiral praising Carvajal's peace-making efforts and declaring that since Carvajal could not convince them to abandon their wicked designs, nothing would do but to grant them the terms they demanded. For such was the spirit of the

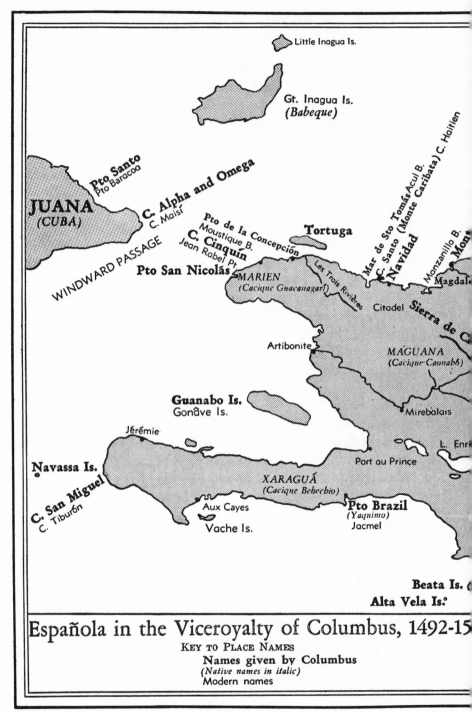

Little Inagua Is.

Gt. Inagua Is.
(Babeque)

C. Haitien

C. Santo (Monte Caribata)

Mar de Sto Tomás Acul B.

Pto Santo
Pto Baracoa

JUANA
(CUBA)

C. Alpha and Omega
C. Maisí

Pto de la Concepción
Moustique B.
C. Cinquín
Jean Rabel Pt.

Pto San Nicolás

WINDWARD PASSAGE

Tortuga

Les Trois Rivières

MARIEN
(Cacique Guacanagarí)

C. Santo **Navidad**

Manzanillo B.

Mont

Magdal

Citadel **Sierra de C**

Artibonite

MAGUANA
(Cacique Caonabó)

Guanabo Is.
Gonâve Is.

Mirebalais

Jérémie

L. Enri

Navassa Is.

Port au Prince

C. San Miguel
C. Tiburón

XARAGUÁ
(Cacique Behechio)

Aux Cayes

Pto Brazil
(Yaquimo)
Jacmel

Vache Is.

Beata Is.
Alta Vela Is.

Española in the Viceroyalty of Columbus, 1492-15

KEY TO PLACE NAMES
Names given by Columbus
(Native names in italic)
Modern names

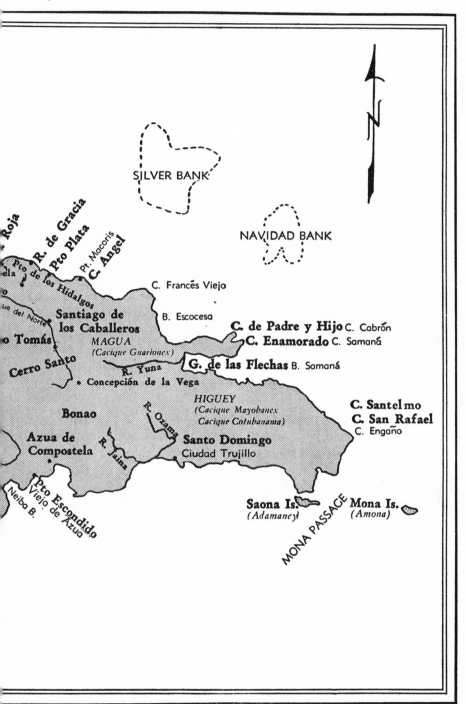

SILVER BANK

NAVIDAD BANK

Roja

R. de Gracia

Pto Plata

Pt. Macoris

C. Angel

Pto de los Hidalgos

ela

ua del Norte

C. Francés Viejo

Santiago de
los Caballeros

o Tomás

B. Escocesa

MAGUA
(Cacique Guarionex)

Cerro Santo

C. de Padre y Hijo C. Cabrón

C. Enamorado C. Samaná

R. Yuna

G. de las Flechas B. Samaná

• Concepción de la Vega

HIGUEY
(Cacique Mayobanex
Cacique Cotubanama)

C. Santelmo
C. San Rafael
C. Engaño

Bonao

R. Ozama

**Azua de
Compostela**

R. Jaina

Santo Domingo
Ciudad Trujillo

Pto Escondido
Viejo de Azua

Neiba B.

Saona Is.
(Adamaney)

Mona Is.
(Amona)

MONA PASSAGE

rebels, he (Ballester) was certain the majority of the Admiral's men would go over to them; and though the Admiral might have confidence in his servants and the honest men about him, they could not resist that great force of rebels, whose number was daily increased by new recruits.

This the Admiral already knew from experience, for in view of Roldán's being so near Santo Domingo the Admiral had mustered up all the men who were fit to bear arms. He found that between those who pretended to be lame and those who claimed to be sick he had less than seventy men to go out against the rebels, and of these less than forty could be relied on. Next day, October 17, 1498, Roldán and the other rebel leaders who had wanted to confer with the Admiral sent him a letter bearing their signatures in which they wrote that they had quit the Adelantado because he plotted to slay them; and that they had awaited the coming of his Lordship, their master, thinking that he would consider what they had done as a service to him. For this reason they had prevented their men from doing any injury to his Lordship or his possessions, as they might easily have done. On his arrival, however, his Lordship not only showed displeasure at their actions, but even sought to harm them. Now, wishing to do honorably that which they had resolved to do and enjoy freedom of action, they were quitting him and his service.

Before the Admiral received this letter, he had already sent Roldán a personal message through Carvajal, expressing his confidence in Roldán and assuring him of the favorable account he had given of him to the Catholic Sovereigns; he added that he had not written to him for fear that if some of the common people saw his letter, they might do Roldán some mischief. Instead of a letter he was sending the alcaide Ballester, in whom (as Roldán knew) he placed great trust, and with whom Roldán could speak as if he were the Admiral himself. Roldán should therefore consider what was proper for him to do, and he would find the Admiral ready to discuss every reasonable proposal.

On October 18th the Admiral dispatched five ships to Spain, and by them he sent the Catholic Sovereigns a detailed account of all that had happened, saying that he had delayed the departure of those ships since his arrival in the belief that Roldán and his men would leave in them as they had announced they would do. The other three ships were being readied for the Adelantado to continue the exploration of the mainland of Paria and to organize the fishing and trade in pearls, samples of which he sent to the Sovereigns with Carvajal.

CHAPTER 80

How Roldán Came to Treat with the Admiral, and How They Failed to Reach Agreement

Three days after he received the Admiral's letter, Roldán replied, expressing readiness to comply with the Admiral's wishes. However, as his men would not consent to his going to see the Admiral without a safe-conduct, he asked that one be sent him in the form described in the letter that he and his lieutenants had signed and sent to the Admiral. The Admiral promptly sent him a safe-conduct (October 26th). Roldán then came to confer with the Admiral, but his insolent demands showed that he was more interested in suborning as many of the Admiral's men as possible than in reaching an agreement. He therefore left the Admiral without any accord, saying he would report everything to his men and would inform the Admiral of their decision. In order that the Admiral might have a representative who could negotiate and conclude an agreement in his name, a major-domo of his, Diego de Salamanca, went with Roldán.

After much debate, Roldán sent certain articles of agreement for the Admiral to sign, and on November 6th he wrote that this agreement was the best he could get from his men. If his illustrious Lordship approved of it, he should send his acceptance to Concepción, because the Bonao no longer supplied enough food for Roldán's people; he (Roldán) would await a reply until next Monday. Having seen this letter and the articles, with their insolent demands, the Admiral would on no account sign them lest he bring justice into contempt and dishonor both himself and his brothers.

But that the rebels might have no further reason to complain or say that he treated them harshly, on November 11th the Admiral ordered publication of an amnesty which was affixed for thirty days to the doors of the fort. Its tenor was that in spite of some differences having arisen during his stay in Castile between the Adelantado and the alcalde mayor Roldán and some other persons who had fled to him, all in general and each individually could safely return to the service of the Catholic Sovereigns as if nothing had happened; and whosoever desired to return to Castile would be provided free passage and given an order for payment of their wages as was customary, providing they presented themselves in the space of thirty days to receive the protection of this amnesty. He warned that if they did not appear within that space of time, he would proceed against them as the law required. Then he sent Carvajal to Roldán with this assurance, signed by himself, together with a written explanation of why he (the Admiral) neither could nor should sign the articles sent to him; he again reminded the rebels of what they should do if they wished to serve the Catholic Sovereigns as their duty required.

With this writing, Carvajal went to Concepción to see the rebels, who acted very proud and haughty, mocking the Admiral's pardon and saying he would soon be seeking a pardon from them. All this happened in the space of three weeks. During that time, on the pretext of wanting to seize a man that Roldán wanted to put to death, they kept Ballester under siege in the fort and cut off his supply of water, thinking that for lack of it he would surrender; but on Carvajal's arrival they raised the siege, and after much dispute between the two sides they reached the following agreement.

CHAPTER 81

The Agreement Made Between the Admiral and Roldán and His Rebels

The agreement made with the alcalde mayor Francisco Roldán and his company for their departure and voyage to Castile:

First, that the Lord Admiral will give him two good ships, vouched by seamen to be properly equipped, to be delivered to him at the port of Xaraguá, because most of his followers are there and because it is the most convenient harbor for securing and getting ready provisions and all else that may be necessary. From that port, with God's favor, the said alcalde mayor and his company will embark for Castile.

That his Lordship will order paid the wages due them up to the day of sailing, and will write to the Catholic Sovereigns attesting to their good service, that they may be paid.

That he shall grant them slaves from the distribution made to the people as compensation for the sufferings they have endured on this island, and for the services they have rendered, confirming this grant. And as some of the said company have mates who are pregnant or have borne them children, if they wish to take these women, they may go in place of the slaves; and their children shall be free and may go with them.

That his Lordship will order the said ships loaded with all the provisions they may need for the said voyage, as has been done with others; and since they cannot be supplied with bread, he will permit the alcalde mayor and his company to secure bread at their own expense wherever they may be, and will see that they are given 3,000 kilograms of biscuit or, in lieu of it, thirty sacks of wheat, so that if their cassava bread should spoil, as might easily happen, they could subsist on the said wheat.

Item, that his Lordship will give safe-conducts to the persons who come to obtain orders for the payment of their wages.

Inasmuch as some of the persons with the alcalde mayor have had some goods taken from them and embargoed, his Lordship will order these goods returned to them.

Item, that his Lordship will give them a letter for the Catholic Sovereigns in which he will attest that certain hogs belonging to the said alcalde mayor have been left behind to provision the people of this island, these hogs numbering one hundred and twenty large and two hundred and thirty small, and will pray their Highnesses to cause him to be paid the price they would have brought on the island. These hogs were taken from him in February, 1498.

That his Lordship will give the said alcalde mayor license to sell some things that he must sell in order to depart, doing with them as he pleases or leaving them in charge of such person as he may designate.

That his Lordship will order the judges to settle speedily the case of the horse.

That if his Lordship finds the claims of Diego de Salamanca to be just, he will write the said judge to cause them to be paid.

Item, that the question of the slaves belonging to the captains will be negotiated with his Lordship.

That inasmuch as the said alcalde mayor and his company fear that his Lordship or some other person acting for him may seek to do them some mischief with the ships remaining on the island, he will give them a safe-conduct, promising in the names of the Catholic Sovereigns and on his faith and word as an hidalgo (as is customary in Spain) that neither his Lordship nor any other person will harm them or prevent their sailing.

Having seen this agreement, made by Alonso Sánchez de Carvajal and Diego de Salamanca with Francisco Roldán and his company, this day, Wednesday, November 21, 1498,[1] I [the Admiral] agree to observe it in its present form on condition that the said Francisco Roldán or any other of his company, in whose names he signed and ratified the capitulation given by him to the aforesaid Alonso Sánchez de Carvajal and Diego de Salamanca, shall not admit into their company any other Christian on the island of any state and condition whatever.

And I, Francisco Roldán, alcalde mayor, in my name and that of all the persons in my company, promise and pledge my faith and word that the above conditions will be observed and carried out without any fraud, loyally and truly, as set down here, his Lordship observing all that has been treated and agreed upon between Señor Alonso Sánchez de Carvajal, Diego de Salamanca, and myself, as is set forth in the articles.

First, that from this day till he gives his reply, which will be in a space of ten days, I shall not admit into my company any of the Lord Admiral's people.

Item, that within fifty days after the said reply is brought and delivered to me in Concepción with his Lordship's approval of what has been agreed upon and signed (which shall be within ten days), we shall embark and sail for Castile.

Item, that none of the slaves that were given us in the distribution shall be taken from us by force.

Item, that if the Lord Admiral should not be present at the port whence we are going to embark, the person or persons sent thither by his Lordship shall be honored and respected as ministers of the Catholic Sovereigns and of his Lordship; these persons will be given an accounting of all that is embarked on those caravels that they make note thereof or do what seems best to his Lordship, and that they may set apart the things in our charge that belong to the Catholic Sovereigns. It is understood that all the said articles are to be signed and executed by his Lordship just as they are carried in writing by the said Alonso Sánchez de Carvajal and the said Diego de Salamanca. I shall await his reply here in Concepción for eight days from this time. And if he should not reply, I shall not be bound by anything said herein.

In witness whereof, and that I and all the men of my company shall observe and carry out all that I have said, I have signed this instrument with my hand.

Done in Concepción this day, Saturday, November 16, 1498.

CHAPTER 82

How, after Making the Agreement, the Rebels Went to Xaraguá, Saying That They Would Embark in the Two Ships the Admiral Was Sending Them

Matters having been arranged as told above, Carvajal and Salamanca returned to Santo Domingo, and on November 21st, at their urging, the Admiral signed the articles that they brought and again granted safe-conducts to all who did not wish to go to Castile with Roldán, promising them wages or land grants on the island, as they chose, and inviting the others to come and arrange everything to their liking. On November 24th Ballester delivered the Admiral's letter to Roldán and his comrades at Concepción, whereupon they set out for Xaraguá to prepare their departure. The Admiral knew how wicked were these men, and he was grieved that by giving them those ships the Adelantado was prevented from continuing the exploration of the mainland of Paria and putting in order the pearl fishery and its trade; but he did not want to give the rebels any excuse for charging that he did not intend to give them the free passage home he had promised. He therefore began to fit out the ships, and the work being slowed by the lack of provisions, in order not to lose time he ordered Carvajal to go overland to Xaraguá with full power to collect supplies and do whatever was necessary to have the rebels ready to sail while the ships were voyaging thither. He then set out for Isabela to look after the safety of that place, leaving Don Diego in charge at Santo Domingo.

At the end of January, 1499, following the Admiral's departure, the caravels *Niña* and *Santa Cruz,* provided with all they needed for the voyage, finally sailed to embark the rebels; however, a great storm that arose on the passage forced them to put in another port till the end of March. As the *Niña* was in bad need of repairs, the Admiral ordered Pedro de Arana and Francisco de Garay [1] to proceed to Xaraguá in the *Santa Cruz* without her. Later Carvajal sailed to Xaraguá in the *Niña* instead of going overland; the voyage required eleven days, and he found the *Santa Cruz* awaiting him there.

CHAPTER 83

How the Rebels Resolved Not to Go to Castile and Made a New Pact with the Admiral

Meanwhile, since the ships were delayed in coming, and most of Roldán's men did not really wish to leave the island, they charged the Admiral with having delayed the dispatch of those ships, and used this delay as a pretext for remaining there. When he learned of this, the Admiral wrote Roldán and Adrián de Mújica, urging them to abide by their agreement; and Carvajal, who was with them in Xaraguá, protested on April 20th before a public notary named Francisco de Garay, later governor of Pánuco and Jamaica, that the Admiral had sent those ships in good order; they should therefore take them and embark according to the agreement. As they would not do it, on April 25th he ordered the ships to return to Santo Domingo, because the shipworms were destroying them and the crews were suffering severely from lack of provisions.

This did not dismay the rebels; on the contrary, they were gay and puffed up with pride that so much was being made of them. Not only did they show no gratitude for the Admiral's efforts in their behalf but they wrote, charging him with responsibility for their staying. They declared that out of spite he had delayed sending the caravels, which in any case were in such wretched state that they could never reach Castile; and even if the ships were seaworthy, they had consumed their provisions in waiting and could not get more for a long time. They had therefore decided to stay and seek redress from the Catholic Sovereigns.

Carvajal returned overland to Santo Domingo with this answer. At the time of his departure Roldán told him that if the Admiral sent another safe-conduct, he would gladly confer with him in an effort to reach a satisfactory agreement; Carvajal transmitted this message to the Admiral in a letter that he sent from Santo Domingo on May 15th. The Admiral replied on the 21st of May, thanking Carvajal for his efforts in this business and sending the safe-conduct he had asked for, together with a brief but strongly worded letter for Roldán, appealing to him to live in peace and obedience to the Catholic Sovereigns. After the messenger had left for Santo Domingo, he wrote again in more detail on June 24th.

On August 3d, six or seven of the Admiral's lieutenants sent Roldán another safe-conduct that he might come to confer with his Lordship. The distance being so great, however, and the Admiral having occasion to visit that country, he decided to sail with two caravels to the port of Azua, which is west of Santo Domingo, in order to be nearer to the province where were the rebels, many of whom came to the port. The Admiral arrived at the end of August and entered into negotiations aboard his flagship with the rebel leaders. He urged them to abandon their evil courses and promised them great rewards and favors. They replied they would do what he asked if he granted them four things. First, he should allow fifteen of them to return to Castile in the first ships that should come from Spain; second, those who chose to stay should be given houses and grants of land in lieu of their pay; third, he should publicly proclaim that all that had happened was caused by false testimony of a few evil men; fourth, he should restore Roldán to his office of perpetual alcalde mayor.

After the Admiral had agreed to these things, Roldán returned ashore and submitted the new articles to his followers. So arbitrary and unreasonable were these articles that a final one empowered the rebels to use force or any other means to make the Admiral comply if he was remiss in carrying any of them out. But the Admiral was eager to put an end to this wretched business, which had dragged on for two years; for he saw that the number and obstinacy of his foes were growing and that many of his own people were plotting to form new gangs and go off by themselves as Roldán had done. So he decided to sign whatever they put before him, and issued two orders, one appointing Roldán alcalde mayor for life, and another granting the aforesaid four demands. He also confirmed all that was contained in the text of the letter given above.

On Tuesday, November 5th, Roldán began to exercise the duties of his office, and by the authority vested in him he appointed Pedro de Riquelme judge of Bonao, with power to punish culprits in all except capital crimes; capital offenders were to be sent to the fort of Concepción for trial by Roldán. Master and man being cut out of the same cloth, Riquelme set about building a stronghold in Bonao, but was stopped by Pedro de Arana, who understood that this work was to the detriment of the Admiral.

CHAPTER 84

How Hojeda, Returning from His Voyage of Discovery, Caused New Disorders on Española

Having settled his dispute with Roldán, the Admiral appointed a captain with a force of men to patrol and pacify the island. They were to compel the Indians to pay tribute and at the first sign of a revolt by Christians or Indians hasten to crush it and punish the rebels. He did this because he wanted to leave for Castile, taking the Adelantado with him, for he knew that if the latter remained as governor it would be difficult to bury old grudges.

As he was preparing to embark, Alonso de Hojeda arrived at the island from a voyage of exploration with four ships.[1] September 5th Hojeda put in the port that the Christians call "Brazil"[2] (and the Indians Yaquimo[3]) to cut logwood and capture Indian slaves. While busied with this, he did all other mischief he could. To show that he was Bishop Fonseca's minion he attempted to cause a new revolt by giving out that Queen Isabella was at death's door and that on her death the Admiral would be without a protector; and that he, as the bishop's good and loyal servant, could do what injury he pleased to the Admiral because of the enmity between those two. In addition to spreading this rumor, he began to write to and have dealings with some men who had played a dubious part in the late troubles.

Being told of Hojeda's actions and plans, Roldán, by order of the Admiral, marched against him with twenty-six men. On September 29th he learned that Hojeda was only one and a half leagues away, in the village of a chief named Haniguayabá, where he was making cassava bread and biscuit; wishing to catch him unawares, Roldán journeyed all that night. Discovering that Roldán was in pursuit of him, and lacking the means to resist his pursuer, Hojeda made a virtue of necessity and came out to meet Roldán with the plea that want of provisions had forced him to seek supplies in this land which belonged to his royal masters the Catholic Sovereigns, but that he meant injury to none. He gave Roldán an account of his voyage, stating that he had come from exploring for a distance

of six hundred leagues westward along the coast of Paria; there he had encountered Indians who fought the Christians very bravely, wounding twenty of his men. This had prevented him from exploiting the riches of that country, where he found stags, rabbits, tiger skins and paws, and *guanines;* he showed Roldán samples of these things aboard the caravels. He said he wanted to depart immediately for Santo Domingo to report to the Admiral about all he had seen and done. At this time the Admiral was much troubled because Riquelme, judge of Bonao by appointment of Roldán, had begun, with the pretext of building a fold for his cattle, to build a stronghold on a hill from which he could sally with a few people to do what mischief he pleased; Arana had therefore stopped him from continuing that work. Riquelme then began a lawsuit, taking the testimony of witnesses and sending the proceedings to the Admiral with a complaint that Arana had used force against him; he prayed the Admiral to intervene in order to avoid greater disorders. The Admiral suspected him of harboring worse designs, but he thought best to dissemble his suspicions while remaining on guard, for he felt he had enough to do to handle Hojeda's open defiance.

Meanwhile Hojeda persisted in his wicked course. In February, 1500, taking leave of Roldán, he sailed for Xaraguá, where lived many of the men who had revolted with Roldán. As greed and self-interest are the most certain means of inciting men to evil, he announced to those people that the Catholic Sovereigns had appointed him and Carvajal to be the Admiral's advisers lest the Admiral do something harmful to the royal interests; he said, moreover, that one of the things the Sovereigns had ordered was that the Admiral should immediately pay in ready money the wages of all who served their Highnesses on the island. Since the Admiral appeared unwilling to do this, he (Hojeda) offered to lead them to Santo Domingo to force him to pay up immediately; afterward they could throw the Admiral out of the island dead or alive. In no other way could the Admiral be made to keep his word or the pact he had signed.

With these promises Hojeda persuaded many to follow him, and with their aid he fell one night on those who opposed his plan, and there were dead and wounded on both sides. Being convinced that Roldán, having rejoined the Admiral's service, would not support this new conspiracy, the rebels decided to attack him unawares and make him prisoner. But Roldán got wind of their scheme and marched with a strong force to punish Hojeda and crush the revolt. Hojeda took fright and retreated to his ships; and the one from shore and the other from aboard ship wrangled where they should hold their conference, each fearing to place himself in the power of the other.

As Hojeda would not come ashore, Roldán offered to come aboard to speak with him; he asked Hojeda to send him a boat, which Hojeda did. After the boat had taken Roldán and his men in, the latter rose up and fell upon Hojeda's men, killing some and wounding others; then they rowed the boat ashore. Hojeda now was reduced to a single boat for all his ships; he therefore decided to go peacefully ashore to negotiate with Roldán. He sought to excuse his misdeeds and agreed to release some of Roldán's men that he had captured; in return he asked Roldán to restore his boat and crew, for he faced certain ruin, having no other boat fit for use. Roldán wanted to give Hojeda no cause for complaint, so agreed, but he first drew from Hojeda a pledge that he and his men would leave Española in a certain space of time; to ensure compliance he kept a strong guard ashore until Hojeda left.

But just as a bad weed is not so easily uprooted that it will not grow again, so men of evil habits are with difficulty kept from relapsing into their old courses, as happened with some of the rebels after Hojeda had sailed away. One Don Hernando de Guevara, who was in disgrace with the Admiral as a seditious person, had joined Hojeda out of hatred for Roldán, because the latter had restrained him from taking for wife a daughter of Anacaona, the principal queen of Xaraguá. He lured many into a conspiracy to capture Roldán, planning to succeed him as lord of misrule. He especially egged on Adrián de Mújica, one of the principal rebel leaders, and some other villains; and in mid-June,[4] 1500, they agreed to imprison or kill Roldán. But Roldán was on his guard, penetrated their designs, and managed to capture Don Hernando, Adrián, and the other leaders of the gang. He then notified the Admiral of what had happened and asked him what he should do with the ringleaders. The Admiral replied that they had disturbed the peace without cause and it would be the ruin of the country if they went unpunished; Roldán should punish them as their crimes and the law required. The alcalde mayor promptly brought them to trial, summarily ordered Adrián de Mújica, the author of the conspiracy, to be hanged, banished the others from the country as their offenses required, and held Don Hernando in prison until June 13th,[5] when he handed him over with other prisoners to Gonzalo Blanco to convey to the Vega, where the Admiral was at the time.

This chastisement served to quiet the country. The Indians once more obeyed and served the Christians; and so many gold mines were discovered that all left the royal service and went out prospecting for gold, paying the King a third of all they found. They did so well that one man gathered 5 marks of rather large gold nuggets in a single day; one of them was worth more than 196 ducats. The Indians obeyed and feared the Admiral. They were so eager to please him that they voluntarily offered to become Christians; and if an Indian chief had to appear before him, he took care to come dressed.

For the greater security of the island, the Admiral decided to make a tour of it,[6] and on Wednesday, February 20, 1499, he and the Adelantado left Santo Domingo for Isabela, where they arrived on March 19th. From there they departed on April 5th for Concepción, arriving there the next Tuesday. From this place the Adelantado left for Xaraguá, Friday, June 7th.[7]

> The day after Christmas Day, 1499, all having left me, I was attacked by the Indians and the bad Christians, and was placed in such extremity that fleeing death, I took to sea in a small caravel. Then Our Lord aided me, saying, "Man of little faith, do not fear, I am with thee." And he dispersed my enemies, and showed me how I might fulfill my vows. Unhappy sinner that I am, to have placed all my hopes in the things of this world!

February 3, 1500, the Admiral set out for Santo Domingo, intending to return to Castile and give the Catholic Sovereigns an account of all that had happened.

CHAPTER 85

How, as a Result of False Reports and Complaints of Certain Persons, the Catholic Sovereigns Sent a Judge to the Indies to Learn What Was Happening There

While these disorders went on, many of the rebels, writing from Española, and others who had returned to Castile continually made false charges to the Catholic Sovereigns and their royal council against the Admiral and his brothers, claiming they were cruel and unfit to govern because they were foreigners and had no experience in governing men of quality. These rebels declared that if their Highnesses did not intervene, it would lead to the total ruin of the Indies. And even if ruin were avoided, the Admiral would in time rebel and form an alliance with some foreign prince, claiming the Indies were his possession because he had discovered them by his own efforts and industry. That, said they, was why the Admiral sought to conceal the wealth of that country and did not allow the Indians to serve the Christians or be converted to our faith, hoping thereby to win them to his side and use them against their Highnesses.

With these and similar calumnies they importuned the Catholic Sovereigns, complaining that the Spaniards on Española had not been paid for these many years past; this was the subject of complaint and grumbling by all the malcontents at Court. I remember that when I was at Granada, at the time of the death of Prince Miguel,[1] more than fifty of these shameless wretches bought a quantity of grapes and sat down to eat them in the court of the Alhambra, loudly proclaiming that their Highnesses and the Admiral had reduced them to that pitiful state by withholding their pay, adding many other insolent remarks. They were so shameless that if the Catholic King rode out, they would crowd about him, shouting, "Pay! pay!" And if my brother and I, who were pages to the Queen, happened by, they followed us crying, "There go the sons of the Admiral of the Mosquitoes, of him who discovered lands of vanity and illusion, the grave and ruin of Castilian gentlemen," adding so many other insults that we took care not to pass before them.

As a result of these endless complaints and appeals to the King's favorites, the King decided to send a judge to Española who should inform himself about these matters; in case this judge found the Admiral guilty of the things charged, he should send him home and remain as governor of the island. The Catholic Sovereigns selected as their agent Francisco de Bobadilla, Knight Commander of the Order of Calatrava. On May 21, 1499, at Madrid, they granted him full and unlimited powers, with orders in blank bearing the signature of the Sovereigns and commanding the persons on Española to whom they were shown to extend him all aid and favor.

Bobadilla arrived at Santo Domingo at the end of August, 1500. At the time, the Admiral was in Concepción restoring order in that province, where the Adelantado had been attacked by the rebels and where there were the greatest number of Indians, superior in all respects to all the others of the island. So Bobadilla, finding no one whom he must take into account, promptly took the Admiral's home and all that he found there as if it were his by lawful succession and inheritance. He gathered about him all the former rebels and many others who hated the Admiral and his brothers, and proclaimed himself governor. To gain popularity he issued an order exempting all from payment of tribute for twenty years. He summoned the Admiral to appear before him without delay, in the name of the Catholic Sovereigns. In proof of this, on September 7th he sent Fray Juan de Trasierra to him with the following royal order:

Don Christopher Columbus, our Admiral of the Ocean Sea. We have sent the Knight Commander Francisco de Bobadilla, the bearer of this letter, to say certain things to you in our behalf. We desire you to give him full faith and credit and to act accordingly.

From Madrid, May 26, 1499.

I the King   I the Queen

By their order, Miguel Pérez de Almazán.

CHAPTER 86

How the Admiral Was Imprisoned and Sent to Castile in Chains, Together with His Brothers

As soon as he had read the letter from the Catholic Sovereigns, the Admiral left for Santo Domingo. On his arrival, Bobadilla, who was most anxious to remain in office, neither held a hearing nor took any evidence. Instead, early in October, 1500, he put the Admiral and his brother Diego in chains aboard ship under a strong guard; he forbade anyone publicly to mention them, on pain of very severe penalties. He then held a farcical inquest, taking testimony from their open enemies, the rebels, and showing public favor to and even egging on all who wished to speak ill of the prisoners. From the wicked and shameless things these people said, one had to be blind not to see that they were guided by prejudice rather than truth.

That is why the Catholic Sovereigns would not believe the testimony and ultimately cleared the Admiral of those charges. Indeed, the Sovereigns repented they had ever sent Bobadilla on that mission, and with good reason; for he destroyed the island, and dissipated the royal revenues and tributes in order to gain popularity for himself, proclaiming that the Catholic Sovereigns wanted only the title of dominion for themselves, and their subjects to have all the profits. But Bobadilla did not neglect his own interests. He hobnobbed with the richest and most powerful men on the island, assigning Indians to work for them on condition that they share with him all they got by that means; and he sold at public auction the property and estates that the Admiral had gained for the Catholic Sovereigns, declaring the Sovereigns were not laborers or merchants and wanted no profit from the Indies, but only wished to help and relieve the needs of their subjects. With this pretext he auctioned off everything, but saw to it that some of his cronies acquired this property for one third of its value. He subverted justice to the same end of enriching himself and gaining popularity, because he still feared that the Adelantado, who had not yet returned from Xaraguá, might stop his progress and free the Admiral by force. Actually, the brothers of the Admiral had displayed much self-restraint in this regard, for the Admiral advised them that in order to serve the Catholic Sovereigns and not cause disorders they should surrender to Bobadilla peaceably. Thereby, on arrival in Castile they would the more easily secure Bobadilla's punishment and the righting of their wrongs.

This moderation did not deter Bobadilla from seizing the Admiral and his brothers; he even permitted the malcontents and rabble to shout innumerable insults at them in the public squares, to blow horns in the harbor when they were being taken aboard, and to post scandalous handbills about them on the street corners. Although he knew that one Diego Ortiz, the governor of the hospital, had publicly read a handbill in the town square, he not only did not punish him but showed much glee over it, which made all the others seek to outdo each other in devising taunts and insults.

At the time of the Admiral's departure, Bobadilla, fearing he might escape by swimming ashore, ordered the shipmaster, Andrés Martín, to turn him over to Bishop Fonseca bound in chains; it was generally believed that all Bobadilla did was with the approval and advice of the bishop. As soon as they had put to sea, the skipper, who had come to know Bobadilla's malice, offered to remove his chains, but the Admiral refused. He had been placed in chains in the Sovereigns' name, he said, and would wear them until the Sovereigns ordered them removed, for he was resolved to keep those chains as a memorial of how well he had been rewarded for his many services. And this he did, for I always saw them in his bedroom, and he wanted them buried with his bones.[1]

On November 20, 1500, he wrote the Sovereigns that he had arrived at Cádiz. As soon as they learned that he came in chains, they ordered him set free and wrote expressing their good will toward him and their displeasure at Bobadilla's harsh treatment of him. They requested the Admiral to come to Court, assuring him that he would be treated with honor and his affairs settled with dispatch.

Yet I cannot absolve the Catholic Sovereigns of responsibility for selecting for the post of governor such a bad and ignorant man as Bobadilla. Had he been a person who understood the duties of his office, the Admiral himself would have rejoiced at his coming, for in his letters he had pleaded with the Sovereigns to send out someone who should inform himself of the wicked deeds committed by the rebels, in order that they might be punished with fitting severity by another than himself—who might be charged with partiality because the outbreaks had been directed against his brother. It may be urged that even if the Catholic Sovereigns had unfavorable reports about him, they should not have given Bobadilla such unlimited powers; on the other hand, in view of the many complaints they had received against the Admiral, it is not strange they did so.

CHAPTER 87

How the Admiral Went to Court to Report to the Catholic Sovereigns

As soon as the Catholic Sovereigns learned of the Admiral's arrival and that he came in chains, they gave orders (December 17th) that he be placed at liberty and wrote him to come to Granada. There their Highnesses received him with friendly and affectionate greetings, assuring him that his imprisonment had not been by their wishes or command, that they were much displeased by it, and would see to it that the guilty parties were punished and he was given satisfaction for his wrongs.

With these and similar gracious words they ordered his business promptly attended to: In fine, they decided to send out a governor to Española who should right the wrongs done to the Admiral and his brothers. Bobadilla should be commanded to make restitution of the Admiral's property; the Admiral would receive all that belonged to him according to the capitulations between him and the Sovereigns; and the rebels were to be tried and punished as their offenses deserved. Accordingly, the Sovereigns sent out Don Nicolás de Ovando, Knight Commander of Lares, a wise and prudent man, yet a crafty one, inclined to credit the words of malicious and scheming men and capable of cruelty and a vengeful spirit, as he showed in putting to death the eighty caciques in Xaraguá.[1]

At the time the Sovereigns decided to send out the said Knight Commander, they also resolved to dispatch the Admiral on another voyage from which they might derive some profit and with which he might be occupied only until Ovando had pacified the island of Española. They did not think it fair to keep him from his rightful possessions any longer than was necessary, knowing as they did that the charges made against him by Bobadilla were compounded of malice and falsehood and were no just cause for him to be stripped of his rights and privileges.

The start of this voyage being somewhat delayed, and knowing that some of his enemies were urging that the Sovereigns delay it further pending the arrival of new information against him, the Admiral in October, 1501, asked the Sovereigns in person to promise to defend and protect his rights and privileges; he later made the same request of them in a letter. They made this promise to him on the eve of his departure in a letter containing the following:

> Be assured that your imprisonment was very displeasing to us, as we made clear to you and to all others, for as soon as we learned of it we caused you to be set free. You know the favor with which we have always treated you, and now we are even more resolved to honor and treat you very well. All that we have granted you shall be preserved intact according to the privileges that you have received from us, and you and your heirs shall enjoy them, as is just, without any contravention. And if it should be necessary to confirm them anew, we shall do so, and we shall order your son placed in possession of everything, for it is our wish to honor you and reward you in more than this. And be assured we shall look after your sons and brothers as is just, and your office shall be vested in your son. But all this can be attended to after you have sailed; we therefore pray you not to delay your departure. From Valencia de la Torre, March 14, 1502.
>
> I the King.   I the Queen.

The Sovereigns made these promises and offers to the Admiral because he had resolved to have nothing more to do with the affairs of the Indies and to turn them over to my brother,[2] concerning which he reasoned well. For, said he, if the services he had already performed did not suffice to secure the punishment of those wicked men, his future services would avail even less. He had already accomplished the main thing that he had offered to do before his discovery of the Indies, namely, to show that there were islands and a continent to the west, that the way thither was easy and navigable, the advantages plain, and the inhabitants very gentle and unarmed. And since he had personally verified all this, it remained only for their Highnesses to continue what he had begun, sending out people to discover the secrets of those countries. Now the gate was open, anyone could follow the coast, as some were already doing who improperly called themselves discoverers, not considering that they had not discovered any new land but only followed in the wake of the Admiral after he had shown them the way to those islands and the province of Paria, which was the first part of the continent to be discovered. However, since the Admiral had always had a great desire to serve the Catholic Sovereigns and especially the most serene Queen, he was content to return to his labors and make the voyage to be told of hereafter. For he was convinced that new treasures would be found daily, as he had earlier written to their Highnesses in reference to the discovery: "It must be followed up, because it is certain that if not now, then later some new thing of great value will be found." New Spain and Peru have since shown the truth of this observation, but at the time nobody believed what he said. Yet he said nothing that did not prove in time to be true, as the Catholic Sovereigns wrote in a letter that they sent him from Barcelona on September 5, 1493.

CHAPTER 88

How the Admiral Left Granada for Seville to Outfit a Fleet for His Voyage of Discovery

After the Admiral had taken leave of the Catholic Sovereigns, he left Granada for Seville in the year 1501, and on arrival there set about preparing the fleet. In this he showed such diligence that in a short time he had rigged and made ready four ships with roundtops, the largest one being of seventy tons' burthen and the smallest of fifty tons, with one hundred and forty men and boys all told, myself being one.[1]

On May 9, 1502, we set sail from the harbor of Cádiz and made for Santa Catalina,[2] whence we sailed again on Wednesday, the 11th of the month, for Arcila [3] to succor the Portuguese; they were said to be in dire straits, but when we arrived, the Moors had already raised the siege. The Admiral sent ashore his brother the Adelantado Don Bartholomew Columbus and myself, together with the ship captains, to call on the captain of Arcila, who had been wounded by the Moors in an assault. He gave profuse thanks to the Admiral for this courtesy and for the offer of help, sending aboard certain of his gentlemen; some of these proved to be cousins of Dona Felipa de Moniz, who had been the Admiral's wife in Portugal.

That day we set sail and arrived at the Grand Canary on May 20th, anchoring in the Isletas. The 24th we proceeded to Maspalomas, which is on the same island, to take on water and wood for the voyage. The next night we set course for the Indies, with God's aid making a prosperous voyage, so that without having to touch the sails we arrived at the island of Matininó [4] on the morning of Wednesday, June 15th, with a rather rough sea and wind. There, as is the need and custom of those who come from Spain, the Admiral took on wood and water and made the men wash their linen, staying until Saturday, when we stood to the westward of the island and came to Dominica, which is ten leagues distant. Running down the Caribbee Islands, we came to Santa Cruz; and on the 24th of the same month we ran along the south side of the island of San Juan.[5] Thence we took the way to Santo Domingo, the Admiral wishing to trade one of his ships for another because she was a crank and a dull sailer; not only was she slow but she could not load sails without bringing the side of the ship almost under water, which caused a good deal of trouble on that voyage.

The Admiral's intention had been to reconnoiter the coast of Paria and cruise down it until he came to the strait, which he felt must be in the vicinity of Veragua and Nombre de Dios,[6] but because of that poor ship he had to go to Santo Domingo to trade her for a better.

The Knight Commander of Lares, governor of the island,[7] who had been sent by the Catholic Sovereigns to hold an inquest into Bobadilla's administration, took no notice of our unexpected arrival on Wednesday, June 29th. Having come to off the harbor, the Admiral sent Captain Pedro de Terreros, captain of one of the ships, to explain to the Knight Commander that because he had to replace one of his ships and also because he expected a great storm, he wished to take shelter in port. The Admiral also advised him not to permit the homeward-bound fleet to sail for eight days because of the great danger. The Knight Commander, however, would not permit the Admiral to enter the port; much less would he detain the fleet that was homeward bound for Castile. This fleet, consisting of twenty-eight ships,[8] carried the Knight Commander Bobadilla, who had made prisoners the Admiral and his brothers, Francisco Roldán, and all the other rebels who had done the Admiral so much hurt. God was pleased to close the eyes and minds of all those men so that they did not heed the Admiral's good advice. I am certain that this was Divine Providence, for had they arrived in Castile, they would never have been punished as their crimes deserved; on the contrary, as protégés of Bishop Fonseca, they would have received many favors and thanks. But their departure from that port for Castile prevented this. On reaching the eastern end of Española the storm assailed them with such fury that the flagship carrying Bobadilla and most of the rebels went down, and it did such havoc among the rest that only three or four out of the twenty-eight weathered the tempest.

This happened on Thursday, the last day of June, and the Admiral being forbidden the harbor, anchored as close as he could under the land in order to save himself. This caused much grief and chagrin to the ships' crews, who on account of being with the

By His Son Ferdinand

Admiral were denied the hospitality that should be accorded to foreigners, and all the more to men of the same nation; they also feared that if some disaster should befall, they could expect no aid from ashore. Inwardly the Admiral felt the same grief and bitterness, especially when he reflected that in a time of mortal danger he was being denied refuge in the land that he had given to Spain for its honor and exaltation.

By his skill and good judgment he managed to keep the fleet together till the next day, when, as the storm gained in intensity and night came on with deep darkness, three ships were torn from their anchorages, each going its own way; and though all ran the same danger, each thought the others had gone down. The worst sufferers were the men on the *Santo,* who to save their boat, in which Captain Terreros had gone ashore, dragged it astern by cables, until they were forced to cut it loose in order to save themselves.

Still greater was the danger of the caravel *Bermuda,* which ran out to sea, where water washed over her deck—from which it is easy to understand why the Admiral wanted to trade her for another. All concluded that the Adelantado, the Admiral's brother, was under God the saving of her; for there was not at that time a more skillful sailor than he. After all the ships save the Admiral's had taken great punishment, it pleased God to bring them together the next Sunday to their rendezvous in the harbor of Azua, on the south side of Española. As each captain related his misfortunes, it appeared that the Adelantado, experienced seaman that he was, had weathered that great storm by going out to sea, while the Admiral had saved his ship by lying close to shore, like a sage astrologer who foresaw whence the danger must come.

That is why the Admiral's enemies charged that by his magic arts he had raised that storm to take revenge on Bobadilla and others of his enemies who were with him, seeing that not one of his four ships went down, while of the twenty-eight which had left with Bobadilla, only one, and that one of the meanest, the *Aguja,* reached Spain safely with 4,000 pesos of gold from the Admiral's revenues that his factor [9] was bringing home. Three others that rode out the storm had to return to Santo Domingo in a battered and pitiful state.

Chapter 89

*How the Admiral Departed from Espa-
ñola to Continue His Voyage and Discovered the Guanaja Islands*

During their stay in the harbor of Azua, the Admiral permitted his men to rest from the ordeal of that storm. And since fishing is one of the pleasures offered by the sea in such time of idleness, I shall describe two remarkable kinds of fish among the many they caught. One I recall with amusement, the other with wonderment. The first was a ray as large as a medium-sized bed, which the men on the *Vizcaína* stabbed with a harping iron while it slept on the surface, and held fast so it could not escape; and being tied to the boat by a long thick rope, it drew the boat through the harbor as swiftly as an arrow. The men aboard ship, not knowing what went on, were astounded to see the boat running about without oars; eventually the fish died and was hauled aboard with tackling gear used for raising heavy objects. The second fish was caught by another means; the Indians call it manatee, and it is not known in Europe. It is big as a calf and resembles one in taste and color, but is better tasting and fatter; and those who believe that all manner of land animals live in the sea argue the manatee is not a fish but a calf, since it does not look like a fish and feeds only on the grass it finds along the shore.

After the men had rested and the ships had been repaired, the Admiral departed from Azua harbor and went to the harbor of Brazil, which the Indians call Yaquimo, to take shelter from an impending storm. He left this port on July 14th, and ran into such a flat calm that he could not hold his course, and the currents carried him to some small sandy islands near Jamaica; he called them the Puddles because though they had no wells his men found enough water for their needs by digging puddles in the sand. Then, sailing south toward the continent, we came to some islands and went ashore on the largest; it was called Guanaja, which name the map-makers later gave to all the Guanajas; these islands lie twelve leagues from the mainland, near the province now called Cape Honduras, but which the Admiral named Caxinas Point. But as the map-makers have not traveled in this part of the world, in their depiction they fall into a grievous error of which I wish to speak, though it break the thread of my story.

They depict those islands and that part of the mainland twice on their charts, as if they were different lands; thus, although Cape Gracias a Dios is the same as that which they call Cape Honduras, they make two of it. The reason for their error is this: After the Admiral had discovered those lands, one Juan Díaz de Solís, after whom the Río de la Plata is called Río de Solís because he was slain by Indians there, and Vicente Yáñez Pinzón, who commanded a ship on the Admiral's first voyage, set out together in 1508 on a voyage of discovery with the intention of following westward the coast that the Admiral had discovered on his voyage to Veragua. Holding on that course, they sailed along the coast of Cariay, up past Cape Gracias a Dios to Caxinas Point, which they named Cape Honduras. The islands they called the Guanajas, giving the name of the principal island to the whole group. From there they proceeded onward, never admitting that the Admiral had been in those parts, in order to assign the discovery to themselves, although one of their pilots, Pedro de Ledesma, who had sailed with the Admiral on his voyage to Veragua, told them he knew that country and had helped the Admiral discover it; this I later had from him. The charts clearly show this, for they depict that island twice with the same shape and in the same position. The reason is that they brought back a map on which that country was accurately sketched, but they claimed it lay beyond the one the Admiral had discovered. That is why the same land is shown twice on the map, as will become manifest when the navigation of that coast, with God's help, is better known.

Having come to the island of Guanaja, the Admiral sent ashore his brother Bartholomew, with two boats. They encountered people who resembled those of the other islands, but had narrower foreheads. They also saw many pine trees and pieces of earth called *cálcide* which the Indians use to cast copper; some of the sailors thought it was gold and kept it concealed for a long time. The Adelantado being eager to learn the secrets of that island, by good fortune there arrived at that time a canoe long as a galley and eight feet wide, made of a single tree trunk like the other Indian canoes; it was freighted with merchandise from the western regions around New Spain.[1] Amidships it had a palm-leaf awning like that which the Venetian gondolas carry; this gave complete protection against the rain and waves. Under this awning were the children and women and all the baggage and merchandise. There were twenty-five paddlers aboard, but they offered no resistance when our boats drew up to them.

Our men brought the canoe alongside the flagship, where the Admiral gave thanks to God for revealing to him in a single moment, without any toil or danger to our people, all the products of that country. He took aboard the costliest and handsomest things in that cargo: cotton mantles and sleeveless shirts embroidered and painted in different designs and colors; breechclouts of the same design and cloth as the shawls worn by the women in the canoe, being like the shawls worn by the Moorish women of Granada; long wooden swords with a groove on each side where the edge should be, in which were fastened with cord and pitch, flint knives that cut like steel; hatchets resembling the stone hatchets used by the other Indians, but made of good copper; and hawk's bells of copper, and crucibles to melt it. For provisions they had such roots and grains as the Indians of Española eat, also a wine made of maize [2] that tasted like English beer. They had as well many of the almonds [3] which the Indians of New Spain use as currency; and these the Indians in the canoe valued greatly, for I noticed that when they were brought aboard with the other goods, and some fell to the floor, all the Indians squatted down to pick them up as if they had lost something of great value—their greed driving out their feelings of terror and danger at finding themselves in the hands of such strange and ferocious men as we must have seemed to be.

I should add that they displayed admirable modesty, for if one had his breechclout taken from him, he would immediately cover his genitals with his hands; and the women covered their faces like the Moorish women of Granada. The Admiral was so impressed by this that he ordered his people to treat them well, and gave them some trading truck in exchange for what our men had taken from them. He detained only one, an ancient named Yumbé, who seemed to be the wisest man among them and of greatest authority, to inform him about the secrets of that land and to persuade the others to talk to the Christians; he served us very willingly and loyally all the time we were in the region where his speech was understood. Having come to the limits of the area in which his language was spoken, the Admiral gave him some presents and sent him home very satisfied. This happened before we reached Cape Gracias a Dios, on the Costa de las Orejas.

CHAPTER 90

How the Admiral Decided Not to Go to New Spain but Turn Eastward in Search of Veragua and the Strait Across the Mainland

The find of that canoe and its contents made the Admiral aware of the great wealth, civilization, and industry of the peoples of the western part of New Spain. Reflecting, however, that as these lands were to the leeward, he could sail thither from Cuba whenever he wished, he decided to continue with his search for a strait across the mainland that would open a way to the South Sea and the Lands of Spices. So, like one groping in the darkness, he sailed eastward toward Veragua and Nombre de Dios, believing the strait must be there; and so it was. But his mistake consisted in conceiving it to be a channel running from sea to sea instead of a neck of land or isthmus, as others did. This error may have arisen from a misunderstanding; for being told the strait was in Veragua and Nombre de Dios, and the word "strait" meaning either a land or water strait, he understood it in the latter sense, as the most common and as signifying what he fervently sought for. Be that as it may, that land strait proved to be the doorway through which Spain entered upon the dominion of many seas, and one by means of which great treasure has been discovered and conveyed to Spain. So it was through the finding of that canoe that the existence of New Spain was first made known, for God was pleased that this great end should be achieved in that way and no other.

As there was nothing of importance in those Guanaja Islands, he did not tarry there but made for a point of the mainland that he called Caxinas Point, from the name of a tree that grew there; this tree produces fruit resembling wrinkled olives with a spongy core that are good to eat, especially when cooked; the Indians of Española call these fruit "caxinas." As this country contained nothing worthy of mention, the Admiral lost no time in exploring a large bay that he found there but held on his course eastward along the coast that runs to Cape Gracias a Dios; this coast is very low and open all the way. The Indians in the vicinity of Point Caxinas were dressed like those in the canoe, in dyed shirts and breechclouts; they also had thick quilted cotton jerkins like breastplates that were sufficient protection against their darts and even withstood some blows from our swords. But the people who live farther east, as far as Cape Gracias a Dios, are almost black in color, ugly in aspect, wear no clothes, and are very wild in all respects. According to the Indian who was our prisoner they eat human flesh and raw fish, and pierce holes in their ears large enough to insert hen's eggs; that is why the Admiral named that country Costa de las Orejas.[1]

On Sunday morning, August 14, 1502, accompanied by the captains and many of the fleet's people, the Adelantado went ashore with his banners displayed to hear Mass. The Wednesday following, when boats were sent ashore to take formal possession of the land in the name of the Catholic Sovereigns, more than a hundred Indians bearing food came down to the shore; as soon as the boats had beached they presented these gifts to the Adelantado and went some distance off without saying a word. The Adelantado ordered them repaid with hawk's bells, beads, and other trifles. He also asked them about the resources of the region by signs and with the aid of the Indian interpreter. But this interpreter, having been but a short time with us, did not understand the Christians because of the distance—short though it is—separating his country from Española, where many of the ship's people had learned the Indians' language; nor did he understand the Indians of that locality. These Indians being pleased with what had been given them, next day more than two hundred others came to the same spot bringing food of various kinds: chickens that were better-tasting than ours, geese, roast fish, red and white beans resembling kidney beans, and other commodities like those of Española. The land though flat was verdant and lovely, with many pines and evergreen oaks, myrobalans of the kind called *hobos* in Española, and almost all the other fruits and foods found in Española. There were also many pumas, stags, and roe deer, and many of the fish found in Española but not in Spain.

The natives of this country are much like those on the other islands, but their foreheads are not so broad and they do not appear to have any religion. They speak different languages and generally go naked except for a cloth about their genitals. Some wear sleeveless shirts resembling ours that come down to the navel. They tattoo their arms and bodies by burning in Moorish-style designs that give them a strange aspect. Some display painted lions, others deer, others turreted castles, and others a variety of other figures. The most noble ones wear certain pieces of white and red cotton cloth instead of caps; others have large locks of hair hanging over their foreheads. When they adorn themselves for some festivity, some paint their faces black or red, others draw stripes of various colors on their faces or put on a beak like an ostrich, and still others blacken their eyes. They do this to appear beautiful, but they really look like devils.

CHAPTER 91

How the Admiral Cruised Down the Costa de las Orejas to Cape Gracias a Dios and Proceeded to Cariay, and What He Did and Saw There

The Admiral sailed along the Costa de las Orejas eastward as far as Cape Gracias a Dios, to which he gave that name because it took them seventy days of sailing to make the sixty leagues from Point Caxinas to that cape, now tacking toward the sea and again toward land, often gaining with the wind and as often losing, according to whether the wind was strong or weak when they came about. If the coast had not had some good anchorages, it would certainly have taken us much longer to make that distance; but as it was clean and had two fathoms of depth half a league from shore, and the water rose two fathoms every league seaward, it was very easy to anchor at night or when the wind was slack, so that the course was navigable though difficult.

When we came up to the cape on September 14th, seeing that the coast trended southerly and that we could easily continue our voyage with the prevailing eastern winds that before had been so contrary to us, all gave thanks to God; that is why the Admiral gave it the name Gracias a Dios.

A little way beyond we passed among some perilous shoals that extended out to sea as far as the eye could reach. As we needed to take on water and wood, on Saturday, September 16th, the Admiral sent the ship's boats toward a river that seemed to be deep and easy of entrance. But as they came out, the wind having freshened from seaward and the sea become heavy, such a surf built up at the mouth that one boat was swamped and her crew drowned. For this reason the Admiral named it Río de Desastres. Along the banks of this river and in the vicinity there were canes as thick as a man's thigh. On Sunday, September 25th, we continued southward and anchored at an island named Quiribirí, off a village on the mainland named Cariay.[1] Here we found the best country and people that we had yet seen; because the land was high and abounded in rivers and great trees, and the island itself was very verdant, full of groves of lofty trees, palms, myrobalans, and many other species. For this reason the Admiral named it La Huerta.[2]

This island is a short league from a village called Cariay that lies near a river; to this village there came a great number of Indians of the vicinity, many armed with bows and arrows, others with palm-tree spears black as pitch and hard as bone and tipped with fish bones, and still others with macanas or clubs. They seemed determined to resist our landing. The men wore their hair braided about their heads, while the women wore theirs cut as we do. Seeing that we came in peace, they appeared eager to trade their weapons, cotton cloaks and shirts, and the *guanín* pendants which they hang about their necks as we wear an Agnus Dei or other relic, in exchange for our things. They swam out to the ships with all their goods, for the Christians did not go ashore that day or the next. The Admiral did not allow his people to accept any of their articles, since he wanted to show them that we did not covet their possessions; instead he ordered presents to be distributed among them. The less interest we showed in trade, the more they showed, inviting us ashore by making signs and holding up their cloaks like banners. At last, seeing we would not come, they left all the truck we had given them neatly tied together at the boat landing; there our men found it when they went ashore on Wednesday.

Thinking that we distrusted them, the Indians sent aboard an old Indian of venerable presence bearing a banner tied to a stick; two girls, one eight and the other fourteen years old, accompanied him. In response to his pleas, the Admiral sent a boat ashore for water, and the Christians were very careful to make no sign or gesture that might scare the Indians. When they were returning aboard, the Indians urged them by signs to take the girls, who had *guanines* about their necks; at the entreaties of the old man who had brought them, we agreed to let them come along. This stratagem reflected much intelligence on the part of those Indians; and the girls displayed much courage, for though the Christians were completely strange to them in aspect, manners, and race, they showed no fear or grief but always looked pleasant and modest. On this account they were well treated by the Admiral, who caused them to be clothed and fed and then sent them ashore, where the old man who had brought them and fifty more Indians came out to receive them with much rejoicing.

When the boats went ashore again that day, they found the same people there with the girls, who, as the other Indians had done, returned all the things the Christians had given them. Next day, when the Adelantado went ashore to get what information he could about those people, two principal men approached him at the boat landing, and, each taking him by an arm, they sat down with him on the grass on the shore. When the Adelantado asked them some questions and ordered the scribe to record their replies, the Indians were so terrified by the sight of the pen and paper that most of them ran away. The reason was that they were afraid of being bewitched by words or signs. Yet it was they who impressed us as being great sorcerers, for on approaching the Christians they scattered a certain powder in the air; they also burned this powder in censers and with these censers caused the smoke to go toward the Christians. The fact that they refused to take anything of ours was more evidence that they suspected us of being enchanters, con-

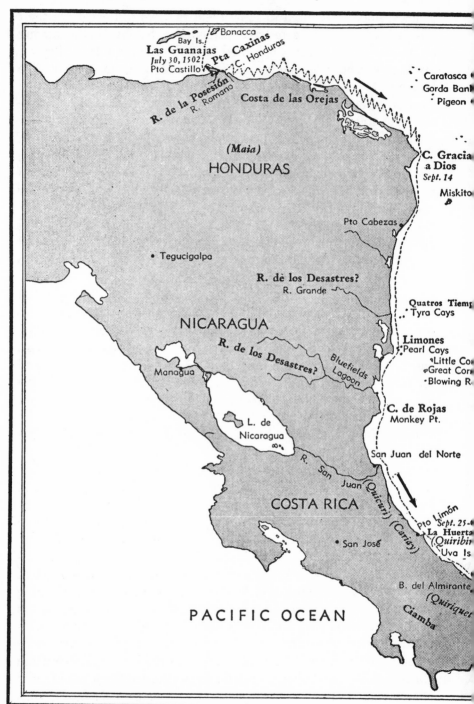

The High Voyage to Central America and Panama, 1502-1503

KEY TO PLACE NAMES
Names given by Columbus
(Native names in italic)
Modern names

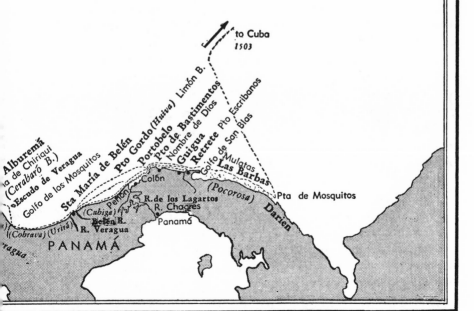

Quita Sueño Bank
North Cay

S.W. Cay

CARIBBEAN SEA

· Roncador Cay

δ

·

θ St. Andrews

Albuquerque Cays

to Cuba
1503

Alburemá
la de Chiriquí
(Cerabaró B.)
Escudo de Veragua
Golfo de los Mosquitos
Sta María de Belén
Pto Gordo (*Huiva*) Limón B.
Portobelo
Pto de Bastimentos
Nombre de Dios
Guigua
Retrete
Pto Escribanos
Golfo de San Blas
Golfo de Mulatas
Las Barbas
Pta de Mosquitos
Colón
(Cabiga)
(Urira)
Peñón
R. de los Lagartos
R. Chagres
(Pocorosa)
Belén R.
R. Veragua
Panamá
Darién
(Cobrava)
PANAMÁ
ragua

firming the adage that says a rogue sees himself in every other man.

Sunday, October 2d, after the ships had been careened and provided with all that the voyage required, the Admiral sent the Adelantado ashore with some men to survey the country and especially to learn of the Indians' dwellings, customs, and mode of life. The most remarkable thing they saw was this: In a large wooden palace roofed with canes were some tombs, in one of which was a corpse, dried and embalmed, and in another two more bodies, with no bad odor, wrapped in cotton cloth; over each tomb was a tablet carved with figures of beasts, and on some the effigy of the dead man, adorned with many beads, *guanines,* and other things they most prize.

Because these were the most intelligent Indians they had seen in those regions, the Admiral caused some of them to be captured that we might learn the secrets of that country. He selected two leading men from the seven who were seized; the others he sent home with gifts in order not to throw the country into an uproar. He told the captives that he needed them to guide him down the coast, after which he would set them free; they, however, thought he was holding them for ransom. The next day many Indians came down to the shore and sent four emissaries to the flagship to treat for the ransom of those men; they offered various things and brought as a present two native wild boars [3] that are small but very savage. The Admiral admired the intelligence of those people, but this only made him more eager to learn what he could about them through an interpreter. He paid no heed to their offers, but ordered them paid for the boars and sent them home with gifts. One of these boars provided fine sport, as I shall now relate.

Among the animals of that country there are certain cats of grayish color [4] the size of a small greyhound but with a longer tail, so strong that if one coils its tail about something, it holds it as tightly as if it were fastened with a rope. These animals move about in the trees like squirrels, leaping from tree to tree and grasping the branches not only with their claws but also with their tails, by which they often hang for rest or for sport. A crossbowman brought one out of the forest that he had knocked down from a tree with a shaft, and because it was still so fierce that he dared not get near it, he cut off one of its legs with a knife. The sight of it scared a valiant dog we had aboard but frightened even more one of those boars the Indians had brought, and it backed off in great fear; this surprised us because hitherto it had run at everybody on deck, including the dog. The Admiral then had boar and cat thrown together, whereupon the cat coiled his tail around the pig's snout, seized him by the neck with his remaining foreclaw, and bit him so that he grunted with fear. From this we concluded that these cats hunt other animals, like the wolves and greyhounds of Spain.

CHAPTER 92

How the Admiral Sailed from Cariay to
Cerabaró and Veragua, and Thence to
Portobelo, All Along a Very Fertile Coast

Wednesday, October 5th, the Admiral set sail and proceeded to Cerabaró Bay,[1] which is six leagues long and more than three wide; it is studded with islands and has three or four channels that are very convenient for getting in and out with every kind of wind. The ships sailed as if in streets between one island and another, the branches of the trees brushing the cordage of the ships. After we had anchored in this bay, a landing was made on one of these islands. The boat's people found twenty canoes beached on the shore, and encountered Indians who were as naked as they came from their mothers' wombs. Some wore only a gold mirror at the neck, and others a *guanín* eagle. They showed no fear, and with the aid of the Indian interpreter from Cariay they traded a gold mirror weighing 10 ducats for three hawk's bells; they said this gold was very abundant and that they got it on the mainland, not far from there.

Next day, October 7th, the boats were sent to the mainland, where they found fifteen canoes filled with Indians. Because these Indians refused to sell their mirrors to us, two of their principal men were seized and brought before the Admiral that they might inform him about their people with the aid of the interpreters from Cariay. One of them wore a gold mirror weighing 14 ducats, and another a gold eagle weighing 22. The Indians said that one or two days' journey inland much gold was found in certain places that they named; they said, too, that there were many fish in that bay, and ashore many of those animals that we had seen in Cariay and many of the things the Indians eat, such as roots, grains, and fruit. The Indians are painted all over face and body in different colors, white, black, and red. They go completely naked, only covering their genitals with cotton clouts.

From this bay of Cerabaró we proceeded to another next to it and quite like it, called Alburemá.[2] On the 17th of the same month we put to sea and continued our voyage. On arrival at the Guayga,[3] which is a river twelve leagues distant from Alburemá, the Admiral sent his boats ashore. As they approached they saw over one hundred Indians on the beach, and these rushed at them with fury, entering the water up to their waists brandishing spears, blowing horns, beating a drum, splashing water toward the Christians, and squirting toward them the juice of some herb that they were chewing. Our men sat quietly and finally succeeded in pacifying them, after which the Indians bartered the mirrors they wore about their necks for two or three hawk's bells apiece. In this way we obtained sixteen mirrors of pure gold worth 150 ducats.

Next day, Friday, October 21st, the boats again went ashore to trade, but before landing the Christians called out to some Indians who were lurking on the beach behind some shelters that they had built during the night from fear of an attack by the Christians. The Indians would not come out, nor would our men land without assurance of a friendly reception on their part; for, as was later learned, they planned to assault the Christians if they made a landing. On seeing that our men would not leave the boats, they began to sound horns and drum and with ferocious yells rushed into the water as they had done the day before, threatening by signs to hurl their spears if our men did not return to the ships. These actions angered our men, and in order to teach the Indians a lesson they wounded one Indian in the arm with an arrow and fired a lombard which so frightened them that they fled in confusion. Then four Christians landed; and after they had again called out to the Indians, the latter laid down their arms and came toward our men very peacefully. They traded three mirrors and said they had not brought any more because they had come prepared to fight and not to trade.

As the Admiral had no other end in view on this voyage than to gain information, without further delay he took the shortest route to Cateba and anchored in the mouth of a great river. They could see the natives of that place assembling to the sound of horn and drum, and presently a canoe containing two men came out to the flagship. After they had spoken with the Indian interpreter from Cariay they came aboard without signs of fear. On the advice of the interpreter they gave the Admiral two gold mirrors they had about their necks, and the Admiral presented them with some of our truck. Immediately after they had returned ashore, another canoe containing three men came out; these traded their gold mirrors as the others had done. After gaining their friendship our men went ashore, where they found many people with their king; he was dressed like the others but was protected from the drenching rain by a huge leaf. By way of example to his subjects he traded a mirror and bid them trade theirs; the Christians obtained a total of nineteen mirrors of fine gold. This was the first place in the Indies where the Christians saw signs of a building; it was a great mass of stucco and appeared to have been made of stone and lime. The Admiral ordered a piece to be taken as a souvenir of that antiquity.

From there he continued eastward and came to Cobrava. The villages of that province lie on the banks of its rivers. As the people did not come down to the shore and the wind was fresh, he held on his course and came to five villages of active trade. One of them was Veragua, where according to the Indians, gold was found and the mirrors were made. The next day he came to a village named Cubiga; this, said the Indian from Cariay, marked the end of the trading country that extended for fifty leagues along the coast, from Cerabaró to Cubiga. The Admiral made no stop there but continued on his course till he entered the harbor of Portobelo; he gave it that name because it is very large, beautiful, thickly populated, and surrounded by cultivated country. He entered it on November 2d, passing between two small islands. Within the harbor, vessels may lie close to shore and beat out if they wish. The country about the harbor is well tilled and full of houses only a stone's throw or crossbow shot apart, all as pretty as a picture, the fairest thing one ever saw. During the seven days that we were detained there by rain and foul weather, canoes came from all about to barter all sorts of food and skeins of fine spun cotton for trifles of brass such as lace points and tags.

CHAPTER 93

How the Admiral Came to the Puerto de Bastimentos and Nombre de Dios, and How He Held on His Course till He Put in the Harbor of Retrete

Wednesday, November 9th, we left Portobelo and sailed eight leagues eastward, but the next day were forced back four by a contrary wind, and so put in among some islets near the mainland where Nombre de Dios now is. Because all the land about and the islets were full of maize fields, the Admiral named it Puerto de Bastimentos.[1] In this harbor one of our boats hailed a canoe of Indians; they, thinking our people meant them harm and seeing the boat only a stone's throw away, cast themselves into the water and tried to escape by swimming. And no matter how hard our men rowed they could not catch them over the half-league that the chase continued. When they caught up with one, he would dive like a waterfowl and come up a bowshot or two distant. It was really funny to see the boat giving chase and the rowers wearing themselves out in vain, for they finally had to return empty-handed.

We remained there until November 23d, repairing the ships and mending our casks; then we sailed eastward to a place called Guiga (which is also the name of another place situated between Veragua and Ciguare).[2] When the boats went ashore, they met a crowd of more than three hundred Indians who wanted to barter eatables and some gold pendants that hung from their ears and noses.

We did not tarry there, and on Saturday, November 26th, we put in a little harbor that the Admiral named Retrete [3] because it was so small that it would not hold more than five or six ships. The entrance was only seventy-five to one hundred feet wide, with rocks as sharp as the points of a diamond sticking up on either side, but the channel was so deep in the middle that if you drew a little closer to one side than the other on entering, you could jump ashore on the rocks. This it was that saved the ships from destruction, for the boats sent to sound the harbor before the ships put in lied about its width, so eager were they to go ashore to trade; if the Indians had wanted to attack us, they could have done so in that narrow channel.

In this harbor we stayed nine days, with miserable weather. At first the Indians came peacefully to trade, but later, when they saw the sailors sneaking ashore from the ships, they withdrew to their huts; for the sailors, a greedy and dissolute set of men, committed innumerable outrages. This provoked the Indians to break the peace, and some fights occurred between the two sides. The Indians gathered in growing numbers about the ships, which lay alongside the shore, and evidently intended to do some harm. The Admiral tried to placate them by patience and civility; but at last, perceiving their arrogance, he sought to strike terror in them by causing some pieces of artillery to be fired. To this thunder they responded with shouts, beating the branches of the trees with staves and uttering great threats to show they did not fear that noise; for they really believed that it was only meant to scare them. In order to temper their pride and teach them not to scorn the Christians, the Admiral ordered a shot fired at a group of Indians on a hilltop, and the ball, falling in their midst, let them know that this thunder concealed a thunderbolt. After that they hardly dared peep out at us from behind the hills.

The people of this country were the best favored Indians the Christians had yet seen, being tall and spare, not potbellied, and handsome of face. The land was covered with small plants, but there were few trees. In the harbor there were large lizards or crocodiles that come out to sleep ashore and give out an odor as strong as if all the musk in the world were collected together; they are so ravenous and cruel that if they find a man asleep they will drag him into the water to eat him, but they are cowardly and flee when attacked. These lizards are found in many other parts of the mainland; some say they are crocodiles like those of the Nile.

· 245 ·

CHAPTER 94

How the Admiral, Harried by Storms, Again Stood Eastward to Get Information About the Mines of Veragua

Monday, December 5th, the Admiral, perceiving that the violence of the east and northeast winds did not abate and that no trade could be carried on with these people, decided to turn back and verify what the Indians had said about the mines of Veragua. He slept that night at Portobelo, ten leagues to westward. The next day, as he was continuing on his course, the wind changed to the west again, but thinking that it would not last, he decided not to alter course but bear up against the wind for a few days. Never was seen more unsettled weather. Now the wind was fair for Veragua; now it whipped about and drove us back to Portobelo. And just as we were most hopeful of making port the wind would change again, sometimes with such terrible thunder and lightning that the men dared not open their eyes and it seemed the ships were sinking and the heavens coming down. Sometimes the thunder lasted so long that we were sure some ship of the fleet was firing signals for help; at other times there fell such a storm of rain that it poured torrents, like another deluge. All suffered greatly and were in despair; for they could not get even half an hour's rest, being wet through for days on end, sometimes running one way and sometimes another, struggling with all the elements and dreading them all. In such terrible storms they dread the fire in the lightning flashes, the air for its fury, the water for the waves, and the land for the reefs and rocks of that unknown coast—which sometimes rears up at a man near the port where he hopes to find shelter, and not knowing the entrance, he chooses rather to contend with the other elements.

Besides these different terrors, there befell one no less dangerous and wonderful, a waterspout that on Tuesday, December 13th, passed between two ships. Had the sailors not dissolved it by reciting the Gospel according to St. John, it would surely have swamped anything it struck; for it raises the water up to the clouds in a column thicker than a water butt, twisting it about like a whirlwind. That night we lost sight of the *Vizcaína,* but fortunately sighted her again after three very dark and dangerous days, during which time she lost her boat and once anchored near land, but had to cut her cable. On that occasion it was noted that the currents along that coast always run with the wind, east with a west wind, west with a wind from the east, and again flowing in the opposite direction when the wind changes.

After such troubles of wind and sea, after the fleet had been half destroyed by the battering storm, with the men's sufferings so great as not to be borne, we had two days of calm during which so many sharks surrounded the ship that it was frightening, especially to those who believe in omens. For just as some say that vultures recognize the presence of a corpse by its smell many leagues away, so some believe that sharks have the same divinatory power. These beasts seize a person's leg or arm with their teeth and cut it off as clean as if with a knife, because they have two files of saw-like teeth. We made carnage among them with a chain hook until we could kill no more, and they still followed us making turns in the water; so voracious are these beasts that not only will they eat carrion but one can catch them by simply attaching a piece of red cloth to the hook. Out of one shark's belly I saw a turtle taken that afterward lived in the ship; from another they took a whole shark's head that we had cut off and thrown into the water because the head, unlike the rest of the body, is not good to eat. It may seem strange that an animal should be able to swallow the head of another of the same size, but their heads are very elongated and the mouth extends almost to the middle of the belly.

Some viewed it as an evil omen and others thought it poor fishing, but all did shark the honor of eating it; for by that time we had been over eight months at sea and had consumed all the meat and fish that we had brought from Spain. And what with the heat and the dampness even the biscuit was so full of worms that, God help me, I saw many wait until nightfall to eat the porridge made of it so as not to see the worms; others were so used to eating them that they did not bother to pick them out, for they might lose their supper by being so fastidious.

Saturday, the 17th, the Admiral put in a port that the Indians called Huiva,[1] three leagues east of the Peñón.[2] In this harbor, resembling a great channel, we rested for three days. When we went ashore, we found that the people here lived in the tops of trees, like

birds; their cabins or huts were built over frames of poles placed across branches. We could not learn the reason for this strange custom but judged that it was caused by their fear of the griffins that inhabit that country or of their enemies, because along that whole coast each league apart the people have great feuds.

The 20th of the same month we left this harbor with fair but unsettled weather, for hardly had we put out to sea when the winds and storms returned to vex us, so that we were forced to enter another harbor, which we left three days later when signs of better weather appeared. But the weather, like an enemy that lies in wait for a man, suddenly attacked us with such fury that it drove us almost to the Peñón, when, as we were hoping to enter the harbor where we had first taken refuge, the wind whipped about so violently that it blew us into the harbor where we had been on Thursday, December 12th. There we stayed from the second day of Christmas until January 3, 1503. After we had repaired the *Gallega* and taken on much maize, water, and wood, we again steered for Veragua, with foul weather and contrary winds that actually grew worse each time the Admiral altered his course. So strange and unheard-of a thing was this that I would not have believed it if I had not been there and had not read the account of it by Diego Méndez,[3] he who sailed in a canoe from Jamaica to Española, as will presently be told. And in the letter sent by the Admiral to the Catholic Sovereigns, that has since been printed, the reader may read how much we suffered and how fortune persecuted him who most merited its favor.

I return to the troubles and changes of wind and weather that caused us so much suffering between Veragua and Portobelo, which is the reason that coast was afterward called La Costa de los Contrastes.[4] On Thursday, it being the Feast of the Epiphany, we anchored near a river that the Indians call Yebra and the Admiral named Belén after that day, it being the Feast of the Three Kings. He sent boats to sound the bar of that river and of another farther west that the Indians called Veragua, and found the entrance of the Veragua very shallow, with four fathoms of water on the Belén bar at high tide. So the boats went up the Río Belén to a village where the Christians were told the gold mines were in Veragua, though at first the Indians would not speak to them and even gathered with their weapons as if determined to prevent their landing.

The next day the boats ascended the Río Veragua to the village of Veragua and received the same treatment from the Indians, for they prepared to fight us not only on land but on the water, from their canoes. But an Indian of that coast who had sailed some time with the Christians and understood a little of their language told the others that we were good people and would not take anything without payment; then they quieted down somewhat. They bartered twenty gold mirrors, some quills of gold dust, and gold nuggets; they tried to enhance the value by saying the gold came from far-off rugged mountains and that during the time they collected it they could not eat or have the company of their wives. The Indians of Española at the time of its discovery also had those customs, according to their own account.

CHAPTER 95

How the Admiral's Ships Went Up the
Río Belén, Where He Determined to
Found a Town, and Leave His Brother
the Adelantado in Charge

Monday, January 9th, the Admiral's flagship and the *Vizcaína* crossed the bar of the Río Belén, and the Indians immediately came to barter their commodities, especially fish, which at a certain season enter that river from the sea, an incredible thing to one who has not seen it. They also exchanged a little gold for pins and larger quantities for strings of beads and hawk's bells. The other two ships, which had missed flood tide that day (though even at highest tide the water does not rise there more than half a fathom), passed over on the 10th. Because the mines and wealth of Veragua enjoyed great fame, on the third day after our arrival the Adelantado took the boats down the coast and ascended the river to the village of the Quibián, which is the name those Indians give to their king. When he learned of the Adelantado's coming, he came downstream with his canoes to meet him. They treated each other with much friendship and civility, each giving the other the things he most prized; and after they had conversed for a long while, the Adelantado and the Quibián each went their own way very peacefully.

Next day the Quibián came aboard the flagship to visit the Admiral, and after they had talked for over an hour the Admiral gave him some things and his men bartered some gold for hawk's bells; then the Quibián returned without ceremony the same way he had come. On Tuesday, January 24th, while we felt very easy and secure, the Río Belén suddenly flooded, so that before we could prepare for it or run a hawser ashore the fury of the water struck the flagship with such force that she broke one of the two cables and drove with such impetus against the *Gallega,* which lay astern, that the blow carried away her bonaventure mizzen; then, fouling one another, they drifted so as to be in great peril of going down with all hands.

Some thought this flood was caused by the great rains which fell incessantly that winter throughout the land, but if that had been the case, the water would have risen little by little and not so fast and furiously. We therefore suspected that a great shower had fallen on the mountains of Veragua. To these the Admiral gave the name San Cristóbal because the summit of the highest mountain towers up into the region of the air above the clouds, where weather changes originate. This summit has the appearance of a hermitage and lies at least twenty leagues inland among very dense woods. The flood was very dangerous, for though it made it possible for the ships to go out to sea, which was half a mile distant, so violent a storm raged there that the fleet would have been shattered to pieces at the mouth of the river.

While this storm lasted we could not secure or lash down the ships; and the waves broke with such fury on the bar of the river that the boats could not go out to explore the coast in search of mines and a suitable site for a town. The Admiral had decided to leave the Adelantado and most of his people here to settle and conquer the land while he returned to Spain for reinforcements and supplies.

Monday, February 6th, the weather being calm, the Adelantado with sixty-eight men rowed down the coast to the mouth of the Río Veragua, a league to the west of the Belén, and then went up the river to the cacique's village, where they passed the day getting information about the way to the mines. The Wednesday following, they marched four and a half leagues and passed the night near a river, which they had crossed forty-three times. Next day, after marching a league and a half with guides provided by the Quibián, they reached the mines; within two hours after arrival each had collected some gold among the roots of the trees, which are very luxuriant there and tower to the skies. They were much pleased with their finds, as none of them had any digging tools or had ever looked for gold before. As their journey had no other aim than to gain information about the mines, they went back very content to Veragua, where they slept that night, and next day returned to the ships.

We later learned that these were not the mines of Veragua, which are nearer, but those of Urirá. Because the people of Urirá were at war with the Veraguans, the Quibián had guided the Christians thither in order to annoy his enemies and in the hope that the Christians would go to that country and quit his own.

C H A P T E R 9 6

*How the Adelantado Visited Some Towns
in That Province, and of the Things and
Manners of the People of That Country*

Thursday, February 16, 1503, the Adelantado went overland up the coast with fifty-nine persons, a boat following with fourteen more. The next morning they reached the Río Urirá, which is seven leagues west of the Belén. When they were one league from the village, the cacique accompanied by twenty Indians came out to meet the Adelantado and presented him with food; the Indians also bartered some gold mirrors. All the time they were there the cacique and his leading men never stopped chewing a dry herb; sometimes they also put in their mouths a powder that they carried, together with the dry herb; it seemed a dirty habit. Presently they went to the village, where many people came out to meet them; they assigned the Christians a hut to lodge in and gave them much food. Shortly the cacique of Dururi, a neighboring village of many Indians, called on them bringing some mirrors to trade. From these Indians they learned that in the interior there were many caciques who had much gold and warriors armed like ourselves.

Next day the Adelantado sent most of his men overland back to the ships while he continued with thirty men to a village called Cobrava, where were cornfields stretching over an extent of six leagues, and then he proceeded to Cateba. In both places they met a friendly reception and were given much food. They also got by trade some gold mirrors like the paten of a chalice, each weighing 12 ducats more or less; these they wear hanging by a string about their necks, as we do an Agnus Dei or other relic.

Being now a great distance from the ships, and not finding along that whole coast a harbor or river larger than the Belén on which to found a town, on February 24th he returned by the same route he had come, with many ducats' worth of gold, obtained by trade. On his return he began diligently to work on the founding of the new town; and the eighty men who were staying, having formed into groups of about ten men apiece, set about building houses on the banks of the Río Belén about a lombard shot from its mouth, beyond a gully that comes down to the river, at the foot of which there is a little hill.

Besides these houses, which were of timber and thatched with the leaves of palm trees that grow on the shore, they built a large house for use as a storehouse and arsenal, in which they placed many pieces of ordnance, powder, and foodstuffs; but the necessities of life, such as wine, biscuit, garlic, vinegar, and cheese, being all the Spanish food they had, they stored for greater security aboard the *Gallega,* which the Admiral intended to leave for the Adelantado's use. He also left all the fishing equipment, such as nets and hooks, because all the rivers of that country swarm with fish. At certain times of the year various kinds of fish come in shoals up the rivers and to the seashore; these fish are the main food of the Indians, since the animals of that country are not numerous enough to live on.

These Indians have much the same customs as those of Española and the neighboring islands, with these differences: The natives of

Veragua and its vicinity turn their backs when they speak to each other; and even while eating they are always chewing an herb; we decided that must be the cause of their rotten teeth. Their main food is fish, which they catch in nets and on hooks cut or rather sawed out of tortoise shell with pita thread; they have the same practice on the other islands. They had another way of catching small fish, like those called *titi* of Española; these fish swim close to shore during the rainy season and are so fiercely pursued by the larger fish that they rise to the surface, and then the Indians catch them in small nets and mats. They wrap them in leaves as apothecaries roll electuaries in paper, and after being dried in an oven the fish keep for a long time. They catch sardines in a similar way; for at certain seasons the sardines, fleeing from larger fish, jump ten or fifteen feet out of the water onto the beach, and all the Indians have to do is gather them up. They have another way of catching sardines: First they set a palm-leaf partition about fifty-four inches high in the middle of the canoe from stem to stern; then they row down the river making a great din and striking the side of the canoe with their paddles. The sardines, trying to save themselves from the larger fish that pursue them, leap toward the canoe, hit the partition, and fall in. In this way they catch all they please. Jurel, shad, and even skate, as well as other kinds of fish, come here at certain seasons. It is truly wonderful to see how they swarm in these rivers at the time of their migrations. The Indians catch great quantities of them, and after being dried they keep for a long time.

The Indians also eat much maize, which is a grain that like millet grows to a tassel or ear. From this they make white and red wine in the same way that beer is made in England, adding spices according to taste; then it has a pleasant flavor resembling that of sour wine. They make another wine from the juice of a tree that I believe to be a palm, although it has a smooth bark like other trees and the trunk bears thorns as long as the spines of the porcupine. From the heart of this palm or palmetto they extract juice by scraping and squeezing, which juice they boil with water and spices; this wine they greatly prize. They make still another kind of wine from a fruit that we had already seen on the island of Guadalupe and that resembles a large pineapple; they cultivate it in extensive fields, planting the shoots that grow out of the top of the pineapple, as we do with lettuce. This plant lives for three or four years, bearing fruit all the while.

They also make wine from other kinds of fruit, especially one that grows on very high trees as large as cedars; each fruit has two, three, or four kernels in the shape of nuts; they are not round, however, but like the garlic or chestnut. The rind of this fruit is like that of the pomegranate, and it resembles the pomegranate exactly when taken from the tree, save that it has no corona; its taste is like that of the peach or a very good pear. Some specimens are better than others, as happens with other fruit. This fruit is also found on the islands, where the Indians call it mammee.

CHAPTER 97

How the Quibián and Many Leading Indians Were Made Prisoners to Ensure the Security of the Christian Town, and How the Quibián Made His Escape Through the Carelessness of His Guards

When the affairs of the settlement had been put in order, with ten or twelve houses put up and thatched with palm leaves, the Admiral prepared to depart for Spain; but the river, which had before placed us in grave peril by its flooding, now placed us in even worse plight by a sharp drop in its water level. The reason was that the January rains having ceased, the mouth of the river became so choked up with sand that instead of four fathoms, which had barely permitted our entrance, there was only half a fathom of water over the bar. We thus found ourselves trapped and without hope of relief, for it was impossible to haul the ships over the sand. And even had we had the equipment to do it, never was the sea so quiet but that the least wave could break a ship to pieces against the shore—especially ships like ours that were already like honeycombs, riddled through and through by the shipworm. So we commended ourselves to God and asked Him to send us rain, as before we had prayed for fair weather; for we knew that rain would swell the river and open up the bar, this being customary in those rivers.

At this time we learned through the interpreter that the Quibián planned to set fire to the houses and kill all the Christians, the Indians being greatly offended that we had settled on that river. It was decided to teach him a lesson and strike fear into his neighbors by taking him and all his leading men prisoners and sending them to Castile, and to make his people serve the Christians. Accordingly on March 30, 1503, the Adelantado set out with seventy-four men for the village of Veragua (I call it a village, but be it noted that the houses are not together, for the people of that country, like those of Biscay, live apart from each other).

When the Quibián learned that the Adelantado was coming, he sent word he must not come to his house, which was pitched on a hill above the Río Veragua. The Adelantado did not want him to flee, so he decided to come with only five men; however, he ordered the others to follow by twos, each pair a certain distance apart from the other. Having come within a musket shot of the house, they were to surround it and allow no one to escape. When he was quite near, the Quibián sent word that the Adelantado must not enter his house, that although suffering from an arrow wound, he himself would come out to speak with him. He did this to keep the Christians from seeing his wives, for the Indians are very jealous. So he came out and sat down in the doorway, saying none but the Adelantado might approach, and this the Adelantado did, telling the other Christians to attack as soon as he had grasped the Quibián by the arm.

The Adelantado walked up to the cacique and inquired about his wound and other matters through an Indian interpreter whom we had captured in those parts three months before, and who now chose to stay with us. This Indian was much concerned for our safety, for he knew that the Quibián planned to kill the Christians. The Quibián did not appreciate the extent of our power and counted on the great number of men at his orders to ensure the success of his design. But the Adelantado felt no fear; pretending he wished to see the Quibián's wound, he seized him by the arm, and though the Quibián was a strong man, he managed to hold him until the four other Christians ran up and made him captive. There-upon the fifth man fired off his gun, and all the Christians rushed out of their ambush and surrounded the house. Inside they found fifty people, most of whom they captured without inflicting a single wound, because seeing their king made a prisoner, they offered no resistance; among them were some of the Quibián's wives and children and other leading Indians. These offered a rich ransom for their freedom, saying they would give us a great treasure that was hidden in a nearby wood. But the Adelantado paid no heed to their promises and decided to send the Quibián, his wife, and the leading Indians aboard ship before the Indians of the vicinity could gather, with himself and most of his men staying to mop up the Quibián's subjects and relations who had escaped.

After some discussion as to who should take the prisoners to the mouth of the river, the job was assigned to Juan Sánchez of Cádiz, chief pilot of the fleet and a highly regarded man, who offered to take the cacique bound hand and foot. The Adelantado warned him not to let the Quibián escape, and he replied he would permit the hairs of his beard to be plucked out one by one if the cacique got away. So he set out down the river with the cacique. About half a league from the mouth the Quibián complained his bonds were hurting him, and out of pity Juan Sánchez untied all the ropes but one that he held in his hand. Soon after, observing that Juan Sánchez was somewhat abstracted, the Quibián jumped overboard, and Juan Sánchez had to let the rope go in order not to be drawn in after him. By this time it was dark, and the other prisoners made such a racket that the Christians could neither see nor hear the cacique swim ashore, and he vanished like a stone fallen in water. Fearing the others might attempt to escape, they continued their way toward the fleet, much chagrined by the result of their carelessness.

Next day, April 1st, perceiving that the country was mountainous, densely wooded, and devoid of villages, with only a hut here and there, and that they might have difficulty getting home safely if attacked, the Adelantado gave up the pursuit and returned to the fleet without the loss of a single man killed or wounded. He presented the Admiral with about 300 ducats' worth of booty in gold mirrors and eagles, gold twist that the Indians wear around their arms and legs, and gold cords that they wear about their heads in the manner of coronets. After the Christians had deducted the royal fifth, they divided the rest among the members of the expedition, giving the Adelantado one of the aforesaid crowns as a token of victory.

CHAPTER 98

How After the Admiral Had Sailed from Belén for Castile, the Quibián Attacked the Christian Town, in Which Combat There Were Many Dead and Wounded

After the Admiral had done all that was necessary for the proper support and administration of the town, God was pleased to send heavy rain that swelled the river and raised the water on the bar so the ships could go out. Therefore the Admiral decided to leave immediately for Española with three ships, in order to be able to send help to the settlement as quickly as possible. We waited for calm weather, so that the sea should not break or beat on the bar, then took the caravels out, the ship's boats going in front. For all our care the ships dragged their keels on the sandy bottom, and had it not been shifting sand, even with good weather the ships would have been in great peril of destruction. We then quickly loaded the ships with the ballast that had been taken off to lighten them while crossing the bar. When we reached the open coast, a league from the mouth of the river, and were about to depart, God put it into the Admiral's mind to send the flagship's boat ashore to take on a supply of water and some other necessary things— whereby the boat was lost but many men were saved both on land and sea.

When the Indians and the Quibián perceived the caravels had sailed and we could not help the men who remained behind, they attacked the Christian town at the very time the ship's boat was approaching the shore. The dense woods allowed the Indians to creep up unobserved to within fifty feet of the huts; they attacked with loud cries, hurling darts at every Christian they saw and through the wattles of the huts, by which they wounded several. The Adelantado first seized a lance and, followed by seven or eight others, boldly charged the Indians, forcing them to retreat to the forest that bordered the huts; thence they sallied to hurl their darts and retreated again, as Spaniards do in the game of jousts. At last, more Christians having joined the fight, and the Indians being punished by the edge of the sword and by a dog who pursued them furiously, they fled, leaving one Christian dead and seven wounded, one being the Adelantado, who received a dart wound in the chest. Two Christians kept out of harm's way: I tell the story of these two to show the rascality of the one, an Italian from Lombardy, and the Castilian severity of the other.

As the Lombard, named Bastiano, was running at a great pace to take refuge in a hut, Diego Méndez called out to him, "Turn back, Bastiano! Where are you going?" He replied, "Let me alone, damn it! I'm running to save my hide!" The Spaniard was Captain Diego Tristán, who had been sent ashore by the Admiral as told above, but who remained in the boat during the entire duration of the fight, although he was near the river where it was taking place. Asked by some why he did not help the Christians, for which some reproved him, he replied that if he had rowed ashore, the Christians might have rushed in panic for the safety of the boat, swamping it and causing the destruction of all, since if the boat were lost, the Admiral would run great danger at sea. Besides, said Tristán, his orders were to obtain water, and he would do nothing more, at least not until our men were in sorer need. When the fight was over, he rowed upstream for fresh water, intending to return immediately to give the Admiral an account of what had happened. He was warned not to go because of the great danger from Indians; he replied he had his orders and could take care of himself. So he continued upstream to where the river turns very narrow and dark, lined with such heavy foliage on both banks that it is almost impossible to go ashore save in a few places where fishermen's trails end and the Indians beach their canoes.

When he was about a league upstream, the Indians sallied from the densest part of this foliage in their canoes with loud cries and blowing on horns, and attacked Tristán from all sides. They possessed a great advantage because their canoes are very light, especially the smaller fishing canoes holding three or four men, so that one could paddle while the others hurled darts and spears (I call them spears, but they are really pieces of wood tipped with fish bones rather than iron).

The ship's boat held seven oarsmen, as well as the Captain and two or three soldiers more, but as they could not protect the rowers from the rain of darts, the rowers soon had to lay down their oars and take up their shields. So great a number of Indians beset them from all sides, darting up in their canoes and retreating when they pleased, that soon they had wounded most of the Christians and especially the Captain, on whom they inflicted many wounds. He remained undaunted to the end and boldly urged on the others; but it was no use, for they hemmed them in so that they could not move or use their muskets. They finally killed Tristán with a spear stroke through the eye, and all the others except a cooper from Seville named Juan de Noya. He by great good fortune fell in the water in the thick of the fight and by swimming under water reached the bank unobserved by the Indians and escaped through the woods to bring the news to the town. At this news our men were beside themselves with fear, for they saw themselves so few and many of their comrades dead and others wounded; and as the Admiral was at sea without a boat and unable to send them aid, they resolved to leave that place immediately. They would have done this, too, in disorderly mutinous fashion, if not prevented by the closing of the river through the onset of bad weather. As a result they could not take out the caravel that had been left for their use; they could not even send a boat to inform the Admiral of what had happened because the sea broke so heavily on the bar.

The Admiral's plight was equally grave, for he was anchored in an open roadstead without a boat and with crews sadly reduced by losses in battle. Therefore he and all the rest of us were as troubled and perplexed as the men ashore. They, observing the issue of the fight and seeing the corpses of Diego Tristán and his men floating downstream covered with wounds and attended by croaking carrion crows, regarded all this as an evil omen and feared they would come to the same end, especially as the Indians were flushed with their victory and gave the settlement not a moment's peace because of its very vulnerable situation. Their affairs would have turned out even worse if they had not wisely decided to move to a large cleared space on the eastern bank of the river, where they constructed a rampart with casks and other materials, planting artillery pieces at strategic places. Thus they kept their enemies at bay, for the Indians dared not leave the shelter of the woods because of the great havoc the cannon balls did among them.

CHAPTER 99

How the Indian Captives Aboard the
Bermuda *Escaped and the Admiral*
Learned of the Defeat He Had Suffered
on Land

While these events were taking place ashore, the Admiral spent ten days in anguished waiting for the weather to clear so he could send another boat to learn the reason for the first boat's delay in returning, though he already suspected what had happened. But fortune was unkind in this as in all else. We could not learn what had happened to the people in the settlement, nor could they learn what had happened to us. To add to our difficulties, some of the Quibián's children and relations, who were prisoners on the *Bermuda,* managed to escape. At night they were confined below deck, but one evening some sailors who wished to sleep on the hatch, and thought the hatch cover was too high for the prisoners to reach, failed to secure it with chains. Some of the captives heaped up ballast below; then, standing on the pile of stones, they forced the hatch open with their shoulders, tumbling the sleepy sailors on the deck; and before the noise had attracted other seamen some of the principal prisoners had climbed out and leaped overboard. The sailors then secured the hatch with a chain and set about keeping better watch.

The remaining captives were filled with despair because they had not escaped with their comrades, and next morning it was found they had hanged themselves to the deck beams with such ropes as they could find, bending their knees because they had not enough headroom to hang themselves properly. Their death was no great loss to us of the fleet but seriously worsened the plight of the men ashore; the Quibián would gladly have made peace for the return of his children, but now that we no longer had hostages, there was reason to fear he would wage even crueler war on the town.

In the midst of these misfortunes and vexations, with our lives hanging by the anchor cables, and ourselves completely in the dark on the state of affairs ashore, some seamen volunteered to swim ashore if the boat took them to where the water broke. This was the *Bermuda's* boat, for the *Vizcaína's* had been lost in the fight; it was the only boat that remained to the fleet.

The Admiral accepted their offer, and the boat carried them to within a musket shot of land; closer they could not come because of the waves that broke on the beach. There Pedro de Ledesma, a pilot from Seville, boldly leaped overboard and swam across the bar to the settlement. There he learned that the garrison to a man refused to stay in that hopeless situation; they begged the Admiral to take them aboard, for to leave them behind was to condemn them to death. Moreover, there were stirrings of mutiny among them, with some refusing to obey the Adelantado or the captains, and only awaiting a break in the weather to go off by themselves in a canoe, since their single boat could not take them all. They said if the Admiral did not take them aboard, they would risk their lives in this way, rather than wait for death at the hands of those cruel butchers, the Indians. Ledesma returned with this reply to the waiting boat and then to the fleet, where he related to the Admiral all that had happened.

Chapter 100

How the Admiral Took Aboard the Men He Had Left in Belén, and How He Proceeded to Jamaica

When the Admiral learned of the defeat suffered by those men, and how discontented and dejected they were, he decided to wait for a turn in the weather and take them aboard. He had to do this with great danger to himself because he was lying off the coast with no possibility of saving them or himself if the weather grew worse. But it pleased God that after eight days during which we were at the mercy of the prow cables the weather so improved that the garrison could begin to transport themselves and their gear over the bar, using their single boat and two large canoes lashed together so as not to overturn. None wished to be among the last to come aboard, and in two days nothing remained ashore except the worm-eaten hulk of the *Gallega*.

Rejoicing that we were reunited at last, we set sail[1] eastward along that coast. All the pilots thought that Española lay to the northward; only the Admiral and the Adelantado knew that it was necessary to sail a good space along the coast before crossing the sea that lies between the mainland and Española. This decision caused much grumbling among the seamen, for they thought the Admiral intended to sail a direct route to Spain with unfit and ill-provisioned ships.

We held on our course till we reached Portobelo; there we had to abandon the *Vizcaína* because she was drawing much water and because her planking was completely riddled by the shipworm. Following the coast, we sailed on beyond Retrete and a country near which there were many islands that the Admiral named Las Barbas;[2] the Indians and the pilots, however, called it the Land of the Cacique Pocorosa. Going on, we reached a headland that the Admiral named Marmóreo[3] and which is ten leagues beyond Las Barbas.

Monday, May 1, 1503, we stood to the northward with winds and currents easterly, always endeavoring to sail as close to the wind as possible. All the pilots insisted that we had passed eastward of the Caribbee Islands, but the Admiral feared he would not be able to fetch Española. So it turned out, because Wednesday, May 10th, we sighted two very small low islands full of turtles (as was all the sea thereabout, so that it seemed to be full of little rocks); that is why these islands were called Las Tortugas.[4] Passing northward by them, we arrived on Friday afternoon at the Jardín de la Reina, which is a great number of small islands on the south side of Cuba.

As we lay here at anchor, ten leagues from Cuba, suffering greatly from hunger because we had nothing to eat but biscuit and a little oil and vinegar, and exhausted by working three pumps day and night to keep the vessels afloat (for they were ready to sink from the multitude of holes made by the shipworm), there came on at night a great storm in which the *Bermuda*, being unable to ride it out, fouled us and broke our stem, nor did she get off whole, but smashed her stern almost to the helm. With great labor on account of the heavy rain and high wind, by God's favor the ships got clear of each other, and although we let go all the cables and anchors we had, none held but the ship's sheet anchor. The next morning we found intact but one strand of her cable, which must have parted if the night had lasted one hour longer; and since that place was full of rocks we could not have avoided running on some of those astern of us. But it pleased God to deliver us then as He had delivered us from many other dangers.

Departing from there with much labor, we put in an Indian village on the coast of Cuba, called Macaca; and having obtained some refreshment there, we stood over toward Jamaica because the easterly winds and the strong westward-running currents would have never let us make Española—especially since the ships were so riddled by the shipworm that day and night we never ceased working three pumps in each of them, and if any broke down, we had to supply its place while it was being patched up. For all our efforts, the eve of St. John's Day the water in our ship rose so high that it was almost up to the deck. With great toil we continued in this state until daybreak when we made a harbor in Jamaica named Puerto Bueno.[5] This harbor was well protected but had no source of fresh water, nor was there any Indian village in the vicinity. So, keeping afloat as well as we could, the next day we sailed eastward to another harbor, named Santa Gloria,[6] that was enclosed with reefs. Having got in, since we were no longer able to keep the ships afloat, we ran them ashore as far as we could, grounding them close together board and board, and shoring them up on both sides so they could not budge; and the ships being in this position the tide rose almost to the decks. Upon these and the fore and sterncastles we built cabins where the people could lodge, making our position as strong as possible so the Indians could do us no harm; for at that time the island was not yet inhabited or subdued by the Christians.

CHAPTER 101

How the Admiral Sent Canoes from Jamaica to Española with Word That He and His People Were Marooned There

When we were thus fortified in the ships as strong as we could be, a crossbow shot from land, the Indians of that country, who proved to be kind and gentle people, presently came in canoes to barter their wares and provisions for our truck. That the trade might be on an equal basis and neither side gain more than was just, the Admiral placed two men in charge of the traffic; and it was agreed that whatever the ship's people obtained by trade would be divided among all in shares. By that time we had nothing aboard to eat, for we had already consumed the greater part of our provisions; much had spoiled, and as much again had been lost in the haste and disorder of the embarkation from Belén.

We being in such straits, God was pleased to bring us to an island abounding in eatables and densely inhabited by Indians eager to trade with us, so that they came from all directions. For this reason, and that his people might not disperse throughout the island, the Admiral preferred to fortify himself aboard and not ashore. Our people being by nature disrespectful, no punishment or order could have stopped them from running about the country and into the Indians' huts to steal what they found and commit outrages on their wives and children, whence would have arisen disputes and quarrels that would have made enemies of them; and if we had taken their food from them by force, we would later have suffered great need and privations. But this did not happen, for the men were confined in the ships and no one

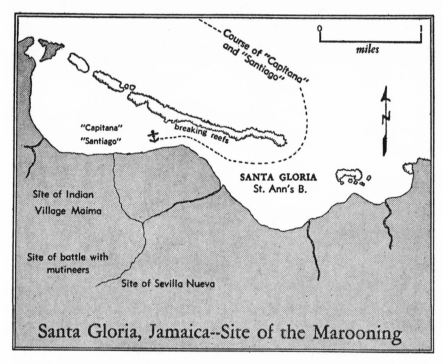

Santa Gloria, Jamaica--Site of the Marooning

could go ashore without getting permission and signing out. The Indians were so grateful for this that they freely brought all we needed in exchange for our things. For one or two hutias we gave them a lacepoint; for a large cake of cassava bread, which is made from grated roots, we gave two or three strings of green or yellow beads; and for a large quantity of anything a hawk's bell, with an occasional gift of a mirror, red cap, or a pair of scissors to the caciques or nobility to keep them happy. By these means we were assured of a plentiful supply of provisions, and the Indians were glad to have us as neighbors.

As some means had to be found of returning to Castile, the Admiral held several meetings of his captains and other leading men to discuss how this might be done. It was idle to hope that some ship might come that way; and there was no possibility of building a new vessel, for we had neither the implements nor the artisans needed for the task, unless we allowed ourselves a long time —and even then such a makeshift vessel would not do, considering the westward-running winds and currents among those islands, so it would only be a loss of time and cause our total ruin instead of averting it.

After many conferences the Admiral determined to send messengers to Española with the news that he was marooned on Jamaica and the request that a rescue ship laden with provisions and ammunition be sent to him. For this mission he chose two reliable and courageous men. Certainly courage was required to make that crossing in the only way it could be done, that is, in Indian canoes made by hollowing out a large log; when heavily loaded, these dugouts are three fourths under water. Moreover, the crossing had to be made in medium-sized canoes, for the smaller ones were too dangerous and the larger ones too slow and cumbrous for such a long voyage.

In July, 1503, having found two suitable canoes, the Admiral ordered Diego Méndez de Segura, chief clerk of the fleet, to sail in one, and Bartolomeo Fieschi, a Genoese gentleman, to sail in the other, each taking a crew of six Christians and ten Indian paddlers. On reaching Española, Diego Méndez should proceed to Santo Domingo, and Fieschi should return to Jamaica with news of Méndez's safe arrival in order to spare us worry and fear that he might have perished. This could easily happen with such flimsy craft if the sea turned at all rough; Indians do not run such great risk, for they can right a capsized canoe while swimming in the sea and get back in. However, honor and necessity incite men to face the greatest risks, so Méndez and Fieschi set out down the coast of Jamaica toward the east end of the island, which the Indians call Aomaquique after the cacique of that province; this end was thirty-three leagues from Maima, the place where we had beached our ships. The distance from Jamaica to Española being thirty leagues,[1] with only one little island or rock along the whole course, and that some eight leagues from Española, they had to wait for a perfect calm before starting to cross that great space in such frail craft. By God's favor this calm soon came.

The Indians having entered the canoes with their gourds of water, some cassava bread, and some other native food, and the Christians having taken their places equipped only with their swords, shields, and provisions, they put out to sea. The Adelantado, who had accompanied them to the eastern end of the island to protect them against attack by Indians at the take-off, watched the canoes until at nightfall they vanished from sight; then he leisurely returned to the fleet, urging the Indians he encountered on the way to be friends and trade with us.

CHAPTER 102

How the Brothers Porras and Many of the People Rose Up Against the Admiral, Saying They Wanted to Go to Castile

After the canoes had left for Española, the people in the caravels began to sicken, both because of the hardships they had endured on the voyage and because of the change in their diet. By this time all the Spanish food had been consumed, and they had no wine to drink or any meat to eat save the flesh of an occasional hutia that they got by trade. Even those who were healthy thought it a hardship to be confined so long to the ships and began to conspire and grumble, saying the Admiral had no intention of returning to Spain, whence the Catholic Sovereigns had banished him; and they said he had even less intention of returning to Española, where he had been forbidden to land at the start of that voyage. His true purpose in sending those canoes was not to obtain ships or relief but to enable Méndez and Fieschi to go to Spain to try to fix up the Admiral's business with the Catholic Sovereigns; while those negotiations were going on, he proposed to pass his exile right there. Otherwise, why had Bartolomeo Fieschi not yet returned as he was supposed to do? And suppose that Méndez and Fieschi had perished at sea, what then? Why, in that case they must help themselves, for no one else would. They could not count on the Admiral to help them escape, for the reasons stated and because he was so afflicted with gout that he could hardly get out of bed, much less endure the hardships of a canoe voyage to Española.

There was nothing for them to do, then, but go off by themselves while they still enjoyed good health, for the Admiral could not stop them; and in Española their reception would be all the better for coming without him: The whole world knew of the bitter enmity and hatred of Governor Ovando, the Knight Commander of Lares, for the Admiral. And when they got home to Spain, they would enjoy the favor of Bishop Juan de Fonseca and the High Treasurer of Castile, Morales (whose lady love was a sister of the brothers Porras, the ringleaders of the conspiracy). As for the Catholic Sovereigns, they would doubtless look on them with favor, being easily persuaded that it was all the Admiral's fault, as they had been at the time of Roldán's mutiny on Española; they would be glad of an excuse to strip the Admiral of all his privileges and free themselves of all their commitments to him.

Made bold by these and similar arguments of the brothers Porras, one being captain of the *Santiago* and the other comptroller of the fleet, forty-eight men signed the articles of the mutiny, choosing Captain Porras for their leader; and they carefully prepared for the day and hour of the outbreak. On the morning of January 2, 1504, the mutineers being armed and ready, Captain Francisco de Porras entered the Admiral's cabin and said to him, "Señor, what do you mean by making no effort to get to Castile? Do you wish to keep us here to perish?" From his insolent tone, so unlike his usual manner, the Admiral immediately guessed what was afoot and replied calmly that he knew no way of going home until a ship was sent; that he was second to no man in his desire to leave, both for his own good and that of the men for whom he was responsible; that if he (Porras) had any other plan to propose, he should submit it to a council of the captains and other officers for discussion; and that he would call as many meetings as were necessary. Porras replied there was no time for talk; the Admiral must decide either to embark or stay with God. Then, turning his back on the Admiral, he cried out, "I'm for Castile, who's with me?" All his henchmen immediately set up a cry, "We're with you!" and running about in great disorder, arms in hand, without any order or plan, they quickly occupied the castles and the roundtops on the mainmasts, some crying "Death to them!" and others "To Castile, to Castile!" and still others "Sir Captain, what do we do now?"

Although the Admiral was in bed so crippled with gout that he could not stand, he nevertheless got up and hobbled to the scene of the mutiny; but three or four honest fellows, his servants, fearing the mutineers might slay him, forced him with great difficulty to return to bed. Then they ran to the Adelantado, who lance in hand was bravely defying the mutineers, and they took the weapon from his hand by force and shut him up with his brother. They begged Captain Porras to go with God and not be the cause of a murder which was bound to harm them all and for which he would certainly be punished. They said none would seek to hinder him from going.

When some degree of quiet had been restored, the mutineers took ten canoes which were tied up to the ships—the Admiral had scoured the islands to procure them in order to keep the Indians from using them against the Christians and also to have them for our use—and they set out in them as gaily as if they were embarking from a harbor in Castile. At this, many who were not mutineers but were desperate at the thought of being abandoned there by the greater and healthiest part of the company also piled into the canoes, to the great distress of the few loyal men and of the many sick, who were convinced they were doomed to remain and perish there. If all had been in good health, I doubt that twenty of those people would have stayed with the Admiral.

The Admiral now came out of his cabin to comfort his men as well as the posture of their affairs allowed. Meanwhile the mutineers under Captain Francisco de Porras cruised in their canoes toward the east end of the island, from which Diego Méndez and Fieschi had begun their crossing to Española. Wherever they called, they inflicted outrages on the Indians, robbing their food and other possessions; they told the Indians to collect their pay from the Admiral and authorized them to kill him if he would not pay. They also told the Indians he was hated by the Christians and was the cause of all the misery of the Indians on Española and would inflict the same suffering on them if they did not kill him, for it was his intention to stay and settle the island.

On the first calm day after the mutineers reached the east end of Jamaica they set out for Española, taking some Indians to paddle the canoes. But the winds being variable and the canoes overloaded, they made slow progress and were not four leagues out when the wind turned contrary; as a result they grew frightened and decided to put back. Since they were not skilled in handling canoes, water began to come over the sides, and in order to lighten them they threw overboard everything except their arms and enough food to get ashore. But the wind grew rough, and becoming more frightened, they decided to kill the Indians and throw them overboard. Some they killed right away; others leaped overboard and swam until exhausted, and when they tried to rest by clinging to the gunwales, their hands were hacked off by the mutineers. They killed eighteen in this way, sparing only a few needed to steer the canoes; this was the Indians' reward for listening to their false promises and their pleas for aid.

Having come ashore, the mutineers were of divers opinions as to what they should do. Some were for going to Cuba, believing that the easterly currents and winds at the place where they were would swiftly bear them there, and that from Cuba to Española was an easy jump; they did not know the two islands were seventeen leagues apart. Others favored returning to the ships and either making peace with the Admiral or taking by force all his arms and goods; still others thought they should wait for another period of calm weather and again try to cross to Española. They decided this last was the best course and stayed in the village of Aomaquique over a month in wait of a fair wind, living off the Indians. When a calm set in at last, they made two more efforts to cross, but both failed because of contrary winds. So they gave up that vain attempt and started back westward on foot, very chopfallen and downcast, sometimes eating what they could find and at others robbing food from the Indians, according to the power or show of resistance made by the local cacique.

CHAPTER 103

*What the Admiral Did after the Muti-
neers Had Left for Española, and of the
Shrewd Use That He Made of an Eclipse*

After the mutineers had departed, the Admiral did all he could
to hasten the recovery of the sick. He also took care to treat the
Indians well that they might continue to bring in provisions for
barter. He was so diligent in this work that the Christians presently
recovered full health, and for a time, at least, the Indians continued
to bring food. But as they are an indolent people who will not
cultivate on a large scale and we consumed more in a day than
they in twenty, and as they were now well supplied with our goods
and saw so many of us there, they began to be influenced by the
arguments of the mutineers. As a result, they began to bring in
less food than we needed. This posed a serious problem, for in order to get food from them by force most of us would have had
to go ashore prepared to fight, leaving the Admiral to face great
danger in the ships. On the other hand, to depend on their good
will meant privation and having to pay twice what we had paid
before; for the Indians understood our situation and their business
very well, and believed they had us at their mercy. So we were
greatly perplexed and did not know what to do.

But God does not forget one who trusts in Him (as the Admiral did), and suggested to him a means whereby we might get all
the food we needed. The Admiral recalled that in three days' time,[1]
at midnight, there would be a total eclipse of the moon. So he sent
an Indian from Española, one of our company, as a messenger to
summon the principal men of the province to a feast and palaver.
The day before the eclipse, the chiefs having arrived, he told the
gathering through an interpreter that we were Christians and believed in God, Who lives in Heaven, and were His servants. God
rewarded the good and punished the wicked, as he had punished
the mutineers by not permitting them to cross over to Española,
as Méndez and Fieschi had done, and by causing them to suffer
many trials and dangers, as the Indians well knew. As for the Indians, God was very angry with them for neglecting to bring us

food for which we paid them by barter, and had determined to punish them with famine and pestilence. To convince the incredulous, God would send them a clear token from Heaven of the punishment they were about to receive. They should therefore attend that night the rising of the moon: She would rise inflamed with wrath, signifying the chastisement God would visit upon them. The Admiral having spoken, the Indians departed, some frightened and others scoffing at his threats.

But at the rising of the moon the eclipse began, and the higher it rose the more complete the eclipse became, at which the Indians grew so frightened that with great howling and lamentation they came running from all directions to the ships, laden with provisions, and praying the Admiral to intercede with God that He might not vent His wrath upon them, and promising they would diligently supply all their needs in the future. The Admiral replied that he wished to speak briefly with his God, and retired to his cabin while the eclipse waxed and the Indians cried all the time for his help. When the Admiral perceived that the crescent phase of the moon was finished and that it would soon shine forth clearly, he issued from his cabin, saying that he had appealed to his God and prayed for them and had promised Him in their name that henceforth they would be good and treat the Christians well, bringing provisions and all else they needed. God had now pardoned them, in token of which they would soon see the moon's anger and inflammation pass away. Perceiving that what he said was coming true, they offered many thanks to the Admiral and uttered praises of his God as long as the eclipse continued. From that time forward they were diligent in providing us with all we needed, and were loud in praise of the Christian God. For they believed that eclipses were very harmful, and since they were ignorant of their cause and of their regular recurrence and did not suspect that men living on earth could know what was happening in the sky, they were certain that his God had revealed that eclipse to the Admiral.

CHAPTER 104

How Another Conspiracy Was Formed
Among the Admiral's People, and How
This Conspiracy Was Quenched by the
Arrival of a Caravel from Española

Eight months had now passed since the departure of Diego Méndez and Bartolomeo Fieschi, without any news of them, and this
caused the Admiral's people much anxiety. Some, suspecting the
worst, said they had drowned or had been killed by the Indians
of Española or had died on the way from sickness and hardships.
They knew that from the east end of Jamaica to the town of Santo
Domingo in Española stretched over one hundred leagues of very
difficult navigation by sea on account of contrary winds and currents and of travel over very rugged mountains by land. To heighten
their fears, some Indians claimed they had seen a derelict boat
drifting down the coast of Jamaica; the mutineers may have spread
this rumor to cause the Admiral's people to lose all hope of rescue.

Being quite certain that all chance of relief was gone, one Master
Bernal, an apothecary from Valencia, secretly began to hatch another conspiracy on the order of the first one, into which he drew
the majority of the men who had been sick. But Our Lord, seeing
the great danger the Admiral was in, was pleased to avert it by
the arrival of a small caravel sent by the governor of Española.
This ship arrived one afternoon and anchored near the grounded
ships; the captain, Diego de Escobar, came aboard and informed
the Admiral that the Knight Commander of Lares, the governor
of Española, sent his compliments and regretted that he had no
ship large enough to take off all the Admiral's men, but hoped to
be able to send one before long; the captain then presented the
Admiral with a barrel of wine and a slab of salt pork and immediately returned to the caravel, sailing away that same night without even taking letters from anyone.[1]

The Admiral's people were much comforted by the coming of
that caravel and covered up the plot they had been hatching,
though the speed and secrecy with which the ship departed made

them suspicious, and they were easily persuaded that the Knight Commander Ovando did not want the Admiral to return to Española. This coming to the Admiral's notice, he told them it had been his doing because that caravel was too small to take them all, and he did not want to leave without taking them all; nor did he wish to stay behind lest it cause new quarrels and negotiations with the mutineers.

The truth was that the Knight Commander feared the Admiral's return to Castile, for he suspected that the Catholic Sovereigns would restore the Admiral to his office and deprive him (Ovando) of his government. That is why he would not help the Admiral go to Española, sending instead that little caravel to spy on him and report how he might be totally destroyed. This the Admiral knew from a letter sent by Diego Méndez in that caravel in which he told of his voyage and what happened to him thereafter. This is the story he told.

CHAPTER 105

How the Admiral Learned What Happened on the Voyage to Diego Méndez and Fieschi

The first day out of Jamaica, Diego Méndez and Fieschi had a fine calm through which they cruised till evening, urging the Indians to paddle as hard as they could with the sticks they use for paddles. The heat being intense, the Indians refreshed themselves from time to time by swimming in the sea. Moving over tranquil waters, by sunset they had lost sight of land. At nightfall half the Indians took their turn at paddling and as many Spaniards at guard duty; this last was a precaution against any betrayal by the Indians. They paddled all that night without resting, and by daybreak were utterly fatigued. Each captain urged on his men and sometimes took a turn at the paddles; and having taken some food to regain their strength after such a hard night, the rowers returned to their work, seeing nothing but water and sky.

It could be said of them what was told of Tantalus, who, having water but a few inches from his lips, could not quench his thirst; our men suffered greatly on account of the folly of the Indians, for in the great heat of the past day and night they had

Mass on Shore

drunk all the water, heedless of future needs. As the sun rose in the heavens the heat and their thirst grew ever worse, so that by noon they were completely exhausted. By good fortune the captains had each brought along a small water cask from which they kept doling out a few drops of water to their Indians, just enough to sustain them till the cool of the evening; they encouraged them with the hope of soon raising Navassa, which is eight leagues from Española. The Indians were not only worn out from thirst and from having paddled two days and a night but were thoroughly discouraged and convinced they were off their course, since by their reckoning they had paddled twenty leagues and should already have sighted Navassa.

It was exhaustion and faintness that deceived them, for even with hard paddling a canoe cannot make more than ten leagues in a day and night on account of the currents running counter to the course from Jamaica to Española. That night one of the Indians died of thirst, others were stretched out on the bottom of the canoes, and the rest were so weak and dejected that they made almost no way at all. Still they pushed along, wetting their mouths with salt water, which was the comfort afforded to Our Lord when he said "I thirst"; and so they continued until night fell for a second time without sight of land.

They being emissaries of one that God wished to save, He caused it to pass that at the rising of the moon Diego Méndez observed that a small island covered its lower part like an eclipse. Had it not been for this, he could not have seen the island, which was very small and looked even smaller at that hour. Méndez joyfully pointed it out to the others, and by doling some of the contents of the water cask to the paddlers so strengthened them that the next morning they were up to the island.

They found it a bare rock, half a league around. Landing as best they could, they offered up thanks to God for His mercy; and as the island was treeless and without springs, they scrambled from cliff to cliff gathering water in gourds, and found such an abundance of it that they could fill their stomachs and vessels. Although advised not to drink too much, some Indians drank their fill and died; others were made dreadfully sick.

Overjoyed at being within sight of Española, they rested that day till the afternoon, larking about and eating shellfish that they found on the shore and cooked, for Méndez had brought flint and steel for making fire. Then, fearing the onset of rough weather, they prepared for the last leg of their voyage, and in the cool of the evening pushed off for Cape San Miguel, the nearest point on Española, and made it the morning of the next day, being the fourth day since their departure.

After resting two days, Bartolomeo Fieschi, standing on his honor as an hidalgo, proposed to return as the Admiral had ordered. But since his people were mere Indians and sailors, exhausted and ill from their labors and from drinking sea water, not a man would come with him; for the Christians regarded themselves as having been delivered from the whale's belly, their three days and nights corresponding to those of the prophet Jonah. Diego Méndez, who was in great haste, had already left in his canoe along the coast of Española, though he was suffering from a quartan ague caused by his great privations by land and sea. Striking inland, he proceeded with his men over wretched paths and rugged mountains to Xaraguá, a western province of Española, where the governor then was. Ovando pretended to be pleased by his arrival, but delayed sending him forward for a long time for the reasons indicated above. By great persistence Diego Méndez at last secured his permission to proceed to Santo Domingo to purchase and outfit a ship with funds and revenues the Admiral had there. Having made a caravel ready and provisioned it, he sent it to Jamaica at the end of May, 1504, and himself took ship for Spain, as the Admiral had ordered, in order to report to the Catholic Sovereigns the happenings of his voyage.

CHAPTER 106

How the Mutineers Spurned the Admiral's Offers and Refused to Treat with Him

The Admiral and his people being much relieved by news of the safe arrival of Diego Méndez and the coming of the little caravel, by which they had assurance of their rescue, the Admiral decided to inform the mutineers of what had happened in the hope of bringing them to obedience. He sent as emissaries two respected persons who were on friendly terms with them; and as proof that the caravel had actually arrived, he also sent them a portion of the salt pork that Ovando had presented to him. When these emissaries came to where Captain Porras and his trusted lieutenants awaited, Captain Porras came out alone to meet them because he feared they brought an offer of a general pardon which his men might be persuaded to accept. But he could not keep his men from learning of the arrival of the caravel, of the excellent health and spirits of the Admiral's people, or of his offer of such a pardon. After several parleys between the emissaries and Porras and his lieutenants, the latter declared they did not trust the Admiral's offer of a safe-conduct and pardon. However, they would gladly leave the island if the Admiral promised to give them a ship in case two arrived; if only one was sent, he should assign half the space to them. Meanwhile, since they had lost at sea all they had gained by barter, he should share with them what he had.

The envoys began to say that these conditions were unreasonable and unacceptable, but the mutineers broke in with threats that if the Admiral did not give them what they asked, they would take it from him by force. Then they dismissed the envoys, rejecting the Admiral's offers. They told their followers the Admiral was a cruel and vengeful man; for themselves they had no fear, as they had friends at Court, but he might vent his wrath on the others, calling it condign punishment. That was why Roldán and his men had not trusted the Admiral's offers on Española. And see how well their enterprise turned out; assuredly it would be the same with them. In order to dispel any effect the coming of the caravel with news of Méndez' safe arrival might have on them, they assured their men this was no real ship but a phantasm conjured up by magic arts of which the Admiral was a master. Clearly a real caravel would not have left so soon, with so little dealing between its crew and the Admiral's men, and surely the Admiral and his brother would have sailed away in it. With such words they hardened their followers' mutinous spirit and egged them on to march on the ships to take by force all they could find and make the Admiral their prisoner.

Chapter 107

How the Adelantado Sallied Forth to Meet the Mutineers Near the Ships and Defeated Them, Capturing Captain Porras

Persisting in their wicked design, the mutineers marched to within a quarter-league of the ships, to an Indian village called Maima, where the Christians later founded a city named Seville. When he learned of their intention, the Admiral sent his brother the Adelantado in an effort to bring them to their senses with soft words, but backed him up with a large enough force to repel any attack. So the Adelantado selected fifty well-armed men who were ready to strike hard blows if the need arose.

Having come to a hilltop a crossbow shot from the village where the mutineers were, the Adelantado sent two men who had gone on the first embassy in another effort to make peace, inviting their leader to a conference. But the mutineers were not at all inferior in numbers to the loyalists, and being for the most part sailormen who held the Admiral's men in contempt as cowards who would not fight, they would not even allow the envoys to address them. Drawn up in battle formation and crying "Kill! Kill!" they fell upon the Adelantado and his men; six of them had earlier sworn to keep together and seek out the Adelantado, thinking that once he was slain the others would give no trouble.

It pleased God, however, that the affair turned out very differently; for at the first encounter five or six of the mutineers were struck down, most of them being men who had sworn to kill the Adelantado. He fell on his enemies so fiercely that in a short time were slain Juan Sánchez of Cádiz, he who let the Quibián escape, and Juan Barba, who first drew his sword at the time of the mutiny; a number were badly wounded, and Captain Francisco de Porras was made prisoner. Seeing themselves so roughly handled, those vile mutineers turned tail and ran away with all their might. The Adelantado wished to pursue them, but his lieutenants restrained him, saying that it was well to punish, but in moderation.

If they killed too many, the Indians, who could be seen looking on, arms in hand, might get it into their minds to attack the victors. The Adelantado followed their advice and returned to the ships with Captain Porras and other prisoners; he was joyfully received by his brother the Admiral and those who stayed with him, all offering up thanks to God for this great victory by which those proud wicked men were punished and abased. On our side the only hurt was suffered by the Adelantado, who was wounded in the hand, and by the Admiral's chief waiter, who died from a slight lance stroke in the side.

As for the rebels, Pedro de Ledesma, the pilot who had gone with Vicente Yáñez to Honduras and who swam ashore at Belén, fell over a cliff and was hidden from sight that day and till nightfall of the next, only the Indians knowing where he was. Curious to know how our swords cut, they opened up his wounds with little sticks. He had a cut on the head so deep that one could see his brains; another on the shoulder, which was almost severed, so that his arm hung limp; one thigh was cut to the bone down to the shin bone; and the sole of one foot was sliced from heel to toe so that it resembled a slipper. Despite these wounds, when the Indians annoyed him, he would growl at them, "Get away, or I'll do you a mischief," and these words alone caused them to run away in great alarm. When the ship's people learned of his plight, they came and brought him to a palm-thatched hut nearby, where the dampness and mosquitoes alone should have finished him off. Having no turpentine, the ship's people used oil to cauterize Ledesma's wounds, which were so numerous that during the first eight days of his cure the surgeon swore he was always discovering new ones. Yet he recovered at last; but the chief waiter, for whose life none feared, died.

Next day, Monday, May 20th, the other mutineers sent envoys to plead humbly with the Admiral to be merciful to them, for they were repentant and wished to rejoin his service. The Admiral granted them a full pardon, but insisted on keeping Captain Porras a prisoner that he might not be the cause of new disturbances. As so many people could not be comfortably lodged and fed and kept at peace aboard the ships, where there was not enough food for even one of the two bands, and as he wanted to avoid the exchange of insults that might revive buried quarrels, the Admiral decided to place the former mutineers under the command of a captain who should tour the island with them, trading with the Indians and keeping them occupied until the coming of the ships, whose arrival was daily expected.

CHAPTER 108

*How the Admiral Crossed Over to Es-
pañola, and Thence to Castile, Where
Our Lord Received Him into His Holy
Glory in Valladolid*

A few days after these events, which reduced the mutineers to obedience and made the Indians better disposed to provision us with food, it was one year since our arrival at Jamaica. At this time the ship that Diego Méndez had purchased and provisioned in Santo Domingo with the Admiral's money arrived; in this ship we embarked, friends and enemies alike. We set sail on June 28th, and experienced considerable difficulty because of the contrary winds and currents on the course from Jamaica to Santo Domingo, where we joyfully put in on August 13, 1504. The governor received the Admiral very hospitably and lodged him in his own house; but it was a scorpion's kiss, for at the same time he released Captain Porras, the ringleader of the mutiny, and proposed to punish those who had been responsible for his imprisonment. Ovando also proposed to intervene in other matters and offenses which concerned only the Catholic Sovereigns, who had sent the Admiral as captain general of their fleet. So the governor's compliments to the Admiral were as false as his smiles and pretense of joy at seeing him. Matters went on in this way until our ship had been repaired and another vessel chartered in which sailed the Admiral, his relations, and servants, most of the others choosing to stay in Española.

We sailed on September 12th. After we had left the river and

proceeded two leagues out to sea, the mainmast of the ship split
right down to the deck. The Admiral then sent this ship back, and

The Paulus Jovius Portrait of Columbus

we continued in our ship toward Castile. After sailing with fair
weather almost a third part of our course, we had a terrible storm
that placed us in great jeopardy. The next day, Saturday, October

19th, the weather having cleared and we being easy, the mainmast broke in four pieces; but the valor of the Adelantado and the ingenuity of the Admiral, who could not rise from bed on account of his gout, contrived a jury mast out of a lateen yard, which we secured firmly about the middle with ropes and planks taken from the stern and forecastles, which we tore down. In another storm the foremast was sprung. It pleased God that we sailed seven hundred leagues in this manner, until we reached the port of Sanlúcar de Barrameda.¹ From there we went to Seville, where the Admiral had relief from his many hardships and exertions.

In May, 1505, he set out for the court of the Catholic King. The glorious Queen Isabella had passed to a better life the previous year.² Her death caused the Admiral much grief; for she had always aided and favored him, while the King he always found somewhat reserved and unsympathetic to his projects. This was clearly shown by the reception that His Majesty accorded him. He received him courteously and professed to be restoring all his rights and privileges, but it was his real design to take them all away; and this he would have done but for his sense of shame, which is a powerful force in noble souls. His Highness and the serene Queen had dispatched the Admiral on his voyage of discovery. Now, however, that the Indies were giving signs of that which they were to become, the Catholic King begrudged the Admiral the large share that he had in them by virtue of his capitulations with the Crown. The King wished to regain absolute control over them and dispose as he pleased of the offices that were only the Admiral's to grant. He therefore proposed to negotiate a new capitulation with the Admiral, but God would not permit it, for at that very time the most serene King Philip I came to the throne of Spain.³ And even as the Catholic King departed from Valladolid to receive him, the Admiral, who was much afflicted by the gout and by grief at seeing himself fallen from his high estate, as well as by other ills, yielded up his soul to God on the Day of the Ascension, May 20, 1506, in the city of Valladolid, having received with much devotion all the sacraments of the Church and said these last words *in manus tuas, Domine, commendo spiritum meum.* God, in His great mercy and goodness, assuredly received him into His glory. *Ad quem nos cum eo perducat. Amen.*⁴

By His Son Ferdinand

[His body was afterwards borne to Seville and buried in the principal cathedral of that city with funereal pomp. By order of the Catholic King, over his tomb was placed an epitaph in the Spanish language that read:

TO CASTILE AND LEÓN,
COLUMBUS GAVE A NEW WORLD

These words and that gift are truly worthy of note. History knows of no man who ever did the like, wherefore the world will ever remember the first discoverer of the West Indies. Afterwards, passing over to the mainland, Hernando Cortés and Francisco Pizarro found many other provinces and great kingdoms. Thus Cortés discovered the province of Yucatán, together with the City of Mexico, called New Spain, then held by the great Montezuma, the emperor of that part of the world. And Francisco Pizarro discovered the kingdom of Peru, which is very large and wealthy, possessed by the great king Atabalipa. From those provinces and kingdoms there come to Spain every year many ships laden with gold, silver, brazilwood, cochineal, sugar, pearls, and precious stones, and many other things of great value, on account of which Spain and her princes today are in a flourishing condition.]

Notes

Editor's Preface

1. The shortened title by which Ferdinand's book is generally cited. The lengthy full title of the first Italian edition, published in Venice in 1571, is *Historie del S. D. Fernando Colombo; Nelle quali s'ha particolare, & vera relatione della vita, & de' fatti dell'Ammiraglio D. Cristoforo Colombo, suo padre: Et dello scoprimento, ch'egli fece dell' Indie Occidentali, dette Mondo Nuovo, hora possedute dal Sereniss. Re Catolico: Nuovamente di lingua Spagnuola tradotte nell'Italiana dal S. Alfonso Ulloa.*
2. A domain of 25 square leagues in the western part of the Isthmus of Panama.
3. John Boyd Thacher, *Christopher Columbus, His Life, His Work, His Remains* (N. Y., 1903-1904, 3 vols.), III, 430.
4. In 1960 the Rumanian scholar Alejandro Cioranescu launched a new attack on the authenticity of Ferdinand's book in a work entitled *Primera biografía de Cristóbal Colón. Fernando Colón y Bartolomé de Las Casas.* Cioranescu argued that the book was a preliminary draft of Las Casas's *Historia.* Although David Henige, *In Search of Columbus: The Sources for the First Voyage*, p. 35, claims that Cioranescu's book is "the most serious, extensive, and effective attack" of its kind, leading European scholars have found its arguments unconvincing and lacking in probative value.

Dedication

1. Baliano de Fornari, a wealthy and philanthropic physician of Genoa.
2. Giuseppe Moleto, Sicilian mathematician and professor at the University of Padua.
3. Giovanni Battista di Marini, Genoese patrician, member of the Senate of the Republic from 1543 to 1556.

Chapter 1

1. Ferdinand's claims of a distinguished lineage for his father are without foundation. Note, however, that he does not say that his father was descended from a Roman consul, but attributes the suggestion to others. The two "illustrious Coloni" or Colombos were corsairs not related to each other or to Christopher Columbus, one being Guillaume de Casenove, nicknamed Colombo, Admiral of France in the reign of Louix XI. It is known that the father of the Discoverer was a master weaver who occupied a modest position in the lower middle class of Genoa.

Marcantonio Coccio (1435-1506), better known as Sabellicus, wrote a history of Venice, *Rerum venetiarum ab urbe condita* (Venice, 1487), that was used by Ferdinand.

Notes to Chapters 1-5

2. Columbus was probably born in the city of Genoa sometime between August 25 and the end of October, 1451.

Chapter 2

1. Agostino Giustiniani (1470-1536), Orientalist, historian, and Bishop of Nebbio in Corsica. In 1516 he published a *Polyglot Psalter* containing (in a note to Psalm XIX) the phrase that aroused Ferdinand's wrath, *Christophorus cognomento Columbus, patria Genuensis, vilibus ortus parentibus* ("Christopher Columbus by name, a native of Genoa, born of common parents"). He repeated this phrase in his *Castigatissimi annali . . . della eccelsa e illustrissima Republica di Genova* (Genoa, 1537).
2. "Born in a lowly place, or of very poor parents."
3. The Italian text is clearly garbled at this point. My rendering of the above passage follows the revision suggested by Rinaldo Caddeo, ed., *Le Historie della vita e dei fatti di Cristoforo Colombo per D. Fernando Colombo suo figlio* (Milan, 1930, 2 vols.), I, 118 n.
4. Astronomical hours, of fifteen degrees.
5. There is no record of such action by the Republic of Genoa.
6. The letter from which this fragment is quoted has not come to light. The phrase "first Admiral of my family" probably refers to Guillaume de Casenove. As noted above, there was no relationship between this man and Columbus.

Chapter 3

1. According to S. E. Morison, matriculation records of the University of Pavia do not support Ferdinand's claim that his father studied at that institution.

Chapter 4

1. René of Anjou, called "the Good" (1409-1480). René, supported by Genoa, disputed the crown of Naples with Aragon. The episode described by Columbus would have taken place in 1472, when he was twenty-one. Some scholars have questioned the truth of the story.
2. Thule (Iceland).
3. The Genoese *braccio* or fathom was equivalent to 22.9 inches.
4. The coast of present-day Liberia in West Africa, from which the Portuguese obtained a variety of pepper of commercial value. The "sirens" were probably seals.

Chapter 5

1. See Chapter 1, n. 1.
2. Ferdinand's account of this affair is sadly confused. The combat, which took place in 1476, was actually between a convoy of five Genoese vessels and a

French armada commanded by the corsair Guillaume de Casenove. Morison, and more recently the Italian scholar Emilio Taviani, believe that Columbus shipped aboard one of the Genoese vessels as a common sailor and accept the authenticity of the story that he was cast ashore in Portugal, as told by Ferdinand.

3. The Convento dos Santos in Lisbon belonged to the knights of the military order of Santiago. By this time, according to Morison, it had become "a fashionable boarding school for the daughters of the Portuguese aristocracy." Ferdinand has confused the names; Dona Felipa was the daughter of Bartholomeu Perestrello and Isabel Moniz.

Chapter 6

1. Greek geographers of the second century A.D. Ptolemy was the great geographical authority of Europe at the opening of the Age of Discovery. Marinus of Tyre buttressed Columbus's theory of a short sail westward from Europe to Asia by his immense overestimate of the size of the known world.

2. Strabo, Greek geographer (64 B.C.?-24 A.D.), author of a text describing Europe, Asia, Egypt, and Libya.

3. Ctesias, Greek historian of the fifth century A.D., author of a history of Persia and a work on India.

4. Nearchus, an officer of Alexander the Great, commanded the fleet that sailed from the mouth of the Indus to the head of the Persian Gulf (325-324 B.C.). Onescritus, historian of Alexander the Great, accompanied Nearchus on this voyage.

5. The reference is to Pliny's great encyclopedia of natural science, *Historia naturalis*, widely read in the Middle Ages.

6. Alfragan (al-Farghani), Moslem astronomer and geographer of the end of the ninth and the beginning of the tenth centuries. It should be noted that Alfragan's miles were Arabic, or 1,973.5 meters. As a result, Alfragan's calculation of the circumference of the Earth was approximately correct, but Columbus reduced it by one third. This led him to conclude that from Spain to the end of Asia was but a short distance.

7. Rodrigo Fernández de Santaella y Córdoba (1444-1509), church official and confessor to the Catholic Sovereigns, and first translator into Spanish of Marco Polo's travel account. The passage to which Ferdinand objected appears in the introduction to this work.

Chapter 7

1. Lucius Annaeus Seneca (4 B.C.?-65 A.D.), Roman philosopher and dramatist, born in Córdoba.

2. The pilot of the Argonauts.

3. Gaius Julius Solinus, Roman poet and grammarian, probably of the third century A.D., author of a description of the world, *Collectanea rerum memorabilium*, based largely on Pliny's *Historia naturalis*.

4. The famous *Book of Ser Marco Polo Concerning the Kingdoms and Marvels*

of the East fired Columbus's imagination with its depiction of the wealth and wonders of China and Japan and contributed materially to his geographical ideas.

5. The pseudonym of the fourteenth-century compiler of a book of travels, combining geography with fantastic yarns, that enjoyed an immense popularity in the Middle Ages. Its real author is now generally believed to have been Jean d'Outremeuse, a citizen of Liège.
6. Pierre d'Ailly (1350-1420), French Cardinal, theologian, and geographer, from whose *Imago mundi* Columbus derived much of his acquaintance with the Greek and Roman texts favorable to his thesis of a narrow ocean between Europe and Asia.
7. Julius Capitolinus, Roman writer of about 300 A.D., one of the authors of the Augustan History.
8. Paolo dal Pozzo Toscanelli (1397-1482), renowned physician, mathematician, astronomer, and geographer of Florence. The authenticity of his correspondence with Columbus (as distinct from his exchange of letters with Fernão Martins) remains a matter of scholarly controversy.

Chapter 8

1. Some scholars question the authenticity of these letters.
2. A reference to a dynastic war between Portugal and Castile (1475-1479) that ended in a Castilian victory.
3. Identified with modern Tsinkiang, on the inlet of Formosa Strait.
4. Identified with modern Hangchow.
5. In the book of Marco Polo, on which Toscanelli drew heavily for his description of the East, Mangi is southern China, and Cathay the northern part of the Chinese Empire.
6. A mythical island in the Atlantic, shown by medieval map-makers on the parallel of Lisbon or that of Cape St. Vincent, toward latitude 40 degrees N.
7. Japan.

Chapter 9

1. On the west coast of Africa, in latitude 10 degrees N.
2. A group of mythical islands in the Atlantic.
3. Bartolomé de las Casas gives this source in his *Historia de las Indias* as "the book called *Inventio fortunata*."
4. Perhaps Fernão Domingues de Arco, to whom King João II in 1484 granted an island which he had sighted west of Madeira, and to which he proposed to sail on a voyage of discovery.
5. Morison gives this man's name as "Pedro Vasques." Palos is in Spain, not Portugal.
6. The Franciscan monastery where Columbus stayed on his first coming to Spain.
7. One of the Azores.
8. Newfoundland.
9. The promised account is not given by Ferdinand.

10. Another omission by Ferdinand (or his translator) occurs at this point, for the story told by Oviedo in his *Historia general y natural de las Indias* is not that of Vicente Dias but of the anonymous pilot who was carried by storms to the Indies, returned to Spain in shattered health, found refuge in the home of Columbus, and shortly before his death informed his benefactor of his discovery and aided him to make a chart of the land he found. "As for me," adds Oviedo dryly, "I hold it to be false."

Chapter 10

1. The first part of Gonzalo Fernández de Oviedo's *Historia general y natural de las Indias* was published in 1535. The material that provoked Ferdinand's anger is in Book II, Chapter 3.
2. This is the pseudo-Aristotle of the work *De mirabilibus auscultationibus*, of unknown authorship, written between the second and sixth centuries A.D.
3. The Casiterides are usually identified with the Scilly islands, northwest of Brittany.
4. A reference to the great voyage of Ferdinand Magellan and Juan de Elcano (1519-1522).
5. This is Morison's salty version of the Portuguese adage.
6. Ferdinand confuses the Greek island of Atalante, severed from the mainland of Euboea by an earthquake, with the mythical subcontinent of Atlantis told of by Plato.
7. Sebosus was a Roman writer on geography, of about 50 B.C.
8. Gaius Julius Hyginus (*circa* 65 B.C.-17 A.D.), Roman author of a chiefly mythological treatment of astronomy, *Poetica astronomia*.

Chapter 11

1. Dom João II (1481-1495).
2. Diogo Ortis de Vilhegas, called Calzadilla, Bishop of Viseu and Tangier, theologian and geographer, member of a small powerful council that advised the King on scientific and maritime matters.
3. Rinaldo Caddeo accepts the truth of this story; Morison rejects it as apocryphal, noting that Columbus invariably speaks of Dom João with respect and esteem.
4. The following translation of Bartholomew's Latin verses was kindly made for me by Professor Charles Sleeth of Brooklyn College:

   Whoever you are who wish to know for your profit the shores of the lands, [this] fine picture will learnedly teach [you] everything, [this picture] which Strabo confirms, [also] Ptolemy, Pliny, and Isidore: not every opinion [of any one of these authorities is], however, one and the same [with the opinions of the others]. Here is pictured even that torrid zone, recently furrowed by Spanish keels, [which was] formerly unknown to the people, [but] which now at last is very well known to many.

   For the author, or painter:
   He whose native place is Genoa [and] whose name is Bartholomew

Columbus of the Red Land published this work in London in the year of our Lord one thousand four hundred ninety and eight, on the thirteenth day of the month of February.

Let praises be sung to Christ abundantly.

The line "that torrid zone, recently furrowed by Spanish keels" probably refers to Portuguese voyages down the west coast of Africa.

Chapter 12

1. In the province of Huelva in Andalusia, not far from the Portuguese frontier.
2. Aragonese *converso* and supporter of Columbus; he lent about half the money needed to launch the Enterprise of the Indies.
3. Fray Hernando de Talavera (1428-1507), Jeronymite friar, prior of the monastery of Nuestra Señora del Prado near Valladolid, and confessor of Queen Isabella.

Chapter 13

1. Don Enrique de Guzmán, Duke of Medina Sidonia, then the wealthiest man in Spain. This negotiation was apparently proceeding satisfactorily when the Duke was banished from Seville by the Monarchs for brawling with a fellow grandee.
2. An indirect reference to Ferdinand's own birth in Córdoba, about August 15, 1488. The reference to "children" may be a translator's error.
3. Alonso de Villalón, member of the Royal Council.

Chapter 14

1. An allusion to a letter of King João to Columbus (March 20, 1488), calling him "our special friend" and inviting him to return to the King's service. Ferdinand evidently forgot to return to the matter.

Chapter 15

1. Moorish Granada had already fallen, the Catholic Sovereigns making their triumphal entrance into the city on January 2, 1492.

Chapter 16

1. The following chart, based on the pertinent chapters in S. E. Morison's *Admiral of the Ocean Sea*, presents some basic facts (and conjectures) about Columbus's ships. No plans, drawing, or dimensions have come down to us; the measurements given here represent Morison's "educated guesses." All three ships were one-deckers. The Spanish *tonelada* or ton was roughly equivalent to 40 cubic feet.

	Santa María or *La Gallega*	*Pinta*	*Niña* or *Santa Clara*
Class and Rigging	Flagship. Three-masted, square-rigged *nao* or ship, a larger and slower boat than a caravel.	Three-masted, square-rigged caravel.	Three-masted caravel, lateen-rigged from Palos to Gomera, square-rigged from Gomera on.
Master	Juan de la Cosa of Santoña	Martín Francisco Pinzón	Juan Niño of Moguer
Captain	Christopher Columbus, captain general and captain	Martín Alonso Pinzón	Vicente Yáñez Pinzón
Pilot	Peralonso Niño	Cristóbal García Sarmiento (or Xalmiento)	Sancho Ruiz de Gama
Tonnage	100 tons	55-60 tons	60 tons
Over-all Length	?	73-75 feet	70 feet
Beam	?	25 feet	23 feet
Depth of Hold	?	11 feet	9 feet
Complement	About 40 men	About 26 men	About 24 men

Chapter 17

1. Cristóbal Quintero.

Chapter 18

1. Probably the small Arctic tern or a young boatswain bird.
2. The boatswain bird.
3. They were entering the Sargasso Sea.

Chapter 19

1. A seagull of gray color.

Chapter 20

1. The two brightest stars of the constellation of the Little Bear or Little Dipper, β (Kochab) and γ.

Notes to Chapters 22-28

Chapter 22

1. Columbus's action in claiming the lifetime pension for himself has rightly been called "a rather cruel abuse of power."

Chapter 23

1. In his Journal of the First Voyage Columbus tells that the banners were marked with an F (Fernando) and Y (Ysabel) with each letter surmounted by a crown.
2. Much controversy surrounds precisely where Columbus made landfall, with the most likely candidates reduced by recent research to Watlings Island and Samana Cay.
3. The name given to the American aborigines by Columbus in the belief that he had reached the eastern end of Asia or India.

Chapter 24

1. Small round bronze bells, about the diameter of a quarter dollar, that were attached to the hawks used in falconry. Other standard trading goods of the Spaniards in the Antilles included lace points, the metal tips of the laces then used to fasten men's clothing; red caps; and brass tambourine jingles.
2. A copper coin of the smallest value.

Chapter 25

1. Modern Rum Cay.
2. Modern Long Island.
3. The reference is to tobacco.

Chapter 26

1. Modern Crooked Island.
2. A lacuna in the Italian text.
3. The supposed aloe wood was actually useless agave.

Chapter 27

1. "The River of Seas"; modern Puerto Gibara.
2. Columbus, dominated by his pathetic illusion, at first identified Cuba with Japan, later with the Asian mainland; the embassy was sent to visit the Great Khan or Emperor of China!

Chapter 28

1. Sweet potatoes or yams.
2. Tobacco.

3. These small dogs, whose bark was limited to a kind of grunt, were bred by the Indians principally for use as food.
4. This passage is badly mixed up. Bohío, the Arawak word for the native hut, was later identified by Columbus with Haiti; Babeque was apparently the Indian name for Great Inagua Island.

Chapter 29

1. Probably modern Júcaro Bay.
2. Modern Tánamo Bay.
3. The supposed mastic was gumbo-limbo resin; the aloes, agave.
4. Probably the coati.
5. A trunkfish.

Chapter 30

1. Modern Puerto Cayo Moa.
2. Modern Puerto Baracoa.
3. A light-oared vessel of not more than 300 tons, sometimes having one or two masts.

Chapter 31

1. Meaning that this was Alpha and Omega, the beginning or the end of the continent of Asia, depending on whether one journeyed toward it from the East or the West. Modern Cape Maisí.
2. Modern Moustique Bay.

Chapter 32

1. A coin struck by the Catholic Sovereigns.

Chapter 33

1. Modern Acul Bay and Picolet Pt.

Chapter 34

1. The gold-bearing central zone of Española; Columbus believed "Cibao" to be a corruption of the name Cathay.

Chapter 35

1. "Port of the Nativity."
2. Cape Haitien.
3. Modern Río Yaque del Norte.

Notes to Chapters 36-42

Chapter 36

1. Modern Cape Samaná.
2. This man was not a Carib but one of the Ciguayo, who wore their hair long and were less peaceful than the Taino that Columbus had previously met.
3. An alloy of gold and copper smelted by the Indians on the South American mainland, and apparently imported by the Taino of Española. A pendant or other ornament made of this alloy was also called a *guanín*.
4. Probably modern Martinique.
5. "Bay of Arrows"; modern Samaná Bay.

Chapter 37

1. Given as San Theramo in Las Casas, *Historia de las Indias*; modern Cape Engaño.
2. In Estremadura, Spain.
3. In Italy.
4. Near Palos, the starting point of the voyage.

Chapter 38

1. João de Castanheda.

Chapter 39

1. Las Casas, *Historia de las Indias*, reports that the Portuguese delegation included two priests and a notary public.

Chapter 40

1. The outer port of Lisbon, about four miles below the city.

Chapter 41

1. He was Bartholomeu Dias, perhaps the discoverer of that name of the Cape of Good Hope.
2. Columbus declined, perhaps fearing for his life. According to the Portuguese chronicler Rui de Pina, some of Dom João's courtiers proposed to assassinate the Discoverer and later to claim that he had picked a quarrel and caused his own death. Pina relates that the King forbade such an action.

Chapter 42

1. This name, appearing in both Ferdinand's *Historie* and the *Historia* of Las Casas, is regarded by Caddeo as a misprint or an error in translation. Iglesia, however, cites Antonio Ballesteros as noting that the Infante Don Enrique de Aragón, King Ferdinand's cousin, was called "Fortuna."

Notes to Chapters 44-52

Chapter 44

1. For the capitulations of April 30, 1492, and May 28, 1493, I have used with some changes the translation in the magnificent facsimile edition of *Christopher Columbus: His Own Book of Privileges*, compiled and edited by Benjamin F. Stevens (London, 1893), pp. 53-62.
2. Councilmen of Seville and other cities in ancient Andalusia.

Chapter 46

1. They were in the Lesser Antilles.
2. Modern Mariegalante.

Chapter 47

1. Puerto Rico.
2. Many modern historians and anthropologists are skeptical of Columbus's ascription of cannibalism to the Carib Indians, noting that there is little or no believable evidence for the claim.
3. Yaramaqui is modern Antigua. There is no clue to the identity of the other islands.
4. Alonso de Hojeda (*circa* 1466-1515 or 1516), future explorer of the coast of Venezuela and one of the rebel leaders on Española.

Chapter 48

1. Later called Nuestra Señora de las Nieves; still known as Nevis, birthplace of Alexander Hamilton.
2. The Virgin Islands.

Chapter 50

1. The mark weighed 230.04½ grams.

Chapter 51

1. Don Diego (1468-1515), the youngest of the Columbus brothers, was summoned from Genoa to Spain by Christopher on his return from the First Voyage.
2. "The Pass of the Hidalgos."
3. "River of Canes." Actually the Río de Oro (modern Río Yaque del Norte), whose mouth Columbus had explored on the First Voyage.
4. A twining plant that yields a resin used as a purgative.

Chapter 52

1. An affluent of the Río Yaque del Norte, of uncertain identity.
2. "Green River."

Notes to Chapters 54-58

Chapter 54

1. Fray Bernal Buyl or Boyl, first apostolic vicar in the Indies, had been entrusted by the Catholic Sovereigns with the work of conversion of the Indians.
2. The *alguacil mayor* (chief constable) of the fleet.
3. A close friend of Columbus, and his factor or business agent.
4. Guacanagarí feared the Admiral's wrath; he had aided the Indian women captured in the Caribbees to flee from the ships and had taken one of them for a wife.
5. The modern Trois Rivières River.
6. Modern Guantánamo Bay.
7. A West Indian rodent.

Chapter 55

1. Modern Dry Harbour.
2. The *Niña* or *Santa Clara*.

Chapter 56

1. Elsewhere Ferdinand calls it Cape Cruz, the name given to it by Columbus.
2. "The Queen's Garden," an archipelago extending for over 150 miles from the Gulf of Guacanayabo to Trinidad and twenty to fifty miles off the south shore of Cuba.
3. These birds were flamingoes.
4. The pilot fish (*Echeneis naucrates*), which has a sucker on its head by which it attaches itself to its prey.

Chapter 57

1. A hallucination caused by a flight of cranes, suggests Washington Irving; probably an instance of Castilian crossbowmen "pulling the long bow," thinks Morison.

Chapter 58

1. Modern Isla de Pinos.
2. Ferdinand tactfully omits mention of the fact that before leaving Cuba, Columbus had his crews sign a statement that Cuba was a part of the continent of Asia.
3. Perhaps the modern Mangles.
4. Morison explains this phenomenon as caused by fine white sand stirred up by the waves and mixed with the water up to the surface.

Chapter 59

1. Modern Portland Bight.
2. Modern Morant Point.

Chapter 60

1. After his friend Michele de Cuneo of Savona, the first to sight it.
2. Named by Columbus La Bella Saonese, after the Italian town of Savona; now Saona.
3. Given in the *Historia* of Las Casas as Mona, its present name.
4. Perhaps a nervous breakdown, brought on, as Morison suggests, by "his extreme exertions, lack of sleep, and bad nourishment."

Chapter 61

1. There is no evidence that such an agreement was reached.
2. Charles VIII.
3. These ships carried to Spain the first shipments of Indian slaves, numbering more than 500; of this number only half arrived alive.
4. Ferdinand is in error; Caonabó neither participated in nor was made prisoner in this battle, but was captured by Hojeda by a ruse.

Chapter 62

1. Edward Gaylord Bourne, one of the founders of Latin American historical studies in the United States, was apparently the first to appreciate the importance of Columbus's contribution to American anthropology. "Christopher Columbus not only revealed the field of our studies to the world but actually in person set on foot the first systematic study of American primitive custom, religion, and folklore ever undertaken. He is in a sense, therefore, the founder of American anthropology." "Columbus, Ramón Pane, and the Beginnings of American Anthropology" (*Proceedings of the American Antiquarian Society*, Sec. Ser., XVII, April, 1906, 310-348).
2. That is, Cuba, which Columbus then believed to be the mainland.
3. According to Las Casas (*Apologética historia de las Indias*, in *Docs. inéditos para la historia de España*, LXVI, 435-436), Fray Ramón Pané came to Española with Columbus on his Second Voyage in 1493. He adds that he was a Catalan by birth and did not speak Castilian perfectly, and that "he was a simple-minded man so that what he reported was sometimes confused and of little substance." Despite its limitations the treatise of Fray Ramón is of fundamental importance as the earliest study of the American Indian and the only source for the ethnology of the Taino of Española at the time of the Conquest. In the words of Bourne, "the range of its contents is considerable. It contains a cosmogony, a creation legend, an Amazon legend, a legend which offers interesting evidence that syphilis was an indigenous and ancient disease in America at the time of its discovery, a flood and ocean

legend, a tobacco legend, a sun and moon legend, a long account of the Haitian medicine men, an account of the making of their cemís or fetishes, of the ritualistic use of tobacco, a current native prophecy of the appearance in the island of a race of clothed people and lastly a brief report of the earliest conversions to Christianity in the island and of the first native martyrs." I have changed the spellings of some names in Pané's treatise to the terms assigned in José Juan Arrom in his scholarly edition of the *Relación* (México City, 1978).

4. Bourne supplies the fifth name, "Iiella," from Peter Martyr's epitome of the original treatise in the ninth book of the First Decade of his *De rebus oceanicis.*
5. Syphilis.
6. A lacuna in the Italian text, but later he is called Deminan.
7. Bourne supplies this gap from Peter Martyr's epitome of the original treatise.
8. A lacuna in the Italian text.
9. A lacuna in the Italian text.

Chapter 65

1. Henry Harrisse, *Fernando Colón* (Seville, 1871), pp. 83-84, calls attention to a discrepancy in Ferdinand's account. The marriage referred to did not take place till April 3, 1497, almost a year after Columbus's return from the Second Voyage.
2. The correct year is 1497.
3. Ferdinand evidently forgot to tell of these matters.
4. The Infante Don Juan died October 4, 1497, five months after his marriage.

Chapter 66

1. The port of Seville.
2. Brother of Beatriz Enríquez de Arana, Ferdinand's mother. Ferdinand carefully avoids all mention of his relationship with his mother's family.
3. Giovanni (or Juan) Antonio Colombo, son of Columbus's uncle, Antonio. Of him Las Casas says, "a very capable and clever man, and of much authority, with whom I frequently conversed."

Chapter 67

1. In sailing so far south Columbus was apparently motivated by the prevailing notion that gold, precious stones, and spices were found most abundantly in the hot zones.

Chapter 68

1. Modern Galeota Point.
2. Modern Erin Point.

3. The coast of Venezuela.
4. Modern Bombeador Point.

Chapter 69

1. "Sandy Point."
2. The Indians interpreted the Spanish song-and-dance as a preparation for combat.

Chapter 70

1. The Dragon's Mouth.
2. The Serpent's Mouth.
3. "The Rooster"; modern Soldado Rock.
4. They were in front of the Orinoco. Ferdinand does not mention his father's belief that it was one of the four rivers of Paradise and had its source in the Garden of Eden.

Chapter 71

1. This, the first documented landing of Europeans on the American continent, is believed by Morison to have been made at Ensenada Yacua, on Paria Peninsula, Venezuela.
2. Probably *chicha*, made from maize.

Chapter 72

1. These were the mouths of the Río Grande, Venezuela.
2. "Cape Blunt"; actually modern Monos Island.
3. "Cape Barnacle."
4. "Gulf of Pearls," the name Columbus gave to the inner part of the Gulf of Paria.

Chapter 73

1. "Of Shells"; perhaps modern Punta Escudo Blanco.
2. "The Guards"; modern Los Frailes.
3. "Witnesses."
4. Columbus had been absent from Española two and a half years.

Chapter 74

1. Chief Justice.
2. Poverty, chastity, obedience.

Chapter 75

1. Columbus had built the fortress of Concepción on a height in the province

of Cibao, between Isabela and Santo Tomás, and had placed it under the command of Miguel Ballester.

2. A native of the island of San Salvador who had been taken away by Columbus to serve as interpreter, and who had been baptized a Christian. The Admiral had rewarded him for his services by giving him possession of a small district in Española.

Chapter 77

1. The Italian text gives the incorrect figure "eighteen."

Chapter 79

1. The correct date is September 12, 1498.
2. Governor of a fort or castle.
3. The Italian text has the erroneous date "February 24th."
4. An error by Ferdinand or the translator, for Ballester never captured Roldán.

Chapter 81

1. The correct date is November 14, 1498.

Chapter 82

1. Francisco de Garay, later governor of Jamaica and rival of Cortés in the conquest of Mexico.

Chapter 84

1. Hojeda had contrived to obtain license from Bishop Fonseca for a voyage to Paria, although shortly before the Sovereigns had reaffirmed the authority of the Admiral over all the lands and seas that he had discovered or would discover.
2. Because of the abundance of brasilwood found there.
3. Modern Jacmel.
4. The Italian text has the clearly erroneous date, "July."
5. This date should probably be "July 13th."
6. The material that follows, down to the close of the chapter, is out of its proper place, since it refers to events that happened in 1499, after Ferdinand has related events that took place in the year 1500.
7. At this point, as Caddeo notes, the narrative jumps without transition from the Adelantado to the Admiral, and from June to December. The source of the quotation that follows is unknown. Caddeo, accepting its authenticity, believes Ferdinand took it from the Admiral's letters, memorials, or journals, and notes its close resemblance to the wording of the Admiral's *Lettera rarissima*, addressed to Doña Juana de la Torre. He believes it refers to

Christmas Day, 1499, when Hojeda, at the head of a force of rebel Spaniards and Indians, was threatening Santo Domingo.

Chapter 85

1. Prince Miguel, grandson of the Catholic Sovereigns, died before reaching his second year, in Granada, July 20, 1500.

Chapter 86

1. There is no evidence that these chains were actually buried with the Admiral.

Chapter 87

1. On the basis of a report that the Indians of Xaraguá were forming a conspiracy, Ovando summoned the caciques and notables of the province to a feast in the village where he was staying. At a given signal Spanish soldiers fell upon the Indian guests and put them to death, burning many alive in the house of the native queen, Anacaona.
2. Diego Columbus, the Admiral's first-born son and principal heir.

Chapter 88

1. Ferdinand at the time of this voyage was not yet fourteen years old.
2. The castle guarding the entrance to the port.
3. On the coast of Morocco.
4. Martinique.
5. Puerto Rico.
6. In Panama.
7. Nicolás de Ovando.
8. According to Las Casas, there were thirty-one ships.
9. Alonso Sánchez de Carvajal.

Chapter 89

1. Ferdinand wishes to credit his father with discovering the existence of the wealthy realm of the Aztecs. Modern students believe the Indians encountered by Bartholomew came from the coast of Honduras, an area of relatively high Indian culture that had been part of the Maya empire of the Cocomes, and that they were trading with the island of Bonacca.
2. Pulque, a drink in widespread use in ancient Mexico and Central America.
3. Cacao beans.

Chapter 90

1. In modern Honduras.

Notes to Chapters 91-100

Chapter 91

1. Probably Puerto Limón, in Costa Rica.
2. "The Garden"; modern Uva Island.
3. The peccary.
4. The spider monkey.

Chapter 92

1. Or Zorobaró, the Indian name for modern Isla Colón, mistakenly applied by Columbus to the modern Almirante Bay.
2. Chiriqui Lagoon.
3. This river marked the beginning of the rich gold-bearing region called Veragua (Panama) by the Indians.

Chapter 93

1. "Harbor of Provisions"; modern Nombre de Dios.
2. In his *Lettera rarissima* to the Catholic Sovereigns, Columbus reports that the Indians had told him that "the sea surrounds Ciguare, and that from there it is ten days' journey to the river Ganges"—suggesting that he realized that he was on an isthmus between two seas. In any case, from this point on he ceased his search for a water strait and concentrated on the search for gold. The Guiga above was probably the mouth of the modern Río Culebra.
3. "Closet"; modern Puerto de los Escribános.

Chapter 94

1. Probably modern Limón Bay or the adjacent Manzanilla Bay.
2. Meaning "cliff" or "cape," believed by Morison to be the headland at the mouth of the Río Chagres.
3. His letter from Jamaica of July 7, 1502. There is a translation in Cecil Jane, ed., *Select Documents Illustrating the Four Voyages of Columbus* (London, 1930-1933, 2 vols.), II, 112-43.
4. "The Coast of Contrarieties."

Chapter 100

1. April 16, 1503.
2. The modern Archipelago of Las Mulatas.
3. "Marble."
4. Modern Little Cayman and Cayman Brac, about 115 miles northwest of Jamaica.
5. Modern Dry Harbour.
6. Modern St. Ann's Bay.

Notes to Chapters 101-108

Chapter 101

1. The actual distance between Jamaica and the nearest land on Española is about 108 nautical miles.

Chapter 103

1. February 29, 1504.

Chapter 104

1. According to Las Casas, by this ship Columbus sent a letter to Governor Ovando, "hoping for the succor of God and yourselves."

Chapter 108

1. On November 7, 1504.
2. Queen Isabella died November 26, 1504.
3. In 1506 Philip the Fair, husband of Juana the Mad, daughter of the Catholic Sovereigns, ascended the throne of Castile, which had been ruled by Ferdinand of Aragon as regent.
4. Ferdinand's text ends here. The remainder of the chapter is an addition probably made by the translator Ulloa, and contains a number of errors. The remains of Columbus were interred, not in the Cathedral of Seville, but in a monastery in Valladolid; three years later the body was transferred to the Las Cuevas monastery in Seville. More than a decade later, in compliance with Diego Columbus's wishes, it was moved to the cathedral in Santo Domingo. In the course of the next four centuries the bones of Columbus were twice moved again, first to Havana in 1795, then, after Cuba gained its independence in 1898, to a tomb in the Cathedral of Seville. It is possible, however, that the wrong coffin was transferred to Havana in 1795. "All or part of Columbus's remains," concludes John N. Wilford, "could be in Seville, Santo Domingo, Havana, or Genoa. Each city has laid a claim, and the boasts of Seville and Santo Domingo ring with authority, especially in their tourist literature. But the record, as in nearly everything concerning Columbus, is far from clear."

Index

Acul Bay, 81
Adamaney. *See* Saona
Adelantado, The. *See* Columbus, Bartholomew
Afonso V, King of Portugal, 19
Africa, 6, 18-19. *See also* Carthage; Guinea
Agesingua, 35
Aguja, 229
Alburemá Bay. *See* Chiriqui Lagoon
Alexander VI, Pope, 102
Alfragan, 16
Almirante Bay, 241-243
almonds. *See* cacao beans
Alonso, Rodrigo, 177
Alpha and Omega. *See* Maisí, Cape
Alta Vela, 144
Alvarez, Fernán, 108
Amayauba (cave), 153
Amazons, 170-171
Amona. *See* Mona
Anacacuya, cacique, 154
Anacaona, Queen, 218
Angel, Cape. *See* Macoris Point
Antigua, 113, 116
Antillia, 21, 25
Aomaquique, 267, 271. *See also* Jamaica
Arana, Diego de, 82, 85, 120, 123, 149, 176
Arana, Pedro de, 176, 199-200, 212-213, 214, 217
Arana, Rodrigo de, 85
Arcila, 227
Arco, Fernão Domingues de, 290
Arenal, Punta del, 182-183
Aristotle, 17, 25, 29
Aristotle, pseudo-, 29-32
Arteaga, Captain, 165
Arubeira, 113

Atabalipa, 285
Atlantis, 29
Aumatex, cacique, 164
Averroës, 17
Ayala, Juan de, 166
Azore Islands, 15, 24, 25, 31, 32, 33, 90, 93, 106, 143, 172, 179. *See also* names of islands
Azua, 213, 229-230

Babeque. *See* Great Inagua Island
Ballester, Miguel, 75, 193, 201, 203, 206, 208, 211
Baracoa, Puerto, 74, 75
Barahona, friend of rebels, 193
Barba, Juan, 280
Barbary Coast, 33
Barbas, Las. *See* Mulatas, Archipelago de las
Barcelona, 101, 108, 226
barter, between Indians and Spaniards, 60-61, 64, 65-66, 77-80, 83, 120, 123, 126, 127, 128, 145, 170, 185, 232, 234, 236-237, 241-244, 249, 250-251, 253, 265-266, 272-273
Bastiano, the Lombard, 259
Bastimentos, Puerto de. *See* Nombre de Dios
Bay Islands. *See* Bonacca
Beata Island, 144, 189
Beccaria, Antonio, 30
Behechio, cacique, 148
Belén (river and town), 249-263 *passim*, 265, 281
Bella Saonese, La. *See* Saona
Benzoni, Girolamo, xvii
Bermuda, 229, 261-262, 264
Bernal, Master, 274
beverages, Indian, 185, 232, 254-255

Note. For the convenience of the reader, most obsolete place names are cross-referenced to the modern names.

Index

Cipango, 21, 56
Clear, Cape, 27
Coaybay, 157
Cobrava, 243, 253
Cod, Land of. *See* Newfoundland
cohoba, 157, 159, 162-163
coiro, 170-171
Colchis, 32
Coloma, Juan de, 44, 105
Colombo, Juan Antonio (Giovanni Antonio Colombo), 176, 199-200, 202
Colombo the Younger (George Bissipat), confused for Guillaume de Casenove, 12, 13, 287, 288
Columbus, Bartholomew (Don Bartolomé Colón), viii, 6, 7, 36-37, 146-147, 149, 167, 190-208, 212, 215, 219, 222-223, 227-270 *passim*, 280-281, 284 ·
Columbus, Christopher (Cristóbal Colón, Cristoforo Colombo)
  ancestry and early occupation, 3-14
  death and burial, 284-285
  First Voyage, 44-100
  Fourth Voyage, 227-282
  interest in Portugese voyages, 14-15
  negotiations with Portugese King, 35-36
  negotiations and agreement with Catholic Sovereigns, 37-44
  privileges granted by Catholic Sovereigns, xi, 44, 102-108, 174, 225
  reasons for undertaking Enterprise of the Indies, 15-29
  Second Voyage, 108-173
  Third Voyage, 174-223
Columbus, Diego (Giacomo Colombo), 123, 130, 192-193, 194, 197, 222, 228
Columbus, Diego (Don Diego Colón), vi-vii, viii, xi, xiii, xvi, xx, 36, 37, 40, 146, 175
Columbus, Don Diego, Indian cacique, 194
Columbus, Ferdinand (Don Fernando Colón), vii-ix, xi-xii, xxi, xxiii-xxiv, 146, 173, 175, 220-221, 227-284 *passim*

Columbus, Ferdinand (Cont.)
  biography of his father, v-vii, xi-xiii, xv-xvi
  library of, viii-x, xxiv
Columbus, Luis (Don Luis Colón), i, xiii-xvi, xx
Concepción (fort), 166, 168, 193, 195-196, 201, 202, 207-208, 210-211, 214, 219, 221
Concepción, Puerto de la. *See* Moustique Bay
Concepción, Santa María de la. *See* Rum Cay
Conchas, Cabo de. *See* Escudo Blanco, Punta
Contrastes, Costa de los, 249
Convento dos Santos (Convent of the Saints), Lisbon, 14
copper, 150, 321, 232
Córdoba, vii, 37, 40, 42, 92
Coronel, Pedro Fernández, 130, 174, 198
Correa, Pedro, 24
Correo, 184, 187
Corte-Real, Gaspar and Miguel, 29
Cortés, Hernando, 285
Costa Rica. *See* Cariay
cotton, 60, 64, 66, 70, 89, 112, 114, 150, 170, 185, 232, 234, 236, 240, 244
Crato, Prior of, 100
crocodiles, 245
Crooked Island, 24, 66-67
Cruz, Cape, 134, 135, 142
Ctesias, 16
Cuba, 8, 29, 32-34, 67, 68-75, 131-132, 134-143, 233, 264
Cubagua, 189
Cubiga, 243
Cugureo, 4, 5
customs and beliefs of Indians, 60-61, 69-70, 75, 78, 80, 82, 88, 113, 114-116, 117, 118, 124, 126, 141, 148, 150-168, 170-171, 182-183, 185, 187, 231-232, 234-235, 237, 240-241, 242, 247, 249, 252, 253-255

D'Ailly, Pierre, 18
Damão, Alvaro, 99
Desastres, Río de, 236

Index

Index

Index